THE GREAT BRITISH
ALL-NIGHTER OF THE YEAR

SOUND
AND
RHYTHM
MEMBER

THE SOULFUL SHACK
MOD SOCIAL CLUB
MEMBER- E.K HOOR

SCOOTER RALLY
NEWHAVEN

JUST 5 MILES EAST OF B

TURDAY OCTOBER 27

ENSED BARS - TRADE STAN
AMUSEMENTS - SNO

turday 12.00 Mid-c

VE ON STAG

STARS
ul Bar
TRUT
T EDDIE

GHT AWAY - CAMP IN THE FO

-IN ADMISSION £ 5
On Arrival

THE RIGHT TO ALTER THE PROGRAMME WITH

..FREEMAUS..SCOOTER..CLUB..

OFFICIAL NON-PAID MEMBE

Name EDDIE PILLER
Type of scooter VESPA 90
Reg ERO 90 E
Membership number 23

"I CAN'T PAY FOR THAT"

T0243196

PRESENT
Groovy
cellar
YOU
41, Alderbrook Rd,
SW12

SOUTHEND RHYTH
SOCIETY
Name EDDIE PILL
Address 15 CONN
LOUGHT

Ready Steady Go!
'1983'
Name EDDIE Piller
Address 15 CONNAUGHT Av
LOUGHTON ESSEX

ship No: 157___ 1981

K. G. Promotions
60's Soul Night
at BOGARTS
NAME EDDIE
MEMBERSHIP NO.......1.0.1.

FRAN & YVONNE
THE SMALL FACES FAN CLU
DELL
RD WELLS

marquee 25th Anniversary
90 Wardour St. W.1 437-
Privilege Card
EXPIRING DECEMBER 31s
Not Transferable - Not valid until sign
Name EDDIE PILLER
Address 15 CONNAUGHT
LOUGHTON ESSEX
Signature

Ready Stea
'198
Name EDDIE PILLER
Address 15 CONNAU
LOUGHTON ESS

EXCEPTION OF ♥

IRS 115

'STEREO' CERT 'A'

IF EVER YOU
FIND LOVE!

Produced by Dennis Weinreich.
Remixed by Hein Hoven.

READY STEADY GO
MOD CLUB
"FAST EDDIE"
Name_____
Address 15 Connaught Avenue, 5 NOV 1981
Loughton, Essex..
EADY GO MEMBER 1981

CHARD PARFITT / ALLAN FIELDER / THE TRUTH
Special thanks to Gary and Brian for the past and good luck in the future.
photos by H.T. Murlowski   Sleeve by Terry Rawlings, Eddie Piller.

CLEAN LIVING
UNDER DIFFICULT
CIRCUMSTANCES

EDDIE PILLER

CLEAN LIVING UNDER DIFFICULT CIRCUMSTANCES

A LIFE IN MOD

monoray

First published in Great Britain in 2023 by Monoray,
an imprint of Octopus Publishing Group Ltd
Carmelite House
50 Victoria Embankment
London EC4Y 0DZ
www.octopusbooks.co.uk

An Hachette UK Company
www.hachette.co.uk

ISBN 978-1-80096-059-6

A CIP catalogue record for this book is available from the British Library.

Printed and bound in the UK.

1 3 5 7 9 10 8 6 4 2

Typeset in 11.5/17pt Sabon LT Pro by Jouve (UK), Milton Keynes

This FSC® label means that materials used for the product have been responsibly sourced.

In Adversis Puritas

This book is respectfully dedicated to Peter Meaden and Randy Cozens. Sleep well.

CONTENTS

CONTENTS

FOREWORD BY PAUL WELLER

The truth is that none of us second-generation mods can lay claim to being the first at any of it. We were copying the tribal originals: learning about what they wore, what they listened to, what drugs they took, what books and films they liked.

Their influences! Influences that have led me on to so many great things. That have made me question everything I was ever taught at school or told about on TV.

A liberation most definitely!

I'm amazed at how mod has kept going; it's been over 40 years for us second-gens! And I think it's still strong. I've been glad to see how adaptable mod is, how every generation that gets into it adds something to it. It's Kept Its Faith.

We might not have invented the wheel, but we've definitely kept it turning.

Eddie was there very early doors. His story is of the many.

PW. KTF

INTRODUCTION

S o just what does 'clean living under difficult circumstances' actually mean? What an odd title for a book – it makes absolutely no sense, surely?

Well, that's a fair question. It might seem confusing. Unless, that is, you have ever been touched by the hand of mod, and then it makes perfect sense. If you know what mod is, everything falls into place.

The Sixties mod world had its own guru. A philosopher-poet who saw the Soho mod scene as a total, all-consuming way of life. A place where teenagers could leave the strictures of their dysfunctional suburban family and embrace a new one of their own choosing. The Soho modernist family.

His name was Peter Meaden, and he was the man who truly defined what mod was – or rather *is*.

Originally partners with The Rolling Stones manager Andrew Loog Oldham, Meaden rose to prominence as the proto-manager of The Who. He was the man who changed their name to The High Numbers and shaped them as the mod superstars they would soon become. As Townshend's guru, Meaden both articulated and lived the totality of a mod life. Like many of the early followers on the path, he was an evangelist, encouraging others to join him on the journey.

After losing The Who to managers Lambert and Stamp, Meaden instead moulded Jimmy James and the Vagabonds – who were black and therefore more 'authentic' than his previous charges – into the perfect mod band, directing them and the burgeoning mod scene from his Soho bedsit. The Flamingo Club, The Scene, Scotch of St James . . . he saw mods as his own personal army; like fellow traveller DJ and A&R man Guy Stevens, he truly believed in the movement and its ability to change the world.

Peter Meaden had a point. Mod manifested itself in Swinging London, Carnaby Street and *Ready Steady Go!*, and shaped Britain's self-image in the Sixties. It was a sociopolitical youth explosion that swept the world, and Meaden, along with his original partner Oldham, advocated the concept of 'art as commodity as business'. It did him no good, though. An addiction to amphetamines eventually led to a mental breakdown and incarceration in a North London mental institution – and this, bizarrely, is where I come in.

In the late Seventies, a journalist called Steve Turner had remembered this fragile and rather broken Svengali, and took the time and trouble to track him down to interview him about his life. Peter Meaden was by now hospitalised in Southgate and undergoing electroconvulsive therapy (ECT), which has long since been frowned upon but was, at the time, seen as a way of 'resetting' a patient's brain. Despite his treatment and mental health issues, Meaden came across in Turner's interview as both erudite and a rare visionary; a Byron-esque mod poet-philosopher who was able to define just what it was that the very concept of mod meant to him at the time.

He compared the young mods' sartorial outlook with the peacock style of Spanish bullfighters, and their subversive nature to that of the Viet Cong, fighting against the establishment from the left field. But most importantly he defined the concept of mod thus: 'Modism, or mod living, is an aphorism for clean living under difficult circumstances.'

It means nothing, but at the same time it means everything.

Turner's interview was eventually published in the *NME* in 1979 off the back of the mod revival. And, as a young mod at the time, I was captivated. Meaden's words seemed to join the dots and fill in the gaps. He gave me something to believe in and that was this rather indefinable and dysfunctional thing called mod. Meaden and Paul Weller made me the person I am now.

Strangely, by the time I read those words, I had already met Meaden. In 1978, when he was with his son Sascha at the home of my childhood friends Jackie and Mickey Curbishley, whose dad Bill was by then managing The Who. Peter was back in the game, looking after The Steve Gibbons Band for Curbishley's Trinifold management company. He'd been a consultant on the film *Quadrophenia*, saying, 'This film's about me, man; this is my life,' after reading the script. But he took his own life just two months later, never having seen it.

His *NME* interview had such an overwhelming impression on me that I named this book in his honour.

Clean Living Under Difficult Circumstances.

PART 1

1

ALTERNATIVE ULSTER

I t started innocently enough.

In the early months of 1983, a letter arrived at my mum's house in Loughton. It was addressed care of *Extraordinary Sensations*, the mod fanzine I'd been running since 1980 just before I left school. Now up to Issue 8 with a circulation pushing 3,000 copies a time, this home-made magazine had become one of the mod scene's leading publications, taking over from the legendary but long defunct *Maximum Speed*.

I received an enthusiastic postbag of around 25 letters a week. Teenagers wrote from all over the world: unsolicited articles for publication, futile pleas for long-out-of-print back issues, demos and fanzines for review or forthright views for the letters page. The fanzine was part of an underground network catering for the young but seemingly ever-growing mod scene that had appeared organically on the streets of London in early 1979.

Dubbed the 'mod revival' by a cynical and generally hostile music press, the scene initially coalesced around The Jam before an explosion of like-minded bands appeared on London's gig circuit that spring. Mod enjoyed its brief time in the spotlight. The Jam, the film *Quadrophenia*, the two-tone phenomenon and dozens of hit bands like Secret Affair, The Lambrettas, the Purple Hearts and The Chords ensured a loyal teenage following, but by 1982, ignored by the music press, mod had retreated back underground.

And it was here in the shadows that – even after The Jam split in December of that year – the scene continued to grow, word spreading through a growing network of teenage fanzines and newsletters. It's estimated that at the scene's peak in 1983 there were more than a thousand of these home-made magazines serving a youth culture that had spread to more than 20 countries.

Mod was underground, unfashionable and, apart from the occasional tabloid 'Bank Holiday riot' exposé, invisible.

But it was thriving . . .

This particular letter to *Extraordinary Sensations* was postmarked Belfast South.

Make no mistake, at this point Ireland was at war. An ugly, brutal civil war that saw a demented catalogue of religious and political murder forced onto an embattled population. In London we were somewhat insulated from the insanity, which hid behind the almost innocent-sounding euphemism of the 'Troubles'. The English had, to a degree, lost interest in the constant atrocities being committed by both sides.

IRA, UDA, UDR, INLA, UVF, SDLP, UUP, DUP. Always those endless fucking initials. Of course, we *knew* it was happening, but unless there was a bomb in London or Warrington or Brighton it tended to pass us by.

Of all the regions of the UK, Belfast was where the mod influence was biggest. Stylistically the scene may well have been a year or so behind what went on in London – and the adherents correspondingly younger – but the passion and commitment was total. I received plenty of letters from Ireland, often in envelopes decorated with targets, the colour of which was the only reference to religion, political persuasion or tribal loyalty: from the Republic in the south and the Catholic areas of Northern Ireland, the targets were invariably green, white and orange; from Northern Irish Protestant communities, they were red, white and blue.

How quaint, I'd thought. Like the random graffiti left by Arsenal or Spurs fans. Except that it wasn't quaint. It was deadly fucking serious. I was a naive 19-year-old who certainly wasn't aware of the internecine politics of Ulster.

The letter came from an *Extraordinary Sensations* subscriber called David Holmes, Homer to his mates. He lived on the Ormeau Road in Belfast in a mixed area (and by that I mean it was a suburb where Catholics and Protestants lived side by side) and was still at school. He made me an offer: he said a group of Belfast mods had taken it upon themselves to club together to hire a venue so I could come over and play some of the latest London tunes. Belfast's various independent record shops that stocked my fanzine agreed to sell tickets. *Crikey*, I remember thinking to myself. *This might actually work!*

I'd been DJing since 1981 and by this time regarded myself as a proper mod-soul DJ. I was part of a setup of similar-minded teenagers from East London who hosted regular club nights and sold-out alldayers at the Ilford Palais. My partners were Ray Margetson, the editor of *Patriotic* fanzine, Dean Port from Hainault and Mappy from Walthamstow, and we were starting to make a name for ourselves at Ilford clubs like Barons and the Regency Suite.

It was a great scene, but did I want to do something different for a weekend and go to Belfast? Damn right.

I wasted no time contacting mates in Dublin. Sean O'Gorman and Robbie McDonald were *Extraordinary Sensations* subscribers hosting their own gigs under the aegis of the Emerald Society. Mods were big on clubs and societies back then; that was the way of our world in the early Eighties. We did everything ourselves and built up excellent channels of communication in those pre-internet days. I duly posted my missives on that wafer-thin blue paper reserved for international correspondence: could they tie something up for me in Dublin over the same weekend?

Some three weeks later, again by airmail, they replied in the affirmative and I set to planning my trip. We chose the upcoming Easter weekend, although on reflection we might not have thought things through properly!

This was the plan: I'd ride my Vespa over to Wales, catch a ferry to Dublin, attend a scooter ride-out on Good Friday, DJ, wave goodbye to my Dublin friends and make my way up to Belfast cross-country – spending Saturday night with another fanzine subscriber who lived in a small village somewhere en route before ending up with David Holmes and the lads in the 'Fast for a DJ session on Easter Sunday. Next day, I'd join 50 other scooters on a run to Bangor on the Irish east coast and ride back to London the day after that. A simple enough journey on paper, but over 800 miles and a ridiculously long way in practice. The thought of going abroad on my scooter for the first time was appealing, but my naivety was appalling.

I'd recently lost my job and found myself with some extra time on my hands. As a result, I'd become a junior NCO in the Territorial Army.

Malcolm Knox, a mod mate from Epping, had suggested joining him in the TA – specifically the regiment where he was a full-time sergeant, the London Scottish. Apparently the advantages were legion. You could fit your service in with real work or stay on the dole and do as much or as little training as you liked. It paid regular army wages and, best of all, on completion of a paltry 14 days' training a year they paid you a tax-free 'bounty' of £250, which was more than enough bunce for a decent scooter at the time. What was there not to like?

Initially five of us – all mods from Essex – signed up and were shipped off for basic training at Cultybraggan, a former German POW camp in west Perthshire. Once briefly the home of Hitler's doolally henchman Rudolph Hess, the camp gained notoriety in the spring of 1945 when five Waffen-SS were arrested for the murder of a fellow inmate suspected of being a British spy. Yep, our temporary home had once played host to an incident that resulted in the largest multiple execution in 20th-century Britain! It was that kind of place.

Those two weeks in the Highlands came as a shock. It was the height of winter, with 2 feet of snow on the ground, and conditions were not just beyond basic; they were bordering on barbaric. No heating in the World War II Nissen huts (the same ones the Nazi prisoners lived in!), a temperature of -10°C, awful food and quite literally crap, substandard equipment. The camp's commanding officer was a former SAS lunatic who began each day at 5.45am with a three-mile run dressed in full combat gear wearing an eyes-only balaclava, the unfit jokers of the London Jocks stumbling through the snow in his wake.

Unsurprisingly, the cockneys in G Company, London Scottish were hated Sassenachs and given a hard time by the genuinely Highland instructors. It wasn't just us, though – they hated the scouse and Geordie Jocks too!

Surprisingly, I loved it.

Map reading, forced night marches, weapons training, orienteering, combat tactics – all outside my 19-year-old comfort zone. Word about the easy wages spread and, bizarrely, within six months there were 25 London mods in our ranks. I got super fit, and the old Euston sleeper train, flights or occasional road trips every other Friday for training in Perth, Dundee or Kirkaldy instilled an enduring love for Scotland. But one thing we hadn't done was consider the politics of it all – at least I certainly hadn't. I was doing it for the craic and the money.

There was a permanent notice pinned to the board at our HQ, a beautiful 19th-century drill hall in London, close to Victoria Station. Standing orders proclaimed that *any* soldier was obliged to inform his company commander if he intended to visit Ireland, either the Republic or Ulster. Being a good lad, I left a note in the boss's pigeonhole.

Alarm bells didn't ring even after I received a summons from the colonel. Such communication was extremely rare; our OC occupied dizzy heights and didn't deign to mix with us mortals overmuch. It was unusual for him to enter a training session and unheard of for him to pull a junior soldier out of one.

'Corporal Piller?' I put down the workings of a Carl Gustaf anti-tank weapon and came to attention. 'Come with me. I've got someone in my office who would like a word.'

Gulp. What had I done? Or could it be a promotion? A couple of months earlier I'd been awarded the Messines Trophy (given to the 'most promising' soldier in the regiment and the only thing I've ever won in my life). Maybe I was about to be promoted to 'full screw', which would mean a pay rise!

I followed the colonel up the stairs to his office and waited outside for a minute to be summoned.

'Enter.'

I marched inside and saluted. The office was a small, flyblown room painted antiseptic grey and in it my OC was sitting behind an enormous desk, a large coronation portrait of the Queen on the wall behind him. All I could remember about the boss was that his tam-o'-shanter appeared to be made from a far softer material than mine. The perks of command, I supposed.

'Ah, Corporal Piller. Take a seat.' He gestured to an ancient elbow chair with sagging upholstery. It's an anachronism that the rank of lance corporal, the second lowest in the army, is always referred to as 'corporal'.

A second man was sitting to his left. It was him who addressed me.

'I'm the army intelligence officer attached to 1st Battalion, 51st Highland . . . blah . . . blah . . . blah . . . And your CO has told me that you've a trip to Ireland coming up?'

'Er, yes, I do,' I spluttered. Where was this going?

He paused and I had a chance to study him. Light-brown hair cut in a short back and sides, an ordinary face with a clipped moustache; dressed in a ubiquitous dark-grey pinstriped suit with an off-white Aquascutum mac folded over the wooden arm of his chair. He raised an eyebrow and looked at his fingernails.

'Do you mind telling me the purpose of your visit?'

'I'm going on holiday . . .' I told him that as well as a part-time soldier I was a DJ and had been invited to Dublin and Belfast to play soul records to a bunch of teenage mods. He smiled indulgently, obviously amused. I was probably the only DJ he'd ever met.

'Well, corporal . . .' A long pause as he stared at me. 'I'd prefer it if you cancelled your trip. The situation in the province is becoming increasingly dangerous for members of the armed forces. I understand that I can't force you, but I'd strongly advise against going.'

He emphasised the word *strongly* and looked hard at me as he delivered it.

Mind racing, I blurted out a defence. This was ridiculous.

'Sir, I'm sure there's nothing to worry about. See, on our scene we really don't care about that kind of stuff . . . I mean sectarianism or the Troubles . . . er . . . things like that. In fact, it's probably the only place in Ireland where everyone's come together regardless. I'm sure I'll be fine. I'm staying with friends every night . . . erm, just ordinary people.'

I tailed off, aware that it sounded pretty weak. For fuck's sake, I didn't even consider myself a proper squaddie. We were just a bunch of mates having a laugh and getting paid for playing at soldiers – kind of like Scouts with benefits. Weren't we?

'All right, if you really insist on going, then I've a few words of advice. Under *no* circumstances are you to mention to *anyone* that you're in the British Army.' Stressing the word *anyone* as if an overearnest delivery would drum home the seriousness of the situation I'd be putting myself in.

'You may well find yourself approached in social situations and asked seemingly innocuous questions. This is extremely important: you're not to discuss religion with anyone. Avoid questions as to your schooling; if your primary school's name was St Something-or-other, this could imply a Catholic education. Similarly, profess ignorance to any aspect of Scottish football . . . Under no circumstances mention you're in the TA. Do I make myself clear?'

This was a joke, right?

Silence hung in the air until: 'By the way, just what religion are you?'

'Well, sir . . .' I hesitated. What religion was I anyway?

'I've a Catholic mum and my dad's Church of England . . . I was brought up Catholic but gave it up when I went to senior school. I suppose I switched to C of E . . . Well, that's what we had in assembly . . .' Uncertain now. 'But that was donkey's years ago and I haven't given it a thought since I left school. I find it all a bit boring.'

'But, Corporal Piller, they certainly don't find it boring in Ireland. If asked, I would suggest you say you're Jewish. You're from the East End, so it's not entirely implausible.' I smirked, recalling the family legend that we had a healthy dose of frummer somewhere in our distant Bethnal Green past.

'However, if anything untoward happens, anything at all, you're to contact me as soon as you can. Your colonel here will pass on any messages. I may need to debrief you on your return. Ireland can be a very dangerous place for members of the services. *Do not* forget what happened to Captain Nairac.' Again, heavy emphasis, this time on *do not*. Although who Captain Nairac was and what'd happened to him was a complete mystery to me.

The interview ended and I was dismissed none the wiser. I remember thinking at the time how odd the whole conversation had been. Of course, mods didn't give a shit about religion. To us the philosophy of mod had pretty much replaced the church – hadn't mod guru and The

Who manager Peter Meaden called modism the 'New Religion' in 1965? We were mods first and anything else a very distant second. I was going to stay with mates; mostly boys I'd been penfriends with for years. All would be fine, wouldn't it?

I didn't give the matter another thought.

The Wednesday before Good Friday, I sorted out the records I was going to take to Ireland. 'What's Wrong With Me Baby?' by The Invitations, 'Ain't There Something That Money Can't Buy' by the Young-Holt Trio, 'My Baby Must Be a Magician' by The Marvelettes and Tony Clarke's 'Landslide' were typical of the set I took, and there were a few of the big hits too – 'Never for Me', 'I Can Feel It' and 'Seven Days Is Too Long' – along with some classic organ jazz from Jimmy Smith and Jack McDuff.

I carefully packed my rucksack with four days' worth of clothes, a washbag, wet-weather gear, sleeping bag and my army bedding mat, which meant that the trusty Vespa P200E was truly overloaded. I could have taken the infinitely cooler Lambretta GP175, but to be honest it was unreliable and had neither front nor rear racks, which I needed to strap my kit to. No, the less fashionable workhorse, my P Range, would do the job. Always started first kick and never let me down.

As well as riding half the length of Ireland, I'd be traversing the whole width of the UK. I spent the night planning my route to Fishguard, where I'd catch the ferry to Rosslare and then cross-country to Dublin.

I rose before dawn to a dull, grey and rainy day so typical of Easter weekends. It always looks like the weather will hold but it never quite does. By now, the Bank Holiday trip had become an established tradition – mods had ridden out to most British seaside towns since the cinema release of *Quadrophenia* in the summer of 1979. Prior to that, the majority of us had got the train for a day trip.

Without fail, weather-wise, Easter seemed to always promise more than it delivered. My old nan used to say, 'Ne'er cast a clout till May is out'. It wasn't until I was halfway to Great Yarmouth on Good Friday in 1981 that I'd realised what she was on about. Sun does not equal warmth – at least not in April!

The journey to Wales before Easter 1983 was uneventful, if cold, wet and uncomfortable. Motorways in the early Eighties weren't what they are now and a long journey like that in drizzle on an overloaded scooter with wheels the size of dinner plates was a terrifying thing. In spite of this, I arrived at the port in good time, lashed my bike to a strut on the ferry's main deck and took my place at the bar for one of the most uncomfortable four-hour journeys of my life.

As I soon discovered, the Irish Sea can be an unforgiving bastard. Always windy and bitterly cold, dirty grey waves with their spume-flecked 'white horses' incessantly pounding the hull; it made an irregular passenger feel more than a bit sick. Relieved to reach land, I disembarked and headed north.

By the time I reached Dublin, the sun had returned and the day was really quite pleasant. I searched out my correspondents: Sean O'Gorman first and from there we rode to Robbie McDonald's, whose family lived somewhere up in the north of the city and had generously offered me a bed. I remember how different the countryside was to what I was expecting; a magnificent estuary with rolling dirty-green hills created a majestic backdrop to my first taste of Guinness in a proper Irish pub. That first night passed pleasantly. I met a few of the people whose names I knew so well from our regular letters and we resolved to meet again next morning, Good Friday, to go on the ride-out around the streets of Dublin.

Rising early, we were sent on our way with a hearty breakfast cooked by Robbie's mum, who was, like all the mums I met in Ireland on that trip, generous and kind.

'Why's it so busy?' I asked Robbie, who did his best to fill me in.

By the time of the Easter Rising in 1916 there had been any number of heroic but unsuccessful insurrections by a host of freedom fighters, revolutionaries and secret societies, long forgotten by us, the English, but cherished and revered by them, the Irish. The cause of Irish freedom was much more complicated than I'd understood and, as Robbie told me, Easter was always a big weekend in the Republican calendar.

In a Georgian square some way off the beaten track we met up with 40 or so mods gathered together and sitting astride their scooters. They were chatting, some revving engines, waiting for the metaphorical dropping of a handkerchief that would signal the mass hornet-buzzing of hairdryers as they roared off in a pack for our ride-out.

I asked where exactly we were going. Rory (or more properly Ruraigh), a tall, be-parka'd lad with a fine collection of two-tone patches sewn up one arm, laughed and slowly looked me up and down.

'Jeez, Eddie, so you mean they've not told you where we're off to . . .? There's only one place we can go on a Good Friday . . . And that's the GPO.'

I looked at him blankly, as if the further meaning of what he'd said would become instantly apparent if I stared hard enough. It didn't of course. My knowledge of Irish history was negligible at best. He sighed and spelled it out.

'Eddie, we're going to join the Bhoys . . . You know, the Republicans . . . Every year, they commemorate the Rising down at the post office on O'Connell Street. There's a big march and bands and stuff . . . It's a grand old party, son – you'll love it!'

Well! That told me. This was my first inkling that the weekend would be political.

The scooters snaked through side roads until we reached the wide-open avenue that was O'Connell Street, where crowds had already gathered. Sure enough, I spotted Sinn Fein banners being carried among the several hundred people milling about. Speakers were addressing the crowd and the vibes were something akin to a carnival.

We pulled up. Although the Dublin pubs were shut (this being a religious holiday), several lads produced cans of beer from pockets or scooter toolboxes and lit up fags. I took in my surroundings. I didn't smoke, but happily tucked into a proffered can of Harp lager. Friendly banter ensued and we were soon joined by others with no scooters who'd arrived to take in the atmosphere and watch the ride-out. I'm sure we listened to some of the speeches, but I zoned out, relaxing in the sun. We were just doing what groups of mods did: rejoicing in our shared fellowship, talking about records, gigs, fanzines and clothes.

I pulled out a few dozen copies of the latest *Extraordinary Sensations*, the sale of which pulled in a handful of punts for my beer and petrol. In those pre-Euro days, Eire still used its own currency – the punt being the equivalent to the pound sterling. The one-punt note even looked suspiciously like our quid but without the Queen's head!

As things wound down, we mounted up and rode our scooters round the city again. Exhilarating.

The rest of the day went to plan. We'd dumped the bikes off and I got stuck into DJing at the pub for the Emerald Society. The atmosphere was electrifying. Everyone was sporting their best clobber: boys in sharp-cut tonic suits and girls in minidresses and white tights or more formal in A-line skirts and white knee-length socks. There were even a few with feather-cuts and those long, three-quarter-length jackets favoured by suedehead girls. A brilliant night.

I rose late on Saturday and met some of the lads for breakfast. Before long, it was time to be on my way: I was in an unfamiliar city with 50 miles to cover before I reached my next stop, where I'd arranged to crash with another young mate – well, a pen pal actually. He lived in a village halfway between Dublin and Belfast. I had a map but wanted to arrive early as I didn't fancy searching out his house in the dark!

At 1 o'clock I reloaded the Vespa and said my goodbyes. Robbie had plans and arranged to meet me later, so Sean O'Gorman, Jeff Lefroy and a few others rode with me for 20-odd miles before leaving me to press on to Ulster alone.

The sun was shining as I headed north and it was warm enough to take off the US Army parka, roll it up and strap it to the Vespa backrest with a bungee. Riding a scooter through lush countryside is a beautiful thing and it was now that I truly understood why Ireland is known as the Emerald Isle. Somehow, the grass really did seem greener. Fields took on a lushness seldom seen in England, and as for the coppices and woods, they invited short comfort breaks when another can of Harp was whipped out of the rucksack.

I was searching for a small town in County Monaghan called Castleblayney, as my friend Micky had given me specific directions to his place from there. His village was a couple of miles further along, still deep in the countryside.

This was where my lack of knowledge of Irish geography became something of an issue!

I made it to Castleblayney with no problems. It was still early evening and the pubs were open, so I stopped to check the directions. I later realised from the map that Monaghan was part of the province of Ulster but, along with Cavan and Donegal, was in the Irish Republic and not Northern Ireland.

The place I was looking for was the next village along, just over the border in South Armagh.

I never really noticed a specific border, no obvious rivers, walls, fences or barriers. I knew I'd arrived in Northern Ireland by the fucking great watchtower that rose some 40 feet up by the side of the road. It reminded me of a deer hideout that hunters might use in the culling season except that it was made of steel, three times as big, painted a dull grey and looked menacing and sinister. Half a mile further along I rode past an imposing concrete and metal fortress set back from the road, with steel gates some 12 feet high. I was just on the edge of the village, so kept going for another 200 yards until I came to a square. I pulled up, dismounted and stretched my legs.

About 30 yards opposite was a pub with maybe 20 men gathered outside. It looked like they were celebrating something. I assumed there must have been some kind of local sporting victory but had no idea what. Hurling? Gaelic football? Certainly it seemed like someone local had excelled at a particularly Irish sport. Again, my ignorance about the fact that sport had been a weapon in the Irish war for over a hundred years is both damning and slightly shaming.

It was a balmy evening and the group across from me looked boisterous but good-natured. I decided to sample a pint of Guinness and walked towards the pub, pulling my map out as I went. Perhaps one of the lads could give me directions to Micky's gaff?

A few seconds later things went wonky.

I was halfway across the road when I became conscious of a change in the atmosphere. I stopped and looked up to see a handful of the previously jubilant and apparently friendly crowd pointing and beginning to move in my direction. My initial reaction was curiosity and, as you do, I looked over my shoulder to see what they were pointing at.

Shock and surprise, there was nothing behind me. The 20 or so men across the square were pointing and shouting at *me*. Worse, they were moving towards me now and with real intent. It became obvious that I was their object of interest – and for some reason I couldn't quite fathom, they looked pretty pissed off.

I acted instinctively: did a quick about-face and sprinted back to the scooter. All I could think was thank Christ it was the Vespa or I'd have been fucked. The Lambretta would surely have seen me pushing the bike up the road trying a jump-start. But my P200E burst into life first kick and I jumped on.

I U-turned and roared back the way I'd come, heading the 100-odd yards to the police station I'd passed on the edge of the village. Glancing back, I saw the lads had given up the chase but were still jeering and shouting. What the fuck was that about?

To be on the safe side, I pulled into the police station. I say 'police station' but the building looked more like a fort. Behind those 12-foot steel doors was a normal police station, except that it wasn't in any way normal to me or to anyone else unacquainted with a police station planted foursquare in the middle of a civil war. I roared in, stole a quick look behind and, with a flat feeling in my gut that the lads from the pub might still be after me, jumped off and ran towards the entrance.

I bounded up the five steps and was immediately confused. There was some kind of three-way glass porch with a push-button intercom preventing me from getting inside. I ignored it and banged on the door.

'Quick! Some people are after me – can you shut the gates . . .?'

I was shouting and panting at the same time, heart bursting out of my chest.

I doubted that anyone was still after me but was shit scared and freaking out, feeling very much alone and not understanding what was going on. Someone inside the lobby had taken a decision, though, and across the courtyard behind me the massive grey steel gates began to slide slowly shut . . .

Thank fucking Christ, I thought.

'Move away from the door. Put your hands behind your head and lay face down on the floor.'

What the fuck?

A soldier (and member of the Ulster Defence Regiment, going by the Harp insignia on his collar) barked the order at me. He opened the convoluted three-way door system and walked out. An FN 7.62 SLR held confidently in his hands.

'Who the fuck are you?'

The broad, guttural working-class Ulster twang did nothing but reinforce the surreal nature of the situation I found myself in. The man was a sergeant, sporting a long Merv Hughes moustache and, judging by his demeanour, didn't think much of me at all. He gestured at me with the rifle.

'Stand up.'

'Now, sonny, just what the fuck do you think you're doing?'

'Well, I, er . . . I mean, I drove into the village and . . . er . . . a load of blokes chased me and started shouting, so I thought it best if I . . .'

'They would have ripped you limb from limb if they'd caught up with you, you total wee fuckwit? Are you really that fucking stupid?'

He pointed at the Vespa with his rifle.

I looked down at my scooter. Fuck me, he was right. Just below the white lettering proudly proclaiming me from Woodford was a Union Jack sticker perhaps 5 inches across. It was not intended to be political; it was just a Who-type pop-art adornment on my flyscreen. All mods used the Union Jack, didn't they?

The burly sergeant bawled me out for being such a fucking twat. He made it very clear that he had better things to do than deal with someone who'd just ridden around what they called 'bandit country' virtually waving a Union Flag.

He could see I was in shock, though, and after a couple of minutes' shouting and berating me he relented, pointed to a chair and offered me a cup of sweet tea. The first thing he advised me to do was to peel off that sticker. I was embarrassed, of course; I'd given no real thought to life on the border.

What an idiot.

*

'So, Edward, let's just run through this again. What the fuck are you doing in Crossmaglen on Easter weekend?'

I'd been in the police station (or was it a barracks?) for close on an hour now and was still having trouble explaining exactly what I was doing there. They couldn't believe that anyone, least of all an Englishman and a soldier at that, could come *on holiday* to one of the most dangerous places on earth to stay with people he'd never met. Apparently, the sergeant's senior officer, a lieutenant who was obviously another battle-hardened veteran of the Troubles, had been in favour of opening the gates and kicking me straight back out into the village. The crowd had long dispersed, but until I could find Micky's house I'd be a target for any revellers looking for an English idiot on a scooter to beat up. The officer asked me for the address of where I was staying and, after some discussion and rolling of eyes, gave me directions, wished me luck and told me to be very, very careful.

Eventually, slightly shell-shocked, I rolled up at Micky's, parked up the Vespa and knocked on the door.

Thank fucking Christ.

I'd made it to the family's small and cosy home on the outskirts of Crossmaglen with no further incident. I was in two minds about relating what had happened but in the end decided against it. There was no point.

The terraced house they lived in was too small for a large family, but again I was welcomed with a warmth that I was coming to realise was the default setting for all Irish families.

Micky was a real diamond, maybe just 16, smart with closely cropped black hair and a small, wiry frame. He was dressed in a green and blue tonic jacket, short-cut blue Sta-Prest with a pair of desert boots. We'd corresponded before but never met, and the first thing that struck me was his softly spoken voice with its lilting accent – the border accent is like that; nothing like the hard, guttural sound of Belfast.

It was dark by now. After unpacking the scooter and having the obligatory cup of tea, I set off with Micky, his dad and brothers to their local. Robbie McDonald was yet to arrive on the train, so was going to join us there later.

I was still somewhat shaken by my initial reception and was now advised by Micky to follow instructions from his dad: 'Keep your voice down and don't speak to anyone unless they talk to you first . . . Do you know your Hail Mary? Good. Oh yeah: you're my cousin from London, OK?'

Well, it was certainly OK with me – more than OK. The penny had finally dropped and I now knew that I'd underestimated the Irish political situation and was completely out of my depth. In fact, the name Crossmaglen was starting to ring bells. As was that of Captain Robert Nairac, mentioned by my OC. It had suddenly come back to me. Nairac was a legendary undercover SAS soldier who'd somehow inserted himself into a border village in bandit country. One particular night, he'd been drinking and singing rebel songs in a Republican pub close to where I was now and had somehow been identified (or 'made') and executed, his body fed to pigs. *Oh, that Captain Nairac*, I thought to myself.

Fuck, wasn't Warrenpoint where that IRA ambush took out a Para patrol just a few miles up the road?

Sweet Jesus! I was going to have to be very careful indeed.

The pub was small. All Formica tables and unmatched chairs but vibrant and warm with good Guinness. The bar was fuggy with a heavy layer of cigarette smoke and packed with working-class men and boys, all hard faces with smart jackets, shirts and ties. I don't mean smart as in fancy, I mean smart as in Sunday best. Simple three-button affairs that were still the choice of working men back then. Invariably dark, they were worn for work – often manual labour – as well as socially and, probably most importantly, for Mass.

The evening passed amiably and without apparent incident. A couple of pints of Guinness relaxed me somewhat. Robbie arrived from Dublin and my set-to at the police station was long forgotten as I tucked into the beer and became more gregarious, enjoying the social situation. I remembered Micky's dad's caveat and did my best to appear invisible and keep my telltale cockney voice down. I assumed I'd been successful because it was way beyond the draconian official closing time when we walked back through the light drizzle for a nip and a nightcap. Whiskey was the drink of choice. My time in Scotland had taught me the difference between whisky and whiskey. The former was Scottish and the latter most definitely Irish. Powers, Bushmills, Jameson and Paddy were the brands of choice and, like everything else in the country, your drink was subtly political. As I climbed into my sleeping bag that night, I reflected that I was learning the nuances as fast as I could.

Saturday broke to a clear, cloudless sky. The sun was up and it was a fine morning. The house was all abustle and I was soon shifted from the sofa by Micky's mum.

'Here's a wee cup of tea for you, Edward. Get yersel' up and dressed because we're off to church in a minute.'

Church?

Sure enough, the house was already crowded with men everywhere. Soon a couple of lads appeared and were dressing in the front room. Drummer-boy uniforms. I made myself scarce and sat outside on my scooter to wait.

The village had come alive and it seemed everyone was getting ready for church. As if at some prearranged signal, people began to assemble in the street. Fifes and drums to the front, families to the rear and in the middle a coterie of six men dressed in black polo-neck jumpers and berets. More to the point, each of them sported a Sam Browne belt – the leather over-the-shoulder arrangement worn by British officers to hold their small-arms holster – and all those belts contained a pistol.

It was clear these guys were heavy. I assumed that they were probably some of the volunteers from the South Armagh Provisional Irish Republican Army. The most feared unit of the IRA – the ones who apparently took no notice of the Army Council in Belfast.

Fuck, fuck, fuck! What was I doing? I was now at an Easter church parade with the IRA in Crossmaglen. Scared. Beyond shocked.

I looked across at Robbie McDonald, who simply shrugged his shoulders with a nervous grin. He told me later: 'It wasn't so bad for me because at least I was from the south. You on the other hand were a Brit and intruding on something very, very private . . .'

Although the sky was clear with no clouds, a cold breeze made me wish I'd worn my parka.

The helicopter rose above the trees some 300 yards away. It looked like a Lynx, but I was no expert on NATO aircraft. I'd spent hours memorising the bare silhouettes of Soviet Bloc hardware and could tell that this one bore no resemblance to a Hare, a Hat or even a Hermit (NATO code names for Russian helicopters all began with an H). No, this was one of ours all right and it was on a mission, of sorts. It was heading towards us.

Micky pulled me aside and pointed up at it, still 100 yards from the church and hovering at 200 feet, the noise of its rotors aggressively loud, almost deafening.

'They do it on purpose, the bastards! They fly as close as they can to disrupt the feckin' parade. Y'know, with the noise and stuff, straight over the feckin' church . . . They never come close enough to get shot at, but they have long-range cameras. They're looking for volunteers, men on their lists . . .'

He turned away, frowning.

The march was approaching the church now and I assumed we'd be led inside by the fifes and drums. But no, we weren't.

The church was an enormous, imposing whitewashed 19th-century Catholic job just off the main street, surrounded by a large expanse of open green. As we got closer the band fell silent – but instead of parading through the main gates, the marchers veered off to the right and entered the graveyard opposite. The rest of the crowd, now maybe 100-strong, surged after them into the enclosed space and arranged themselves in orderly lines around what looked like, well . . . what had to be a freshly dug grave.

Robbie McDonald pointed across and told us to look. Sure enough, several men were gathered under the corrugated-steel mortar defence of the army watchtower on the outskirts of the village. 'They're spying on us!' he shouted, as the telltale glint of binoculars sporadically flashed in the sun's reflection.

The regular *thok-thok-thok* of the helicopter grew steadily louder as it inched its way closer, drowning out all but shouted conversation. A dark-green monster adorned with the blue and red roundel that seemed to have replaced the classic mod target of World War II vintage.

From there things happened so quickly that I can't be sure of their order. A priest spoke for some minutes and handed over to a politician. At least, I took him to be a politician and he was warmly greeted. I was too far from the grave and the helicopter was making too much noise for me to hear what was said. What on earth was happening here? Was it some kind of memorial service?

No, it was an IRA funeral.

Jesus.

Robbie reached across, squeezed my arm in reassurance and shuffled closer as I tried to imagine myself invisible. The atmosphere was highly charged and I realised it was imperative no one sussed I was a Brit.

Suddenly, as if directed by an invisible hand, the crowd began to move backwards and away from the open grave. It was apparent that this manoeuvre had been performed before and probably on a regular basis. Into the gap, with a semblance of a regular army drill, proudly marched the black-clad volunteers of the Provisional wing of the IRA – only now they'd pulled balaclavas down over their faces beneath their berets. One thing stuck in my head: for some reason I noticed that, although their drill movements were tight, they didn't have matching combat trousers. Some wore olive green, a couple DPM camouflage and one was wearing jeans.

At the command, they came to attention, removed their pistols from the Sam Browne holsters and pointed them skyward. Another command and three volleys were discharged in quick succession. At this, the helicopter edged closer to the graveside as if to get a better look. The crowd surged forward and mobbed the shooters, crowding in on all sides and shielding the volunteers from the army observers.

As one, the six men dropped to the floor and pulled off their balaclavas and berets. It was over in a second. As the crowd split into smaller groups there was no longer any sign of the volunteers. They'd slipped on civvy jackets and blended in with the crowd now making its way out of the churchyard and back onto the street.

Seemingly frustrated, the helicopter gained height and roared off.

It was time to leave for Belfast.

Belfast rocked.

My first memory of the divided city was of riding my scooter into the town centre, parking up and passing through some kind of security gates. They were painted red and the only thing I can equate them to is the turnstiles you clanked through to enter Seventies football grounds. In London in 1983, the idea of walking through security gates to bowl up Oxford Street would have been plain ridiculous, but in Ulster it was the norm. Of course, there were many bombings during the Troubles; in the space of just a couple of days I heard what I assumed was an explosion and there was certainly the sharp crack of distant gunshots.

Most bizarrely, within four hours of my arrival I witnessed a riot – its genesis and subsequent suppression – at first hand.

The riot was in a nondescript terraced street just 100 yards long. I was riding past on the scooter and what I saw was so shocking that I had to pull over, park up and just watch. I saw a squad of soldiers in classic 'fighting in built-up areas' (FIBUA) deployment spring into action. The soldiers, weapons drawn, appeared to be well organised, with the obvious objective being containment: keeping the rioters within the confines of the terraced street. They had clearly done this many times.

Then I saw *it*.

I think the local term was Flying Pig. A hybrid vehicle, painted a drab grey-green; a cross between a standard army Land Rover and 1-ton armoured car. The oddest thing was that it appeared to have an extendable wall made of steel attached to one side. With a dexterity no doubt perfected in countless practice sessions, in one swift move the Pig swung round and neatly blocked the end of the terrace. At the same time, a similar vehicle performed an almost identical move at the other end. It was done. The riot was contained, the youths would soon get bored of throwing their stones or petrol bombs and the army could deploy elsewhere – probably to perform the same perfect industrial ballet in another part of town.

How on earth could this dysfunctional, fucked-up city have become the biggest and most vibrant exponent of the mod revival? It seemed near impossible.

My guide – one of my fanzine correspondents riding his own scooter alongside mine – didn't bat an eyelid. This was apparently normal life in early-Eighties Belfast and I soon realised that the Troubles actually fuelled the *need* for a mod scene. The mod philosophy empowered these young kids and somehow gave them the confidence to reject the sectarian attitudes of their elder brothers and sisters.

Many early-Eighties mod boys and girls took a lot of stick for not following their siblings down their own particular sectarian path. It really did appear that the paramilitary gangs were on the verge of losing control of an entire generation. They were hostile to youth culture specifically because it had its own values and rules that had nothing to do with the entrenched bitterness of the struggle. This independent spirit initially manifested itself in the late-Seventies punks who gathered around Terri Hooley's Good Vibrations record shop and continued with the next generation of teenagers who just happened to be mods and rudeboys. Committing themselves to an alternative youth culture made kids less susceptible to pressure from the older generation to get involved.

In direct contrast to the chaos and tension, the people of Belfast – at least the ones I met – were warm, funny, stoic and generous.

I was to stay with David 'Homer' Holmes's enormous and welcoming family on the Ormeau Road in south Belfast. The area had originally been a Protestant stronghold – indeed, it was where the first of the famous sectarian murals appeared (King Billy sat astride his horse in 1908 in the days before partition) – but by the time I'd arrived it was a 'mixed area'. Even then, though, the tension was palpable, and I resolved to keep myself to myself and my accent under wraps.

Just as in Dublin with the McDonalds and the O'Gormans, and on the border with Micky's family, the Holmeses welcomed me into their home. Homer had nine brothers and sisters, an unimaginable number to an Englishman, even among us left-footers! To be honest, I thought it must be something of a novelty for them to have an English lad staying in the 'Fast, but again the warmth I experienced was profoundly humbling.

The evening was soon upon us and before David took me down to the venue we got dressed in his front room, as smart mods must.

He was a few years younger than me with pale skin and dark, burnished-copper hair, and tall – almost as tall as I was and certainly tall enough to take his trousers and indeed whole appearance seriously. I'd brought my chocolate-brown tonic suit, but it'd been folded in my rucksack and was creased beyond redemption. I borrowed an iron from David's mum and did my best to make my gear presentable. I wore a pink pin-collar shirt with a claret tie, while Homer dressed in a blue-green tonic. We spent ages trying to look good and I can't stress how important that was at the time. Because we were mods, we both felt the need to make a sartorial impression; the whole thing, at least back in the early Eighties, was to look the absolute bollocks. I was in Ulster and, as I saw it, representing the East London mods to a whole host of kids that knew nothing about us. I needed to dress like I was the best. We took an inordinate amount of time over our look and style; if these Belfast boys had never met a proper English mod before, I wanted them to remember me by my clothes and my records.

The gig itself was at a legendary Belfast pub called the Abercorn, which was legendary for all the wrong reasons. In 1972, at the height of the Troubles, the place had been blown up; two people were killed and over a hundred injured. No one ever claimed responsibility and even today a mention of the place elicits frowns and hard stares. I knew nothing of this of course, nothing at all. Just that it was close to the Europa Hotel, famous for being 'the most bombed hotel in the world'.

It was the first time the crowd had heard 'Smokey Joe's La La' by Googie René Combo on a dance floor, a jazz/R&B track I'd snaffled from Randy Cozens' Mod Top 100 (Cozens was a particular hero, and his chart, published in *Sounds* in August 1979, became the definitive list of mod-soul records and was what I based my early sets on) and introduced into my set at Barons in Ilford. As with many of those rare early mod tracks, I'd picked up a US issue (on Class) – they were always cheaper than the UK pressings – with a 'dinked' hole, which meant that you needed a 'spider' or a 'donut' to insert into the large hole so it would play on a record player!

The pub was packed. By 1983 Northern Ireland had thrust its way to the pinnacle of the British mod scene and, like in Dublin, everyone had dressed up in their finest for the gig. Sweat was dripping from the ceiling and people were dancing on the tables.

This was why I was here – the incredible atmosphere was what it was all about. The night was a massive success.

Northern Irish licensing laws being draconian at that time, the night ended at 11 o'clock. I'd been drinking with a trio of Belfast girls who appeared to have adopted me as their pet, and Geraldine, Karen and Marie were now walking me towards a burger van a couple of hundred yards down the road to grab some food before bed. There were plenty of people milling about when suddenly a white Escort van sped round the corner. It was driving too fast and at the last minute swerved onto the pavement towards the food queue. Most people managed to throw themselves out of the way but one girl of maybe 17 years old wasn't so lucky. The van clipped her and she spun round screaming, collapsing into the road as the driver sped off and chaos descended. People were shouting and crying and the girl looked in a bad way. We were 30 yards from the impact site and my instinct was to run and help her. I'd recently finished an army medical course and, with trauma injury fresh in my mind, thought of nothing else as I ran across the road.

Geraldine kept pace with me but grabbed my arm and pulled me to a halt.

'Eddie, what do you think you're doing? Just leave it; let the medics deal with her.'

It was obvious the injured girl needed some first-responder treatment and I wanted to apply my training. It was then that Karen uttered a sentence that made me realise how fucked the situation had become.

'You can't. You're gonna have to be careful. This is what happens sometimes. They wait until the ambulance arrives. If it's military, they've been known to top the medics.'

Fuck me.

This was the defining moment in a weekend of defining moments. Properly fucked up.

We waited for the ambulance from across the road and it was indeed military. It had been a great night up until now, but I'd had enough of Northern Ireland.

The next day, Bank Holiday Monday, I reluctantly joined the inaugural scooter run to Bangor in County Down, just 20 miles away on the Irish east coast, but to be honest my heart was no longer in it. I really wanted to get home to my dysfunctional mates in Woodford.

That weekend was a formative one for me. I'd seen so much, learned so much. Throughout it I'd seen mods acting as one, loving the music, scooters and clothes, and trying to create their own society among the literal rubble of their own grown-up world. I'd also seen and experienced much more politics than I'd bargained for. I even joined an Orange march on the way back from the Bangor rally as we rode into Belfast city.

Of course, the Vespa died on the way home – but what did you think was going to happen?

There is a postscript to all this.

In 2012 I'd just been diagnosed with cancer and had one more DJing gig before I began a rigorous regime of surgery, radiotherapy and finally chemotherapy. I'd be out of action for at least a year, if I made it at all.

Luckily, I survived! But I'd been told at the time that statistically my chances weren't great, so in the back of my mind I was worried.

Still, this last gig was at the Voodoo Lounge in Belfast and one I didn't want to miss, because I was spinning alongside my old mate and

DJ partner David Holmes. David had, of course, gone on to be an incredibly successful musician and producer, who'd had his first big hit a decade and a half after we first met with the groundbreaking 'My Mate Paul', its lazy drums and upfront jazzy piano deftly sampling 'Smokey Joe's La La'.

It was raining when I arrived and I was pleasantly surprised to bump into Micky, the very boy I'd stayed with in Crossmaglen back in 1983. He was standing in a doorway, sheltering from the weather, and we immediately recognised each other even though I hadn't seen him for over 25 years. He greeted me warmly and before long the conversation inevitably turned to the events of the Easter I stayed with his family.

'Ah, Eddie, it's grand to see you!' Still with his soft, sing-song border accent. 'Actually, I've been meaning to tell you something about that weekend.'

I laughed. 'Yeah, fucking mental, wasn't it? I'm probably the only person who's ever been on a Sinn Fein rally at the GPO, an IRA funeral in bandit country and an Orange march in Belfast on the same weekend!'

He gave me a long, quizzical look. 'Well, Eddie. Ah . . . Y'see, there was a bit more to it and I didn't want to tell you at the time as it would just have made you . . .' He was searching for the right word. 'Erm . . . *panic*, which would have made things much worse. Actually, if I'd known you were in the feckin' TA, you bloody idiot, I'd never have let you come in the first place. It would have been far too dangerous and, well, as it was you nearly came a cropper anyway.'

'Eh, what do you mean?' My interest was immediately piqued.

'Well, remember when we went for that drink in my local?' He paused and exhaled slowly, giving me another of those long, sideways looks. 'Actually, Eddie, the leader of the South Armagh ASU [Active Service Unit] of the IRA was in the pub that night and your presence had been noted. They were sizing you up and called my da out to have a word with him. They said they didn't like the look of you, a Brit in the village on Easter weekend. They were thinking about taking you for a drive and asking you a few questions . . . You know, in that situation they could be pretty heavy . . .'

Another pause.

'Erm . . . What do you mean, "pretty heavy"?' I spluttered.

'Put it this way, if they'd asked you some questions and you'd given the wrong answers – and believe me, being in the British Army of occupation was most definitely a wrong fucking answer . . . Well, it's quite simple. They would have nutted you. Shot you in the back of the head . . . Worse, they might have shot me as well for bringing you into the village. The only reason they didn't was because my da persuaded them you were my cousin from London. I think you were pretty lucky there, son . . .' He laughed. 'Anyway, that was a very long time ago now, so let's get inside and you can buy me a beer.'

And with that he went into the club, leaving me dumbfounded on the pavement in the rain.

2

EDDIE'S DREAMING

In truth, I was always going to be a mod.

Born slap bang in the middle of the coldest winter since the retreat from Leningrad, I spent my first few days in the intensive-care unit at Wanstead Hospital. From there it was plain sailing. I don't have a sorry tale of abuse, alcoholism or violence in my family, and I didn't grow up on the mean streets of Bethnal Green, which was where my dad's family were from. Instead, I experienced an idyllic upbringing in Woodford just five miles further east, where my mum was a housewife – a housewife who ran the Small Faces fan club, but a housewife nonetheless. My dad was a cockney bookmaker.

Cockneys love their traditions and since the 1850s each first-born Piller boy child was christened Edward, albeit with a different diminutive. My great-grandfather was Edward, his son was Ted, my dad was Eddie and I was Ed. My son is Ned.

We were a typical successful East End family, lower middle class and aspirational. The old man was born on Bethnal Green Road and my mum off the beaten track in Tottenham, and together they had made their way to the sunny uplands of the Essex border when I was a baby.

E. Piller & Son, Bookmakers of Distinction (Established 1889) was the name of the business, set up as racecourse 'SP merchants' at the arse end of the 19th century. By the time the 1961 Gambling Act was introduced, the Pillers had established a position of considerable advantage and soon amassed a chain of 11 shops in a crescent stretching from Waltham Abbey to Plaistow via Hackney. The Piller brand espoused the more acceptable shop-based bookmaking, which provided a fig leaf of legitimacy to what had been long considered 'sharp practice'.

Back then, people referred to bookies as 'starting-price merchants' or 'turf accountants' – both terms sounding like the euphemisms they undoubtedly were. The game was definitely *not* the comfortable, (almost) socially acceptable business it is now. Bookmakers were frowned upon and polite society in the Sixties gave them a wide berth.

I never got the chance to understand how the business worked, but I do remember my dad's frustration at the extremely tough conditions attached to his licences. No one under 18 was allowed to witness the internal workings of a bookie's in case they were corrupted, so the shops all had frosted windows with etched images of greyhounds and horses. I was certainly never allowed beyond the back room.

The main nugget of wisdom my dad imparted to me as a child was simple: 'Just one rule, son. Never gamble. You'll struggle to find a poor bookmaker, but the world's full of potless punters.'

I twigged early doors that the whole thing was almost certainly fixed.

Given that we were based in the East End, one would expect a certain amount of interference from the established crime networks that preyed on businesses such as ours, but truth be told, it wasn't too much of a hardship as long as you played by the rules.

By the time I was at junior school in 1969 the Krays were in prison and had lost control of their traditional cockney heartlands. Indeed, my sister was in the same class as Charlie Kray's nipper at a posh public school (she got a scholarship to Bancroft's). All that remained were tales of how the only Piller shop not liable to pay 'protection' was the one 50 yards from the Krays' modest childhood home in Valance Road. It was said that this was because Violet, the Kray matriarch, enjoyed the occasional flutter and the twins left our Bethnal Green shop well alone just in case she witnessed anything untoward. Obviously our other premises were subject to the same terms and conditions as everybody else's.

The reason the Krays passed into legend is because of the misplaced rose-tinted nostalgia that saw them as 'our boys'. They might well have been brutal thugs, but at least they were *our* brutal thugs. The reality is that they *were* of course brutal thugs, but if you paid your protection and kept out of their way they left you alone.

There was no getting away from it, the Pillers were relatively dodgy. Inevitably I heard rumours: my grandad being in trouble over some horserace-fixing shenanigans, the old man falling foul of the Old Bill on a couple of occasions and even whispers of armed robbery in the family. As I said, we were a typical East End family!

Born in late 1963, I came into the world just as the second wave of mod was getting out of the blocks. Of course, I was oblivious to the fact. My dad, Eddie, rode a Lambretta in the late Fifties and followed Ivy League style; he listened to Tubby Hayes or Joe Harriott at the Flamingo Club in Soho and regarded himself as a modernist in the classic sense, but by 1963 when his son Edward was born, any thoughts he'd had of jazz had been replaced by graft.

It was here that fate lent a particularly prescient mod hand.

On the East Ham/Manor Park border, next to the head office of E. Piller & Son and opposite Steve Marriott's dad's fish stall, was a traditional public house. Not just any pub but the most important cockney pub in mod history. This was the Ruskin Arms, owned by Mr and Mrs Langwith, who were the parents of a teenage mod called Jimmy and his brother Derek. The Langwiths were good friends with the Pillers, and when young Jimmy formed a band called Small Faces, my mum took an almost proprietorial interest in their fledgling career.

Jimmy Langwith couldn't really play an instrument, so Steve taught him the basics of rhythm guitar and organ, and in exchange Jimmy's parents let the new band rehearse in the Ruskin Arms. While West

London's The Who had been styled and dressed as mods by Townshend's guru and former Marriott's Moments manager Peter Meaden, Small Faces, from the East End, were the real deal: grassroots mods.

Almost immediately Jimmy switched his surname to the snappier-sounding Winston (his middle name), while his mum and dad bought the group a van and his elder brother Derek was drafted in as road manager. The band (now four strong) furiously rehearsed at the Ruskin Arms, putting together a short but high-octane set of mod-influenced R&B covers with a couple of originals and, before they were even properly ready, played their debut gig at the pub in front of family and friends with an enthusiastic Fran Piller, my mum, in the crowd.

Things moved quickly and despite still having no booking agent or manager Small Faces resolved to play as many shows as possible, wherever they could.

Within a month the band came to the attention of a heavyweight impresario called Don Arden, who quickly assumed the role of manager and Svengali and set about making them stars.

Just a whirlwind ten weeks after they'd formed, Small Faces reached a heady Number 14 in the charts with their debut 45 'Whatcha Gonna Do About It' and were attracting lots of attention from fledgling fans. Looking around for help with their son's band's newfound fame, the Langwiths – who were already running a very busy pub – turned to their neighbours the Pillers. Fran and her friend Yvonne stepped into the breach, first answering letters and then creating an actual fan club; and so began a bizarre rollercoaster of gigs, newsletters, television shows and screaming teens.

A band logo and headed notepaper were commissioned, and a number of newsletters were drafted. These were typical of the time: 'Your fave Small Face' and 'Where Steve gets his clobber' typed on a rusty Remington and copied on a primitive Xerox machine. Fans sent a couple of shillings in postal orders to our house in Woodford, along with a stamped addressed envelope, and in return would receive letters and photographs. Within months the job, which was supposed to have been a bit of fun, had become all consuming – and expensive.

Mum and Yvonne lasted less than a year. The overwhelming pressure of replying to 50 or so letters a week eventually took its toll and the end, when it came, was swift.

Stationery had become an issue. The early expenses were met by Jimmy Winston's parents, but he'd already upset the applecart by 'acting up' on stage and deflecting attention away from Marriott. Jimmy, essentially a rhythm guitarist, was unceremoniously dumped by the new manager and replaced by Ian McLagan, an organist from a West London mod band called The Muleskinners whose Hammond became an essential part of the band's developing sound.

This move caused all kinds of internal ructions. The Langwiths had bought the band's van and their other son, road manager Derek, had been sacked too. They were understandably furious and went as far as to threaten legal action against both the band and Don Arden.

The fan-club girls weren't sure what to do; things were a mess and they obviously felt loyalty to Jimmy and his parents. After much soul-searching the pair continued running the club, but it wasn't to last much longer. Interestingly, in the Small Faces newsletter that dealt specifically with Jimmy Winston's sacking, the girls put a massive up-spin on the story, announcing his departure as if it was a step up to a brilliant new solo career with Decca.

Arden proved less than accommodating and the girls were now meeting a large part of the fan club's costs themselves. The early hustle and bustle of exciting gigs and the feeling of being part of something special had been replaced by a screaming, hysterical wave of rapacious 13-year-old dollybirds and endless letter writing.

While the manager screwed down his teenage charges with a mixture of threats and intimidation – at one point even telling the families that their kids were heroin addicts – he also gave the lads a house in Pimlico, accounts in Carnaby Street clothes shops and a generous weekly wage. Most importantly, he made them pop stars; mod faces with the gear to match.

Yes, Arden manipulated Small Faces and yes, they didn't get properly paid – but on the other hand he was an expert at rigging the charts and, unsurprisingly, under his tutelage the band had a string of big hits.

Small Faces had made the big time, but the fan-club girls were out on their arses as Arden brought their operation in-house and under his control. Fran remained friends with the Langwiths and the rest of the band, particularly drummer Kenney Jones, who visited our home throughout the Seventies. (His extraordinarily exotic Bentley S3 Continental 'Chinese Eye' had originally belonged to Douglas Fairbanks Jnr. It was instantly mobbed by the local kids whenever it was parked up outside our house in Woodford.)

But for Fran the intense and exciting period of the Small Faces fan club was well and truly over.

While my mum was pondering her post-Small Faces future, within the year the band found themselves at the centre of a tug-of-war between Don Arden and the modish Australian entrepreneur Robert Stigwood. Arden won by famously having his minder, Mad John, threaten the interloper with physical violence, but the end was on the cards. Andrew Loog Oldham had been waiting in the wings with his new Immediate label and made a move. As he seduced Small Faces with promises of unlimited studio time, he set about releasing the 'Itchycoo Park' single.

This, dear reader, is where I come in! I know, I was only four years old, but incredibly found myself drafted into a Gered Mankowitz photo session for the 'Itchycoo Park' sleeve (Mankowitz remembers my mother as 'pushy'), which was used on the single's sheet music as well as on the US-only album release *There Are But Four Small Faces*. The photo is of four young boys holding a mocked-up Itchycoo Park road sign in a 'rural setting' that was actually Hampstead Heath. It was a windy day and the sign, being made out of paper, kept blowing about and was difficult to hold straight.

Nevertheless, by the age of five I'd been dressed by Small Faces – or rather by my mum with Small Faces in mind – for most of my life. Rupert Bear-check tweeds with crew- or polo-necks and baby guardsman jackets. I have vague memories of playing with the band on the swing in the garden at home. If that sounds unlikely, bear in mind that for Christmas in 1967 the mischievous Steve Marriott bought me a fully functioning air rifle.

Fran definitely enjoyed her time in the magic circle. In later life she was regularly interviewed for a number of rock & roll books and if you pushed her on the right day she might recount some of her more interesting stories. Countless tales of fun parties with the in-crowd, screaming teens storming dressing rooms, lazy days with the band in Essex or Pimlico and, just for that one moment, being in the centre of Swinging London's cultural whirlwind.

Without a doubt her favourite experience was meeting Wilson Pickett backstage at *Ready Steady Go!*, ITV's premiere rock & pop show. It was November 1965 and she'd been lounging in the green room with Ronnie Lane when the suited and booted American made a beeline for her orange pixie crop. She had no idea who the charming man was, but they chatted for a few minutes until the show started filming. On the spur of the moment, Pickett dragged her on stage to dance to his latest single, 'Don't Fight It'. She loved the experience and I still have the Rediffusion scrapbook that was handed to all *RSG!* attendees as they left the studios. Sadly, the majority of episodes of the most important British music programme of all time were wiped in the late Sixties and Season 3, Episode 11 is one of them. I've never seen her moment of glory. But she was there, and she lived it.

*

By 1968, in the Piller household at least, mod had been put firmly back in the box. My dad never lost his love of modern jazz and Italian tailoring, but the pressures of work meant the scooter-riding days were long gone. This was the way of the world in the late Fifties and early Sixties. Youth culture meant what it said on the tin: it was for youth. Boys and girls enjoying themselves before career and family got in the way.

As for me, as the colourful and exciting Sixties came to an end I was sent to Loyola, a Jesuit Catholic junior school in Buckhurst Hill.

If you aren't up to speed on the vagaries of the Church of Rome, the Jesuits are the stormtroopers.

The headmaster, a Mr O'Gara, was an aloof figure who occasionally dispensed the wrath of God with a 12-inch slice of leather-covered whalebone called the Ferula, which was stingingly administered to the open palm or the back of the leg. But we had no real complaints – discipline was fair and you knew where you stood. Miscreants were punished quickly and effectively and the matter not mentioned again. On the whole, the teachers were kind and of Irish extraction, committed to the betterment of their charges. I loved my time there.

Gareth Barnard and Damien Cronin were my two special school friends. Gareth was my mum's best mate's son and seemed to be going through a pyromaniac phase, setting fire to anything he could, while Damian was a big lad who loved his rugby (he eventually went on to represent Scotland and the British Lions). Both became close friends and joined me on our mod journey a few years later.

For me, though, it was football. But despite being a goalkeeper for the school team, I was never much cop as a player.

My mum's family were Spurs and, hoping to claim me, whisked me off to White Hart Lane as soon as I could stand. The Pillers, however, were thoroughly West Ham. My dad owned the bookie's closest to the Boleyn Ground, mixed with players of all London teams and had season tickets in the west side at Upton Park and took me along weekly. He was always coming into my room at night with another autograph he'd blagged at some booze-up. My collection was unrivalled at school: John Radford, Martin Peters, Martin Chivers, Geoff Hurst, Noel Cantwell, Nobby Stiles, Phil Parkes, Clyde Best, Billy Bonds and dozens more. Pride of place in my bedroom was a signed first edition of Bobby Moore's *Moore On Mexico*.

My parents were friends with Bobby and Tina, and me and my sister would occasionally 'play' with their kids Roberta and Dean in the school holidays. We were usually dragged to Bobby's private members club, Woolston Hall (which became Epping Forest Country Club), where our mums drank G&Ts by the pool in swimwear. It was the only licensed premises we could visit where I wasn't confined to the car park with a bottle of Pepsi and a packet of Golden Wonder.

The boy who sat next to me in class was Danny Greaves, son of the legendary Spurs striker Jimmy, who'd recently moved to West Ham; us boys regularly fought for a glimpse of the great man as he dropped Danny and his brother Andy off at school.

My eighth birthday was fast approaching, and when dad asked me what I wanted for a present, I told him I *needed* that super-cool West Ham away kit: the sky-blue long-sleeved shirt with two claret hoops on the chest. Dad said he'd sort it and would pull his various connections to rustle one up (we very rarely paid for anything; everything in dad's life was based on favours, drinks and deals). Jimmy Greaves apparently had connections to a sports shop, so Dad had a word with him and I waited and waited . . . and waited.

Two weeks after my birthday had been and gone, I heard a knock at the front door and a couple of minutes later Dad popped into my bedroom with a brown paper bag that'd been hastily dropped off by Mr Greaves. Jesus. England's greatest striker was hand-delivering a West Ham away kit. Just for me! Thrilled, I ripped open the package. But wait . . . What the fuck was this? The socks were yellow with a royal-blue band. I pulled them out and scrabbled with the white tissue paper to get to the shirt underneath. This wasn't right. The shorts were royal blue. Eh? I unfolded the shirt to see the blue cannon of the Arsenal on a yellow shirt. Jimmy Greaves had delivered a fucking Arsenal away kit!

To say I was disappointed was an understatement. I picked up the offending rags and ran downstairs to my dad, who was sitting in the lounge watching television.

'Dad, I think there's been some kind of mistake . . .?'

He wasn't even listening and barely looked up from *The Goodies*, grunting a non-committal reply. I was heartbroken – and this was possibly the first time the young pre-mod Piller realised that the wrong clothes were . . . well . . . *wrong*. The Gunners kit sat in a drawer for at least a year until my mum gave it to a charity shop! And, sadly, I never went to see the Hammers with the old man again.

Early football-related sartorial disasters aside, I experienced an idyllic childhood. Holidays in Jersey with my grandparents or Ibiza with my mum. At times it seemed like life couldn't get any better. But then, one day, Dad poked his head round the bedroom door.

'Pack your bags, son, you're off to boarding school on Monday!'

3

I'M STRANDED

When you find yourself on your own at the age of nine, you soon work out you have to sink or swim. There's a multitude of conflicting messages from just about everyone who's suffered it but, if you can cope with the bullying and the misplaced interest from 'adults', then boarding school can be the making of you – like it was for me.

Looking back now, I realise that the 'idyllic' home life I'd perceived was far from it; things hadn't been quite so rosy in the garden. I'd spent almost all of my time staying with my nan and my relationship with my parents was somewhat fractured. They spent most of their time socialising and had little time for their kids.

I was still somewhat naive about my dad's role in East End life. I genuinely thought he worked in a shop and the exotic fruit, trays of fillet steak, electrical gadgets and other luxuries he brought home were purchased in the market and not the result of dodgy connections in the docks. It would be some time before I understood the subtleties of the real situation.

On top of that, I wasn't getting on particularly well with my sister, Vicky. She was three years younger than me, and we spent most of our time arguing and fighting. I assumed I was sent away to give my parents some peace, but it later transpired that my maternal grandfather had insisted I was removed from the loving bosom – his motive being to break the Piller family tradition of life in the slightly tarnished world of East End bookmaking. He wanted better for me.

So, in 1973, I was suddenly removed from my carefree existence at Loyola and dispatched to board at Chigwell School.

Back then, Chigwell had none of the 'fast buck, poor taste' connotations it has today. The school was 350 years old and sat in a sleepy village on the Essex and East London border, just seven miles from my house. I was even allowed to escape the spartan regime with regular trips home at weekends. In truth, the place was a down-at-heel home for affluent cockneys who'd made it out to Essex, but I'd read *Tom Brown's Schooldays* and *Malory Towers* and therefore found myself looking forward to the idea of midnight feasts and self-sufficiency. I also relished the chance to get away from my family.

So boarding school was actually OK. In fact, I got into it at first, in a happy if directionless way, though I gradually began to lose interest as I got older. By the time I was 13, I still had no idea what I wanted to do for a job despite being regularly asked.

There was pressure to 'do something in the City', but I quickly realised that that life wasn't for me. The City of London was the main destination for bright boys from the East London and Essex fringe, and my school churned them out like a conveyor belt. It was the mid-Seventies and the 'bowler hat and old school tie' mentality had been replaced by a thrusting meritocracy. The City was now a results-based game and big money was being made in the futures markets, and the middle-class barrow boys of Chigwell were perfect cannon fodder. While all this might have appealed to some of my mates, I knew quite early doors that I wanted no part of it.

In 1976 I auditioned for a part in the school play and was surprised to be offered the lead. It was called *The Thwarting of Baron Bolligrew* and I was cast as the baron. Yes, he was a nasty, pompous bully with an impressively high opinion of himself, so it was obvious typecasting, but as an egotist I relished the idea of mincing about on stage.

It was during rehearsals for that play that I first got an inkling that there might be something more to the Pillers' setup than I'd previously thought. A number of scenes called for the baron to gesticulate with a shotgun. You know the kind of thing: lording it over the peasantry and scaring the local maidens. The teacher in charge of the play asked if anyone had anything we could use as a prop for the shotgun.

'Oh, I think I can help there, sir,' I said, eager to establish my credentials in this exciting new world. 'I'm sure we've got something at home I could borrow.'

We did indeed have 'something' at home. The coming weekend I was on one of my semi-regular home visits, so the first thing I did was to sneak upstairs to have a look about. Would it still be there? Indeed it was!

Buried under some clothes in the back of my dad's wardrobe was a real shotgun. I wasn't supposed to know it was there but had come across it while being nosey one time. I sneakily stuffed the gun in my cricket bag and took it back to school with me.

The teacher was thrilled – it was a *very* convincing prop. Not knowing the dimensions of 'normal' shotguns, I wasn't aware that this one's barrel had been shortened by some 8 or 10 inches. All I remember was that my prop was a beautiful thing: double-barrelled with gorgeous chasing on the side plates and a sharkskin pattern etched onto the stock.

The teacher, clearly also no firearms expert, was equally unfamiliar with the true length of a shotgun barrel. We used the gun for around three weeks, right up to a special dress rehearsal scheduled two weeks before the first performance so a photographer from the local paper could turn up and take some publicity shots to facilitate a full-on marketing campaign. The following Friday, an article was duly published announcing the forthcoming first night, with me and the shotgun taking centre stage in the accompanying photo.

This was just the beginning of my problems.

Up to now, I'd yet to hear my dad utter a profanity. In spite of his Bethnal Green upbringing, he'd always appeared quiet and considered; certainly polite and something of a gentleman. He was always smartly dressed and well presented, although by the mid-Seventies he'd succumbed to the fashion for large mutton-chop sideburns and a Zapata-esque moustache. However I looked at it, I hadn't heard him swear or even lose his temper.

The Sunday morning three days before I was due to tread the boards in *The Thwarting of Baron Bolligrew*, the cool and polite demeanour I'd projected onto my dad was irrevocably shattered.

'Oh my God . . .! Fuck . . .! We've been burgled!'

Shouting at the top of his voice, he sounded very angry indeed. This might be serious. He was normally in bed eating poached eggs on toast and reading the papers at 8 o'clock on a Sunday, waiting for my mum to clear off to church with my sister and me. No, this was definitely serious.

My room was next to my parents', so I jumped out of bed and tiptoed to the door. I could hear their conversation quite clearly.

'Calm down and compose yourself.' My mother sounded reassuring. 'I'm going to call the police . . . What have they taken? They weren't after my jewellery because it's all still here . . .'

'Do *not* phone the police!' Dad snapped. 'It's the bloody shotgun. It's gone. They've touched nothing else. I reckon they knew what they were after. *Don't* call the Old Bill!'

'Oh, I never liked you having that gun in the house. I wouldn't worry about it; it's not even yours.'

'I know it isn't mine. That's the whole fucking point: I'm looking after it for someone. If the Old Bill find it I'm in the shit, and properly.' My dad was still shouting. I quailed.

Silence while my mind raced.

I'd borrowed a real sawn-off shotgun and used it for three weeks in a fucking school play. Not only that, but a photographer from the local paper had taken a dozen pictures of me pointing it at people. Dad now thinks it's been nicked and is going doolally in the other room at the shit he's going to be in should word get out, either from the bloke he's looking after it for or the Old Bill. It wasn't lost on me that a licensed bookmaker was supposed to be a man of moral standing and hiding a sawn-off from the Sweeney would probably invalidate that licence.

Time to step up and take the rap. I was crapping myself.

In my defence, like all other non-farm-dwelling schoolboys I didn't know that shotguns even needed a licence and assumed everyone had one tucked away in the garage or the wardrobe. Secondly, my dad was a remote figure who I generally avoided, so I couldn't predict where this was going. I did suppose (correctly, as it turned out) that he was going to be massively pissed off when I told him that we hadn't been burgled but that I'd borrowed the gun to use in a play and there were photos of me pointing it in the current edition of the local paper.

I took a deep breath and knocked on my parents' bedroom door. I could almost hear the old man take a deep breath and compose himself.

'Come.'

I poked my head round the door and was relieved to see all looked normal. My mum was in her dressing gown over the far side of the room and dad was standing to the left of the bed in pyjamas.

'What is it, Edward? I'm busy at the moment.'

Edward again: the default setting for when older people were cross with me!

'Erm, well, Dad, I couldn't help but hear . . . Are you looking for the shotgun?'

I took a deep breath and ploughed straight on. I thought it best to lay it all out and see what happened. I mean, it wasn't my fault, was it? I wasn't to know.

The excuse sounded thin. The words tumbled out in a torrent. He coloured slightly at the cheeks.

'You did *what*? For your fucking *play*?'

Mother again. Rarely the voice of reason, but on this occasion . . .
'Oh, Edward, how could you? That was very stupid.'

I glanced over my shoulder for the door, preparing to bolt, but Dad had other ideas.

'What on earth have you been up to?'

He inched round to stand between me and the potential escape route and then, quite calmly, insisted I tell him the whole story.

When I'd finished, I realised that I'd done something impossibly stupid. And the teacher allowing a 13-year-old to parade around on stage with a shotgun, sawn-off or not, was – fortunately for me – more of an offence than my taking it to school in the first place. He hadn't even broken the stock to check if it was loaded. I could've taken a loaded shotgun to school and *shot someone*! Gulp. I was fucked. Just as bad, the first of the three performances were scheduled for the following Tuesday night – what on earth was I going to use as a shotgun now?

My mum was charged with coming up to school on the Monday afternoon to remove the shotgun from the props cupboard, preferably without any attention from passing teachers. I kept badgering away at her, trying to find out who owned the gun; she did eventually fess up, but as you can imagine I'm sworn to secrecy.

This family row took the shine off my acting debut – as did the fact that a very hasty and unconvincing shotgun had been fashioned out of a broom handle and some cardboard! I hadn't appreciated it at the time, but *The Thwarting of Baron Bolligrew* was a big deal. The play was written for the Royal Shakespeare Company and scripted by Oscar-winning writer Robert Bolt, who'd written *Lawrence of Arabia* and *Dr Zhivago*. *Baron Bolligrew* was Bolt's first children's play and one he remained very fond of – so fond, in fact, that he was attending the first night. The pressure was on . . .

I shouldn't have worried. I learned later in life that practice and experience will overcome the nerves associated with public performance, but *Bolligrew* was my first-ever uttering. I was chronically nervous but excited at the same time. It was a buzz!

Like most exciting landmarks, the performance flashed by; and my lines came out more or less right.

Robert Bolt came backstage after the performance to congratulate the cast. While shaking his hand and basking in his compliments, I took a momentous decision. I was going to be an actor!

My career plan got off to a good start. Ian Holm had been at my school in the Sixties and got his first experience with the very drama society I was now a member of. I threw myself into learning what I could about my chosen craft and a couple of other parts in school plays followed.

Then fate took a hand.

In February 1978, two weeks before I was due to play my next role, Puck in *A Midsummer Night's Dream*, I was laid up with chicken pox. It's not a great illness to contract when you've passed puberty; in fact, it's a shit. I took it hard and within days was immobilised. I covered myself with calamine lotion and weathered the storm. All thoughts of acting were binned and I spent a month at home in isolation. The play came and went with an understudy playing my part.

Revision was boring, so I listened to a lot of music. Slade and The Sweet, the pop of my youth, had progressed to more cerebral stuff like Pink Floyd, Queen and ELO. The Beatles and my parents Motown and jazz LPs made more than a passing impression. To cap it all I discovered late-night radio.

I was not yet 15 and there were two radio DJs I was interested in back then. The first was the gnome-like Nicky Horne, who hosted a show called *Your Mother Wouldn't Like It* playing proggy-rock on

Capital. The second was John Peel, whose late-night Radio 1 show was different gravy. He played a bit of everything from his bluesy instrumental theme music through roots reggae and punk. I liked punk and of course was aware of it – it had, after all, been everywhere for the previous 18 months – but it hadn't really connected much. I liked the Sex Pistols and The Stranglers, but it was all very much on the periphery of my world.

My mum had a friend called Jenny Morris who was a PA at EMI Records and when she heard I was laid up with chicken pox she responded with a package of promos snaffled from work. Not just vinyl but posters and badges too. She thought they would cheer me up and she was right: they did.

Although it was Britain's biggest label, by 1978 EMI wasn't too clever. There was loads of stuff in the box, maybe 30 records. A promo of the as yet unreleased *Some Girls* by The Rolling Stones was top of the pile and beneath that were new offerings from Elton John, Queen and Barclay James Harvest as well as a whole host of old people's stuff. Also included among a handful of uncool mustard and red EMI 7-inches was a 45 on the Power Exchange label in a basic black and white picture sleeve.

I worked my way through the albums. Nothing special, but nice of her to think of me – although I loved the way *Some Girls* sort of sounded, it was well put together and the sleeve with the holes juxtaposed over the boy/girl faces looked pretty cool too.

Once I'd listened to all the LPs I came to the 45s. Again, nothing particularly grabbed my attention. The first four singles seemed run-of-the-mill and bland. Then it happened . . .

Enlightenment.

I was struck by a flash of exploding, angry noise. My ears were assaulted by a wall of raw, angry sound; ear-bleedingly heavy and yes, heartfelt. No crackle, no burn, just straight into the track.

Nothing – and I mean *nothing* – could've prepared me for the sound that came blasting out of the speakers. Shocked, I lifted the needle and put it back to the beginning, turning the volume up as loud as it could go.

This was different from anything I'd properly listened to before.

'Like a snake calling on the phone / I got no time to be alone . . . / 'Cause I'm straaaanded on my ownnnn / Stranded far from home . . .!'

What the fuck was this?

What I was listening to was The Saints and their anthemic punk snarl '(I'm) Stranded'.

Written in 1974 and performed by a bunch of Brisbane misfits from the fucking outback – a world more normally associated with flying doctors, 'Waltzing Matilda' and Rolf fucking Harris – this three minutes and twenty-eight seconds of righteous anger blew my head off and forced me to acknowledge life beyond the normal. Never again could I listen to ELO, Queen, Elton John or any of that old shit.

This track spoke to my teenage self. It was what I'd been searching for without even knowing I was looking.

Fuck acting. I wanted music – *this* kind of music. I wanted more of it and I wanted it now.

4

MARQUEE MOON

I t was April 1978, I was 14 years old and I had some catching up to do.

Music at school was polarised. Older boys were into AC/DC, Rush or Black Sabbath and no one in my year was interested in anything at all.

I, on the other hand, was keen to broaden my horizons – but to do this I needed money.

The Saints experience had kick-started my voracious musical development and now, along with a coterie of schoolmates, I began to greedily absorb as much as I could. From that point on, every penny I could blag or earn was put towards buying records or going to gigs. To further this aim, I was working every available moment at my part-time job.

Mister Byrite was a well-known East London fashion chain, and while people laugh about it now, at the time Byrite's was exotic – or at least it *seemed* exotic to me. Owned by a sharp-eyed East End schmutter merchant called Barry Levy, the chain consisted of a dozen or so shops selling cut-price versions of the latest men's fashions. It was in the Byrite warehouse on Blackhorse Road, Walthamstow, that I got my first job. Meaning that now, for the first time, I had my own source of income.

A few months earlier, a sixth-former with the improbable name of Dirk Blackguard had approached me for a chat, which was unusual in that the older boys didn't usually acknowledge our existence. Dirk was also a boarder was looking for kids to accompany him to a gig – he'd heard that Bob Dylan was going to tour the UK and did I fancy it?

Bob Dylan?

I knew nothing of Dylan, but fancied the idea of going to a concert. I'd never been to one before.

The gig was at Earls Court Exhibition Centre and three of us decided to make the trip: me, Dirk and a boy in the year above called Tim Golborn. Tim was one of the few boys at school who appeared even vaguely interested in music and we'd end up taking in many gigs together, but this was our first.

To get tickets for Dylan we headed up to Earls Court at eight in the morning on the day they went on sale, which fortunately for us was a Sunday. Bob hadn't been to the UK for a while, and even though he was playing six dates, demand for tickets was intense and they sold out in just one day. In that pre-internet era, ticket applications had to be in person, and I remember queuing for over eight hours. I didn't mind as it was a completely new experience and just seeing all those people – most of them clinging for dear life to the lost world of the hippy – was fascinating. To me, a middle-class boarding-school boy, they looked like exotic freaks. It was only later that I realised most of them were also middle-class boarding-school boys just like me!

Army greatcoats, denim flares and long, hand-knitted scarves were the fashion items of choice among those standing in the queue and with their greasy, unkempt hair I thought the lot of them looked a proper state.

It was a bitterly cold day spent with a packed lunch and a Thermos flask. Inching ever closer to the front of the long twisting snake of humanity brought its eventual reward when we arrived at the box-office window and passed our cash across to the attendant. He told us that there were only a handful of tickets left for our chosen night and most of the other nights were sold out already. Thrilled, we'd secured three seats as far from the stage as it was possible to be.

I had a three-month wait until the gig, which was plenty of time to get to know a bit about Bob Dylan. I checked the local record shop in Woodford and they had nothing, but I did manage to pick up a secondhand copy of his 1966 orange CBS 45 'One of Us Must Know (Sooner or Later)' at a junk shop in Ilford a week later. I played it repeatedly over the next few weeks, trying to pick up some of the legendary Dylan vibe – everyone talked about him, but I was having trouble getting beyond that first single.

Once I'd discovered The Saints, everything else seemed monochrome and got pushed to the back of the queue – and that included Dylan.

My ticket-buying partner Tim Golborn immediately suggested going to another gig. The whole Earls Court queueing experience had enthused us both, and as it was still a couple of months before Bob Dylan arrived in the UK, why not go and see someone else?

Tim suggested trying a band more in tune with our recent shift in musical direction. After all, the Dylan gig had been Dirk's idea and I for one was not feeling it in the same way as I did the exciting new world revealed when I first heard The Saints.

'Great idea,' I responded. 'But who?'

I'm not sure why, but your choice of the available 'inky' music papers made an important personal statement back then, almost like an extension of your personality. There were three weekly music tabloids on newsstands in the late Seventies and I was fervently *Sounds*. I couldn't stand *Melody Maker* and would only pick up the *NME* when *Sounds* was unavailable.

We trawled through *Sounds* and spotted that the New York punk(ish) band Television were soon to play the Hammersmith Odeon. We'd heard tracks from *Marquee Moon* on John Peel, and while they weren't what we thought of as punk rock, they were angular, hypnotic and best of all supported by a home-grown punk band called The Only Ones. That swung it for us and next morning we set off to Hammersmith on another ticket-buying mission.

My neighbour and Scalextric partner Cliff Dowsett had snaffled his sister's New York punk compilation, which featured tracks from Patti Smith ('Piss Factory') and Richard Hell ('Blank Generation'). Hell was a co-founder of Television, so we listened to the compilation constantly in an attempt to absorb the New York arthouse flavour. I genuinely liked this stuff!

We got to the Odeon to buy tickets but, unlike at Earls Court, there was no queue here – in fact, we didn't see anyone who could've been in the least bit interested in a punk concert. There were loads of tickets left, so we chose the cheapest, high up in the circle, and decided to stop to buy some records on the way home. The only experience of note that day came after we'd left the box office and were waiting on a deserted platform at Hammersmith Tube Station.

We were approached by what used to be known as a 'dirty old man'. My only previous experience of this type of random perversion had been in the public toilet on Loughton High Road while my mum waited outside, when a middle-aged man jumped out of the cubicle mid wank and did a little dance in front of me. I had absolutely no idea what he was up to (I was about seven) and assumed he was in some sort of agonising pain! I ran away as quickly as possible.

This time a dishevelled, unwashed and bearded man of about 50 wearing an unfashionable and grubby leather jacket inched towards us on the otherwise empty platform. Once he'd drawn level with our bench he made a great show of dropping some change directly in front of us. Still bemused, we waited to see what he was up to.

We didn't have to wait long, as he bent over so forcefully that his dirty camel-coloured Farah's split from fly to belt loop. Of course, our new friend wasn't wearing pants and the vision of his crusted ring-piece and low-slung bollocks as he went through the charade of trying to pick up his change while pushing his hairy arse in our faces has stayed with me these 40-odd years.

From there, feeling somewhat shell-shocked, we took the train across London to a record shop we'd read about in *Sounds*.

Small Wonder was in Hoe Street, Walthamstow, and was the type of emporium that served up records you couldn't buy in Woolworths. The place was a poky lock-up and didn't look too special from the outside, but as soon as we pushed open the door our senses were assaulted. Loud, booming dub reggae on the stereo, the heady smell of joss sticks (or was it spliff? I was too young to tell) and a multitude of records in their often-outrageous picture covers stuck to the walls.

'Hello, lads, what can I do for you?'

Nervous and unsure of myself in this new world, I stuttered out: 'Erm . . . Well, I'm just looking, erm, you know . . . for stuff.'

'Oh really?' said the guy behind the counter. 'Well, feel free. If there's anything that takes your fancy, just ask me and I'll play it for you.'

The late Seventies was the golden age for vinyl. There were record shops on every corner and all the department stores hosted disc departments. There was even a 'singles bar' in Rumbelows, the electrics rental chain. But sadly, we soon realised that not all record shops were created equal. In the spring of 1978 our local, Penny Farthing in Woodford Broadway, offered little more than a conservative mix of chart-based fare and albums by exotic-sounding groups like Curved Air, Kiss, Jethro Tull and Heart. Mainly rubbish.

Small Wonder was about as different from Penny Farthing and the like as it was possible to be.

Often forgotten in favour of its West London rival Rough Trade, Small Wonder was in 1978 an oasis in a desert of musical mediocrity.

It was cramped and untidy, and the second you stepped inside you realised you were somewhere special. Today Rough Trade is rightly remembered with much love and fondness, often by people who never went there, but in my opinion (and having spent many hours in both) Small Wonder beat it hands down. The shop was rather nondescript and grubby, slap bang in the middle of a shopping terrace, and the man offering to help us out on our first visit was the owner, a friendly bloke with long blond hair and wearing a beanie hat. His name was Hippy Pete and he was a bone fide legend.

We discovered later that Pete Stennett had bunged his savings and redundancy money into a shop that, in his words, would 'sell the kind of records I'd want to buy myself'. Pete was hoping to introduce a new generation to the dark, German-prog sound of Amon Düül II but, fortunately for us, the shop had quickly become the local haven for independent punk rock.

From our first visit that afternoon, Stennett took an almost fatherly interest in us. If in 1978 staff in Rough Trade could greet the casual and inexperienced visitor with aloof distain, at Small Wonder you'd get the opposite.

In order to answer Pete's question, I took in the singles pinned to the wall above the counter. 'Safety-pin Stuck in My Heart' by Patrick Fitzgerald, 'Homicide' by 999, The Lurkers, The Users, The Damned, The Stranglers, Albertos y Lost Trios Paranoias, TV Personalities, Buzzcocks, Sham 69 . . . A veritable sweetshop of names, some new to me, some slightly more familiar to Tim, but all, without exception, sounding like they were from a different place to the one I'd been living in. Picture covers, coloured vinyl, home-made sleeves, 12-inch singles! It was indeed a brave new world.

After a nervous ten-minute browse Pete asked us what bands we liked.

'The Saints and The Stranglers, but we're off to see The Only Ones and Television next week. Have you got anything by them?'

He rooted around and pulled out some records. Top of the pile was a 7-inch copy of 'Lovers of Today' by The Only Ones on Vengeance.

'That's their first single, came out six months ago, but the new one's even better – released this week. It's on CBS.'

He also flashed a green vinyl 12-inch of 'Foxhole', Television's forthcoming single. I bought both and so did Tim. Hippy Pete, perhaps sensing he might be on to a good thing, soon pulled other 45s out from behind the counter.

'If you like that, you'll love this . . . "19 & Mad" by a local band, the Leyton Buzzards – or what about this one by Angelic Upstarts? 999? Chelsea?' And he was right, we did.

From that point on, Small Wonder became my regular hangout. Pete could be notoriously rude, but it was taken in good heart. In fact – and I'm still not sure that he didn't do this for every customer – each time I visited he'd pull out a preselected pile of 45s from behind the counter in a bag *with my name written on it.*

'These came out a couple of days ago; I thought you might want them . . .'

Not just flattering but a major entrée to a world I was desperate to discover. Small Wonder was a very special place. Even their shop logo, printed on their bags, was extraordinary. A black American family dressed in their finery sitting posed in a portrait, taken in the 19th century!

Immediately we felt like we belonged. Every time we went to the shop we met kids just like us. Initially we'd been nervous and out of our depth, but Small Wonder gave us confidence to join this new world that we'd been scared of. Those early punk records that Pete Stennett first played us gave me the self-assurance to experiment with so many new sounds. The Stranglers and The Saints were first, but I soon fell in love with the whole lot. John Peel helped of course, but within weeks of our first visit Small Wonder made me feel part of something.

That first afternoon we bussed it back to Tim's house on the 179 in a rush to listen to our first pile of punk purchases in more detail.

The Only Ones' debut 'Lovers of Today' was first. To be honest, the (soon to be banned) sleeve freaked me out a bit. It looked like some weird kinky sex drama with one of the band members (who looked a little like Max Wall) wearing a fishnet body stocking. Musically the record packed a punch: melodic punky pop with a lazy drawl from vocalist Peter Perrett. Their most recent single was the one that hooked me, though. 'Another Girl, Another Planet' was the perfect punk missive, with an awesome intro that slowly built into an incredible crescendo leading into the first verse – and what a fucking guitar solo!

This was what my life was going to be about.

The following week, me and Tim donned our black leather jackets – which were by now adorned with obligatory pin badges – and caught the train up to the Hammersmith Odeon for our first-ever gig. We arrived ridiculously early and sunk a couple of cans on the Tube. For once we couldn't get served in the first couple of pubs we tried. Then we arrived at the bar of the Clarendon Hotel – a notorious rock & roll venue where the barman didn't even look at us twice!

After the Clarendon we crossed the roundabout and headed for the imposing Odeon to take our place in the queue outside, but not before being confronted by a number of touts offering tickets at a substantial markup. Pleased that we'd been shrewd enough to buy ours upfront, we made our way into the venue and climbed the stairs to the circle. The place was still half-empty when we sat down and the crowd was a mixture of punks and new-wave fans who all wore the ubiquitous leather jacket, tight jeans or flares and All-Star baseball boots.

Unsure what to expect at my first rock & roll gig, I initially thought that The Only Ones appeared out of their depth as they wandered onto the enormous stage. The band were greeted with mild, somewhat restrained cheers as they launched into a loud but surprisingly accomplished set. They immediately dispelled the idea that punk bands couldn't play. This lot were inspiring because we had both their singles and felt like we were already a part of their world, that we belonged. Perrett was a brilliant frontman and the hall filled to capacity during their set. There was a short interlude during which the pair of us persuaded a bloke sitting next to us to buy us a beer at the bar and then, before we were even back in our seats, the lights went down, the venue descended into blackness and an expectant hush settled over the crowd as they waited for something to happen.

And happen it did.

Television took the stage to a cacophony of sound and launched into a perfect set. Contrary to what I'd read about them, they certainly weren't a punk band – even less so since Richard Hell left to form The Voidoids. What they were was a technically accomplished, stripped-down rock band whose angular, guitar-driven sound showcased long musical battles between Tom Verlaine and the other guitarist, Richard Lloyd. 'Marquee Moon' was the standout song in the set, but the new single, 'Foxhole', was also met with a hysterical reaction. The gig seemed to be over in just a minute, even though the set lasted more than an hour, and suddenly we found ourselves outside on the pavement in a daze, threading between the cars as we joined the throng heading for Hammersmith Station and the long journey home.

What an incredible way to pop our gig cherry!

If only all gigs were as good as that one. A couple of months later, in June 1978, the Bob Dylan concert came round in a rush but was something of an anticlimax.

The trouble with Earls Court and venues like it was the whole impersonal nature of the relationship between performer and audience. In our case, the seats were so far away from the stage that Dylan appeared no bigger than an ant and the acoustics were poor, as they always are in cavernous halls. On top of that, the 'voice of a generation' droned on for what seemed like three hours. I didn't know enough about Dylan to follow proceedings with too much enthusiasm, but halfway through I brightened and sang along with conviction to 'One of Us Must Know (Sooner or Later)', 'Like a Rolling Stone', 'Hurricane' (a Peel favourite) and a couple of his bigger hits. They were the brief highlights for me but, in truth, I felt out of my depth and something of an imposter.

More than that, I realised that psychologically I'd already moved on.

5

DO THEY OWE US A LIVING?

Things eventually came to a head at the dreamy spires of Chigwell just a week or so after the gig. I was just 14 years old.

Inspired by the legless fighter ace Douglas Bader, who'd given a talk to the pupils earlier that 'Speech Day', I'd organised a clandestine raid on the school's summer party, where three hundred parents congregated in a marquee on the cricket pitch and drunk themselves stupid.

I'd hatched a plot to camouflage my cronies with boot polish, slip under the tent flap, grab as much alcohol as we could and run away. It was to be a real *Boy's Own* adventure.

The operation ran like clockwork. Leaving pillows stuffed under blankets in our beds, we shinned down the drainpipe from our dormitory, ran through the graveyard next door and successfully snaffled several bottles of hard liquor from a couple of tables.

Laughing at our success and looking like escapees from Stalag Luft 14, we settled down in a derelict building in the grounds and guzzled the lot. Some teenage vomiting and passing out was followed by the barking of a dog, which jerked me back to my senses. I looked at my watch. Shit, it was three hours since our raid and a search party led by two coppers with a police dog had eventually found us slumped in a heap. We were still completely twatted.

It hadn't taken long for the younger boys to crack. The shock of an interrogation by the Old Bill at two in the morning after you've been caught wide-eyed and legless might even have done for Douglas Bader himself. It all came tumbling out from them.

'Piller was to blame, sir – he made us do it!'

One by one my erstwhile accomplices distanced themselves. We were caught bang to rights – or rather *I* was. Fortunately, the headmaster didn't want the bad publicity that would accompany the arrest of a paralytic 14-year-old. Instead, we were on the receiving end of a massive bollocking from the coppers about the twin evils of stealing and drinking alcohol but mainly about stealing alcohol.

We were taken back to our boarding house and sent straight to bed by a stern-faced housemaster. I was told to be ready by ten the next morning with my bag packed. I was in serious trouble. I realised I wasn't going to get away with the usual 'six of the best' from a slipper or cane. The night passed slowly and without the relief of sleep.

I'd skipped breakfast and spent the time collecting my things. Rather than treating me as a conquering hero, the other boys were giving me a wide berth as if I was toxic, which of course I was.

I caught a glimpse of my face in the mirror and it still bore traces of boot polish (do you know just how difficult that is to remove?). A quarter of an hour later my mum arrived and I was summoned to the headmaster's office. I sat in the corridor quailing on a plastic chair until they called me in. The head was called Brian J. Wilson. Mum was sitting there with a face like thunder as he pointed to a chair and delivered his judgement: I was to leave the establishment immediately. And permanently.

Mum shooed me out of the office and waited for the door to close before she spoke.

Somehow she persuaded the old goat to rescind my expulsion. She didn't tell me how, but I remember that when we got home I heard her tell my dad that, 'Wilson said there was no shame in having an adopted child and in fact it was something to be proud of.'

Had she really spun the lie that I was a poor, fatherless waif who the Pillers had magnanimously taken to their bosom? Genius if true. Whatever magic she weaved, I found myself allowed to return after a two-week suspension. But I was now a day boy and I'd be there only until I sat my O levels, which were still over a year away.

The school hierarchy was now watching me like a hawk. My card was marked and boredom meant I'd pretty much given up on everything in school apart from history and cricket. Outside school our gig excursions became more regular and I found myself joined by a couple of punk-curious classmates called Richard Habberley and Tris Pitt, both having been drawn towards the music by Tris's elder brother, who was friends with a local band called Crass.

Crass somehow bucked all the trends associated with the established 'punk scene' and as such were often disliked by the Sid Vicious clones increasingly prevalent at gigs. The band lived in a mysterious pagan-type commune deep in Epping Forest called Dial House. They wore black, paramilitary-style uniforms and were avowed anarchists (not in the Malcolm McLaren/Sex Pistols Situationist way: Crass were serious political anarchists). They also practised what they preached and made sure their records sold for not much more than cost price. We loved them.

A couple of weeks after my suspension and I was back at Mister Byrite's earning some cash. I rose at seven and took the 179 bus to Blackhorse Road (one stop along from Walthamstow), where I was the lowest of the low: a warehouse boy. When I wasn't sweeping up or making tea, I was picking and packing items for daily distribution to the shops. They were a friendly group and many of the men working on the factory floor were older Teds – all tattooed knuckles and full-on greased DAs, relics from the glory days of Gene Vincent and Elvis who just couldn't let go of their rock & roll dream. I secretly laughed and thought them sad; I mean, what 14-year-old could ever imagine middle-aged men clinging to the last vestiges of a dying culture they'd followed religiously since their teens? Oh, the irony!

There were two advantages to the job. The first was that it paid well: in spite of my age I was clearing over 30 quid a week, while the bus fare was probably just 10 pence each way. The other was that the warehouse was only two bus stops from Small Wonder.

The wages fuelled my passion for record collecting but also afforded me the opportunity to head into London's gig land more often to see some of the bands whose records I'd been buying.

The summer was spent going backwards and forwards between sweaty pub gigs and record buying at Small Wonder. The shop was always a regular target for the local plod, who'd famously taken exception to the window display for the Sex Pistols' *Never Mind the Bollocks* album. After a couple of heavy-handed warnings, they threatened to arrest Pete Stennett under obscenity laws (which had been designed to combat pornography), but the resourceful shopkeeper circumvented this by covering the double *l* in 'bollocks' with a piece of paper so the display read *Never Mind the Boocks*. This enraged the Old Bill, but there was nothing they could do. Still, they kept trying.

It was the drug squad that nailed Stennett in the end.

They'd been keeping the shop under observation, long suspecting that cannabis was smoked on the premises. And there were occasional but unsuccessful raids, while plainclothes coppers pretending to be customers loitered to keep an eye out for anything suspicious.

I was only 14 and even I could tell that Pete smoked hash, so it must have been blatant to the drug squad. Sure enough, eventually their persistence paid off and he was nailed for possession. But this didn't deter him; he just became more careful.

The more time I spent in Small Wonder, the more I loved the setup. Pete not only had the shop but had also established his own very independent label, which was both credible and successful, and my first real inspiration. Maybe I could do this kind of thing one day?

Small Wonder Records repeatedly outsmarted major-label A&R departments and built an incredible roster of groundbreaking, future household names from scratch. I suspect this was because Pete was working at the very bottom of the industry pyramid, the coalface, far below the level that major labels considered worth their while, and consequently he ran rings round them. Uniquely, his approach was almost entirely altruistic and that was probably why he discovered so many brilliant bands. He didn't do it for the money; he did it because he could and because the bands needed an outlet.

Punk, metal and goth . . . Small Wonder's roster included the likes of The Cure, The Cortinas, Menace, Angelic Upstarts, Patrick Fitzgerald, Punishment of Luxury, Leyton Buzzards (who became Modern Romance), Cockney Rejects, Anthrax and Bauhaus. And then Pete signed Crass, who of course we already knew – and who were probably the only band in Britain regarded by MI5 as a genuine threat to the security of the nation.

As well as having a vague connection to Crass through Tris's older brother, we also thought Crass co-founder Penny Rimbaud was the closest thing Essex had to a spiritual guru and were somewhat in awe of him.

Take your pick: writer, painter, composer, philosopher, poet, activist, pacifist, anarchist, musician and co-founder of the Stonehenge Free Festival in 1972 alongside Wally Hope, who was murdered by the state for his efforts while Rimbaud got off scot-free. Originally an artist, Penny (then known as Jeremy Ratter) was an enthusiastic young mod when in 1964 he won a national TV competition to paint a portrait of The Beatles to accompany the release of 'I Want To Hold Your Hand' live on *Ready Steady Go!*. At the time, Rimbaud wasn't particularly interested in The Beatles per se, but his younger sister was a fan and so he'd entered the competition just to see if he could win on her behalf. The winning artwork was to be used in a national Beatles exhibition arranged by Mecca Ballrooms (who in fact 'lost' the painting) and the artist would be presented with two records of their choice by John Lennon live on TV.

Come the show, as Lennon handed Rimbaud his carefully considered choices by Shostakovich and Charlie Mingus, he made a flippant aside, 'Each to his own,' then added in Rimbaud's direction, 'Rocker, I'll get you for that.' For once, Lennon had been stumped. Tiring of the whole business, Rimbaud made his way out of the studios pursued by a gaggle of teenyboppers wanting to hold *his* hand. So how mod was that?

A fabulous and fascinating man who was also a handy drummer, Rimbaud joined forces with vocalist Steve Ignorant in 1977 to form Crass, who were without a doubt an important influence on me in the autumn of 1978. Together Ignorant and Rimbaud made angry and aggressive two-minute anthems with surprisingly high-level recording quality, but it was their political sentiments that ruffled the establishment. Along with their open-door commune nestled deep in Epping Forest, their music inevitably drew attention to their political agenda. Crass were equal-opportunity offenders – they didn't give a fuck who they offended, whether it was church, state, the corporate world, left, right, liberals, religion . . . In fact, they railed against just about everyone with vested interests in anything! Consequently, they were targeted by both left *and* right.

Things exploded with the band's first album, *The Feeding of the 5000*. Small Wonder had been using a vinyl broker to manufacture the record, which unfortunately ended up at an Irish pressing plant. The factory workers initially expressed concern at the disrespectful appropriation of Christian symbolism in the album's title, but when they heard the lyrical content of 'Reality Asylum' they became apoplectic. So outraged at (what they regarded as) the intensely blasphemous nature of the song, they downed tools and refused to handle the record. After a long standoff in which the workers refused to back down, eventually a grudging compromise was reached between Small Wonder and the factory: the offending song was removed and replaced with two minutes of silence, tactfully named 'The Sound of Free Speech'.

The Feeding of the 5000 was well received, but the problems with the pressing plant and the censorship issues they'd highlighted prompted Crass to establish their own imprint in order to safeguard their artistic integrity. The band reissued the album in 1980 with 'Reality Asylum' restored to its original position.

Without a doubt Crass were local heroes who we embraced with enthusiasm. I loved their album and spent most of 1978 traipsing round London in a prison-surplus jacket with the band's symbolic logo painted on the back. Unfortunately, I only got to see them once, at the Conway Hall in the summer of 1979 – and even then only very briefly because the gig was smashed up in an enormous fight between the British Movement and Red Action, neither of whom had any love for Crass!

Because my mum's relationship with Small Faces convinced her she was once part of the music business, she was relaxed about me going to gigs – and the West End was only 20 minutes away on the Central Line. The summer of 1978 saw us constantly out, from the smallest pubs to the biggest auditoria, and we were never once turned away, something today's overregulated 14-year-olds would find hard to believe. Buying pints was no hardship either; the oldest-looking lad would be the one to order beers at the bar and it usually worked.

By the end of the summer I'd seen a Pete Shelley-fronted Buzzcocks (Howard Devoto had quit and was now in Magazine, who I'd caught at the Electric Ballroom), Subway Sect, The Damned, Generation X, The Lurkers, 999, Menace, The Mekons, Gang of Four, X-Ray Spex, Joy Division, Lora Logic, Leyton Buzzards, The Slits, The Human League, The Ruts, Patrick Fitzgerald, The Members, Tom Robinson Band, Stiff Little Fingers, Dr. Feelgood, The Fall and Sham 69, and had graced venues such as the Marquee, Dublin Castle, Music Machine, Electric Ballroom, Nashville, Moonlight Club, Lyceum, Hammersmith Odeon, the Fulham Greyhound, Pied Bull and the Global Village.

There was a substantial difference between gigs at massive venues like Earls Court or the Hammersmith Palais and the ones held in small pubs and clubs. Because my first few concerts were in big halls, it took a while before I realised how different and incredibly inspiring shows in small pubs and clubs could be.

Without a doubt the Marquee had the best atmosphere. It was a smallish, down-at-heel club halfway down Wardour Street with black-painted walls. The back bar was adorned with the legend 'SPEED KILLS' in 3-foot letters, a reference to a Steve Gibbons song that checked the dangerous speedball habit that swept London's rock heartlands with tragic consequences in the mid-Seventies.

The sound was always better at small gigs, as was the proximity of the band – you could be standing within touching distance of the lead singer. They were substantially cheaper too, but it was the atmosphere that made these events. Almost all venues cared not a jot for legal capacity at the time and it was common to be shoehorned into a sweaty room with two or even three times as many punters as the place could stand, but we simply didn't care. You'd be drenched in sweat, regularly knocked over by hordes of pogoing teenagers and shouting yourself hoarse for a couple of hours until you found yourself dumped on the pavement at kicking-out time to catch the train or bus home. The sense of belonging to something special and exclusive was my main motivating factor. More so than even the music.

It was this that propelled me on. I loved punk but soon discovered that it wasn't the only way I could experience this kind of feeling. In fact, I didn't even need to go into London to find this level of excitement. Something else was hiding in plain sight, right on my doorstep in Essex.

It was called jazz-funk.

6

DO THE BRITISH HUSTLE

The summer of 1978 was when I fell in love with punk. But it was also the summer that I fell in love with black music.

Woodford was a predominately but not exclusively white suburb, split in half by a railway track. As a rule, south of the line was working class and north was middle class. There were of course exceptions and the main one was Trinity, the Catholic comprehensive on the High Road. The thing about Catholics was that their institutions cared nothing for race, only religion. The place was a veritable cornucopia of ethnicity and the same went for the church next door; my class was full of Irish, Sri Lankans, West Indians, Africans, Poles, Maltese and even a German.

The black kids we knew weren't from school but from the local underage soul discos like the Hawkey Hall or Rovsco Scout Hall. Our teen fashions clumsily copied those of the adult scene at the Ilford Palais or the Lacy Lady: silk-style bowling shirts, plastic sandals or winklepickers, straight cords or pegs, wedge haircuts and even quiffs . . . We did our best and danced enthusiastically, but an admiring circle usually formed around the real dancers, who were almost exclusively black.

Kids like Pedro Sandiford, his brother Lenny, Alan Omakoji, Derek Boland and Andy Campbell were among the local faces, and we were lucky that our under-18 nights pulled DJs like Froggy, Chris Hill, George Power, Steve Walsh and Robbie Vincent. The cream of the DJ world came to play in Woodford and Ilford, just for us kids. From 1977 to 1982, Essex was the epicentre of the jazz-funk scene.

I saw no contradiction in liking both punk and jazz-funk at the same time. Not least because we went to discos to meet girls.

Chigwell was a boys' school and we never, ever managed to get off with members of the opposite sex. There were far more girls our age at teen discos than at gigs. I assumed this was because girls were less interested in sweaty jumping up and down than boys were and even if they liked punk were unlikely to be allowed out except to a local youth-club disco.

In the holidays I socialised with my local mates from Woodford. Chris Page, Andy Boyce, Nick Sharp, Roger Stein (later known as BJ), Cliff Dowsett, Julie Dear and Sally Coulbeck all lived in my road or within the local area, and it was with them and a handful of schoolmates – Stuart Jefcoate, Dave Reynolds and Ash Whitby – that I took my first tentative steps into the world of disco.

The Hawkey Hall was a Thirties-built civic hall; it was the kind of place where the local community put on 'gang shows' and pantomimes at Christmas but somehow also allowed enterprising soul promoters the opportunity to put on gigs for under-18s. Twice monthly the venue was rammed with several hundred teenagers bouncing around on its highly sprung dance floor. I'm surprised they even let kids near the place, what with the vomiting, occasional graffiti and regular fighting, but it was there that we learned our chops.

The best thing about the place was the dance competitions.

These didn't just involve little kids bopping around like headless chickens; they were real proper battles that achieved a life and status of their own. We watched kids battle it out week in, week out. One kid whose life was significantly changed by the Hawkey Hall competitions was Pedro Sandiford; one of his victories led to a real dance-school scholarship that opened the door to a genuine career in the arts and contemporary dance.

You must bear in mind that jazz-funk was everywhere in Essex in 1978. A local hero, Orient's Laurie Cunningham, was an acknowledged dancer at the Royalty in Southgate and was rumoured to occasionally make kick-off at Brisbane Road straight from jazz-funk all-nighters.

Every week, the brightly lit, cavernous hall with its impossibly high ceilings was bursting with teenage hormones and we'd queue up with our 30p entrance fee desperate to meet others of our ilk. It was 'Tuesday night beneath the plastic palm trees'.

I was buzzing one particular night. Still only 14, I'd secured my first-ever slow dance during what the DJs embarrassingly called the 'Erection Section' – a regular spot where they'd play three or four slowies in succession and encourage us to 'pair up'.

These segments were awful. The best-looking girls would be immediately swept up by older boys, leaving us shy kids to pluck up the courage to approach one of the shrinking violets propping up the back wall. It was incredibly humiliating as the girls always turned us down. After all, they were as shy and embarrassed as we were. On this night, the DJ (who may or may not have been George Power) whacked on a new release called 'Three Times a Lady' by the Commodores, which immediately raised the teenage temperature.

Me, Chris Page and Nick Sharp were standing by the cloakroom with some other boys and I realised I needed to make a snap decision about which was worse: to be seen standing with a bunch of luckless boys or to be publicly rejected by a girl? In uncharted territory, I chose the latter. I'd asked girls to slow dance on a dozen occasions but every single time they'd shaken their heads and looked awkwardly at the floor, resulting in burning cheeks and an embarrassed, lonely trudge back to my mates.

I scanned the far wall but the remaining girls looked as embarrassed as I felt. Hold on, though – was that a good-looking soulgirl standing by the bar?

Probably my own age, maybe just 15, she was wearing a pencil skirt, patent court shoes and a white silk blouse, with a long string of beads slung diagonally over her shoulder – along with perms, this was the height of soulgirl fashion in 1978. I thought she looked cracking.

I shuffled over and shyly asked if she'd like to dance. She looked as scared as I felt but stared gamely into my eye. 'Yeah. Sure.'

Whaaat?

We spent the next eight minutes shuffling in uncomfortable circles, awkwardly clutching each other in a vice-like embrace. I wasn't sure what we were doing, but it certainly didn't feel like dancing. As the third slowie came to an end and I heard the opening strains of 'Boogie Oogie Oogie', she leaned forward and kissed me. Fuck! I stole a quick glance at my mates and they were trying hard to avoid my triumphant eye. We had a quick snog and a couple of minutes later she suggested we get a coke. I asked for her number and she scribbled it down, suggesting I call on Saturday morning. Her name was Debbie and she lived in Chingford.

I'd broken my duck. This was easy.

At least I *thought* it was easy. After all, I'd got Debbie's number and she wanted me to call . . .

Just ten minutes later a slightly drunken (having smuggled alcohol in my grandad's hip flask) Eddie was taught a serious lesson.

As the three of us set off for home I noticed some other lads giving us dirty looks. Who they were or why they'd taken against us we'll never know because something just popped out of my mouth unbidden.

'Wankerrrsss!'

Fuck. What had come over me?

So what! Nothing mattered because I'd just swapped numbers with Debbie! I had a girlfriend, so who gives a fuck?

There were six of them, obviously a few years our senior, and to my horror they immediately started chasing us. When I say chasing, I mean they were dogged in their pursuit and even after half a mile hadn't given up. As we passed the Horse & Well, I chanced a backward glance but – *fuck* – they were closing.

Desperate by now, my companions suggested ducking into Woodford Wells Cricket Club, just ahead on the left. Enclosed by a wire fence and with substantial vegetation around the boundary, it certainly had some hiding places but with no obvious exit wasn't a great option. If the chasers followed us in, we'd be trapped and would face a certain beating.

I told the others to go for it; I'd keep going to draw them on.

Chris and Nick peeled off and headed for the bushes on the far side of the cricket pitch. I was so confident our pursuers would follow them into the club that I stayed on the road, running to the end of the cricket ground before looking for somewhere to hide.

I was done in. I'd run at least a mile and couldn't go much further.

Around the corner and all I could see was a single tree. I pressed myself against it. They wouldn't catch me here, surely? Nah, they'd never come this far.

I risked poking my head round the corner.

Fuck. They'd ignored Nick and Chris and all six of them were coming on at full speed, just 70 yards away, sprinting.

I looked frantically around for a better hiding place but there wasn't one. If I made a break for it, they'd instantly see me and I'd be fucked. They were only 40 yards away now. I'd no option but to blend into the tree and hope they wouldn't see me. Hold on: just 5 yards away and in deep shadow I spotted a shallow ditch and without hesitation dived in. It was wet and muddy but I forced myself deeper into the hole.

They ran around the corner as one, coming to an untidy stop and seemingly confused that I'd disappeared. I swallowed to control my breathing; the slightest noise and I'd be done for.

They were just feet away from the ditch, panting and arguing about what to do next. They knew I was close.

'When I find the fucker I'm gonna kick his head in . . . I'll teach the twat . . . Blah, blah, blah . . .'

I was cacking myself. My ditch was a totally inadequate hiding place and they were certain to flush me out. Should I make another dash for it?

Suddenly: 'Oi you fucking wankers . . .'

I was saved by the timely intervention of Nick and Chris, who'd made their way out of the cricket club, seen the lads gathered on the corner and shouted at them.

The shout seemed incredibly loud in the deserted street and had the desired effect. Nick and Chris sprinted down an alley and the Wanstead lads, swearing and absolutely furious, set off in their wake. I waited 30 seconds before standing up and trying to dust myself down. That was impossible because I was covered in mud and soaked, but at least they hadn't got hold of me.

I'd think twice before doing that again.

In 1978 we were still a year or so away from adult nightclubs but our teenage world was growing and by June I was so committed to being a soulboy that I'd bought 'Boogie Oogie Oogie' on its day of release. Most of my local mates had become soulboys too, and as we met more kids with a similar outlook our extended group was joined by the likes of Derek Boland and his mate Stuart Blake. Derek was obsessed with being a DJ and we'd bonded over this skinny ginger bloke from Ilford called Froggy. He'd often play our underage gigs with a set of soul, jazz-funk and disco. Thing was, we were fascinated by him. Not only did Froggy play the records we wanted to hear, he'd also come across some weird DJing technique in the States and brought it back with him. It was called mixing.

I was far too young to understand the power a DJ could wield over a crowd back then, but Froggy had it all worked out. It wasn't just about the records he played; it was about *how you heard* the records he played. For Froggy, it was about the sound system, the PA, the way the bass hit you in the stomach. He'd linked two turntables together with a mixer and somehow made records last longer, missing out the shit choruses and playing only the good bits, swapping from one disc to another. It was unique and exciting.

Even as a kid I realised that Chris Hill was the 'DJ as entertainer', while Froggy was the 'DJ as DJ'. I know he wasn't alone, and he was joined on the path by many others, but from my perspective I just immediately knew that I wanted to do what he did. Towards the end of the year, still only 14 and walking through the backstreets of Ilford one afternoon, I spotted Froggy cleaning his car. It only seemed natural that I walked over and asked for his autograph. The best thing? He gave it to me . . .

Eventually, our crowd got into adult discos and graduated to grown-up clubs like Lacy Lady, Goldmine, Oscars, Zero 6, Dukes, Room at the Top and the Ilford Palais. Essex and East London along with the Old Kent Road and Kent were the soulboy heartlands, but for us it was all about Essex.

You might ask how could I be into TV Personalities and George Benson at the same time. Well, I know this isn't the traditional 'punk changed everything' narrative, but 30 years of oversimplified TV music documentaries can be deceiving. People forget that in 1978 there was a well-established, symbiotic relationship between punks and soulboys. Chris Hill, the Soul Mafia's biggest DJ, was an early champion of punk and promoted gigs at the Lacy Lady by groups like The Damned and The Clash. Longtime Essex soulboys like Mark Sherlock followed the Sex Pistols from gig to gig and it was common to see a handful of punks at soul discos and plenty of soulboys at punk gigs.

It was an easy line to walk and occasionally the line became blurred. Did soulboys nick plastic sandals and mohair jumpers off punks or was it the other way round?

I loved punk for its aggressive and explosive impact. It was angry, loud and full of energy. So imagine my surprise when I discovered that jazz-funk could be just as, if not more, powerful. In the summer of 1978, I saw Hi-Tension playing on *Top of the Pops* and they blew me away. I'd been used to waiting with bated breath for The Stranglers or The Jam (who kept popping up) to creep into the chart countdown, but this lot seemed to combine punk attitude with jazz-funk music and style. Brit-funk was markedly different from what was happening in black America and took its influences from the up-tempo sounds of Brass Construction and War. There were dozens of similar bands pushing the same vibe: Central Line, Incognito, Light of the World, Heatwave, Freeez and even Level 42. We loved them all.

Of course, this didn't mean that I gave up punk; surely both worlds could exist in tandem? But admittedly in terms of clothes it did become tricky. Soulboy gear for Ilford and punkish gear for gigs in town. I tried to make it work for a while.

Later that summer we managed to get hold of tickets to see Buzzcocks at the Hammersmith Odeon on 4 November 1978, just before my 15th birthday. Up to this point I'd dipped into various fashions as I chose; I was still flirting with a sort of punk look but with ever-decreasing enthusiasm. At the Buzzcocks gig I wore a fluffy white mohair jumper over a Last Resort shop T-shirt, straight black jeans and a pair of DMs with a large 999 badge. (I'd recently picked up their 'Feelin' Alright With the Crew' 45 and had added them to my list of must-see bands.) I assumed I fitted into the junior punk world relatively well. I couldn't have been more wrong.

Me and the lads jumped off the train at Hammersmith and ran across the road to join the queue of ticket holders. I was buzzing as I'd just picked up a copy of their (now rare) *Spiral Scratch* EP from the small ads in *Sounds* and was looking forward to seeing both Buzzcocks and Subway Sect, who were supporting. We'd been drinking cans of beer on the Tube and were having a good time. As we joined the queue, though, I couldn't help but hear some of the disparaging comments from the people in front of us who were obviously unimpressed

'Fucking poseurs . . .'

Did I hear that right? We weren't just poseurs; we were apparently *fucking* poseurs.

In the world of 1978 Kings Road punk, there was no bigger insult than 'poseur'. It meant you were adopting a look you had no right to adopt. It meant you were a fake, a mug.

'Did you hear that, Tris? That bloke called us poseurs!'

'Got to be honest, Eddie – no, I didn't. Hurry up or we're gonna miss Subway Sect . . .'

Truth be told, I couldn't let it pass. I felt massively insulted. This was long before I'd ever had a fight, so it didn't mean I was going to clump him – it meant that my face burned a deep red and I wished I could fade into the background. More importantly, it also meant I wasn't accepted as one of the people I'd been cultivating a sense of belonging with for the previous six months. They obviously thought I was beneath them.

I didn't let the insult pass either. Overnight I was finished with punk. We kept going to gigs, and I loved the music, but I never felt comfortable with their scene. To be honest, by this time punk had become a cliché, even an embarrassment. Split between posh people in overpriced Westwood gear at one end or glue-sniffing Sid clones in their studded leather jackets at the other. I was neither.

But something happened that night that also pointed to a new direction. Buzzcocks were simply amazing. Those four angular, skinny and besuited Mancs gave me my first glimpse of a sharp, stylish Sixties-influenced way of life. They wore their clothes and their attitude differently. With their hypnotic chords, genuinely progressive modernist art and design, monotone tonic suits and block-coloured Mondrian shirts, Buzzcocks gave me my first glimpse of a different future – even if I didn't yet really know it.

And by the winter of 1978, the more I thought about it the more certain I became: I wasn't going to be a punk.

If I needed confirmation that I'd fallen out of love with punk, it happened at a gig at the Electric Ballroom in December of 1978. I'd gone to watch Generation X, who were supported by Chelsea. There was a weird relationship between the two bands as Billy Idol and Tony James were founder members of Chelsea but had long since quit to form Generation X, and only vocalist Gene October remained of Chelsea's original line-up. I'd picked up the 'Right to Work' 45 on Mark Perry's Step-Forward label at Small Wonder and was itching to give them a go.

I wish I hadn't. It was the first time I witnessed gobbing, a bizarre gig habit much loved by the more stupid punk-rockers. Musically the band were great, but a large group of leather-jacketed Sid clones with budget bondage trousers spent most of their set coughing up yellowy-green gob and launching it at Gene October (was that a wig? I'd heard rumours . . .). The worst thing was that he appeared to revel in it, not once wiping the spit off his face where half a dozen lumps of phlegm hung in elastic strings. It turned my stomach. Chelsea were a pretty tight band, but the whole punk thing had become awful by then. No wonder there was a hepatitis epidemic sweeping London. Yep, I was done. I didn't even wait to see Generation X.

Then, just a day later, I got to see The Jam for the first time. The band were playing a low-profile Christmas show at Camden's Music Machine. Their single 'All Around the World' was one of my favourite records, and me, Stuart and John Bailey were determined to see them live. I'd even inked their logo on a pair of army greens I was wearing to the gig.

But this is the odd thing.

I loved their *This Is the Modern World* album. I loved The Jam's artwork, the band's outfits, the photographs, the inner sleeves and their music. But what I didn't do was join the dots with what frontman Paul Weller was actually (and probably unintentionally) creating. To me at the time The Jam were just another punk band I liked alongside so many others. The Saints, The Damned, Generation X, 999, The Lurkers, The Stranglers, The Fall, Menace, The Clash, Chelsea, Sham 69 . . . blah, blah, blah. All of them were just bands we loved. The Jam were one of a crowd.

When I finally saw them live, I did notice that there were lots of boys of a similar age to me wearing these new baggy green coats called parkas (I'd seen them at the football too, and at other gigs), but I still hadn't worked out that they were part of something new and totally different from punk.

The Jam didn't dress like other punk bands. Their music might have been hard and fast punk, but it seemed different somehow. They looked smarter, almost proud of how they dressed; completely the opposite of virtually everyone else I'd seen up to that point. Suits, shirts and ties? Rickenbackers and AC30s? I could think that The Jam were a willing bridge to a previous age, between the angry and aggressive blues of Dr. Feelgood or The Hammersmith Gorillas to the Sex Pistols. But even seeing the band live still hadn't opened my eyes to what was happening in front of me.

The gig was fast, hot and sweaty, and I loved it. But did I realise what all these kids in the audience wearing parkas, tonic jackets and target T-shirts were up to? No. The clues to my future were everywhere, but I still hadn't worked it out. Then one particular night, when I was on my way home from a Stiff Little Fingers gig at the Electric Ballroom, it finally happened. It was February 1979, and the bolshie Ulster punks were one of my favourite bands at the time. Crammed into a sweaty

Northern Line Tube carriage, I whipped out an industrial-sized marker and inked 'SLF' on the door. A tall bloke tapped me on the shoulder – bear in mind the carriage was absolutely packed with fellow gig-goers – and asked if he could borrow my pen! I laughed and passed it over. He wrote 'mods' – and drew an arrow on the top of the d.

What the fuck was that about?

Genuinely interested but somewhat confused, I asked him. I mean, I obviously knew what mods were – they were kids who fought rockers at the seaside a generation ago. But why had he scrawled the word on the Tube 15 years later?

He passed the pen back and I looked at him more closely. Tall, much taller than me, he was wearing a T-shirt with a Spitfire RAF symbol on the front, tight blue jeans with a half-inch turn-up, suede shoes and a greeny-yellow shimmering jacket that changed colour with the light. Most weird was his pair of mirror shades. It was night-time and we were on the Underground – could he even see?

The boy, maybe 17, spoke to me like I was an idiot – not rudely, just as if I wouldn't understand what he was telling me.

'Well, mate, it's a bit like this . . . You know The Jam? They're mods . . . See, *we*'re mods too. A bit like the mods in the Sixties but not the same; we're more now, more up-to-date. We've got our own bands . . . like The Jam . . . bands who play just for us. Were you at the Electric Ballroom gig tonight?

'Erm, yeah, I was actually.'

'Yeah, I thought so. See, we like Stiff Little Fingers but they're not a mod band. Nah. We don't like all that punk stuff. Don't get me wrong, I like the music, but when it comes down to it, they don't have anything to say to *me*. I'm no punk and I'm certainly not Irish . . .' He paused and contemplated. 'I like The Undertones, though – they're a bit mod! Nah, I'm an East London mod and I follow The Jam from gig to gig, you know what I mean?'

Well, I didn't but I persevered and so did he. Like many of those early revival mods, he was an evangelist, spreading the word of his chosen way of life and encouraging others to join him. He was chewing rapidly, jaw working away in random staccato movements that appeared to have nothing to do with the gum in his mouth.

'Listen, if you ain't busy, then we're going to a gig next week: Saturday night down in South London, place called the Kings Head; we're going to see our mate's band 'cause they've just got a new drummer. They're proper mods. You wanna give it a go, mate? You can meet us if you want.'

Crikey, a mod band? I had no idea what he meant but I liked the sound of it.

'Yeah, that'd be great. What are they like?'

'They're like us, mate. Called The Chords and I suppose you'd say they're a bit like The Jam. They've only just started; no records out and only played a handful of gigs . . . Pretty raw but loads of energy . . . There's a few of us going.'

I resolved to give the matter some thought. Over the next few days, it dawned on me that the whole mod thing stemmed from The Jam. Suddenly it clicked and I was in!

I poured over The Jam's record sleeves for inspiration and one of the few things I'd managed to work out about these new mods was that they wore the baggy green parkas I'd first spotted at football but without quite understanding their significance. So those kids were actually mods? They also seemed to wear desert boots, button-down shirts, Harringtons and maybe Levi's jackets. It also became apparent that the mod schtick was a well-worn, generational path, so I went through my dad's wardrobe and blagged a thick-striped button-down with suitably large collars. That looked pretty good. However, to really fit in, to be part of this new gang, I knew I needed to find myself a parka.

*

E. Piller & Son's main shop was on High Street North, East Ham. The Army & Navy surplus store was massive, just 100 yards from our shop and on the bus route to Ilford. The morning of the gig, I caught the bus down with Tris and we both bought parkas. I think they cost a tenner. At the time I couldn't understand the fascination with this ugly overcoat – except for one thing: it distinguished you from what went before, the punks with their bondage gear and Sid Vicious leather jackets. We knew the mods from the Sixties wore them, so I suppose if it was good enough for them it was good enough for us. But mainly, when you put on the coat it made you feel like you were on a different path.

The Chords gig was incredible. I'd never been out in South London before and wasn't sure what to expect. A mod band? The pub was heaving and free to get in, the crowd much more friendly than we were expecting; south of the river certainly wasn't as bad as it'd been portrayed. The Kings Head was one of the first venues in London to offer a home to the new movement and unsurprisingly the rest of the crowd were dressed just like us. In parkas!

But it was the warm and friendly atmosphere that sold me: it really felt that we were at the beginning of something special. The band were amazing. To be fair, the frontman looked even younger than I did, and the songs were a melodic take on punk rock. The Chords – and that kid on the train – had showed me what I wanted to be.

I wanted to be a mod.

PART 2

7

THIS IS THE MODERN WORLD

S o how was I going to be a mod?

I wasn't completely in the dark. I realised that they'd been around me at football and gigs but I just hadn't recognised them for what they were.

A couple of the people I stood with on the North Bank at Upton Park were clearly mods, including a beautiful tomboy called Cindy from the tougher part of Dagenham. The following Saturday I began my education.

It was all very entry-level stuff. At the start of 1979 mod was a misunderstood iconography resting heavily on the concept of US parkas and French crops. Musically it seemed to be a mixture of classic and obvious Sixties heroes like Small Faces, The Who and The Kinks alongside some of the later punk from The Jam, Generation X, Buzzcocks or Sham 69 and pub rock like Dr. Feelgood or The Pleasers. The main unifying factor was the clobber. Clothes spoke volumes, certainly louder than the music and substantially more important. It was about proving you weren't a punk – and that was something I was very keen to do.

There were no clothes shops catering for mods, so everything came from junk shops or Brick Lane Market with the main advantage being that secondhand was cheap. It cost nothing to 'turn mod'; it just took commitment. The first real argument I remember having with Richard, Tris and Stuart was over shoes.

We'd been told that Hush Puppies were the ultimate mod footwear, but that never really made sense to me. Genuine Hush Puppies were extraordinarily expensive and in the very early days I never met a mod who had a real pair. Instead, we all bought suede shoes from Brick Lane. Most looked shit, but there was a particular Polish desert boot that managed to trump the rest. I could never work out why we were supposed to wear them because by 1979 they were a grandad staple, but the fact was, Hush Puppies were part of our holy grail – one element of a style triptych, to be critically appraised alongside the button-down and the parka. And this was where I made my first mistake. Before we understood that a parka had to be a specifically American fishtail, I bought a square-bottomed German NATO job at the same time Tris picked up his M51 in March 1979 – and I hadn't even realised I'd blundered.

With my gear, my mates, records from Small Wonder and a copy of *Sounds* in my back pocket for gig listings, it took just weeks for me to transform into a fully paid-up mod.

The four of us spent Saturdays trawling the junk shops of Ilford hoping to find our new uniform on the cheap.

Even in early 1979, the different youth cults could mix without trouble. Sometime in March we'd heard there was to be a protest against the police and council on the Kings Road in Chelsea. I'd picked up a flyer in Kensington Market urging punks, skins, rockabillies and mods to make a stand against the closure of the Beaufort Market, an independent mish-mash of an emporium halfway up the Kings Road that was under threat from that curse of the creative world, redevelopment.

We'd been to the Kings Road a couple of times as it was a great place to generally hang out and try to find cheap mod gear.

The Clash were rumoured to be playing on the building's roof and as I'd yet to see them live we decided to make the trip to West London. I'd loved the band's 'Tommy Gun' single and even today think that *Give 'Em Enough Rope* is their best album. A free Clash gig was certainly worth the effort.

So, on 31 March a few of us answered the distress call, donned our parkas and made our way to Sloane Square to see what might happen. We clocked a dozen punks on the train and a few more milling around in the square itself. There were groups of skins, mods and even Teddy boys all heading towards the Kings Road.

The main thing I noticed as we walked out of the station was the massive police presence in Sloane Square. This lot didn't look like normal Old Bill either; more like that notorious squad of mobile riot police called the SPG. The Special Patrol Group were often dispatched at a moment's notice to 'control' (take out) anyone looking to protest against the establishment: football hooligans, unions, strikers or, more regularly, members of the black community. They looked forbidding and were tooled up.

We weaved our way through the Saturday-afternoon shoppers but soon spotted a dark-blue cordon 100 yards further up the Kings Road. The Old Bill were intercepting young people and turning them back the way they'd come. The three of us quickly jumped onto a slow-moving Routemaster heading towards the World's End (a rather telling name for a brutalist estate with a run-down reputation up the other end of the Kings Road). Hiding on the top deck we could see there was definitely something untoward happening ahead, and as soon as the bus passed the police cordon we ran down the steps, jumped off mid-stop and joined the burgeoning crowd.

Things kicked off immediately.

It was the oddest thing. One moment random sightseers were wandering along the Kings Road oblivious to the growing tension, the next they're being charged by police in groups of two or three with truncheons drawn.

Saturday shoppers were clearly overwhelmed as increasing numbers of kids tried to force their way through to the Beaufort Market itself. It was the first time I'd found myself in this kind of situation and it was actually exhilarating. Suddenly we were in the middle of a full-blown riot. We were carried along in a surge, and as we drew level with Chelsea Town Hall I glimpsed a burly skinhead charging the Old Bill, swinging an A-board in a wide arc. He was taken down by three SPG, but immediately a punk took his place and the disturbance continued. We got nowhere near the market itself because the melee was too great yet as an experience it was extraordinary. Police were snatching lone punks or random tourists and forcing them into one of half a dozen Black Marias lined up outside the Town Hall.

People react in different ways when they find themselves in a riot. Time and again I've seen the same behaviour as trouble develops and the crowd usually divide themselves into three different groups.

There are those who run away from the riot's epicentre (where the trouble is) as fast as they can; then there are people like us, the ones who watch goggle-eyed (for we'd seen nothing like it before – even the rucks at West Ham were nothing like this); and then there are the people for whom the red mist descends, the ones who go on the attack. On this occasion they seemed to be in the majority.

The grievances had been building for a long time. Punks were originally drawn to the Kings Road by the publicity heaped on McLaren and Westwood's shop, Sex (later called Seditionaries), but by 1978, Acme Attractions, Johnsons, the Beaufort Market and an ever-expanding coterie of left-field fashion emporia had turned the area into the punk mecca. Now it was all going to be redeveloped – hence people's anger. In the end, and in spite of the overactive police, not much else happened that day and the Beaufort Market was cleared within the hour. Unfortunately, I still didn't get to see The Clash, though I was sure I heard a few chords from up on the roof.

On the train home we congratulated ourselves as we'd avoided being arrested when so many others were snatched. I'd been impressed with the protest's organiser, a tartan-clad punk called Jock McDonald from The Bollock Brothers, and resolved to keep an eye on him in the future.

McDonald stuck his head above the parapet. He was a motivator, an organiser and an anarchist, leading from the front in his bondage trews and taking no prisoners. It wasn't long before he arranged a further away-day to Brighton, where a few hundred mods, skins and punks came together and much the same thing happened on the seafront. I suspect that this trip in the spring of 1979 might have been the last occasion where all the different youth cults could hang out together without fighting each other. After that there was constant tension.

Despite increasing in number, mods still had no clubs that were specifically for them. There were two reasons for this: firstly, the average age of a mod in April 1979 was still around 16; and secondly, we still didn't really understand what mod music was, especially in a way that might have been recognised by our Sixties forebears. Instead, it was all about gigs – all our exclusive mod nights out were to see bands. To be fair, most of them sounded just like the punk bands we'd been watching a few months earlier. A kind of Sixties wash became the default teen mod sound. Sure, occasional soul records like 'Green Onions' or 'Midnight Hour' surfaced, but lots of rubbish was included just because it was made in the Sixties. Incredibly, one of the biggest mod records of the summer of 1979 was 'Glad All Over' by The Dave Clark Five.

The lack of mod nightclubs meant that we still frequented the under-18s discos of Ilford, where we invariably met more followers of the early mod path.

Our favourite had to be Sunday night at Room at the Top. On the top floor of a department store called Harrison Gibson, and accessed by a lift with a capacity of just 12, the venue held 400 but was often far more crowded. Scary stuff when you remember that *Towering Inferno* had been a cinematic blockbuster just a couple of years earlier.

It was a brilliant night out and by the summer had become the go-to destination for local kids. As the mod population grew, the DJs added a 'mad mod half-hour' and we'd wait for it religiously. The opening chords of 'Green Onions' or Prince Buster's version of 'Madness' signalled a frantic rush for the dance floor, which for 20-odd minutes became a heaving sea of parkas, trilbies and Harringtons. We joined the scrum occasionally but preferred to stand against the back wall trying (without much luck) to look cool for the girls.

Since that first Chords gig in March, our little gang of mates took in as many gigs as we could. Money was no hardship: we'd bunk the Tube and the entry costs were always around 50p. We were out three nights a week, every week, and there was never any shortage of bands to see.

By the end of April 1979, The Fixations, The Merton Parkas, The V.I.P.'s, Speedball, The Mods, Long Tall Shorty, The Killermeters, Sta-Prest, The Crooks, Beggar, The Teenbeats, Back to Zero, The Tickets, The Low Numbers, 6 More Prophets, The Scooters, Squire, Chicane, Les Elite, Sema 4, The Directions and Small Hours had all played in London and were suddenly rubbing shoulders with the big three of The Chords (how quickly they had grown), the Purple Hearts and Secret Affair – all of whom had a presence, power and following that left many other groups in the shade.

The Wellington in Waterloo, Pegasus in Stoke Newington, the Kings Head in Deptford, the Bridge House in Canning Town, the Pied Bull and the Hope & Anchor in Islington, Rock Garden, Global Village and the Marquee in the West End, Windsor Castle in Paddington, Bull & Gate in Kentish Town, the Hop Poles in Enfield and the Dublin Castle in Camden were all hosting regular mod nights. There were several others too and this was just in London – similar things were happening all over the country.

I'd been at school with Dave Cairns, Secret Affair's mercurial guitarist, and although he was a few years older than me his presence had loomed large. You know what it's like at school: an age gap of two or three years represents an enormous, insurmountable chasm (for the elder boy), but the young'uns always gaze adoringly at their cooler seniors. Consequently, when Secret Affair held a band meeting at the Horse & Well in Woodford Green in those spring days of 1979, Cairns had no idea who the scrawny, poorly dressed young mod boy was who approached him at the bar.

I certainly knew who Cairns was, though.

We'd soon realised that this particular pub was the mod haunt in Woodford. I couldn't believe my luck – my suburb had somehow staked its claim as the mod capital of the East London fringe. There were regularly half a dozen scooters lined up outside. The Horse & Well's landlord cared nothing for age-related ID, the concept of which had yet to be invented, so the elder boys (and men) who drank there seven days a week proudly flying the mod flag were soon joined by a younger (14-, 15- and 16-year-old) clientele. The pub was walking distance from my house, so we often made the trip for a pint.

On this particular Wednesday night, I had to do a double-take when I saw the four members of one of the biggest new mod groups, Secret Affair, gathered in the saloon bar! Now, while I say four members, truth be told the band was a dictatorship. All decisions were taken by Ian Page (a resident of Roding Valley, some two minutes from Woodford as the crow flies), the lead vocalist and trumpeter – with a little help and support from the aforementioned Cairns (who hailed from High Beech, a village deep in Epping Forest). These two had already been together for a couple of years before Secret Affair, having founded the proto-mod/power-pop band the New Hearts. Page and Cairns met as students at Loughton College and bonded over shared ideas of style and swagger. The New Hearts were not ultimately successful and, after a short period on the cusp of stardom, split (acrimoniously, from their management at least) with nothing to show for their efforts but memories of some brilliant gigs with The Jam, two fabulous but unsuccessful singles and a hefty (but un-recouped) music publishing deal from the well-established industry hustler Bryan Morrison to carry over to their new band.

In the spring of 1979, Secret Affair launched the legendary Mods Mondays at the Bridge House in Canning Town. This was the first regular mod night in the capital (just ahead of the Wellington in Waterloo) and was organised by Terry Murphy, who came from a famous East End boxing/acting dynasty. The pub's guvnor, more used to hosting pub rock and blues gigs, had spotted the potential in the early revival and offered his venue as a place where this young movement could gather. We'd been there a couple of times already and recognised the band from their early headline slots.

Rather shyly, I walked across the Horse & Well saloon to where Cairns stood at the bar. I said hello and asked if he remembered me from school.

'Er . . . No . . . Should I?' Probably irritated that he'd been intercepted by a kid.

Undaunted, I pressed on. 'Well, I, erm, I was at Loyola with you, but I'm a few years younger . . .'

At that his eyes lit up and the shutters were lifted. 'Ah, did you have Mrs McGoldrick or Miss Sands?' he asked.

'Both,' I replied, losing my inhibitions. He asked me how I was and my initial apprehension lifted as this legend among men (well, among our teenage group of newly minted mods) engaged me in conversation.

'I always thought Miss Sands was a bit tasty!' he said. I reddened but eventually he followed it with: 'We're filming our first video next month; we need a few Glory Boys to come down and be extras – are you up for it'?

Like a shot I was in there . . . Were we up for it? Jesus, the Glory Boys were legendary: a gang of early East End mods and football hooligans who followed Secret Affair from gig to gig. They were way out of my league. Mainly West Ham, their identifying mark was one of two tattoos – either a three-quarter-inch keyhole on the arm or, more commonly, the word 'mods' carved into the lower lip.

Cairns scribbled the information I needed on a beer mat and instructed us to meet the band and the other extras at the Acklam Hall in Ladbroke Grove a month hence . . . I was thrilled; I mean, who wouldn't be? The biggest band on my new scene had asked us to be in their first video!

Back of the net.

I swaggered back to our table bursting with pride. I could tell the lads were envious as I relayed the conversation. My tenuous school link with Secret Affair's guitarist had paid dividends and I was determined to make the most of it. We marked the date down, moved on and turned our thoughts to the coming weekend, when Beggar were playing at a pub called the Duke of Wellington on the Balls Pond Road in Dalston.

Things like this kept happening. Our new mod identity seemed to open up new people and new doors. The more we went out, the more things happened to us.

Dave had called me a Glory Boy . . . I had to take the plunge. Didn't I . . .?

Now, a tattoo on a 15-year-old schoolboy's arm was a no-go, but I wasn't put off and, a few weeks later, caught the bus down to Ben Gunn's tattoo parlour in Chingford with my mate Bunny and asked for the full lip job.

'It's gonna hurt, son,' announced this middle-aged brick shithouse who had not a two-bob bit's worth of un-inked skin on his entire body. He was well known as a 'no questions asked' tattooist and I'd fortified myself with a couple of shots of brandy before we trekked down there. I asked him to get on with it. He was right. It did hurt. A lot. But hey, now I was a fucking Glory Boy, so who cares?

Trouble was, a tattoo didn't suddenly make me a Glory Boy. To be honest, I was just a 15-year-old kid from Woodford with a slightly wonky 'mods' tattooed on my lip. What it did do, though, was make me *feel* like a Glory Boy. I could at least hold my head up in their company.

By June the music papers had cottoned on that something was stirring on the streets.

Many of the same faces appeared at gigs and were now on nodding terms. In the spring of 1979 they were inevitably draped in the ubiquitous parka, still worn as a badge of belonging rather than as a fashion item. Nods of recognition grew into the occasional hello and eventually led to the purchase of one of those home-made, photocopied fanzines that eventually became known as 'modzines'.

Fanzines loomed large in our world in the summer of 1979; they were the glue that held us together. *Maximum Speed* was the first and best but was soon joined by *Get Up & Go!*. While it only ran to two issues, *Get Up & Go!* was an important fanzine for me personally as the editors inspired me to start my own fanzine six months after they quit. It was put together by Vaughn Toulouse and Tony Lordan from the band Guns for Hire (who later morphed into Department S) and the pair were early mod adopters.

Maximum Speed and *Get Up & Go!* weren't the only modzines available that summer, but they were the best. Sadly, both threw in the towel early doors but others soon appeared to take their place: the punkzine *Surrey Vomit* morphed into *Can't Explain* (edited by Roger Allen, who managed Speedball), Gary Crowley ran *The Modern World*, *Direction Reaction Creation* was typeset and looked very professional, *Shake* (run by a 14-year-old called Dominic Kenny) captured the growing scene perfectly and although it wasn't strictly a modzine Tony Fletcher's *Jamming!* was very supportive.

The mod revival initially benefitted from some favourable mainstream press coverage. Garry Bushell from *Sounds* and Adrian Thrills at the *NME* were the men who took the plunge; Thrills saw the scene as a natural progression from The Jam, while Bushell loved the sociopolitical value of a street-level movement that had sprung directly from the inner-London working classes with no apparent help from music-industry Svengalis. In other words, Garry Bushell realised that the mod revival was a real and genuine thing that had appeared spontaneously. He eventually became a lone voice but continued to support it as best he could.

Other scribes initially welcomed the 'revival' (as it had become known), but the love affair with the music press wouldn't last. At ground level, and as the disparate movement quickly grew, mod broadened its appeal, and by the end of June 1979 the mod revival was recognised as a 'thing' in the media.

Sporting our freshly painted parkas – Tris's proper US model sporting the keyhole logo of Secret Affair and (to my eternal shame) my German NATO non-fishtail jobbie with Small Faces on the back – one Tuesday in May 1979 we were tooling down Dean Street on our way to the Rock Garden, a small West End venue that was hosting the fabulously soulful Small Hours. The band were fronted by a sharp-dressing film student called Neil Thompson and I'd adopted them because they'd been formed by Kym Bradshaw, bass player on '(I'm) Stranded' by The

Saints and a man who'd undergone a complete mod rebirth since relocating to London in 1977.

As we crossed Leicester Square, we were flagged down by a journalist who told us she was writing an article about the mod revival for *Observer Magazine*. Could we spare ten minutes to answer some questions? Wow. I was impressed – even I'd heard of the *Observer*.

'Yeah, sure, we'd love to . . .'

Tris Pitt was my classmate and a shy young thing who left all the talking to me. The journalist ran through the obvious. Why were we mods? Where did we go? What bands did we like? Was there any future in the mod scene?

We apparently passed with flying colours. The article was to be included in a 'mod special edition' a month later. The cover would feature a host of scooter riders from Orpington's 5.15 Scooter Club and we were to provide some internal colour. The interview was all very predictable because we were new at this game – the mod game, I mean – and after they'd taken a couple of shots of our parkas we moved off to the gig and forgot all about it.

I was not even six months past my 15th birthday and was becoming increasingly aware of other bands, trying to take in as many live as I could. I'd spotted a short piece in *Sounds* with a picture of the Purple Hearts' drummer Gary Sparks setting up his kit at the Bridge House while wearing a parka. He looked so cool but I hadn't yet seen them play, so I vowed to check out their next London date. Gigs were coming so thick and fast now; their next show was just six days after the Small Hours gig where we'd spoken to the *Observer*.

In only six weeks, the scene had exploded. It was Bank Holiday Monday, 28 May, and on that night we could have seen Beggar at the Saxon, Walthamstow; The Vapors at the Ruskin Arms in East Ham;

The Crooks at the Windsor Castle, Paddington; and Secret Affair and The Numbers at the Bridge House in Canning Town. In that week there were more than 30 mod live gigs in London alone. We chose to take in the show at the Notre Dame Hall in Leicester Square.

The Purple Hearts came from Romford, just a few miles up the road from me, and were only a year or so older. No manager, no hustler behind the scenes. The negligible age difference emphasised the unusual relationship between the revival bands and their fans. Paul Weller from The Jam was just four years older than me and the new groups he inspired were a just year or so my senior. So the Purple Hearts were 16 or 17 years old when I first saw them at the Notre Dame Hall! No wonder there was so little pretention and such an amazing bond between bands and fans. It would be difficult to be condescending to an audience just a year younger than you.

Among both the bands and their fans were kids whose elder brothers may have been punks but who felt no affinity with the bullshit that went with that scene. Many of our groups formed because they'd been influenced by the mod side of punk; The Jam of course but to a lesser extent Buzzcocks, Generation X, Eddie and the Hot Rods and Dr. Feelgood.

It was a drizzly Bank Holiday Monday and half a dozen of us rushed back from an away-day on the coast in Clacton and jumped on the Central Line at half six. Me, Tris Pitt, Richard Habberley, Stu Jefcoate, John Bailey, Andy Gilbert and Martin Smith made the journey, and three of us were wearing our parkas to keep out the rain. Stu was wearing the only other acceptable kind of coat, the olive-green US Army mac, and Richard had a smart half-length leather coat. At each station we'd poke our heads out of the carriage door to see if there were any mods waiting on the platform.

That night the Purple Hearts were joined by three other bands: The Mods, Back to Zero and Squire. The average age of the punters bouncing around in a sea of green was probably just 16 and you could feel the teenage tension in the air. The venue was an extraordinarily beautiful Art Deco church hall in Leicester Square dating back to the Forties that was attached to the Notre Dame de France church next door. I swear that at those early gigs nuns would be manning the cloakroom and the door.

Squire were on first. A four-piece from Woking (better known as The Jam's hometown), they single-handedly instigated that early mod revival fascination with the boating blazer, an archaic Edwardian striped jacket more associated with cricket and rowing clubs from Henley or Winchester than working-class youth. Squire pulled off the look and sung in a soft, harmonic style that was markedly different from most of their contemporaries. They actually reminded me of a teenage Hollies. Lead vocalist Enzo Esposito was a third-generation Italian immigrant and Soho hairdresser who was known to cut Weller's barnet and was well backed by Tony Meynall, who stepped up to lead the band when Enzo later quit. Squire sang unashamedly mod lyrics like 'Walking Down the Kings Road' and 'It's a Mod World' while the seven of us stood at the bar sipping our pints, soaking up the atmosphere.

Next up were Back to Zero. Numerous urban legends have grown up around this Stoke Newington four-piece, many of them true, but the one that sticks in my mind was that their energetic singer, Brian Betteridge (a stage name; he was born Brian Kotz), had won the prestigious BBC Radio 4 competition *Brain of Britain*. This was proper kudos – just to qualify meant you were seriously bright. I later learned that the reality wasn't quite as impressive. Brian had won a Radio 1 pop quiz in 1978 and wasn't the real 'Brain of Britain', but he was certainly a veritable encyclopaedia on all things Sixties and he jumped around the stage like a Duracell bunny on sulphate. The rest of the band, led by Sam Burnett alongside Andy Moore and Mal, were just like us. They dressed like us, were the same age as us and were bloody great. Their angular, chopped chords and melodic, punky sound seemed to be based – as so many were – on the mod template pioneered by The Jolt, a Jam-like three-piece who'd been signed to Polydor in 1977 by Chris Parry (The Jam's A&R man) and had their album produced by Vic Coppersmith-Heaven (The Jam's producer) but who chucked it all in just as the revival gained momentum.

The Mods were from Boreham Wood in North London. They had a serious following of tough-looking older lads who were very vocal, constantly chanting at the gig. I never really understood why The Mods weren't much bigger. I loved the band and their energy. It was during their fast and furious set that I first noticed the mod 'dance'.

Punks, bless their little cottons, tended to violently jump around while grabbing and gobbing at each other, and their dance was dubbed the 'pogo'. For one thing, mods weren't keen on the pushing and pulling – and woe betide anyone caught spitting; they'd receive a hefty clump.

Compared to the punk gobbing I'd witnessed at the Chelsea gig six months previously, the mod revival dance was a joy. Unless you actually partook or at least witnessed it from close quarters, then I'm not sure my explanation can do it justice. You found a small patch of floor facing the band, generally standing in rows in a semi-orderly fashion, and jerked backwards and forwards from the hips up in a violent rocking motion. The feet remained planted firmly on the floor while the arms, fists clenched, moved opposite each other as the body rocked in time to the music. Think Max Wall trying to do Chas Smash's dance with his feet nailed to the floor. See? I told you I wouldn't be able to do it justice! Occasionally, depending on space, the arms remained glued to the side of the body.

This wasn't the only mod dance kicking about in 1979. The Glory Boys had an interesting variation whereby they'd climb onto one another's shoulders and bellow 'Glory Boys!' while doing the same dance from the shoulders up. Well, at least the one on top would do the dance from the shoulders up; the one in the supporting role would do his best not to fall over.

Secret Affair had a healthy female following, mainly in their mid-teens with a penchant for ski pants, shift dresses and massive earrings. They usually danced in rows at the front of the stage and threw in some synchronised Sixties-style go-go moves as if they were extras on *Ready Steady Go!*. On the whole, though, mod girls danced like us but with a little more arm action.

The Purple Hearts closed the evening and were everything I'd hoped they'd be. Punky, mod garage delivered by four kids from up the road. They reminded me of the best of the punk scene but without the bullshit. They were fronted by the charismatic Bob Manton, with Gary Sparks, that cool parka-wearing drummer I'd seen in *Sounds*, Simon Stebbing on guitar and a cocky bass player who'd picked up the moniker 'Just Jeff' in the band's first interview. I was blown away – they were the ultimate mod band.

Unbeknown to me, halfway through the set a photographer standing to the left of the stage captured Manton just as he leaned forward into the crowd. A week later a review appeared in *Time Out* and there I was, bouncing around mid-clap. I was thrilled. The Purple Hearts screamed 'STYLE' in capital letters and were as tight as fuck. Unusually for our scene, the band had been together for a year already – and it showed. They were powerful and angry; everything a 15-year-old could want. They dressed how I wanted to dress and I vowed to improve my wardrobe immediately. Some months later the band released the anthemic 'Millions Like Us', which became one of the mod revival's finest records, but somehow they managed to top it with their second single, 'Frustration'.

> I get frustration!
> I wear it like a suit

But the jacket fits too tightly
And there's lead inside my boots

A genius lyric from an incredibly underrated band.

8

THE REAL ME

The 1979 Bank Holiday season was in full swing and we were abuzz with potential destinations.

We'd all heard about the 1964 set-tos with rockers but, like most mods at the time, we decided to visit a seaside town by train and only for the Bank Holiday Monday itself.

An 18-year-old mod from round the corner called Tim had heard that mods were supposed to be going to Clacton-on-Sea for the coming weekend, so was going to ride there on his Lambretta, the first I'd ever seen close up. We had no scooters but we still wanted to go and see what all the fuss was about. Clacton was a down-at-heel dump on the 'Essex Riviera' that had been in general decline since the late Sixties. In fact, all the seaside towns I visited in those early mod days were in terminal decline.

Five of us made the trip on 28 May, but the most interesting thing about that particular Bank Holiday Monday was the train journey. Absolutely nothing of note happened all day! It was a bright sunny morning and we joined a couple of hundred other kids wandering up and down the promenade wondering what it was we were supposed to be doing. The heavy police presence meant that none of us could get into a pub, so after a confused hour or more, we jumped onto the train and headed back to London in time to take in the Purple Hearts gig at the Notre Dame Hall.

That Bank Holiday was a definite anticlimax and one that we were determined not to repeat. By the time the next one came round three months later, the mod revival was well on its way and this time we recruited a few more of our new friends to join us on a trip to another dump on the Essex Riviera: Southend-on-Sea.

Our excited group of 15- and 16-year-olds from Woodford teamed up with some mod girls (or 'modettes', as they proudly called themselves) from Hainault, a hard council-estate suburb 15 minutes from us by bus. I'd met Simone, Diane, her brother Dean, Maxine and a bunch of mouthy mod girls led by a ginger-haired parka-wearer called Alex at the Room at the Top under-18s disco a couple of months earlier.

Alex was larger than life. Her fiery red hair and oversized parka with a Who patch stitched onto its left breast made her stand out from the rest of us.

Nine of us met at Liverpool Street Station at half past nine on Monday 27 August and soon found ourselves joined by a journalistic team from *Sounds*. Encouraged by their staff writer Garry Bushell, the music paper was keen to get a handle on the growing mod movement and chose a group of kids at random to spend the day with. Bizarrely, they latched onto us!

As soon as we piled into our compartment and the train got rolling, out came the alcohol. Alex had snaffled a bottle of vodka from her dad's booze cupboard and someone else pulled out a Watneys Party Seven. Happy days!

By the time we clambered onto the platform at Southend we were pleasantly pissed. Virginia Turbett, the *Sounds* photographer, wasted no time snapping away and insisted we acted naturally and be ourselves. This was no problem for Alex, who was an extrovert and a drunken one at that. The weather had changed and it was raining a light drizzle, but that didn't put anyone off and we were soon on the beach acting up for the camera.

Contrary to what we were expecting, there was no kind of trouble. At one point a group of a dozen leather-jacketed rockers rumbled along the seafront on big-bore British bikes but paid us not a scintilla of attention. In the main there was a crowd of between two and three hundred mid-teen mods, punks and skinheads ambling around amusement arcades and standing outside pubs. The handful of Old Bill present endeavoured to move everyone along at every opportunity but nothing actually happened. Nothing, that was, until I heard the high-pitched *cough-cough-put-put* metallic whine that was unique to the two-stroke engine of that marvel of postwar Italian engineering, the scooter.

Sure enough, in a cloud of light-blue-grey exhaust smoke, a group of 20 Lambrettas and Vespas turned onto the seafront and started making their way slowly up and down. Parading like carnival floats in a provincial backwater, their riders to a man (well actually, in one case, a woman) clad in that bottle-green coat we had come to know and love, the M51 US Army parka. Most but not all of the scooters were decorated with a handful of lights and mirrors; some had those metallic gold letters proclaiming the model on their leg shields and a few sported flyscreens that boasted of their owner's area. I remember two specifically: Bethnal Green and Deptford Mods.

Up until now we'd known that 'mods liked scooters'. We'd seen the odd handful parked outside the Wellington or the Bridge House on gig nights and even a few lined up at the Horse & Well, but this was the first time I'd seen an actual convoy making its way purposefully down a street and, yes, showing off. I was moved. It was exciting to feel part of this wonderful youthquake that was reinterpreting the past in a way that suited our contemporary future. I resolved to get hold of a scooter at the first opportunity.

The rest of the day passed in a blur until we got the train back to London and parted at the Central Line, happy and buzzing.

Imagine my pleasure and surprise when, the following Thursday, *Sounds* published the promised article on mods. Pride of place was a photo of a sopping-wet Alex walking up the slipway from the beach, arms akimbo, laughing with a gang of kids and a handful of coppers behind her. We worked out that I'd been standing 18 inches out of shot to her right. We were ecstatic.

A week later my own photo appeared in the *Observer Magazine*, sweatily jumping around at the front of the Notre Dame Hall stage. The journalist had even used some of my words in the article. Oh, how I showed off at school! Tris also had his photo in the magazine and our short-lived notoriety only added a few more local recruits to our new, exciting and totally addictive mod world.

The summer holidays gave me a last opportunity to work for Mister Byrite, and because I was now old enough (though still only 15 – I'm sure Health & Safety would dub it child exploitation now but fuck it, I needed the money!), I worked in the Ilford shop and not the Walthamstow warehouse.

Imagine my joy when I turned up on my first day there to see the place kitted out wall-to-wall with tonic suits, Sta-Prest trousers, Harringtons and button-down shirts. I soon realised that a staff discount made an entirely new wardrobe possible and boy, did I fill my boots. I was taking home 45 quid a week, of which, after rent paid to my dad, at least a third went on schmutter and the rest on records and gigs.

That June, five of us – me, Tris, Richard, Stu Jefcoate and John Bailey – made our way to the ABC in South Woodford to watch *The Kids Are Alright*. This was The Who's feature-length documentary, which was screened nationally in cinemas. In the queue we met another gang of local mods, which was the first time outside of a gig that we'd come across people like us. They were from Epping and there were half a dozen of them. The Silvester brothers, Mark Bradford, Smiffy, Dave Stokes and Spencer were the ones who introduced themselves. Surprisingly, South Woodford was their closest cinema even though Epping was at least 12 miles up the road. It was the first step in building our extended group and within the month we'd met others from Chingford, Hainault, Chigwell, Loughton and Wanstead.

As the year progressed, we travelled to West End gigs together and soon worked out the local boundaries, the places that were safe to go to. Epping – good; Harlow – bad. Loughton – good; Debden – bad. Wanstead and Snaresbrook – good; Leytonstone – bad. Chigwell – good; Hainault . . . Well, Hainault was half and half, but generally bad! By the end of the year there were at least 50 of us from the Essex suburbs who met once or twice a week . . .

The Jam were definitely the glue that held our scene together. By the time I first saw them live, they'd moved on from playing small venues and were headlining theatres – although it was possible to capture some of what must have been the incredible atmosphere of their early gigs when they played one of the handful of 'secret gigs' under a false name at venues like the Marquee or the Nashville. If John's Boys or The Eton Rifles ever turned up in the listings, you knew you were in for a treat! Before long, Woking's finest had become the centre of our social world.

It was at a Jam gig at the Rainbow in Finsbury Park that I experienced that rush of teen emotion called love at first sight. I spotted her three rows away from me, sporting a slightly odd geometric barnet and a gorgeous – no, *stunning* – white crochet dress cut slightly above the knee. I was instantly smitten. She was with a group of five other girls, all of whom were around our 15-year-old age group. Now, the policy at Jam gigs (once the band started playing the larger, seated venues like this) was to start off in your own seat but stealthily make your way ever closer to the stage by any means possible (getting 'down the front'), doing your best to avoid the ever-vigilant security who fought a losing battle to keep you in your seat.

As the band walked off at the end of their set, I found myself squeezed up against this vision in white. This had probably been my subconscious intention but wasn't planned as I didn't have the bottle to say as much as a hello to a girl at the time. When the hormonal and hysterical collection of young, parka-clad teens were bellowing 'We want The Jam!', I steeled myself and took the plunge.

'Er, hello . . . Um . . .' I can't remember what I actually said but remember that it took an awful lot of courage to begin a conversation.

We both went equally red, and so began an awkward and rather clumsy love affair. It turned out her name was Paula. She was from Wembley and, like me, a left-footer who also attended a single-sex Catholic school – in her case, a convent.

The gang of girls she was with were all at the same school and collectively answered to the name of the Wembley Girls. Gangs and their names were very popular at the time and ours was the Woodford Mods (which included mod girls Jackie Clarke, Laura Maloney, Clare Richards and Philippa and Petra Winnet), although you couldn't really call us a gang. I suppose we were just an ever-widening group of friends who came from a nebulous geographical area centred on Woodford. Rather like the Wembley Girls – although we never discovered where they actually came from. Wembley? Harrow?

Weller, Foxton and Buckler bounced back on stage and launched into their first encore. By the start of the third tune, Paula was carried away from me in the crush. I felt strangely empty but decided to renew our friendship at the first available opportunity. After all, she was a real mod girl and I'd decided that I wanted a real mod girlfriend. We rushed to catch the train home and that was the last I saw of her that night.

*

I never considered myself a romantic but, inspired by Paula, I wrote my first letter to Paul Weller. I was already a member of The Jam Fan Club and received the regular newsletters, but I felt there was an important question that had never been addressed. Why on earth was there no mention of the beautiful acoustic song 'English Rose' on the sleeve of *All Mod Cons*? Neither the title nor the lyrics. My crush on Paula had spurred me to find out. I mean, the track was a beautiful love song and obviously meant something to its composer. Was he embarrassed?

I never expected a reply, so imagine my surprise when just two weeks later I received a handwritten letter from Paul explaining that 'the song was very personal and I just didn't think that the lyrics would mean anything to anybody else, especially without the music . . .' My god! Had that really happened? Had my hero taken the time out to answer my question personally? How extraordinary! How special . . .

Soon we were regularly bumping into Paula and the Wembley Girls at the Marquee, the Music Machine or the Fulham Greyhound. But it was at a gig watching Small Hours at the impossibly inaccessible Jacksons Lane Community Centre in Highgate that she made a suggestion I jumped at: why didn't we go to a gig together the following week?

Secret Affair were playing out in Acton or Uxbridge, in the wilds beyond the (pre-M25) North Circular Road. Of course I wanted to go! But there was a major logistical problem: I'd never be able to get home to Woodford after the show. While I was almost hoping Paula would ask me to stay at hers (and this when we were both not yet 16), she rather more sensibly introduced me to three of her mod friends who were a few years older than us: two brothers, Peter and Kevin, and their flatmate, Shane, who lived in a shared house up in Harrow-on-the-Hill. While Shane was a scary-looking (but very sweet) lunatic with tattoos on his hands who'd progressed to the Amateur Boxing Association finals the previous year and now had a nose to prove it, Peter and Kevin were somewhat less frightening and offered me their couch for the coming Saturday.

Memories of the gig itself are lost in the depths of time, but I do remember that the four of us and a couple of their mates made it back to the large and ramshackle house by midnight. First thing I noticed was that there were three motorbikes parked in the front garden. Peter saw me eyeing them up and asked whether I wanted to go for a ride and join the ton-up club? Having consumed a number of pints of Carling, I'd lost my inhibitions and so I agreed.

What a twat. He sat me on the back of some monstrous Kawasaki, and gave me a full-face helmet and instructions to hang on tight, very tight. At first all went to plan, but then he took me down the A40 and opened up the throttle.

'Wow, this is fucking great!' I shouted.

As we hit the ton, and with no warning, he bent down flat to the petrol tank and the full force of the wind hit me smack bang in the chest.

'Jesus fucking Christ . . . Aaaarrgghhhhh . . . Slow down, you fucking bastard . . .'

I was screaming like a baby at the top of my voice. I'd nearly been blown from the pillion. Only some desperate adrenaline-fuelled grab for his waist as the wind hit had saved me from certain death.

I was shaking as we pulled up to the house, but all Peter did was laugh. We went inside and I rushed to the toilet, looking in the mirror as I wiped sick from my mouth to see that all the blood had drained from my face. Pulling myself together, I walked back into the front room to grab a beer. Shane the boxer offered me a brandy instead and berated Peter for giving me such a scare. I felt I'd looked stupid in front of my new friends and was obviously out of my depth.

Needless to say, the rest of the night was spent crapping myself, my parka zipped to the neck with the hood wrapped tightly about my face. What were they going to do to me next?

I needn't have worried as it became apparent that Peter was only fucking about with the kid and Shane woke me next morning with a cup of tea. Making my way to the kitchen for the proffered slice of toast, I could see something odd through the frosted-glass back door that led into the sideway. It was light blue and shaped somewhat like . . . Oh my God!

'What's that?' I asked breathlessly.

'Oh, that's Pete's old scooter. He never uses it. Why d'you ask?'

Shane was more interested in his copy of the *Sunday Mirror* than he was me, so I unlocked the door and had a look myself.

To anyone else it was a fucked-up small-frame Vespa 90 fast approaching the end of its useful life, but to me it was beautiful – a marvel of Italian style and engineering with the registration number ERO 90B. And I was going to have her.

When Peter came down for breakfast, I asked him straight out. After all, he was a few years older than me, well over 6 foot and drove a big Kawasaki. What use was a tiny little pop-pop that travelled at 45mph down a very steep hill?

'Oh, that old thing? Really? It's just a little Vespa . . . Tell you what, you can have it. I only bought it for a laugh . . . Fully working too. Just give me 20 quid when you get the chance . . . It's yours.'

I stammered out my thanks and a broad smile cut my face in half.

'I can't thank you enough Pete, you're a star. I really like it!'

Somewhat bemused, he grunted and walked over to the teapot.

I knew not the first thing about scooters. My dad had ridden a Lambretta back in 1959 and both parents had refused my requests to let me have one, not least because I was too young. *Sod it*, I thought. I'd just have to surprise them . . . But how on earth was I going to get it back to Woodford? I sure as hell couldn't ride it – I mean, I wouldn't know how, and even if I did, I'd never find my way back from Harrow.

Slowly an idea formed in my head. It was a Sunday and I knew that Preston Road Station was only half a mile up the road. I was going to take the scooter to Woodford by Tube.

In 1979 there were no Oyster cards or even ticket barriers and on Sundays there were very few guards or inspectors. If I played my cards right, I might just pull it off. I said my farewells to the lads and set off for Preston Road pushing my new acquisition along the pavement. Sure enough, the station was deserted when I arrived. There were no staff anywhere, so I went to the ticket machine and purchased a single. To be on the safe side, I bought the Vespa a half-fare ticket as well. That way if I did meet an inspector I could at least try to convince him that we'd paid for the journey. (Note: 'it' had now become 'she' and part of 'we', and the anthropomorphisation of ERO 90B was complete.) From memory, her ticket was the same as mine: a light-green card, 1 inch by 2.5 inches, except that hers had a diagonal red stripe across it to denote a half-fare.

Preston Road was on the Metropolitan Line but far enough out of London to be an overground Tube station. There were 32 iron-clad steps down to the platform, so I made sure we were heading in the right direction and allowed her to roll slowly down the steps with my hand on the front brake – which was on the handlebars. All went swimmingly and within ten minutes the first train had pulled in. The carriage looked very old and a glance at the map told me I needed to change first at Baker Street, then King's Cross and again at Liverpool Street for the Central Line to Woodford. As I wheeled her over the gap between the platform and the carriage, I realised I didn't know how to put the scooter on her stand. After a couple of fruitless attempts, I gave up, embarrassed, and leaned her up against the glass partition instead.

Over the course of the 25-minute journey to Baker Street a few passengers got on and looked startled to see us but, although we got some odd looks and even a couple of smiles, no one said a word. All was going to plan. So much so that I was becoming slightly complacent. Changing from the Circle to the Central Line at Liverpool Street is quite complicated and involved going up a couple of flights of steps as well as down. Fortunately, a small-frame Vespa isn't a heavy bike and I managed to sort of lift-push her up without too much trouble. *This is easy*, I thought.

Onto the final straight and I was carefully manoeuvring the scooter down the very last (and rather steep) set of steps onto the eastbound Central Line platform. I wasn't being quite as careful as I should have been, though, and halfway down disaster struck: somehow I let the Vespa, which was moving under her own impetus one step at time, briefly slip out of my control. She bumped down the next step on her own as if possessed by a malevolent spirit. In a frantic effort to stop her, my inexperienced hands confused the front brake (on the right side of the handlebars, next to the accelerator) with the clutch and gears (on the left-hand side). This resulted in the scooter slipping into gear and bouncing another couple of steps on her own, which provided just enough momentum to jump-start the engine (there is no ignition switch or key on a Vespa 90; it's too basic). The little bit of throttle I applied while trying to find the brake was sufficient for ERO 90B to roar off solo down onto the platform.

'Aaaaaaaaggggggggh . . .! Sweet fucking *Jesus* . . . Come back, you bastard!'

My life flashed before my eyes – the immediate vision was of my scooter plunging off the platform, onto the live tracks and exploding just as the 2.04 to Epping pulled into the station, causing a major derailment. Arrest would soon follow and I'd be sent to prison . . . I know this seems rather a lot to flash before the eyes in what was probably no more than a second, but I swear it did.

As ERO 90B reached the bottom of the stairs, centrifugal force and momentum kept the now wobbling small-frame Vespa upright as she made her stately and unaccompanied way along the platform, steering ever so slightly closer to the gaping chasm at the platform edge. Screaming and terrified people scattered as entire families returning from what had probably been a pleasant trip to Petticoat Lane Market took evasive action. The *pop-pop-pop* of the scooter's engine sounded deafening in the acoustic amplification of the tunnel-shaped space.

I . . . must . . . get . . . to . . . the . . . And then I had her! But stopping the bastard was another matter.

I couldn't risk the front brake in case, in my panicked confusion, I accidentally twisted the handlebar-mounted throttle again. I did the only thing I could to prevent a front-page disaster scenario: I crashed her into one of those hefty mahogany benches that were once a common feature on the Tube network.

She stopped all right because the bike was still in gear, so the engine stalled. How the flying fuck did that actually happen? People were coming to their senses and one or two were admonishing me. I mumbled my apologies and made my way to the other end of the platform while the thick cloud of two-stroke smoke slowly dissipated. On reflection, I can only assume that in 1979 CCTV had not yet made it onto the Tube because, incredibly, there was no official reaction whatsoever. No guards or inspectors rushed down onto the platform to give me a severe reprimand. No British Transport Police arrived to arrest me. Nothing happened. Well, I wasn't one to look a gift horse in the mouth and when the next train pulled into the station, with my heart beating ten to the dozen, I wheeled my new acquisition on board and thankfully watched the doors close behind me.

The rest of the journey passed uneventfully and the worst I received were a few confused looks until the train pulled into Woodford Station, my final destination. This time there was a guard at the exit. He removed his cap and stood there staring in confusion, scratching his head like some latter-day Will Hay in a Fifties Ealing comedy.

Eventually he spoke. 'What the bloody hell do you think you're doing? You're not allowed to take motorbikes on the Tube.'

'It's not a motorbike, it's a scooter!' I ruefully muttered.

At this he snapped. 'I don't care what it is. You're not allowed to take it on the Tube. It could cause a serious accident.'

I handed over the tickets I'd bought and said: 'But the bloke at the other end said it would be all right as long as I bought the scooter a ticket. Look – here it is!'

'Sorry, laddie, that's a bloody lie and you know it is. You're going to have to take it back to where it came from. Where did you get on anyway?'

'Erm . . . Preston Road.'

He laughed. 'Now I know you're lying. You expect me to believe that you travelled the entire length of the Tube network with *that* and no one stopped you?'

'Erm . . . Yeah . . . And I won't be able to take it back to where it came from either.'

'And just why not?'

'Erm . . .' Gazing wistfully at the opposite platform. 'I won't be able to push it up all those stairs to get it over there . . .' Long pause, wide brown eyes looking up at him. 'Unless you'd like to help me?'

At this he conceded defeat and shouted, 'Just get that bloody thing out of my sight!', but not before snatching the two tickets still proffered in my outstretched hand.

I rolled the Vespa out of the station, relieved. That was the difficult part of the journey over, but I still had to get her back to my house – and that meant a concerted push of over a mile, large parts of it uphill. The afternoon summer sun was at its peak, I was wearing a parka as well as a tonic jacket over my Fred Perry and within 100 yards I was sweating like a pig. After the second hundred I arrived at Woodford's first hill.

Fuck it, I'd had enough of this. I was going to ride the bloody thing!

Well, at least I'd learned the basics from the incident on the platform, and though I didn't have a helmet, I felt my luck was in. You never saw a copper in Woodford on a Sunday. I made sure the scooter was in

On the Vespa 50 borrowed from John Graham, 1979.

Passport photo in
obligatory parka!

In my bedroom in Woodford,
late 1979/early 1980.

Woodford mod (left) plus assorted mates, 1979.

Amphetamine comedown, on the landing at my parents' house.

Wearing a new-old stock
jacket from Davis in Mile End.

On the Brighton Bank Holiday
run with John Halls, 1981.

With the Woodford mods in Amsterdam.

Queuing outside the Ilford Palais mod alldayer, 1982.

A packed crowd inside the Ilford Palais mod alldayer, 1982.

Gathering in the carpark before the Ilford Palais mod alldayer, 1982.

007 playing at the Ilford Palais mod alldayer, 1982.

With my flatmate Bunny and the Americans, 1984.

(Left to right) Me, Ricey, Mark Steers, Garry Moore, Ian Shreeves, Jim Watson, John Halls and 'Big' Bob Morris at Paul Hallam's club Sneakers in 1984.

The Prisoners in Holland, 1984.

DJing at the Formula One club, between Covent Garden
and Leicester Square, in 1984.

In Lowestoft with Jon Cooke, 1985.

neutral, tried the kick-start and, like all Vespas, she spluttered into life first go. I jumped on and pottered off up the hill at about 10mph, learning as I went. Riding a scooter isn't difficult and I contend that absolutely anyone can do it – so I did! After the first 20 yards I'd got the hang of it; a further 30 and I managed a gear change, making my hatless way through the backstreets of Woodford Green until I pulled up outside my front door.

As it was by now late Sunday afternoon, the old man would be snoozing on the sofa, having returned from the afternoon jazz session at the Cauliflower in Ilford. A few pints of ale while taking in his personal favourite, The Tony Lee Trio, usually set him up for a session on the sofa watching West Ham on *The Big Match* with Brian Moore. My mum would be getting the Sunday roast together for the one occasion of the week where we ate as a family. I let myself in.

'Oh, there you are, Edward. I was wondering when you'd show your face . . . What was that noise . . .?' She poked a querying head around the front door. 'What on earth is that?'

Excitedly I said, 'It's a Vespa 90, Mum, and it's bloody great!'

'I can see that, and I didn't ask you how it was. Whose is it?'

'It's mine,' I said rather too proudly.

'I don't think it is, Edward. Just wait until your father finds out.'

And off she went, calling, 'Ed! Ed, come and see what Edward's brought home and before you say anything . . . he's not keeping it.'

Thirty seconds later a shoeless Dad walks out of the front door and looks quizzically at my light-blue first love.

'Terrific.' Not the response my mother was hoping for. 'How much did you pay for it?'

'Twenty quid . . . but it's on tick.'

'That's about right; certainly not worth much more than that,' he said as he made his way around my scooter in his socks, appraising her bodywork.

Now at this point, three months from my 16th birthday, I was still only 5 foot 7 inches tall. My dad, however, was 6 foot 3 inches and as he sat on my tiny Vespa he laughed. 'I knew it'd be too small for me! Not a patch on my last one, a Lambretta TV175, but this is a good starter bike for you. Does it work? Where did you get it from? How did you get it home?'

As the story unfolded, I could tell my mum was getting more pissed off – not actually with me but with my dad for not coming up with suitable admonishments at relevant parts of our somewhat incredulous journey from the other side of London. The only time he appeared even mildly disapproving was at the bit where I'd ridden home from the station without a helmet.

'Well, you can't ride it on the road for another few months because you aren't legal till you're 16 . . .' (He was wrong on this point: only a Vespa 50 was legal at 16; anything with a bigger engine and you had to be 17.) '. . . but I see no reason why you can't teach yourself how to drive and look after it in the garden . . .'

I was chuffed and within five minutes had manoeuvred her down the sideway onto the pristine lawn. An hour later and I'd burned a figure of eight into the topsoil and had the hang of my amazing new toy. I stopped only when I was called in for Sunday dinner and my dad advised a trip to Woodford Scooters in the morning to pick up a crash helmet.

Woodford Scooters had a great reputation for building custom Vespas in the Sixties, rather like its near neighbour Eddy Grimstead's in Gants Hill. The man there explained how to mix petrol with two-stroke oil and found a tatty old manual for me to take home. I taught myself the basics of maintenance and decided to respray the bike, ready for when I took her out on the road after I'd passed my 16th birthday (even though I'd still be too young, my dad thought I wouldn't be and that was good enough for me!). The preparation was a ball-ache, and rubbing the old paint off to bare metal by hand took weeks, but I convinced myself it would be worth it in the end.

Well, it wasn't – anyone who's tried to paint a vehicle using spray paint bought from a car-parts shop will know that it's a complete waste of time. Still, that didn't deter me and eventually I was finished. Trouble was, my scooter looked utterly shit. Oh well, I was still gagging for the chance to ride on the road wearing my new open-face skidlid.

I didn't have to wait long. I was good friends with Jackie Curbishley and her younger brother Mickey, who were part of our small but rapidly growing group of local mods. These two had an advantage over the rest of us in that their dad Bill managed The Who. You wouldn't have known it, though, because they were never flash, didn't talk about it and only their close friends knew. To most people, they were just ordinary mods like the rest of us.

The 14-year-old Mickey Curbishley had a Lambretta in the garage and as soon as he heard of my new acquisition he suggested I bring it round so we could go riding together at RAF Buckhurst Hill, which was just 100 yards from his house. The former World War II Battle of Britain fighter station had been abandoned for a couple of decades and was a favourite for learner drivers and kids who weren't road legal.

Great idea, I thought, but I still had to get the Vespa to his house and, apart from the journey home from the station, I'd not yet driven on the road. Eventually I threw caution to the wind, put on my parka and rode there for an exciting afternoon's fun.

I loved the concept of a scooter, the freedom and rush that two wheels give you as a teenager – the chance to get from A to B without the need for public transport. I realised in those very first weeks that this little machine would be the first of many; that this would be a lifelong love affair.

9

MILLIONS LIKE US

All through the glorious summer of 1979, the mod scene grew. New bands proliferated at an incredible rate and were now sorting themselves out into some kind of hierarchy.

The Jam were at the top of the pyramid. They had a slightly different status from all the others. The media didn't regard them as a mod revival band, and this was probably because Paul Weller had somehow created the entire revival in his own image.

L. Ron Hubbard might have deliberately set about establishing his own religion, but Paul Weller seemed to have inadvertently started one too. He had all the elements in place and our reluctant messiah found he'd created a movement almost by accident.

Weller had been obsessed with mod since childhood. While he was keen to share his personal journey of discovery with others, too late he realised that his love of the Sixties, The Beatles and the minutiae of mod would inspire millions. That was never his intention. But you can never put the genie back in the bottle.

I've seen Paul's school exercise books and they're remarkably similar to mine: doodles of scooters covered with lights and mirrors, RAF targets and Small Faces or Who logos abound. The difference was that I'd got my inspiration from Weller himself, while he was looking back ten or so years to the original Sixties mod scene – or at least to an idealised and iconographic distillation of it. What possessed him to do this I've never quite worked out, and he hasn't been particularly effusive on the subject. I've heard talk that there was a small South London mod revival in 1974, and similar stories have been told about other areas with localised mod scenes – especially in the north, with their long tradition of soul and scooter clubs, which continued into the Seventies, long after the original mod scene in London had been forgotten. Steve Ellis of Love Affair told me that he considered his group to be the last mod band to have a chart hit (a cover of Robert Knight's 'Everlasting Love'), but even they gave up the ghost in 1969.

I assume Paul Weller was part of that 1974 wave. Maybe the photobook that came with The Who's original 1973 *Quadrophenia* concept album was an inspiration? The photobook and album told the story of a young mod, the sort who'd been into The Who the best part of a decade earlier, in 1964. We may never know. What we do know is that Weller's vision inspired a whole generation to follow him down the mod path.

Either way, as far as I'm concerned everything Paul Weller and The Jam ever did *was* mod and defined mod for my generation. While The Clash were fiddling about trying to 'Rock the Casbah', Weller was talking about 'kidney machines that pay for rockets and guns' or the shocking urban violence found in 'Down in the Tube Station at Midnight'. For me, there was absolutely no contest. No Jam, no mod revival – no matter how much Weller himself might have regretted it. Like Dr Frankenstein, he created a monster that made a life for itself.

From his hard-hitting sociopolitical lyrics that painted a perfect portrait of late-Seventies Britain to the photo of the three band members sheltering under the brutalist A40 for *This Is the Modern World*. From the nonsensical arrows taped to Weller's jumper through to the target label and Rickenbacker guitar of *All Mod Cons*, whose inner sleeve featured the Vespa Super wiring diagram . . . The band hadn't just adopted the mod look – they had set it out as some kind of 'action plan' for us to follow. So we did.

I'm certain it was the way The Jam treated their fans that made the difference. It made us love them. Better still, our punk older brothers and sisters were completely split about The Jam, which surely made them even more appealing

The first-ever punk fanzine, Mark Perry's *Sniffin' Glue*, was overtly dismissive of the band's mod attitude. This resulted in The Jam burning a copy of the fanzine on stage at an early gig, but all this did was galvanise the other early punkzines to jump to their defence.

Shane MacGowan's *Bondage* hailed them as the best band of the lot. Gary Crowley's *The Modern World* and Adrian Thrills' *48 Thrills* proclaimed their brilliance to all and sundry, and Tony Fletcher's *Jamming!* wasn't far behind. Suddenly it was the antics of the Sex Pistols's Sid Vicious that was attracting approbation. Weller's first fight with him was at The Jam's Upstairs at Ronnie's gig and they again came to blows at the 100 Club punk festival.

Importantly, this illustrated that The Jam were 'part of punk' but not 'from punk' – and it was this that their fans picked up on. Weller's following were younger and far less tolerant of the Situationism and faux-anarchy of McLaren's Pistols. Indeed, it was initially mooted that Glen Matlock, the most 'mod' Sex Pistol, would eventually join The Jam!

Paul Weller and his two bandmates seemed different from their contemporaries. They offered us a fresh start; they were unique. One thing that John Weller, Paul's dad and manager, encouraged and that reinforced the band's relationship with their growing fanbase was to throw open the doors to the band's sound checks. You could turn up to any venue, anywhere in the country, and at half three the back doors would be opened and anyone who was hanging around outside could come in and watch. These kids might have been too young for the official show, or unable to get hold of a ticket, but they were welcomed with open arms.

The Jam's road crew could certainly be tough (I'd been thrown out by John Weller or Kenny Wheeler on a number of occasions), but on the whole they treated The Jam's fans with great respect. In truth, the whole thing was a family affair. The fan club was run by Paul's sister Nicky, his dad John was the manager and his mum Ann kept a sharp eye on proceedings. In all my later experience of the industry, this was totally unique.

The Jam were in the process of building the most obsessive and loyal fanbase of any band in the country.

In 1965, Peter Meaden had described mod as the 'New Religion'. Now, Paul Weller took it one stage further and made the concept a reality.

After the initial underground explosion of the mod revival, the 'big three' bands following in The Jam's wake – The Chords, the Purple Hearts and Secret Affair – were all in the process of signing record deals by the middle of 1979.

After a false start with Jimmy Pursey's fledgling mod label, The Chords were snapped up by Polydor, as were the Purple Hearts, signed by Chris Parry for his Fiction subsidiary.

Secret Affair were different and had some clout because of their New Hearts experience the previous year. Page and Cairns had the legendary music publisher Bryan Morrison fighting their corner. Morrison encouraged a bidding war between a number of major labels who were suddenly desperate not to miss out on this new phenomenon. To sweeten the pill and secure the deal, frontrunners Arista offered the band their own bespoke label. This generosity tipped the scales, so Secret Affair inked the paperwork and launched I-Spy Records.

All three bands used the summer of 1979 to build their profile through gigging (not least The Chords, who secured a coveted support slot with The Jam) and mod continued its steady spread through the country.

Terry Murphy, the owner of the Bridge House (already well established as the home of the Mods Monday residency), jumped on the bandwagon with his own label, Bridge House Records. The big idea was to record some live sets over the May Bank Holiday and release a compilation showcasing the scene. He booked several of the available bands and the album was hastily recorded, featuring Secret Affair, Squire, The Mods, Beggar (who by now had moved up from South Wales and settled in Leyton, making them another of our 'local' heroes), Small Hours and The Merton Parkas from – yes, you guessed it – Merton Park in Southwest London.

I really liked Danny and Mick Talbot, but their band broke the first rule of marketing.

Never. Ever. Use puns. End of.

Sadly, no one had passed this wisdom on to the unfortunate Merton Parkas, who were consequently viewed as bandwagon-jumpers with a silly name. They weren't actually. Fronted by the genuinely talented Talbot brothers (lead vocalist/guitarist Danny and keyboard player 'Merton Mick', whose nickname lasted significantly longer than the band), they built up a substantial following on the early scene. Originally called The Sneakers, they were a melodic four-piece who wrote surprisingly catchy pop songs. Along with Squire, they were often derided for being lightweight, but I would say that they came from the power-pop side of the revival and were different from many of the rest, who were literally 'punks in parkas'.

The Sneakers quickly attracted the attention of the respected indie label Beggars Banquet, who smelled a hit. The band were immediately signed and an overenthusiastic marketing department changed their name to The Merton Parkas and rushed them into the studio, desperate to have the first 'mod revival hit'. This was an attempt to copy The Damned, whose label Stiff Records made a very big splash by beating both the Sex Pistols and The Vibrators to be the first British punk band onto vinyl. Stiff at least chose the incredible 'New Rose' as their 45, though. The A&R man at Beggars Banquet couldn't have got it more wrong.

The debut single, 'You Need Wheels', was certainly no 'New Rose'! A turgid cod-R&B plodder that relied on an implied reference to scooters, the much-heralded debut 45 from the mod revival limped into the Top 40. The chorus was incredibly uninspiring: 'You need wheels if you wanna make deals / You need a tie if you wanna get high . . .'

While the song was actually about a red sports car, the single came packaged in a sleeve that featured the band perched uncomfortably on borrowed scooters outside Merton Park Station. There was also an embroidered 'parka patch' stapled to the front.

The damage was done, and although the Merton Parkas did indeed have the first (non-Jam) hit of the revival, their long-term credibility plummeted. Even their excellent debut album, *Face in the Crowd*, released a month later, couldn't repair the situation and they never came back from the 'cheesy bandwagon-jumpers' tag. In fact, with the release of 'You Need Wheels', a backlash swept through the whole scene. It was implied that the Parkas had made a laughing stock of the rest of us. Critical photocopied flyers denigrating the band began appearing at gigs, left on tables or in pub toilets. These were issued by the anonymous K.A.M.P. (Kill All Merton Parkas) and the band, who had lost the goodwill of many of their fans, never recovered.

'You Need Wheels' and its marketing campaign provided a sceptical and hostile music press with an excuse to dismiss the mod revival as a joke. It was a terrible start for the scene.

The Merton Parkas's early deal with Beggars Banquet meant that they were pulled off Terry Murphy's *Mods Mayday '79* album at the last minute – too late to redesign the sleeve, which consequently sported thick black lines drawn through the band's photo and song credits.

When the vinyl of *Mods Mayday '79* arrived at my local record shop I proudly bought a copy and took it to school to show the lads.

By now we were following our favourite bands from gig to gig and a well-trodden circuit of down-at-heel music pubs became regular destinations. As well as the originators Secret Affair, Purple Hearts, The Merton Parkas and The Chords, we also followed the incredibly soulful Small Hours, Beggar, The Teenbeats, Dolly Mixture, Long Tall Shorty, The Lambrettas and our own version of John Cooper Clarke called Eddie, Steady, Go!

I first saw the latter south-coast four-piece at their debut London gig at the Hope & Anchor. The Lambrettas were unfairly regarded as latecomers to the party; in reality they were part of a strong Sussex scene that also included The Teenbeats and The Vandells. They were signed by the ever-astute Elton John, who'd long admitted a love for his mod roots. You can just about make me out on the front cover of their debut 45, 'Go Steady', which features some very cool and energetic photos from a stage invasion at the Marquee that really sum up the excitement of that period. Singer Jez Bird looks cool as fuck.

Singles by mod bands were flying out at an incredible rate, and while Pete at Small Wonder had strict instructions to reserve me a copy of all of them, I was finding it hard to keep up.

10

THE KIDS ARE ALRIGHT

On 16 August 1979, something happened to take what had been, up to that point, a thriving but still relatively underground teenage scene and propel it into the outer stratosphere of contemporary culture.

Quadrophenia was released in the cinema.

We were in a somewhat privileged position of course, being friends with The Who's manager's kids, Jackie and Mickey Curbishley; it was Bill who, after years of determined persuasion, eventually brought the project to the big screen.

I'd always assumed that the film was a mid-Seventies tax loss for a load of middle-aged men who fancied a go at reliving their youth. Forty years later, while researching a documentary I wrote about it, I finally realised that I couldn't have been more wrong.

Quadrophenia is a genuine masterpiece, one of a host of films that came to embody the short-lived concept of 'new British realism' – a genre that included *The Long Good Friday*, *Babylon* and *Scum*. Franc Roddam, a relatively young and obscure director from the northeast, had impressed with his bizarre and somewhat dark television play *Dummy*, which was a hard-hitting piece about a deaf girl who is eventually forced into prostitution and degradation on the streets of Bradford. It defined the genre and managed to catch the eye of Bill Curbishley and his partner Roy Baird.

The movie was based on The Who's 1973 concept album – or rather on Pete Townshend's conceptual rock opera of the same name, which was performed by The Who. It had originally been a loose audiovisual fantasy, telling the story of the gradual mental disintegration of a young mod's life and dreams through the medium of song. We'd all pored over the album's original gatefold sleeve for details and clues many times. I'd even been offered the opportunity to appear as an extra in the film but was away on holiday at the time it was shot, much to my eternal regret.

About 20 of us made it to the ABC in Woodford for the opening night and the place was heaving with teenage mods, with a queue stretching round the block. Despite fears of 'mods and rockers' violence, the event passed peacefully but raucously. The atmosphere in the cinema was electric. None of us knew what the film was going to be like, but from the moment Phil Daniels's character Jimmy Cooper walks slowly back from the cliff's edge at sunset and the action cuts to him riding his Lambretta through Shepherd's Bush to the sounds of 'The Real Me', I was hooked. The title sequence alone blew my tiny mind and the audience didn't stop cheering and shouting all through the movie.

We were 15 and what the film did for us was to provide a template, imaginary or not, of what the mod world *could* do for us enthusiastic acolytes. Rightly or wrongly, it became a manual as to how we should dress, dance and live.

Many of the film's throwaway lines – most of which were ad-libbed by Daniels, Phil Davis, Mark Wingett or Trevor Laird – became catchphrases for our generation: 'You lookin' for Ferdie?', 'Party in Kitchener Road . . .', 'Don't fancy yours much!', 'They don't make Levi's in your size . . .', 'Why don't you roll over and do a few underwater farts!', 'I don't wanna be like everybody else; that's why I'm a mod, see?', 'Chalkey – the ponce!' and my personal favourite, 'Do the bastard's motor.'

There are hundreds more, each one contributing a minuscule amount of the humour and glue that kept our scene together. But it was almost impossible to beat the acting in the scene where a spaced-out Phil Daniels as Jimmy Cooper was knocked off his bike by the Post Office van. It was almost as if the entire film had been made just for us – and if it hadn't been, then we were certainly going to try to live our lives just like the mods on the big screen were portrayed as living theirs; it was all we had. The movie and the revival were the perfect synergistic collision.

The reaction the film prompted from within the established scene was varied to say the least. Roddam's interpretation of Townshend's mod vision was certainly not universally popular. Paul Weller for one was famously not a fan. But it was on the early revivalist mods that it seemed to have the biggest effect. Many of the original faces – people who'd been mods since the beginning of the year, maybe even in late 1978 – simply walked away, regarding the expected influx of 100,000 'tickets' (or 'A-bombs', as we also disparagingly called these often clueless interlopers) as the final straw in a world that had peaked a few months earlier and was being infiltrated by bandwagon-jumpers.

But there were also thousands of other youngsters who took it for what it was: a brilliant, evocative, energetic attempt to sum up the excitement and contradictions of the Sixties mod lifestyle. The naysayers' loss was soon forgotten by the rest of us as a whole new generation of mods flocked to the banner and in the process gave the scene a fresh impetus.

More importantly, it had given us some kind of detailed insight into what mods actually did! Bank Holidays weren't supposed to be dull train rides to the coast on a Monday afternoon; they could be full-blown weekends of fun where we'd ride down to the coast and let off a substantial amount of steam before heading back to London on our scooters in the rain.

*

The massive increase in numbers that *Quadrophenia* encouraged brought with it some resentment from other youth cults, especially skinheads, with whom we'd enjoyed a fragile and gradually disintegrating peace throughout the summer. But the first time we were physically attacked just for being mods was actually by the usually far more docile punks.

It happened after a Secret Affair gig that summer. I was buzzing as we filed out of the Marquee, and (par for the course) we were soaked and steaming with sweat. Before we'd even made it 15 yards towards the Tube, we were charged by a gang of punks. They were a few years older than we were and we certainly weren't expecting any trouble from that quarter.

Initially I wasn't sure what had goaded them into attack mode, but eventually realised it must have had something to do with the lyrics to Secret Affair's forthcoming 'Time for Action' single, which had been picking up some radio play. As well as being a rallying cry for the new mods, it famously contained the contentious lyrics: 'We're all dressed up for the evening / We hate the punk elite . . .'

I don't blame the punks, actually – how were they supposed to feel? They went from being the cool kids on the block to being losers virtually overnight.

Secret Affair were talking metaphorically about the punk scene in general, how it'd become so detached from its roots, was controlled by a shadowy elite of Svengali types and would soon be swept away by this new scene of sharply dressed Glory Boys; but punks didn't quite see it like that. They were pissed off and came to the Marquee to give it to some of the arrogant bastards who were coating them off.

The 'punk elite' stormed across the road nursing a genuine anti-mod grievance. Some of the crowd turned to face them, but others sprinted for Old Compton Street and perceived safety. I wasn't sure what was happening, so I didn't run – but before we'd even moved, half a dozen

Glory Boys who'd been walking out of the venue behind us hurried across the road to cut them off.

So began a running battle down Wardour Street, through Chinatown and all the way down the hill, past Charing Cross Station to the Embankment.

The fight was certainly violent and frantic bouts of windmilling were followed by brief spurts of running and then more fighting. Somewhere east of Trafalgar Square I lost a shoe. It flew off over a wall and into a basement space, unreachable. I was gutted. They were my favourite loafers from Blackmans and I'd only owned them for a couple of weeks. This led to a semi-hop to the Tube followed by an embarrassing limp-hobble home from Woodford Station an hour later wearing just one shoe and a white towelling sock!

Something else happened at the gig that night. It was the last time Secret Affair handed out some of what they euphemistically called 'glory pills' to their enthusiastic following from the stage.

This was a highly popular but completely illegal part of the band's early stage show, and how they never got busted by the drug squad I'll never know. Well, in fact I do know, and it's worth digressing to explain.

One of the band's roadies was an occasional drug dealer and at a particular Mods Monday at the Bridge House pulled out a big bag of blues he'd hidden down the back of an amp and forgotten about.

He turned to Dave Cairns: "'Ere, Dave . . . Mods love their speed, don't they? Look what I've found: a bag of blues. You can have the lot for a tenner . . .'

Naively the boys thought it might be a bit of fun to throw a few handfuls of pills into the crowd. At around the same time, Ian Page and Dave had been photographed for some promo shots by Fin Costello that gave the impression Ian was holding some pills in his outstretched hand. Hell, why not? It'd be a laugh!

Sure enough, the crowd at the Bridge House show went mad for the pills and the caper was so popular it was repeated at the next gig. Just as the band launched into 'Time for Action', handfuls of the little blue tablets were launched into the audience, prompting more hysteria.

The Marquee gig was the third time they'd pulled this stunt. I'd suspected that the so-called glory pills were just aspirin coloured with blue food dye but was soon informed that they were most definitely real by one of my schoolmates who'd snaffled a couple. Fifteen minutes later he was flying.

However, the band wouldn't hand out blues in this way again after that night. By now, word had reached the drug squad. Secret Affair's next show was at Vespa's in Charing Cross and was due to be filmed for the forthcoming mod movie *Stepping Out*.

Dave Cairns was tuning up in the dressing room with just ten minutes to stage time, unaware that the roadie had stored that night's pill bag in his guitar case. Suddenly the roadie comes running into the room: 'Dave? Dave! Shit! The place is crawling with Old Bill. I reckon they're drug squad. They must be onto us . . . Come and have a look!'

Cairns crept out onto the balcony overlooking the dance floor and, sure enough, there were at least a dozen old'uns spread incongruously throughout the audience. You can see them in the *Stepping Out* footage itself: the average age of the crowd was 16 and most were wearing parkas, so grey-haired men in their forties and fifties dressed like extras from *The Sweeney* stood out like sore thumbs. Cairns was paranoid at the best of times, and on discovering that the blues were in his guitar case he rushed back into the dressing room, grabbed them and ran to the toilet. He began emptying the bag into the bowl, frantically flushing the handle.

'Hey, Dave, whaddya think you're doing? I need those for the film. It's gonna be the climax of the movie . . . Glory pills for the Glory Boys and all that . . .?'

This was Lyndall Hobbs, the movie's director and the occasional girlfriend of Al Pacino.

'Sorry but I'm flushing them down the bog . . . The drug squad are out there and I don't wanna get nicked. Anyway, I thought you were filming us because we're a great band?'

Hobbs was furious, but I think the potential consequences of their live-show stunt had finally dawned on the band and, sure enough, as the set reached its climax the dozen or so plainclothes Old Bill moved towards the stage, obviously waiting for the opening chords of 'Time for Action'.

It appeared they'd been briefed that this particular song, always the highlight of the set, would be their cue to storm the stage and arrest the band, who'd be caught bang to rights handing out illegal drugs. Unfortunately for the Old Bill, nothing happened. No drugs were offered because Cairns had already flushed them away and after a few uncertain and confused minutes the coppers made their way to the exit and left empty-handed. Secret Affair had learned their lesson and the errant roadie was under strict instructions never to bring drugs to a show again.

More filming for *Stepping Out* took place just a couple of days later, this time in Carnaby Street. Word went round that the film company needed some extras for a feature-length documentary about the scene. We were to meet outside the Shakespeare's Head one particular afternoon and simply walk about 'looking like' mods. The film was a budget 'documentary' B-movie and had been commissioned to accompany the forthcoming blockbuster *Alien* for its cinema release.

I put on my parka, dressed in some obvious mod gear and set off to Oxford Street on the Central Line, determined to grab a piece of the action. As I ambled down Argyll Street, it soon became apparent that something unusual was happening. I'd never been to Carnaby Street before, so I walked its entire length, taking in the various sights before heading back to the Shakespeare's Head. There were already 50-odd parka-clad 16-year-olds milling about waiting for someone to shout 'Action!' I nodded to a couple of familiar faces and spotted a handful of scooters parked outside a shop called Carnaby Cavern.

Ah, this is a famous mod shop, I thought, recognising the name from their shockingly bad adverts in the music papers. The Carnaby Cavern might well have had an endorsement deal with The Jam, but their ads for 'Jam suits' and boating blazers featured a hand-drawn image of a supposed mod looking more like Frankenstein's monster. Still, The Jam went through a period of wearing their gear and you can even see examples on the front cover of the 'News of the World' single. Paul is wearing a sky-blue suit, while Bruce is sporting an unmatched jacket-and-trouser combo. They are both wearing so-called 'Jam shoes', but the Cavern jackets had that odd, unflattering square cut to the front. Rick Buckler had rather sensibly plumped for the biker jacket/target T-shirt combo, which so confused many aspiring young mods at the time!

I couldn't get anywhere near the shop window, so walked towards the parked scooters. Impressed, I spotted a couple of band faces in the crowd. Two I recognised were The Little Roosters' frontman Gary Lammin and Danny Talbot from The Merton Parkas, who was soon joined by his brother Mick and the rest of the band to be filmed walking up and down the street.

Ooh, how exciting!

Us extras pottered round the backstreets for the cameras and a few were briefly interviewed until things generally fizzled out and I headed home. I'd been told that the director was going to shoot a few upcoming gigs and some general interviews before the film would be ready to edit. The day had been exciting and the mass gathering of young mods reinforced the feeling that I was part of something special.

I'm sure that the film provides a brilliant snapshot of the early mod revival, but sadly I never got to see it. I did trek to the Woodford ABC for *Alien*, but there was no sign of *Stepping Out* on the bill. Apparently the film was shown for only a limited time and even then not in every cinema. Surprisingly, as far as I know it has never surfaced since, so I don't even know if I made the cut!

Just a couple of months later it was Jackie Curbishley's 16th birthday, and Bill and Jackie Snr had let their young flower hold a party in the room above the garage at their Essex mansion. My status as 'family friend who knew Jackie Snr' meant I was handed the essential role of beer monitor. Bill wasn't stupid and after stocking the garage with cans of lager ensured that the rest of the crates were stored in the house. My job was to approach the front door and politely request the appropriate resupply when necessary.

Andy Gilbert, Richard Habberley and many of the East London mods were in attendance as well as Jackie and Mick's old mates from Chigwell and Woodford. I'm sure you can imagine, a birthday party at The Who's manager's gaff was the hot ticket that autumn. It was coming up to 9 o'clock and the party was in full flow. There were about 60 or so in attendance, all letting their hair down and acting like they were in Kitchener Road. I revelled in my role as intermediary between the kids and the parents as the magic alcohol provider and was popping over to the big house every 20 or so minutes to pick up another case of Heineken and a couple of bottles of wine. It was a 40-yard walk from the garage to the front door and I could tell Jackie Snr was a little annoyed at the frequency of my bangs on the door, but she took it in good grace.

Bill Curbishley was always very quiet and didn't have too much to do with us kids. We were obviously in awe of him – after all, he managed The Who, was 6 feet tall, built like a brick shithouse and had a Canning Town reputation to match. The other thing about Bill was that he was always proud of his East End mod roots. When I did occasionally get to chat to him I thought he was somewhere up there in the pantheon. After all, he personally pulled The Who back from the brink when he took over from Lambert and Stamp and made the *Quadrophenia* movie in his own mod image. Lambert and Stamp had stolen The Who from Peter Meaden and might well have made them into stars, but as the Sixties turned into the Seventies the pair had increasingly taken their collective eyes off the ball. They'd made a real botch of things and The Who wanted a fresh start following the mess of Ken Russell's arthouse take on *Tommy* and the losses they were incurring with their Track Records label and other businesses. They needed someone they could trust to get their house in order, and although Bill was only the band's road manager at the time, it just so happened that they trusted him.

Of course, we were always speculating on the real identity of Jimmy Cooper.

Irish Jack, an early Who roadie, always claimed it was him. Peter Meaden, my mod hero, was sure elements of the character were based on his own amphetamine-driven descent into mental illness. But the truth was that Jimmy Cooper was an amalgamation of all the mods who shaped Townshend's world (including a young kid found wearing a parka at the bottom of a cliff after a Bank Holiday in 1964, whose story had so appalled Pete Townshend at the time). Bill Curbishley was certainly one of those faces who were incorporated into Cooper's quadrophonic personality.

On the night of his daughter Jackie's 16th birthday, I was to see the other side of our hero Bill.

It was getting dark and I was on yet another trudge to blag yet another case of beer. This time I heard something strange, rather like a football chant – totally out of place. I looked around in confusion and to my horror spotted a gang of 30-odd skinheads climbing over the front gate. I froze. What should I do? Run back to the garage and warn the mods or carry on to the house and alert the Curbishleys? At this stage the partygoers were obviously oblivious and that would mean that the scooters would get a battering before anyone managed to get outside.

In a split second I made the decision to sprint to the front door, banging hard on the knocker six or seven times. Jackie snatched it open, visibly angry.

'Edward, what on earth do you think you're doing?'

Edward again.

I pointed to the drive. The skinheads were over the gate by now and walking in an amorphous mass towards the garage and the scooters.

'Sorry but I didn't know what to do. I think it's the Debden skins and they've come to smash up the party.'

Bless her. Jackie immediately took in the situation and didn't waste a second.

She disappeared back inside and I heard her shouting, 'Bill, Bill, quick – there's a load of skinheads storming up the drive . . . Quuiickkk!'

In a flash there he was, in his socks. He poked his head round the door and disappeared back inside for what seemed like an eternity but was probably no more than five seconds.

When he reappeared, still in his socks, he took three steps from his front door and bellowed, 'Come on, then – who's first? D'ya want some?'

The skinheads stopped in their tracks as Bill's voice carried like a regimental sergeant major's. It had the same kind of mesmerising effect.

As one, the skins looked towards the house to see Bill Curbishley apparently load a shotgun, close the barrel in a single movement and point it in their direction.

'I said, who's *FIRST*?' he bellowed. It was loud.

They turned and ran, plainly terrified. By now some of the mods were out of the garage and chased them to the fence, jeering.

Bill said nonchalantly, 'Eddie, what the fuck was that about?'

'Erm, I think the Debden skinheads found out about the party and were going to smash it up . . .' I stuttered.

'Well, I don't think we'll be seeing them again. Mugs . . .'

'But would you have shot them or what?' I asked.

'Oh, don't be silly, son. It's not loaded.'

With that, Bill Curbishley turned round and walked casually back through his front door.

11

IF THE KIDS ARE UNITED?

In the summer of 1979 I'd become friends with the Warrior Square skins from Manor Park, who were based round the corner from my dad's shop in East Ham. Mods and skins were still two sides of the same coin back then. The Warrior Square lot's leader was a lad called Ray Bruce, a sharp dresser maybe a year or so older than us who we used to meet at the Last Resort shop in Brick Lane on a Sunday morning.

At the end of the Seventies, Brick Lane Market was a completely different experience from the uninspiring 'street food' destination it is today. In 1979 it stretched from Club Row at the top of the Hackney Road to Aldgate. Brick Lane was an extraordinary, fascinating place and many East End teenagers met there every Sunday. It soon became the main weekend destination for young mods.

You could buy absolutely anything in the market – from songbirds or ferrets to Blue Beat 45s or sheepskins through to cut-price furniture and smoked-salmon beigels. You could even pick up *National Front News*, should you be so inclined. There were always a lot of skinheads lurking and most (but not all) were National Front or British Movement types who spent Sundays randomly attacking Asian kids. The market became the centre of what was known as 'Paki-bashing'; as the year went on, increasingly violent skinheads asserted themselves and Brick Lane became a dangerous place for anyone. Including mods.

From my perspective, in 1979 youth was divided first by culture, then area and finally by football. In the East London suburbs it was mainly mods, punks, skins, rockabillies, soulboys and New Romantics. People tended to laugh at New Romantics at the time because of their pretentious outfits and perceived effeminacy, but in Margate in 1980 I once saw a gang of 50 of them steam into twice their number of skins and completely destroy them; make-up and kilts all over the shop. It wasn't what we were expecting, but then someone pointed out that Boy George was a boxer and Chris Sullivan (the man behind the WAG Club and Blue Rondo à la Turk) was one of the hardest men in London. Mods never had any trouble from New Romantics and one of my best friends, Richard Habberley, became a leading light on that scene. Surprisingly, both Spandau Ballet and Wham! started off as mod groups; unsurprisingly, Duran Duran didn't!

Initially, the tribes mixed together. Our particular extended group was made up of skinheads from Epping, Debden and Hainault, soulboys from Buckhurst Hill, Wanstead and Ilford and mods from Woodford, Chingford and Loughton, but we always felt we were part of the same Friday-night crew. From there you could pin down the different football teams involved, but for a brief period football was forgotten as we all headed off to Zero 6, Oscars or the Ilford Palais together.

This came to an end in the summer of 1979 at the Last Resort.

Our hitherto go-to Sunday destination had become increasingly hostile, not just to mods but to everyone. The Nazis were reasserting themselves on the streets of the East End. The Last Resort had originally been a punk emporium but became popular with mods when it purchased many of the clothes used in *Quadrophenia*. For a few weeks we hung around outside, trying on the pork-pie hats and tonic suits but realising that they were all out of our price range. Things exploded a month after the August Bank Holiday trip to Southend with a specific incident involving the Chelsea Headhunters, a right-wing skinhead firm from West London. In a nutshell, they discovered that one of our lot – a skinhead from Epping called Si Spanner – was Jewish, so they stabbed him outside the shop. From that point on we looked after our own and viewed Brick Lane with trepidation.

By now, cultural uniforms had diverged. The introduction of two-tone and the scene that went with it had thrust ska into the spotlight, and initially mods, skins and rudeboys had embraced the sound and look together. Madness had taken over the Dublin Castle's mod residency from The Fixations and we regarded the up-and-coming ska bands like The Selecter, The Beat and of course The Special AKA as part of our shared scene. There were even a couple of out-and-out mod ska bands like The Bodysnatchers (fronted by the girl-face Rhoda Dakar from Brixton) and Tony Lordan and Vaughn Toulouse's Guns for Hire. But by the end of 1979, ska had been completely appropriated by skinheads, which meant that mods made a conscious effort to look different from people we'd previously regarded as our friends and allies.

We were soon put right. The skinheads certainly weren't our friends *or* our allies.

The first real battle took place at the filming of Secret Affair's 'Time for Action' video at the Acklam Hall, again in August 1979. We were three of around 50 East London mods who'd been drafted in as extras in the audience.

The director picked me out to stand against the wall with Tris Pitt and Dave Reynolds from school alongside Gary Wood, who was one of the East End faces. It was for the cut-away shot that went with the line: 'Standing in the shadows, where the in-crowd meet . . .'

I was seriously chuffed. Maybe I was going to make it as a Glory Boy after all!

It was a spectacular day with an atmosphere to match and was where I first met the musical polymath and Kent Records guru Tony Rounce, who was dressed in a leopardskin gilet and flat cap doing a passable impression of a rockabilly.

There were plenty of Glory Boys in attendance. When filming ended, we all shuffled out of the venue in good spirits – only to be ambushed by a gang of Ladbroke Grove skins who seemed to appear from nowhere. There was an incredible set-to, which lasted five minutes, but we managed to escape before the Old Bill turned up. The skins melted back into their estates and somewhat shellshocked we took the train home. My assumption at the time was that this was territorial. The Ladbroke Grove skins (who were apparently non-racist) had obviously heard there'd be a firm of East London mods coming over for the day and decided they weren't having any of it.

Sadly, it became apparent that there was more to it than that. There'd been a number of minor scuffles between different cults as the summer progressed, but the real split came at Southend over the August Bank Holiday. The mod scene had been expanding exponentially and the extra impetus given by the release of *Quadrophenia* two weeks earlier on 16 August meant that by the end of the month mod was everywhere.

Mods and skinheads headed to Southend for the weekend and the atmosphere was initially jovial. Eventually, though, the skins – shirts off and braces down – steamed into the mods, whose average age of 15 or 16 meant they were substantially younger and smaller than their aggressors. At first, we couldn't work out what was happening and assumed it was to do with football or territory, but the reality soon became clear: skinheads were just attacking mods on sight. And so began in earnest what would become a brutal, long-running war lasting five years.

We were stunned. The skins who were part of our crew were still mates, but everywhere else was now dangerous. We could no longer go and see The Specials, Madness or The Selecter and at virtually every gig had to run the gauntlet to get between the Tube and the venue.

Less than a month later, any fragile bonds that remained between the two scenes irrevocably snapped.

It was 21 September 1979 and the irrepressible Jimmy Pursey, Sham 69's vocalist (described by Mark Perry's *Sniffin' Glue* as 'the real face of working-class punk'), was appearing with his band at the Rainbow in Finsbury Park.

Sham 69 had been experiencing increasing hostility from their own following, who were apparently unhappy about the direction the band had taken over the previous couple of months. There were vague rumours that something awful was going to happen.

The band were from the commuter town of Hersham in Surrey and had embraced working-class bootboy culture as a direct response to the art rock pioneered by groups like Joy Division, The Mekons and Gang of Four. Pursey's populist punk proved appealing to the burgeoning skinhead culture and Sham 69 regularly charted with their raucous street-punk anthems. He never realised there would be a price to pay for the band's casual appropriation of an increasingly right-wing cockney culture and their working-class heroes like the gangster and folk hero George Davis. (Sham publicly supported the 'George Davis is innocent' campaign that was in full sway at the time, with the bank robber's name sprayed on virtually every bridge in London. Less than a year after Davis's original conviction was quashed on appeal and he was released from prison, he was caught red-handed on an armed robbery and was back doing bird soon after.)

Alongside their original punk fans, Sham 69 were attracting an extreme right-wing element among the skinheads of the National Front and British Movement. Unlike Angelic Upstarts, who were genuinely industrial working class and radically left, or the Cockney Rejects, who'd famously dissuaded the political right from attending their gigs with fists at 'the battle of Barking', Sham realised too late that their lyrics did little to discourage the growing politicisation of their following. Finally, though, in August 1979, Jimmy Pursey announced that the band's next single would be a cover of The Yardbirds' undoubtedly antiracist single 'Mister You're a Better Man Than I'.

The band's following were less than impressed with this antiracist mod anthem and apparently apoplectic that their one-time hero was now playing benefit gigs for Rock Against Racism.

The British Movement's elite shock troops, known as the Leader Guard, had marked Pursey's card and were waiting for an opportunity to teach Sham a lesson. By 1979, the BM had overtaken the National Front as the face of fascism in Britain and, thanks to their poster-boy organiser Nicky Crane (who later appeared on the *Strength Thru Oi!* compilation album – a disgraceful endeavour if ever there was one), had been attracting attention and headlines for their violent attacks on Asians in Leicester and the East End. By the middle of 1979, skins in green MA1 jackets sporting the BM's sun-wheel symbol were a regular fixture on Britain's high streets.

In a strange and somewhat unexpected twist, Pursey seemed very taken by the emerging mod revival and loved the fact it was an organic movement that had developed with no outside manipulation. Inspired, he'd set up his own mod label through Polydor. JP Productions had already signed The Chords, Long Tall Shorty and The Low Numbers and were in the process of demoing the Purple Hearts. He was perfectly positioned to take the revival overground with some serious major label support. Weirdly, Pursey himself appeared oblivious to the growing tension between mods and skinheads when the band announced a gig at the Rainbow in Finsbury Park.

I'd always liked Sham 69, so arranged to go to the gig with Ray Bruce and some of the Warrior Square skins. Jesus fucking Christ, it was one of the most terrifying nights of my life.

The atmosphere was unlike anything I'd experienced. From the moment we walked in, I realised something shocking was going to happen – you could actually taste it in the air: fear and aggression. And hysteria. The venue had removed the ground-floor seats to allow for a bigger crowd, but this just exacerbated the situation and allowed skinheads to run around randomly punching people.

I'd dressed in a window-pane button-down with Levi's and monkey boots, topped off with my sky-blue Harrington, and didn't look particularly out of place – or so I thought . . .

The skinheads were becoming increasingly pumped up and were chanting, 'There's only one Adolf Hitler!' and flinging out the Nazi salute towards the stage with stiff right arms.

'*Sieg Heil! Sieg Heil! Sieg Heil!*'

Terrifying.

The Low Numbers were the first band Pursey had signed to his label and lasted just two songs before they were canned off. Next up were The Little Roosters, who didn't fare any better – although they dealt with the shower of coins and bottles with remarkable stoicism. Their singer, Gary Lammin, should have had some credit in the skinhead bank because he'd previously been the guitarist in the bootboy heroes Cock Sparrer, but you wouldn't have known it. And neither did the skinheads. He told me later that after the Roosters were forced off stage, he'd snuck back on to pick up the coins that'd been thrown at them. He comfortably collected more in change than the band were paid for the gig!

Just 20 minutes later, the support bands' equipment had been cleared offstage and the audience were baying for blood – specifically Pursey's. By the time the road crew had set up Sham's backline, there were more than 300 shirtless skinheads running around screaming on the ground floor. I was standing by the bar and out of the corner of my eye caught sight of something green crash down from the balcony and slam onto the floor just 10 yards from where I was standing. I couldn't tell what it was at first; it was just a bundle. The skins were kicking it as they ran past. Sickened, I realised they'd thrown a parka-wearing boy from the balcony.

By now the Rainbow was extremely dangerous and the atmosphere hysterical. It was like some kind of dystopian rally; you half expected a brainwashed mob to start screaming, 'Burn him! Burn him!' as they found their next victim.

Sham 69 limped onto the stage and were attacked before they'd finished the first number.

'Tell us the truth / Don't let us down / You're a fool if you do . . .'

More and more skins clambered onto the stage, trying to get past the road crew and security. Pursey tried valiantly to reason with them, but it was hopeless. His fans were beating him up on stage at his own gig. Pop was indeed eating itself!

Ray Bruce grabbed my arm and shouted urgently into my ear: 'Mate, you'd better fuck off. You have hair – these bastards are attacking anyone and you look like a mod. If they grab you, I ain't gonna be able to help.'

I pushed my way through the baying crowd and out the doors, running for Finsbury Park Station without looking back.

That one event marked a sea change in the relationship between the different youth cultures. Suddenly everyone was fair game. The violence was terrifying and it felt like us mods were taking our lives in our hands every time we left the house. It seemed that we were nearly always the victims. I was soon sick of it.

12

WHATCHA GONNA DO ABOUT IT

The more we discovered about original Sixties mods, the more clothes became important to our world. I would guess that 90 per cent of our clothes were secondhand, but even then, one-upmanship was definitely the motivating factor. But just what to wear? In that sweltering summer of 1979 we got the chance to work it out.

The more I researched it, the more I realised that there should be more to our sartorial world than just a parka and a pair of what we euphemistically called 'Hush Puppies'.

Our suede shoes were cheap copies that cost less than a tenner from Brick Lane. I actually preferred Clarks' desert boots to genuine Hush Puppies, but of course in 1979 or 1980 they were also nothing more than a fantasy. Real Clarks were far too expensive for us.

Trainers were also out.

I never saw a mod wear a pair of training shoes before the mid-Eighties. I'm not sure why as there was certainly a precedent: the elusive Chad, the kid in Ethan Russell's photo-story booklet stapled inside The Who's original 1973 *Quadrophenia* LP, was rocking a fine pair of special-edition Gola's with his target T-shirt. But unlike the T-shirt, the trainers never caught on.

In 1979 we might well have owned a pair of Dunlop Green Flash trainers, mainly because we couldn't afford (or, more likely, hadn't persuaded our mums to buy us) Stan Smiths, but would never have worn them out at a gig. If mods wanted to look cool and fit in, there were just a handful of options. Boots were acceptable, but only if the lace-ups were 8-hole Dr. Martens or burgundy monkey boots with yellow trim and laces (at a push we might have had a pair of slip-on dealer boots or even suede Chelseas, but truth be told, in 1979 they too were a bit beyond us as Shellys had yet to make their mark). As the summer wore on, we dropped them as uncool and all except desert boots and the odd monkey boot were left to the skinheads from whom we now needed to massively distance ourselves.

Loafers and brogues were de rigueur, but strict rules still applied. The former had to be tasselled with thick soles (usually from Blackmans on Cheshire Street), while the latter were bog-standard but needed to have been highly polished. Oxfords were considered but soon ditched as uncool, and until the mid-Eighties I never once saw a pair of Bass Weejun penny loafers on a mod foot.

The real footwear dilemma came with what were universally known as 'Jam shoes'.

Christened thus because they were regularly sported by the Woking three-piece, the shoes originally came in a couple of different styles. The first generation were always two-tone, with the bottom black and the top white or occasionally brown and cream, and usually with a waffled top. They could be lace-up or side-buckled slip-ons, pointed or more regularly with a rounded toe. You could pick them up in the original Shellys or the Kings Road Robot (a completely different entity from the Carnaby Street emporium of the same name), or in some of the bandwagon-jumping West End shops that sprang up to cater for new mods. As with just about any other footwear, you could also find them in Brick Lane.

I will cough up to owning a pair, but I bought them for school and never wore them after July 1979. The original design soon dropped out of fashion until bizarrely, a year or so later, the 'son of Jam shoe' burst onto the scene. Like many mod fads, this one was introduced by Paul Weller and the style was instantly dubbed a Jam shoe by shops keen to cash in. Mods had always worn bowling shoes, genuinely nicked from ten-pin bowling alleys: you'd wear crap plimsolls or worn-out school shoes, hand them in to get your bowling shoes and not swap them back at the end of the night; everyone did it. But the second-generation Jam shoes were an abomination.

Paul Weller must have had his pair specially made as I'd never seen anything even slightly similar before, but then all his other fashion ideas were bang-on, so I can forgive him the one slip-up.

We disparagingly called them 'badgers'. They were black suede and, while they shared a tiny bit of bowling shoe in their genetic makeup, in reality they weren't even slightly related – they appeared to be more influenced by a competitive cycling shoe. Firstly, badgers had a hard sole with a stepped heel (whereas proper bowling shoes had a soft, rubberised sole without a defined heel), but the main issue was the bold white stripe stitched down the middle, complemented by a couple of semicircular thinner stripes on the sides. They were shockingly ugly but within a month of Paul sporting them were everywhere. Age was no barrier and it seemed that every parka-clad 12- or 40-year-old was mincing up and down Carnaby Street in a pair. I have vague memories of a red, white and blue version. They were genuinely painful on the eye and one of Weller's few sartorial errors.

The other 'must have' mod accessory in 1979 and 1980 was an odd choice too.

I'm not sure why the trilby was so popular at the time as I never saw a photo of an original mod wearing one. No, I assume the fashion came from Trevor Laird's Ferdy or Mark Wingett's Dave characters in *Quadrophenia*. By June 1979, the rumour mill was rife with stories that Johnsons in the Kings Road and Brick Lane's Last Resort had secured a supply of 'stingy-brim' titfers that had been especially knocked up for the film. Now, these weren't actually trilbies but proper pork pies and I was thrilled to snaffle one for a tenner at the Last Resort one Sunday. I felt vindicated when I saw Chas Smash wearing his on stage at the Dublin Castle just a couple of weeks later. Ten pounds was an extortionate amount for a hat, but Jackie Curbishley confirmed that they were all genuine *Quadrophenia* kit, so I didn't mind. (To be fair, I was less keen on the purple-suede parka she offered me when the movie came out. Ughh . . .)

As the ska and two-tone element of the mod revival grew, trilbies became more common, perhaps because pork pies were so hard to find. Pioneered by Pauline Black from The Selecter and some of the early rudeboys from the spin-off bands, trilbies were suddenly everywhere. My classmate Dave Reynolds was wearing his at the filming of the 'Time for Action' video! Personally, I was never comfortable in a hat, even the pork pie, and always thought that they made my head look bigger, so it was an experiment I never repeated.

Mod jeans were limited to just the one pair. Levi's 501s.

There were several brands knocking around at the time. Brutus, Lee Cooper, Lois and Wrangler were the big ones but weren't vaguely acceptable in our world. Your Levi's needed a three-quarter-inch turn-up, preferably stitched in with the bottom seam cut off so you could iron them properly flat, and early doors they would occasionally be bucket-bleached, which gave the jeans a block-dyed piebald look. Bleaching soon fell out of fashion as the skinhead conflict kicked in and they then had to be dark indigo, preferably dead stock with a 'Big E' tag.

The whole thing about mod was to be pedantic and you couldn't get more pedantic than worrying about the manufacturing year of your jeans. It took a while for me to work this out, but eventually I discovered that the 'Big E' (or 'Capital E' if you prefer) Levi's were discontinued in 1971, so if you wanted original mod jeans, the red tag (and it had to be a red tag) on the back pocket sported a logo that read 'LEVI'S' rather than 'LeVI'S'. I'd been assured by a wise old mod that the denim and the looms they were made on were of far superior quality – which is why a pair of Big Es will cost you up to a grand these days, if you could even find them.

The *Quadrophenia* scene of Jimmy Cooper sitting in a bath hoping to shrink-fit his jeans was something we all tried to emulate at least once!

The only alternative to jeans was a pair of sta-prest slacks, but by 1980 real ones were almost impossible to find. The holy grail was a pair of original Levi's Sta-Prest with tags, but I only ever saw a couple of genuine pairs and they were both too short for me to get away with.

Most trousers sold as 'sta-prest', especially the ones from Carnaby Cavern, Shellys and Melanddi, were nothing of the kind. They were just straight trousers in an inappropriate cotton-type material that had been knocked up and sold as sta-prest to the ignorant – kids who had no idea of what they should have been buying anyway.

Ironically, the one thing these kecks *didn't* have was a permanent crease running down the centre of the trouser, which was what gave the real-deal Sta-Prest their name. That crease meant you never needed to iron them, which was perfect for the young Sixties mod living alone! Trouble was, the genuine article hadn't been on the market since the early Seventies and the only thing us kids knew was that mods were supposed to wear them.

Many an A-bomb or ticket ended up with double or even triple tramline creases where their mum had been forced to iron a pair of not-sta-prest a few times.

And that's the other thing: mods could be very dismissive of young kids that weren't quite cutting it in the style stakes.

The right jacket was essential. Casual priorities were Levi's denim 'truckers' – very occasionally found in suede; they were super popular. Blue denim always had to be dark indigo, but the much rarer white was seriously cool.

Slightly more formal were three-button tailored jackets in either plain material or madras, usually worn with contrasting block-coloured trousers. Monkey jackets with elasticated waists and striped ring collars vied with unbranded Harringtons (I never saw a Baracuta in 1979 or 1980) as the casual jacket of choice.

When I was still 15, Mum told Kenney Jones I was now a mod and he handed me a bottle-green suede jacket with red stitching, a square-cut front with popper fastenings and a suitably large collar. For the first three months it fit me like a glove and I always felt a million dollars when I pulled it on. History right there! Real Small Faces history.

Trouble was, by the end of the year I was 5 foot 9 inches and couldn't do the buttons up. For a while it was consigned to the wardrobe until I reluctantly lent it to Small Faces nut Terry Rawlings (who you'll meet shortly) as he wanted to copy the design. He immediately lost it. It's one of my biggest regrets and I still haven't forgiven him.

For some reason, white towelling socks were de rigueur right up until 1983. Everyone wore them, especially on the ska scene, but they were occasionally replaced with red. Both colours served the same purpose.

Steve Marriott once confessed that he wore his trousers 3 inches short with white or yellow socks because the contrasting colour of the socks in the trouser/shoe gap drew the eye to his dancing feet. This was a trick he claimed he'd nicked off the legendary James Brown, who was certainly the best dancer of his generation. How much dancing Marriott actually did once the band had been swamped by the 13-year-old dollybirds that flocked to Small Faces after their chart hits is a moot point. Fact was, it was a useful stage tool in the band's early arsenal. Why the revival generation picked up on the style I'll never know, but the fact was that *everyone* on the mod scene, from Weller downwards, wore white socks. This was something that was disparaged and even denied later on, but whether people like it or not, it happened.

The overcoat you wore was also incredibly important too.

First and foremost, we chose the M51 US Army fishtail parka of Korean War vintage. These would often be decorated with a hand-painted band logo to the rear and sported a collection of badges or patches sewn onto the arms. Finding them was never a problem; parkas could be picked up for a tenner from one of the dozens of surplus stores dotted around town. Possibly the most important but regularly neglected accessory was the yellow-headed 'Esso Man' plastic figure that was attached to the zipper. It was always super cool but not so easy to find.

As time moved on, parkas gradually lost their iconographic 'badge' status and reverted to their initial function of protecting clothes from the elements. They were warm and weatherproof and I can remember sleeping in mine on a number of occasions. I still have my second one, an M51 with The Chords' logo painted on the back, but it's had a very hard life!

Another decent coat worn by original mods but not particularly embraced during the revival was the sheepskin. If we had them, then they had to be secondhand, preferably from the late Sixties, dark burnt-orange suede with brown leather piping and a creamy off-white sheep's wool lining. I'd nicked my dad's 1967 half-length that hadn't been out of his wardrobe since 1972 and loved wearing it, even if it was slightly too big for me. I felt the coat stood out from the parka-clad crowd and looked super smart with its two 4-inch side vents. Many kids wore the dark brown version with a faux-wool lining; these were fashionable at the time, but I always thought they were a disappointment – more suitable for taxi drivers! An original was essential and looked incredibly stylish.

I was casually acquainted with a couple of old Jewish boys who'd been in the sheepskin game since the Sixties. One day I was parking the Vespa outside their shop to pick up a couple of beigels when one of them saw me and came out to have an enthusiastic chat.

'Eddie, that scooter takes me back . . . I never told you this before, but our shop was very popular with mods in the Sixties. They'd come down to Brick Lane on a Sunday morning, usually straight from one of their all-nighters – speeding off their tits, most of them. Anyway, we'd open at seven in the morning and there was always a queue hanging around waiting. Basically, they'd want their sheepskins altered on the spot. They'd been at a club that weekend and probably spotted a few others wearing similar coats, maybe copied off *Ready Steady Go!* or something they'd seen at the Scene. They'd want us to make their coat look different from everyone else's; shorten it, add a buttonhole, change the edging . . . Every bloody week, it was. Did I ever tell you that our bestselling mod coat was a full-length sheepskin?!'

Wow! The full-length sheepskin was a rare beast and not something that had been seen in public since I was a nipper.

In 1979, vintage sheepskins were always cool – but again, sharing a look with skinheads was never going to be popular for long.

So this, then, was our mod uniform. Eventually, when we could afford a tailor, the three-button suit was added to the armoury but for now this was our basic look. The point is, we had begun to pay attention to detail – and now sometimes found that secondhand just wouldn't cut it for us. We wanted new. Unworn clobber. But just where were we going to find it?

13

IN THE CITY

'Carnaby Street Welcomes the World', read the proud slogan. Obviously erected in the early Seventies, the now tatty sign stretched the whole width of the street and was appropriately close to the public toilets.

From the early days of the revival, the world's one-time 'favourite shopping street' became the main destination for teenage mods.

Punks, by this time almost entirely Sid clones, had long colonised the Kings Road and we needed somewhere different to hang out. Given its rich mod history, Carnaby Street was the obvious choice, but by the time we rocked up the place could only be described as a proper shithole. How Westminster Council allowed such an iconic and unique asset to become a festering embarrassment remains one of life's great mysteries. Too late they realised their mistake and their efforts to rectify the situation since haven't worked.

We knew nothing of the glory days of John Stephen, Lord John or Swinging London, and by 1979 the street was pedestrianised, carpeted with tacky rubberised orange and yellow tiles that were peeling up at the edges. It looked at least five years past its sell-by date, was filthy and packed with those awful tourist-tat shops selling Beefeater tea towels to foreigners for a tenner a pop.

Carnaby Street might have been unfit for purpose, but into this desolate dump stepped the new young mods.

Ours was a brand-new movement made up of enthusiastic teenagers (average age 16) that had developed spontaneously in less than six months. There were no Svengalis managing the bands, no manuals on 'how to be a mod' and no great plan directing us kids. Just the occasional glimpse of a 15-year-old folk memory we didn't really understand. Of course, we had Paul Weller to go on, but all we really knew were the obvious symbols: parkas, scooters, desert boots and . . . Carnaby Street.

I'd spotted a number of interesting-looking shops during my Carnaby Street recce for the filming of *Stepping Out* in May, so I was soon back there.

I also discovered more about the Carnaby Cavern. This (once) marvellous clothing emporium was established by Colin Wild at the height of Carnaby Street's fame and credibility. Set up to cater for genuine pop stars, they turned out flared jumpsuits and stage costumes for the great and the good, but before too long, a disillusioned Wild sold out and set out on his own as a tailor and shirtmaker.

The Carnaby Cavern's new, sharp-eyed owners switched to the far easier youth market just a year before the punk explosion. For a while, bondage trousers and torn shirts were de rigueur, but by 1978, as the punk scene was fading, suddenly The Jam breathed new life into the brand.

Mod was a gift from the gods!

In just a couple of months the growing scene provided an enthusiastic and captive market of kids who wanted to dress in suits but understood nothing about what went into making them. In 1979 nobody even realised that the suit's shape, material, cut, the lapel and vent size, and even the buttonholes and lining were extremely important, but if these new teenage customers only wanted something with three buttons or garish stripes, then you could sell them any old shit. And Carnaby Cavern did.

While the Cavern did actually provide a bespoke 'tailoring service', the bulk of their stock was cheap, poorly made acrylic-blend suits, boating blazers in some kind of striped fuzzy-felt fabric and sta-prest trousers that didn't stay pressed. Surprisingly, I liked the shop and the owners and over the years they flogged a couple of thousand copies of my fanzine, but – and it's a big but – I never bought any clothes off them. That would have been a step too far!

The Carnaby Cavern wasn't alone. A few other hustlers cottoned on to this new market and began to stock equally poor clobber, but it was still possible to discover the odd ruby in the dust.

Colin Wild hadn't moved far from the Cavern. He was a striking, psychedelic refugee from 1968 who made bespoke shirts from a poky first-floor room in Newburgh Street, which ran parallel to Carnaby Street. With his long, tawny-blond hair with pointy-toed Cuban heels and kick-out corduroys, he looked like a cross between Catweazle and an extra from *Here We Go Round the Mulberry Bush*. But Colin Wild made great shirts and instinctively knew what a young mod wanted. The first he made for me was a light-green button-down with long, dagger-tipped collars and shoulder epaulettes, which I copied from a photo of Keith Moon in 1965 and cost 15 quid. (The end result was so perfect that the shirt was eventually lifted by Dom Bassett, a young mod boy from South London who plucked up the courage to admit the theft more than 30 years later.)

Well Suspect was a tiny all-male boutique in Foubert's Place, just off Carnaby Street, which sold the best mod clothes in London. The quality and cut were just right and they used decent material in their limited-production designs. Boy George even worked there for a time! My first purchase was in the late summer of 1979, a few weeks after *Quadrophenia* first hit the cinema. It cost me a full two weeks of holiday-job wages but was definitely worth it: a short-cut, three-button bum-freezer suit in a dogtooth pattern with 4-inch side vents and grey silk lining. It perfectly matched my favourite shoes, a pair of chunky loafers from Blackmans in Brick Lane.

While Well Suspect was the best, it was probably too expensive for the average 15-year-old. My limited-production suit cost 52 quid and took many, many hard hours of work to save for. They also sold real boating blazers, made with proper material (unlike the Cavern, who appeared to use dyed sacking). In fact, I'd set my heart on a boating-blazer suit (yes, with matching trousers) just like the one Brian Jones was wearing to one of his many court appearances and on the sleeve of *Through the Past, Darkly*. Sadly, the shop closed before I could raise the money.

Kingly Street also boasted a mod hairdresser called Barbers Point. It sat just up from the junction with Ganton Street by the Blue Posts. In 1979 and 1980 the 'Weller feather-cut' hadn't yet spread to the masses, but Sue Brady, more of an original suedehead than a mod, had been there for a while already and had a natural understanding of whatever the next mod look was going to be. Indeed, I sported a variety of styles – a college boy, a French crop, a *real* crop (number 4) and even a (soulboy) wedge – but there was not one particular mod hairstyle at the time. The look tended to be short and smart, sometimes college boy or sometimes French crop but without an enforced style. Sue often had to endure the whole gamut of skinhead abuse for cutting mod hair, but as the hairstyle solidified, she came to define it.

Lonsdale was another go-to mod destination. A long-established supplier of boxing gear and equipment, they had their shop close to the junction of Carnaby and Beak Streets. Lonsdale wasn't a mod fashion choice in the Sixties, but once The Jam were spotted wearing their gear the place was mobbed. Paul Weller was keen on their branded sweatshirts and Rick Buckler championed their boxing boots, not particularly as a fashion item but because he loved drumming in them. The band's casual patronage was all it took: The Jam became responsible for yet another mod fashion.

There were a couple of other Carnaby Street shops that catered for us in those early days. The most important of these was at the top of the spiral staircase next to Boots, which led to a mezzanine floor tucked away off the main street.

Run by a genial Singaporean called Jimmy, Robot was special. The shop had originally ridden the fashionable thrift-store wave popularised a couple of years earlier by Johnsons on the Kings Road and Flip in Covent Garden (but from a cheaper, more 'downmarket' perspective). Jimmy was paying attention to what was happening on the street and gradually the Fifties vintage clothes were replaced by mod staples. By late 1979 he was stocking Harringtons, monkey jackets, US Army trench coats, donkey jackets, Crombies, M51 US Army parkas, MA1 green bomber jackets, desert boots, loafers, off-the-peg suits and jackets, button-downs, Fred Perry polo shirts . . . In fact, Robot sold just about anything the provincial mod might need to buy on a day trip to London.

I couldn't afford too much new gear (not after I'd bought that Well Suspect suit, anyway) on my part-time job, so the stalls of Brick Lane still provided the majority of my wardrobe. It felt like we were out almost every night at one point; there was so much going on and so many bands to see. And the more gigs we went to, the more gear we needed. (That's clobber, not speed!)

Clothes were becoming all-important. I realised I could still pick up great secondhand mod gear at junk shops. There were hundreds of these dotted around the East End and I'd trawl them regularly. Button-downs in bold Sixties colours, turtlenecks, Levi's denim or Harrington jackets, even paisley silk scarves. It was all available and cheap if you put in the time and effort.

I always experienced a guilty spasm if I spotted something special hidden in the racks. A burst of adrenaline with a slight rush of blood to the face as I realised it might just be in my size, followed by a furtive look around to see if anyone else had spotted the object of my desire. A rare record, a scarce Richard Allen paperback, a James Bond hardback with an elusive dust jacket or a sought-after bit of clobber . . . It didn't matter – the reaction was always the same. Imagine the buzz that surged through me one afternoon as I came across a beautiful, shiny black tonic silk-mohair suit in an Ilford charity shop.

I wasn't even aware that tonic came in black, but on closer investigation, the material was definitely a silk-mohair blend. Obviously tailor-made with three buttons, two 5-inch vents and 15-inch bottoms, it fitted like a glove and cost just 2 quid. I thrust the notes into the old dear's outstretched hand and jumped on the bus home tightly clasping a brown paper bag under my arm.

I was soon wearing the suit for school, pairing it with some savagely pointed winkle-pickers and the obligatory white socks. It looked the absolute bollocks. At least, I thought it did.

The school's uniform policy was either a badged blazer or a dark-grey suit. Unfortunately, my suit wasn't grey but a shimmering jet black and soon attracted negative attention from teachers. I was told in no uncertain terms that it was inappropriate and I wasn't to wear it again. Advice I consciously ignored because I was now the smartest mod in the village.

Two weeks later I got a bit flash and made the mistake of wearing the suit to a Chords gig at the Marquee.

The venue was hot at the best of times, but on this particular summer night it was steaming. Wardour Street was packed with young mods and the club had definitely been oversold as it was the last time the band would appear there before moving on to bigger things. Leyton's Beggar were supporting and did a great job of warming up the crowd. It was set to be a brilliant night.

Unfortunately, a combination of the intense heat bouncing off the ceiling and my free-flowing sweat somehow unlocked a long-suppressed smell that had been lurking deep within the body of my favourite outfit.

The gig finished, we spilled out of the club on a high with steam evaporating from our sweaty bodies and made our way to the Underground. By the time we'd reached Tottenham Court Road I realised that I absolutely stank. Standard BO wouldn't have been so bad, but this was anything but standard – it was a very pungent type of BO that had somehow allied itself with the putrid stench of ancient curry and, dare I say it, death! No one would even sit next to me on the train.

Next morning, and in spite of leaving the offending item on the washing line overnight, the odour hadn't diminished. What on earth was going on? I conducted a methodical investigation and there it was, in tiny print on an inch-square label stitched to the inside of the sleeve: 'Smart Man Fashions – Made in Lahore'.

Hanging the suit out of the window for three days made no difference, so my mum suggested taking it to the dry cleaners. That didn't work either, so eventually my beautiful mohair work of art was consigned to the dustbin.

This incident prompted my dad to give me some advice.

There's a reason that there was a tailor on every East End street corner in the Seventies and that was because our parents' generation wore formal wear almost every single day; for work or leisure, church or pleasure, most men had suits made to measure and actually wore them, even for manual labour. Most in the East End had a personal tailor and visited him regularly (and yes, in those days a tailor was a him; while women often worked on the body of a suit, the tailor was always a man).

'Look, son,' said Dad. 'If you're serious about this mod thing I think it's time you got a suit made. If you want, I'll send you to see my man. He's been with me for 25 years and is only a couple of hundred yards up the road. I could probably get you a decent price.'

*

And so it was, in the spring of 1980, after a succession of outfits from Mintz & Davis, Well Suspect and Mister Byrite's, I walked the 200 yards up High Street North until I saw the sign above the door: 'Steve Starr, Gentlemen's Outfitters. Bespoke suits for all occasions.'

I pushed through the glass doors and there he was, standing behind the jump: my old man's tailor, surrounded by tottering towers of sample books and roll after roll of material.

Like most cockney tailors, Steve Starr was Jewish. About 5 foot 8 inches tall and in early middle age, he was affable and welcomed me in, moving some material and pointing to a seat. I introduced myself as Eddie Piller, son of his longstanding client Eddie Piller and a lad of not yet 18 who was interested in having his first suit made. Starr was instantly engaged and immediately asked why a boy would want such a thing – surely tailors were for older people?

That broke the ice. I explained that I was a mod and he immediately knew exactly what I wanted.

'Three buttons, 15-inch bottoms and a 5-inch centre vent. I want it in lightweight material but it's got to be in a bright colour? Erm . . . With red silk lining.'

We flicked through a number of books and settled for an ice-blue fabric with an almost invisible white under-weave. Not mohair or tonic but the white sheen made it stand out without being too flash. I instantly fell in love with the material and Steve Starr seemed as engaged as I was.

'Now, Eddie, I'm going to measure you. Take your jacket off, unbuckle your belt and let me get my tape measure round your waist.'

I wasn't the first young mod to visit Steve Starr and he was more than familiar with the required cut. Colin Miller and John Halls of the Manor Park mods had beaten me to it (although Hallsey wasn't a fan; he didn't like the finish, apparently), and both Derwent Jaconelli from Les Elite and Tony Perfect from Long Tall Shorty were also among Starr's customers.

He was enthusiastic and suggested a couple of extra features I might like to consider.

'A ticket pocket? Frogmouth trouser pockets? Rear patch pocket with a flap? Three working cuff buttons on the sleeve? How about a flap on the breast pocket? Or a secret pocket hidden in the lining?'

For the next minute or so Steve took a number of measurements: waist, chest, stomach, shoulder to shoulder, inside leg, outside leg . . . All the time making notes with a licked pencil in his little spiral-bound book. When it came to the shoulder to cuff, his long-sleeved shirt – I remember it was lilac with double cuffs and gold cufflinks – rode up his arm a few inches as he stretched the tape measure.

Fuck me.

I saw it. That one fleeting glimpse of his wrist brought the horror of what Steve Starr must have been subjected to as a child into a sudden, sharp focus.

Just above where the cuff would normally sit was a number inked alongside a small Star of David tattoo. At some stage he'd taken a knife to it as half the number was missing, overlaid with a pale white scar.

This was grown-up stuff.

My tailor had been a prisoner in a Nazi concentration camp.

Up to that point I'd been fairly flippant about the war. Brought up on a diet of *Battle*, *Action* and *Commando* comics, and regularly shown a succession of films like *The Dam Busters*, *The Great Escape*, *Battle of Britain* or *633 Squadron* with their stirring Ron Goodwin-style scores, meant that my view of World War II was simplistic in the extreme. I suppose I viewed it as a game played out between the RAF and the Luftwaffe in the pale-blue sky above Essex or by lantern-jawed, doughty sergeants shouting, '*Hände hoch!*' at the advancing Hun. I never considered what it must have been like for the people who were actually there and had their lives ruined by it. Even though my grandad wouldn't get into a German car until the day he died, I'd barely bothered to really consider why – and even when I asked him, he wouldn't answer but just stared into the distance.

As far as I was concerned, the Nazis had great uniforms (idiot) and better tanks, but we won mainly through British grit and without giving too much credit to anyone else. That was about it. I was never taught what happened to the Jews.

Starr must have been in his teens when it happened, because in 1980 he looked in his mid-forties with a life story tattooed right there on his wrist.

I was gobsmacked.

Auschwitz? Buchenwald? How the fuck did he survive? What happened to his family? How did he get to England? I had a hundred questions but couldn't ask any of them. Steve saw me clock his wrist and quickly look away. He smiled sadly but didn't say a word, just carried on measuring.

The suit was a powder-blue three-button in a lightweight material but came in at £70 quid. The old man bought it as a delayed 16th birthday present.

Ah yes: in November 1979 I had finally turned 16! And ridiculously I already felt something of a veteran on the mod scene. So much had been concertinaed into such a short time, I'd given absolutely no thought to my last few months at school. In six months I would be doing my O levels and be gone for good. There was no chance of staying on to do A levels as I'd already been told I'd have to leave after my O levels. I'd also been told by my form teacher, a Mr Reeder (who we obviously called Bleeder, a short ginger man with a comb-over and a serious Napoleon complex), that I should give up all thoughts of further education regardless of how well I did in exams as 'people like you don't go to university'. Indeed, my lack of commitment to school had seen a constant theme in my reports since the age of 11. The one I remember best was the head's comments attached to the back of my report at the age of 13.

'If he continues like this, I fear Edward will waste his not inconsiderable talents. He is a boy of high intelligence, although his attitude seems to convey the opposite. Edward is at a crossroads and I can see him becoming either Head Boy or being expelled. Only he can decide which path to take.'

Well, I think we know how that turned out!

14

I CAN SEE FOR MILES

I'd read somewhere that amphetamine increases the IQ by an average of 15 per cent. That's why both sides gave it out in spades during the war. Speed not only made you cleverer, it also made you more resilient and more alert. In a school experiment I'd been put forward to take a number of O levels earlier than normal to help manage the workload. I remember leaving the Marquee at 11.20 on a Tuesday night after watching The Merton Parkas (in spite of the backlash, they were great live), dropping a few pills and revising through the night – less than an hour's sleep and I was sitting in the school hall finishing my geography O level at 11 in the morning. Something must have worked as I had done no work but somehow managed a decent pass.

You see, everybody *knew* that mods were supposed to take speed and, even though we were only 16, it was extremely easy to get hold of. In fact, a schoolboy mate of mine from Hainault was knocking out five blues for a quid.

Please don't think I plunged into that world without doing my research first.

There was a useful and well-thumbed book in the school library called *Alternative London*. This was an annual publication, a handbook that laid out everything you could ever need to know about 'alternative' (that is, illegal and left-wing) culture. God knows why it was there. Agitprop, squatting, the free press, Marxism, legal advice centres, abortion, paganism, prostitution, political protest and a very large section on drugs. In a fucking boarding-school library with curious and stupid teens searching for kicks. You couldn't make it up!!

The information was laid out in an impressively non-judgemental way. This hippy bible explained the chemistry, effects, danger, drawbacks and comedowns of every single illegal drug (and plenty of legal ones too). From mandies to quaaludes, opium to acid, mushrooms to smack and dozens of other stimulants I'd obviously never heard of; they even extolled the psychedelic euphoria experienced from ingesting nutmeg! *Alternative London* gave amphetamines a relatively clean bill of health and when it revealed that our own government doled out Benzedrine to the Desert Rats because 'the active ingredients present in the drug boost stamina, the IQ and EQ substantially', my interest was piqued.

The deciding factor was a quote I unearthed in an article about mods published in old copy of the *Evening Standard* from 1964 (in the pre-internet days we were constantly searching for write-ups about original mods in old newspapers, books and university theses). The author of the piece, Anne Sharpley, had been investigating the exponential rise in the use of amphetamine pills for recreational purposes among London's mods, and she shone an interesting light on speed. Drinamyl was the brand name for the pills that were known as 'purple hearts' in the clubs and they were one of the most common forms of the drug.

The establishment and elder generation were outraged at her conclusions, but Sharpley's piece was bravely sympathetic to mods.

> They are looking for, and getting, stimulation not intoxication. They want greater awareness, not escape. And the confidence and articulacy that the drugs of the Amphetamine group give them is quite different from the drunken rowdiness of previous generations on a night out.

That was mod right there and it convinced me to take the plunge.

After I'd finished my mock exams, my mum came across three or four pills wrapped in silver paper in a trouser pocket. She went absolutely doolally. I was carpeted and she lectured me about the evils of drugs, yada, yada, yada. I retorted that they weren't even mine; that I was looking after them for someone else – rather similar to the excuse Jimmy Cooper fed his mum when she found his bag of pills under his mattress in *Quadrophenia*. My mum didn't believe a word but she never told my dad, so I got away with it.

Something I certainly didn't get away with just a few months later was my self-inflicted brush with death. This was so stupid that looking back, I can't believe I actually did it.

I can lay the blame not just on my own stupidity and naivety but firmly on the aforementioned *Alternative London* handbook. On reflection, it was pretty irresponsible for the school to stock that particular instruction manual and make it freely available to teenage boys. I assume it was an attempt by some of the more progressive elements at the school to display their right-on credentials. They nearly killed me.

At the tail end of 1979, I'd secured a couple of advance tickets to the regular monthly mod event that was held on Hastings Pier. There were always three or four great bands playing, but on this particular occasion I can't remember who was on the bill; possibly The Lambrettas or The Circles, and I suspect the Welsh band Seventeen (who later became The Alarm) were supporting. The reason I couldn't remember was because I woke up the next day in hospital without a clue how I got there.

I'd suggested the gig to an enthusiastic schoolmate and the pair of us thought it might be a good idea to pick up a few pills for our night on the coast. We didn't have the money for anywhere to stay and the last train returned to London an hour and a half before the gig finished. We decided that instead of going home that night we'd sleep in our parkas somewhere warm and catch the first train back on Sunday morning. But where to get the blues? My mate from Hainault had been keeping a low profile for a couple of weeks and the only other option we could think of was to head up to the West End and try to score from some randoms.

We'd read in one of the Sunday scandal sheets that drugs were freely available at Piccadilly Tube Station on a Friday night. A maze of subways spread out from the central Underground hub there, which provided ample places to hide and conduct illicit deals. In fact, the tunnels had long been a favourite pick-up spot, well known for both rough trade and drug deals since the Sixties.

Being young and stupid but keen to get our hands on some blues, we made the trip to Piccadilly the night before the gig. We were crapping ourselves and jumping at every shadow. I mean, buying drugs from a street pusher isn't the kind of thing that your average mid-teen boarding schoolboy should be doing . . . But we steeled ourselves, identified some suspicious-looking hippies and tried to approach them surreptitiously. There was nothing for it but to go straight in.

'Erm . . . Excuse me, mate, but we're trying to get hold of a few blues. Can you sell us any?'

The first man we asked was dressed in double denim and had long, lank black hair and a sparse moustache. He just stared at us for about ten seconds and said, 'Oh, fuck off, you little twats.'

That knocked us back somewhat, so we decided to go above ground to regroup, grab a Wimpy and try again in 15 minutes.

This time we had more luck. The next bloke was wearing more traditional hippy gear: flares and a grubby Afghan coat, with greasy ginger hair that almost reached his shoulders. We asked the same question and this time weren't told to fuck off. Instead, he looked us up and down, smirking, and said, 'Yeah, I've got something for ya. Two for a quid, 12 for a fiver. Take it or leave it.'

Well, that was steep but we decided to get eight between us and handed over our pound notes. The bloke reached down the front of his pants and came back with a clear plastic bag, counted out eight pills and handed them over. They certainly didn't look like blues; the capsules were half orange and half turquoise.

'Er . . . These don't look like blues . . .?'

He replied, 'Oh, they're blues all right. They're just made by a different company. Look at that side – it's blue, ain't it?'

With that he scurried away, heading deeper into the tunnel.

Of course, we were naive and had no idea what we were doing; to us, there was no reason to think he'd sold us anything *but* blues. We went home clutching our booty and met the next morning at Charing Cross, where we jumped on the first train to Hastings. We had a great time bumming around the town all afternoon, got served in a pub and tucked into the vodka we'd brought with us. At five we ate some fish and chips and made our way to the pier for the gig.

The doors opened early because there were four bands playing, and we'd even managed to sneak in the rest of the vodka. The pair of us drank a few weak pints at the bar until about 8 o'clock, when we dropped the pills.

Less than an hour later I was gone. Completely twatted. I have vague memories of crashing out in a garage or a tool shed in someone's garden, but that was it. I came round in hospital the next day, oblivious. Apparently, when we'd first arrived, the casualty doctor had asked my friend if we'd taken any drugs. Even though he was worried that we'd get into trouble, my friend reluctantly confessed that we'd dropped some blues . . .

'I don't think so. Blues are uppers and have the opposite effect to whatever he's taken. Can you be more specific?'

Well, I'd dropped five and my friend had only taken two, so he sheepishly handed his last capsule over. The doctor wasn't impressed.

'Oh, for God's sake, you stupid boys. These aren't blues – they're barbiturates. Tuinal, you idiots. Downers. They have the opposite effect to speed. Very dangerous, especially for children. More people die of an accidental Tuinal overdose than any other drug. How many has he had?'

It turned out that five wasn't enough to do me in but, taken with the vodka and four pints of lager, was enough to knock me out. They kept me under observation for a few more hours and I never discovered what (or even if) they gave me to counteract the effects of the barbies. My mate was sitting by the bed when I came round and gave me a brief rundown of what'd happened since I'd passed out. Before I was discharged, the doctor delivered a lecture on the dangers of drugs and how lucky I was. Fortunately, the hospital hadn't informed my parents (who were away), nor my nan, who I was staying with. It wasn't their policy to alert the police either and we'd stuck to the story that we were over 16, which we weren't quite.

My mate was pleased. It had been much warmer in the hospital than the tool shed he'd broken into and he'd even been supplied with cups of tea and breakfast while I'd been crashed out. I was discharged, and we walked slowly up the hill to the station and boarded the next train to London. I was hanging my throbbing head in shame but was genuinely lucky, and at least my 15-year-old self had learned another important lesson. I was back in school on Monday morning.

It was on a long train trip to see a regional gig by The Chords that I first decided to produce my own fanzine. I'd been travelling with a handful of London mods when I found myself sitting next to Goffa Gladding, one of the three editors of our scene's most important modzines, *Maximum Speed*, and a real mover and shaker. I'd collected all the issues religiously, but during our conversation it had become apparent that Gladding was bored of doing it and unlikely to produce a new edition.

'See, Ugs . . .' He used to call me the 'ugly one', for some reason, which I always thought a bit of the old, 'Pot, meet kettle . . .' to be honest. 'It takes an awful lot of work and commitment to get a fanzine together and you don't make any money out of it. Total labour of love . . .'

Dom Kenny, the editor of *Shake*, was in the same carriage and told me that, with the demise of the earliest fanzines – along with *Maximum Speed*, *Get Up & Go!* had also called it a day as Tony Lordan and Vaughn Toulouse concentrated more on their new band, Guns for Hire (who would later morph into Department S) – there would be a gap in the market and he was determined to fill it with *Shake*. The other big player at the time was the more professional-looking *Direction Reaction Creation*. I resolved that I'd give it a try myself.

There had been a few handwritten punk fanzines but they were often unintelligible, and so I resolved to type mine. This was a painful process that seemed to take an inordinate amount of time, hammering out the text with a single finger on the very same typewriter that my mum used to produce the Small Faces' newsletter. But what was I going to call it?

I wanted to name it after a song by one of the bands we followed, but I didn't want to choose something too obvious. This meant that I immediately scrubbed the more well-known songs off the list: 'In the City', 'Millions Like Us', 'Maybe Tomorrow' and 'Time for Action' were all appropriate but could soon lead to overkill. In the end I plumped for a live track by the Purple Hearts called 'Extraordinary Sensations', which surfaced on record a couple of months later as the B-side to 'Frustration'.

Issue 1 of *Extraordinary Sensations* was a bit of a joke as I didn't have a clue what to write about. In the end it was made up of just 14 one-sided A4 sheets: a couple of gig reviews and a two-page piece on the filming of the 'Time for Action' video rubbed shoulders with some cut-and-paste collages of Roy Lichtenstein images, targets and pictures of Cathy McGowan. I'd made only 20 copies, using the photocopier at my mum's work, and they all sold on a single night at a Back to Zero gig down at the Bridge House. Stupidly, I never kept one and had soon misplaced the original pages, so I've not seen a copy since, which is something of a tragedy, *but* . . . fanzines were ultimately disposable. That was the point of them: they were produced and then purchased to be thrown away soon after. Most of that run of 20 were probably read on the train home and then chucked in the bin.

Despite the fact that I had my remaining O levels coming up, the spring of 1980 was incredibly important for me musically and culturally as I'd decided to take the fledgling *Extraordinary Sensations* seriously. While I hadn't received any letters (I soon realised I hadn't included an address!), I did get a lot of encouragement from my mates, so decided it was worth another go.

I approached Issue 2 far more seriously, featuring more gig reviews and a handful of real, structured articles. I'd even sourced a professional printer. Well, that isn't *strictly* true: Dave Stokes was one of the Epping mods, and while he was indeed a professional printer, he'd actually run off my copies in his lunch break on the QT. The level of professionalism was also improved by Stokesy being able to provide double-sided pages, and I even recruited my art teacher to draw a few unique illustrations. This time I sold 150 copies . . . I then managed to finish and release Issue 3 before leaving school in the summer, and felt that the fanzine was beginning to take proper shape. I'd persuaded Brian Betteridge, lead singer with Back to Zero, to craft an article about John Lennon and his poetry. I'd also had a number of letters sent in for publication, so was able to run a real readers letters page as well as include several reviews.

There was certainly a blossoming of this second wave of modzines, with the other players including *Patriotic, Can't Explain, Roadrunner, Go Go, In the Crowd, Shadows and Reflections* and *X L 5.* By the spring of 1980 the mod scene was at its absolute zenith. Bands were in the charts and appearing on television, gigs were coming thick and fast, a plethora of fanzines were springing up all over the country and The Jam were cementing their position as one of the nation's top live bands.

The only small fly in the ointment was that a distinct undercurrent of dislike, distain and even ridicule was directed at mod bands by the established inkie music press. I couldn't understand why at the time, but assumed it was simply because mod was a working-class movement that came from the streets and football terraces with no help from the music papers. Worse, it provided direct competition to the holy trinity of bands coming out of Manchester and Leeds – Gang of Four, The Mekons and Joy Division – all of whom were adored by the politically minded press. When you compared 'At Home He's a Tourist' and 'Where Were You?' with 'You Need Wheels' you could understand why! But still, mod bands were successful and hundreds of thousands of teenagers were still flocking to the banner.

That spring, I paid minimal attention to my exams and instead put all my energy into the important things in life – clothes, music, fanzines and scooters.

I was on top of the world.

PART 3

15

TIME FOR ACTION

At the Bridge House in the early months of 1980 I'd met a mod the same age as me from Ilford.

The area that took in Ilford, Seven Kings, Barking, Goodmayes, Gants Hill and Chadwell Heath was one of the real Essex mod strongholds, and this kid, like all young mods we met at the time, was welcoming to fellow travellers on the path. He was called Steve Butler and told me that a cafe called the Seagull, just opposite his mum's house in Ilford, was the main meeting place for scooter riders on a Sunday morning. Apparently about 20 kids on Vespas and Lambrettas would turn up for breakfast and then go for a drive up to Romford or Stratford.

I was intrigued. Other mods on scooters?

I reckoned I could make my way to Ilford without too much trouble – after all, the scooter was mechanically OK; it just looked crap. So, on Sunday morning I followed the 20 bus route on the Vespa 90, sauntered into the Seagull and ordered a cup of tea. After a few random nods someone sat next to me and started chatting. Apart from Mickey Curbishley, I'd never really spent any time with other scooter riders and was lapping it up. This boy was a tall, rangy mixed-race kid called Adrian from the other end of Ilford and he was interested in my bike.

He asked me how much I'd paid for it and we spoke about the merits of Mason's in Wanstead, another major scooter dealer in the area.

'So how much is your insurance? It's only a 90, so I suppose it's not much?'

'Erm . . . what do you mean, insurance?' What on earth was this guy on about?

'Well, you know, without insurance you can't get it taxed!'

'Taxed?' I was starting to think that perhaps I had missed something.

'Yeah, taxed . . . And MOT'd – you have an MOT, don't you?'

Well, that was it for me. I didn't even know what an MOT was, let alone insurance and tax. *Fuck*. I thought I'd better try to sort it out.

We spent the afternoon threading our way across London to have a look at the new terminal that had just been built at Heathrow. With the scooters pulled up and parked, we grabbed a quick cup of tea and then immediately set off back the way we'd come. There was absolutely no point to the journey other than the joy of riding as part of a large group of scooters. It was an incredible feeling and one that would stay with me for the rest of my life. The 90 held out pretty well, but I could tell that the exhaust was about to blow.

The next day, I took ERO 90B down to Woodford Scooters to enquire about taking an MOT test. The kindly mechanic gently told me that my first love was a heap of shit and that I should dump her straight away. He said I'd be better off starting from scratch and advised me to hunt down a Lambretta LI 150 from the small ads in the local paper.

'Should set you back a ton at most . . .'

I thought I should persevere with the Vespa a bit longer while I got the money for a new bike together. I'd had some trouble with the gearbox, but it was too big a job for me and I had no idea of how to fix it; still, I wasn't prepared to give up yet.

Help was at hand, though, and from an unlikely source. Mr Thomas was my geography teacher, a hulking great Welshman with a passion for rugby who'd heard about my scooter. He approached me one afternoon, revealed that he'd been a mod in the Sixties and knew his way round scooters with his eyes shut. He also told me that he'd been toying with the idea of introducing a motorcycle maintenance club after school. He had a suggestion . . .

'Look you, Piller, I'd every intention of starting with something juicy – you know, maybe a Norton or a Rudge – but it seems that you've something we can use to introduce the concept to the boys. I know it's only a two-stroke, but why don't you bring the Vespa in and I'll get the lads to fix it under my supervision? I'm thinking an hour every Tuesday at four, boyo?' (OK, so he didn't really say 'boyo', but I couldn't resist it!)

A notice was pinned to the board and nine kids turned up the first week, most of them young mods from the two years below me. The Strickland brothers, Andy Mangan, Perry Quai, Andy Jefcoate and Danny Quill were among them. I mention these particularly as they all achieved something in the mod world in future years.

Mr Thomas was true to his word and showed us how to service a scooter and perform basic maintenance tasks, such as changing a spark plug or a throttle cable. His expert attention added a couple of months to ERO 90B's lifespan. I eventually took the scooter for a second MOT test. Sadly, she failed. Again.

I rode round to Jackie and Mickey's and gave my first scooter a proper send-off. They lived very close to a bridge over the M11 and the motorway was still being excavated just 50 yards from the house. We pushed the 90 to the lip, gave the engine some revs (the exhaust had now blown and the little Vespa sounded more like a Harley Davidson) and let the clutch out so that she careered down the mud embankment into a newly dug drainage ditch.

'Farewell, old friend!' I said as we watched my first love disappear into her watery grave.

*

Having been full of enthusiasm when I turned 16, I was now scooterless, and climbing the walls at school. I was desperate to leave Chigwell as soon as I could and waiting impatiently for the last of my O levels to come round. I wasn't expected to do particularly well, as it had been obvious to most that I'd stopped bothering when I 'turned mod'.

I was still a regular at Upton Park, even though they'd been relegated. The spring of 1980 saw them win the FA Cup Final against Arsenal. I bought a ticket off a tout and had an amazing day out, which ultimately provided me with a final dressing-down from school. To celebrate the win, I'd swaggered into assembly the following Monday with two badger stripes beached into my hair dyed claret and blue with food colouring, and I was immediately sent home to dye my hair brown again. Just two weeks later I'd finished my exams and was at last officially free from Chigwell School – and I suspect they were pleased to see the back of me too. Still, I've always thought it odd that, although I didn't enjoy it at the time, like many people I look back on my schooldays as being among the best of my life!

I spent two weeks in Jersey, holidaying at my grandparent's place in St Helier, and then went back to Mister Byrite for a couple of months to raise some money while I worked out what I was going to do with myself.

By the summer of 1980, mod was probably the biggest youth cult in the country.

The initial buzz of the early days had been followed by the incredible *Quadrophenia* explosion and the short-lived cultural zeitgeist where our bands were regularly in the charts.

The Merton Parkas were the first non-Jam mod band to engage with the charts, and were joined not just by Secret Affair, the Purple Hearts, The Lambrettas and The Chords but also the mod-friendly two-tone bands like Madness, The Beat, The Special AKA, The Bodysnatchers and The Selecter. Even Booker T. & the M.G.'s 'Green Onions' climbed into the UK Top 10 on the back of *Quadrophenia*.

Top of the Pops juxtaposed regular performances by The Jam (who can forget Weller's pop-art appearance for 'Going Underground' when he wore a Heinz tomato soup apron back to front because the BBC refused to allow branded clothes?) with angry, shouty minor hits from The Chords and pop-drenched ska novelty Top 10s from The Lambrettas. It was our moment in the sun. And we certainly made the most of it. Pop magazines like *Smash Hits* and *Record Mirror* and after-school teeny-bop TV programmes soon followed. Mod was the biggest thing in the country, or so it seemed . . .

It couldn't last and it didn't. The media backlash was vicious and many of the bands gave up completely after what must've felt like one long round of banging their collective heads against a wall. The Jam were still around, however, becoming more popular by the day; and there was still enough of the bigger groups gigging to make for a healthy event planner.

We'd also worked out that there was a lot more to the *concept* of mod than we originally thought.

This had first came onto my radar one morning when my dad was driving me to school. Gushing about this new world I'd become part of, I'd asked if I could put on a tape. It was a compilation I'd put together myself and featured loud and aggressive music by The Kinks, The Jam and The Who.

'What's this rubbish?' he'd said.

'It's mod music, Dad – and I love it!'

'Ha! This isn't mod music. It's crap. I suppose you think you're a mod then?'

'Erm, yeah, Dad. Absolutely . . .'

'Well, son, if you want to be a mod you should ask your mother about Small Faces. But let me tell you: mod music is modern jazz. Tubby Hayes,

Art Blakey, Gene Krupa and Cozy Cole. It's where they got the name from – *modern* jazz, see? That's what mod music is. Not this stuff!' With that, he'd switched the tape off and tuned the dial to Radio 4.

I'd had no idea what he was on about. Jazz was crap, obviously. What would he know about it anyway? He was just an old bloke.

But by the summer of 1980, mod influences were changing. Suddenly the mod revival gave birth to yet another spin-off, something drawing from a different musical well.

Psychedelic mods, influenced by styles and music of the later Sixties, were beginning to establish themselves. They had their own bands, fashions, clubs and shops but still saw themselves as mods. When the Regal moved from Kensington Market and opened its doors just opposite the now defunct Well Suspect in Foubert's Place, it caused a genuine sensation. Of course, the bold and flamboyant style of their designs certainly didn't appeal to everyone, but the scene-within-a-scene popularised the 1967 Regency look with velvet suits, high-collared double-breasted jackets, tiny shaped sunglasses (worn both indoors and out), Cuban-heeled boots, paisley shirts and their most impressive groundbreaker, the polo-necked shirt. This was an amazing, almost outrageous design, which looked fabulous. Shirt material was not stretchable, so the tall collar needed to be pulled over the head and then fastened by a row of exquisitely crafted side buttons. I think the shop called it a Cossack shirt, but that wasn't quite right; it was certainly similar, but Cossack shirts usually had a strip of brocade somewhere on the neck and the collar wasn't to the height of a polo-neck – more like a turtleneck.

This scene was still a mod scene, but just a year or so after *Mods Mayday '79*, things were changing incredibly fast. A few of the early revival bands were picking up the psychedelic baton and changing their image. This new take on mod gave birth to some incredible clothes shops that catered for this new direction.

London mods were listening to a mixture of the new paisley sound played at the Groovy Cellar in Piccadilly, which was mainly psychedelic tracks, and were sporting Sixties shirts and Regency-style jackets. Even Paul Weller got involved, donning a paisley button-down on the front cover of 'When You're Young'.

Regal and Alice in Wonderland were the main two men's 'boutiques', but the girls had their own, called Sweet Charity. All were based in Kensington Market. The go-to DJ was The Doctor, who later found fame in Doctor and the Medics, and the soundtrack was most definitely *Nuggets*, the 1973 compilation put together by Lenny Kaye in tribute to the America's mid-Sixties garage scene.

One of the original revival faces, Mike Jones, who wrote for *Shake*, led the way and soon picked up the nickname Mike the Psyche. His band The Playn Jayn was the scene's great hope and I was an enthusiastic partaker of it all. Even the acid. The snapshot in time is well portrayed in Clive Solomon's film *The Groovy Movie*, which was made as a promotional vehicle for the bands he managed.

But before it started, it seemed, it was over. The scene didn't last as there was too much competition from all the other musical possibilities that we gradually all began to realise were open to us. Ultimately, the psych scene kind of drifted apart from the mod scene, lost, missing in action.

But as time went on, that conversation with my dad kept coming back to me. Through reading old articles, sharing tips with friends, hearing DJs play records . . . And all of these things started to pick up momentum towards the end of 1980 as the influences began to broaden. I started to realise that the old man was of course absolutely right. Mod music could also be psych, blues, R&B, soul, beat, reggae, punk and a whole host of other stuff – yes, even jazz. It was never exclusive and nor was it meant to be. It was adaptive. You could take out of it whatever you wanted, and the short but bright psych scene showed a tantalising glimpse of what might be possible.

Scooters really came into their own in the second half of 1980 as more people passed their 17th birthday and could ride legally.

The ranks of the Woodford (and associated areas) mods had grown incredibly and as I spent more time in local pubs I began to make friends with a whole host of other followers on the path, many of them a year or two older than me. They were all buying scooters too.

The obvious thing to do as soon as you passed your 16th birthday was to beg, steal or borrow the money to buy yourself a Vespa 50 Special. John Graham did just this – he was the first of dozens who took the plunge, and would often lend it to me – but the trouble was that Graham was 6 foot 4 inches and it was far too small for him. With my 90 gone, I was toying with the idea of trying to get a Vespa 50 of my own, but they were so slow (limited to just 30mph, with a top speed of 34mph down a very steep hill) that I never bothered and kept looking out for a cheap Lambretta to ride illegally until I was 17.

Julian Abbott, Phil Pastell, Rob Casteletti, Terry Stokes, Nick, Kev and Tim were all near neighbours who picked up Lambrettas, while of my former school friends it was only Richard Habberley, John Graham, John Bailey, Tony Wadey (and his sister Amanda) and Yu-Lon Chung who had invested in Vespas. Even my sister got one on her 16th birthday! There were now so many scooters in Woodford that we moved to a pub with a bigger car park and the Castle became our headquarters for the next few years.

Every week, I'd get the local paper and scan the small ads for scooters. Soon I picked up a Lambretta LI150 for 50 quid off an old chap in Highams Park. I didn't bother with the tax, MOT or insurance because

I wasn't actually old enough be on the road. It was so easy to buy scooters for peanuts then; you just had to knock on doors and offer a fistful of notes. By the time I was road legal, I'd owned at least four.

My job at Mister Byrite ended in mid-August 1980. They knew I wasn't going to stay after the summer and they wanted to pick up a permanent shop boy from the current crop of school leavers. I thanked them for a happy three years' worth of holiday and Saturday work, and the staff arranged a leaving do. What they didn't tell me was what they planned to do to me afterwards.

The Ilford High Road store was a lock-up shop with some window gratings that were slipped into place at close of business. We all had a couple of pints in the General Havelock around the corner, and when we got back to the shop, they grabbed me, shoved a broom handle through the arms of my jacket and taped me in a crucified position to the shop grating with a 'Shoplifter' sign draped over my neck on a piece of string. *Oh, for fuck's sake*, I thought. *Still, it won't be for long; they'll be back in a minute* . . . Trouble was, they didn't come back. At all. I was there for at least half an hour with people simply walking past and laughing at me until a couple of blokes took pity on me and cut me down!

When I was up there, hanging on the edge of building, I had time to think to myself that maybe it was time to get a proper job . . .

16

GENO

The mod scene continued to grow during the summer of 1980, but was showing the first signs of splitting again. We'd already had two other scenes breaking away from mainstream mod life to stride out on their own: first it was two-tone that simply outgrew the strictures of the punky-based revival and then the psychedelic mods in their paisley and corduroy. Now there was a third, because soul and R&B started to become part of the mix.

It seems odd now that in the London-based pre-*Quadrophenia* mod revival of early 1979 there was initially no place for soul music. Our world was centred on bands and live gigs. The first time I even realised there was a connection between mods and soul was when I heard Marquee resident compere and parka-wearing band manager Jerry Floyd spin 'Green Onions' and 'In the Midnight Hour' in between The Chords and their support band in June. There certainly weren't any actual nightclubs we could go to at the time.

The first real impact soul music had on the new mod scene came about through the concerted efforts of a Sixties mod by the name of Randy Cozens.

Cozens was a tough, working-class original who'd kept his love for the Sixties soul of his mod teenage years close to his heart. He'd watched these new mod kids popping up all over London and what he'd seen hadn't impressed him; worse, he regarded the punky thrashings of The

Jam, The Chords and the Purple Hearts as a mistaken foray into punk rock. In Randy's forthright view, these kids should ditch the parkas and rediscover their real mod heritage – and that included the black American music of the Sixties along with proper Italian-style tailoring. Randy, who was only just 30 at the time, was not content with simply moaning about the problem as he saw it. He wrote letter after letter – first to the established soul music papers like *Blues & Soul* and *Black Echoes*, and when that didn't deliver any dividends he targeted the three main music papers, *NME*, *Sounds* and *Melody Maker*. He kept writing until a journalist at *Sounds* decided to take him up on his offer to enlighten everyone and asked him to compile a Mod Top 100 chart to accompany their planned six-page mod feature to be run just after the 1979 August Bank Holiday.

The piece appeared to great fanfare and Randy's choices reflected what would become known as 'rhythm & soul', a very mod-centric take on soul music, and noticeably different from the 'northern soul' sound that had been big in the north in the early Seventies (not that we knew anything about that at the time). His list featured 97 soul and R&B numbers from the mid-Sixties, coupled with two ska (often referred to as blue beat at the time, a name derived from the record label many of the UK Jamaican releases appeared on) and one completely fictitious single, called 'Rancid Polecat' by Ian & the Clarks, named after Cozens' friend the soul DJ and collector Ian Clark (who would later contribute the designs for the 6Ts soul club and Kent Records).

Randy's chart fell on deaf ears with a lot of revival mods when it first appeared and it took quite a while before the concept of the music caught on. Of course, the list was discussed and debated, and many of us knew a few of the records, but on the whole, most young mods were still fixated on the music of The Jam and the rest of the revival bands and just didn't get it. Nevertheless, it was through Cozens' chart that the first steps were taken by the scene towards soul music.

The first mod 'discos' were run by three or four promoters who formed a kind of cartel. They included Darryl Hayden, Andy Ruw and Tony Class. Both Hayden and Ruw often relied on bands as a means of attracting their target audience while playing records before and after for people to dance to, but Class didn't. He was different from the others too, or at least seemed to be. He'd been running a mobile disco with his younger brother for a few years and was a frustrated 'almost' rather than ex-mod, who'd been just too young for scooters in the Sixties. His brother Robin was friends with Huggy Leaver from The Teenbeats and after spending a weekend with him in Hastings bought himself a scooter. After studying the burgeoning scene up close, Class realised there was a gap in the market for mod discos – without bands – and as he already had the equipment decided to give it a go.

On my 16th birthday, 8 November 1979, half a dozen of us from Woodford and Epping caught the train over the water to the Hercules Tavern in Lambeth to attend Tony Class's first night. The Hercules was a typical Victorian boozer, all high, tobacco-stained ceilings and sticky carpets, but as we approached from the station, the first thing we noticed were the 25 scooters lined up outside with a buzzing crowd standing on the pavement. So began Tony Class's major role in London mod life.

By the middle of 1980 he was running mod nights all over the capital, six or seven nights a week. His set lists were still a long way from what Randy Cozens had been hoping for, but some of Cozens' suggestions certainly began making an appearance – among them tracks like 'Wade in the Water' (both the Ramsey Lewis and Marlena Shaw versions). Gloria Jones's 'Tainted Love', Curtis Mayfield's 'Move On Up' and 'My Baby Must Be a Magician' by The Marvelettes.

The staple, though, was a mixture of Sixties mod bands like The Who, The Kinks and Small Faces, pop-soul 45s like 'Nothing but a House Party' by The Showstoppers and The Mar-Keys' 'Last Night' alongside Tamla Motown hits from The Supremes, The Miracles and Martha & the Vandellas, records from The Jam and the early revival bands who were now releasing their own singles, plus a smattering of pop from The Dave Clark Five and The Monkees. Bizarrely, I can even remember hearing novelty records like 'They're Coming To Take Me Away' by Napoleon XIV or theme tunes like 'Hawaii Five-0' and 'Joe 90'. There was also a fair amount of ska and two-tone from The Specials, Madness, Desmond Dekker, Prince Buster and The Maytals.

Still, it was a heady mix for us at the time. There was no doubt that Tony Class became the scene's main DJ – and his nights were like a private club, where mods from all over London would meet, sell fanzines, talk and occasionally fight.

Completely independent of the mod revival, at this time there were also stirrings from the northern soul scene, which in the north of England had been going strong throughout the Seventies with its brand of up-tempo Sixties soul music, played at huge all-nighters in towns like Wigan, Cleethorpes and Stoke. The scene had been massive, even pushing soul music into the pop charts in the mid-Seventies as this underground scene was exploited ruthlessly by a music industry that didn't understand it (sound familiar?).

Debatably, the northern scene was past its peak, but in London a Midlands exile by the name of Ady Croasdell, together with Randy Cozens and other soul fans stranded in the south like Cockney Mick, Ian Clark, Terry Davis and Tony Rounce, started to put on the occasional night at the Railway in West Hampstead, playing their rare soul records to a curious crowd that included a number of mods. I'd been invited along to the first night by Charlotte and Claire, a couple of scooter-riding mods who I vaguely remember as being from South London. It was a fabulous experience. After a couple of one-off nights, the collective moved their event to the Bedford in Covent Garden, and in the late summer of 1979, the 6Ts Rhythm & Soul Society was born.

The early events were probably too specialist for the mainstream revival crowd, but band faces like Martin Mason and Billy Hassett from The Chords, Brian Betteridge from Back to Zero and punters like Tony Smith, Skinhead Sean and Goffa Gladding from *Maximum Speed* ensured that the 6Ts, with its brand of club and northern soul, gained a foothold with London mods. But it was still too early for rhythm & soul to make much of an impact on our world. The soul influence had certainly arrived but was still too purist for most.

Mod club nights sprang up just about everywhere, from Kingston and Richmond in the west to Southgate, Camden and Dalston in the north, dozens of small places in the City and the East End, all the way out to Brentwood, Ilford and Romford. We regularly travelled to clubs in Rotherham, Birmingham or Southend. It felt like we were in a golden age with the best of both worlds: live music and discotheques.

The bands were changing too. While mod revival groups like The Lambrettas and Secret Affair were still having hits in the summer of 1980, a number of the bands on the scene had dumped the mod image and quickly distanced themselves. The New Romantic look was particularly fashionable and chart-worthy, and some of the biggest pop stars of the Eighties started out as mods. Spandau Ballet (originally known as The Cut), Wham! (The Executives), The Alarm (Seventeen), Tears for Fears (Graduate) and Blue Zoo (The Crooks) all fell over themselves to dump the mod image as soon as they could. They weren't alone either. Towards the end of 1980, many of those original teenage champions who'd played the mod circuit in 1979 had realised that a hostile music press who encouraged a vicious backlash, coupled with the incredible success of two-tone, meant that their chances of scoring hits had diminished and so they reluctantly threw in the towel.

But despite these deserters, a new type of mod band appeared on the London circuit and attracted our attention. The first and the biggest were called Q-Tips, although they weren't a mod band per se. They were fronted by a charismatic singer called Paul Young, who dressed like a face in tailored double-breasted suits and was backed by some of the tightest musicians in London (including the original Sixties mod Norman Watt-Roy) wearing stage suits reminiscent of those Sixties soul revues we saw on archive television programmes. It was the band's first single that got them noticed, a cover of a Joe Tex record called 'S.Y.S.L.J.F.M.', which they released on their own label – and if that wasn't enough to nail their colours hopefully to the mast, the label had a target logo. Their gigs were always packed, sweaty and atmospheric, and Young, who'd had a novelty hit called 'Toast' a couple of years earlier with his previous outfit, Streetband, was the consummate frontman, with an incredible soulful voice. The Q-Tips always delivered a great night out, but their limitation was that they seemed to rely on covers.

The Step were a mod soul band who concentrated on their own material. Fronted by a bone fide North London mod DJ called Paul Graham, they (like The Q-Tips) boasted a brass section, but The Step were younger and seemed more real, certainly to us. The band were immediately signed by CBS Records, who reactivated their Sixties soul/mod imprint called Direction for the band's singles. They released a couple of cracking tracks, 'Love Letter' and 'Let Me Be the One', and were certainly adopted and followed by us and Paula and the Wembley Girls, but disappointingly failed to break though.

The third and final group of mod-soul hybrids that we followed were of course Dexy's Midnight Runners (they later dropped the apostrophe), who were originally an integral part of the mod revival – although Kevin Rowland later told me it wasn't something he embraced enthusiastically.

I first saw them fourth on the bill to the Purple Hearts and The Teenbeats, and they quite simply blew me away. They became regulars on the revival circuit, and were so totally different from everybody else we saw: super tight with sergeant major Rowland micromanaging everything from their look to their movements on stage; hard and fast brass-heavy anthems with often political and sometimes nonsensical (to me) lyrics about Irish poetry. Their debut 45 'Dance Stance' even crept into the Top 40, becoming the first of their 13 hit records, and was a real game-changer for me. Their set was littered with incredible up-tempo northern soul covers that we were beginning to recognise from the dance floor, like 'Seven Days Is Too Long' and 'The Horse'. Their incredible debut LP catapulted them to superstardom. *Searching for the Young Soul Rebels* is undoubtedly a work of great genius and in my opinion one of the best British albums ever made.

'Geno' was an enormous Number 1 hit, with such power and energy that it never failed to get people up on the dance floor. While Rowland had steered the band away from the overt mod image they started with, their look – that of the New York docker in leather three-button jacket clutching a northern-soul all-nighter bag – wasn't far enough away to alienate the band's original mod fans. In fact, the single, a paean to the great adopted British mod-soul singer Geno Washington with a galvanising chanted intro, was indirectly responsible for a front-page headline in the *Wanstead and Woodford Guardian*.

I'd arrived home from my summer holiday in Jersey to be confronted by an angry mother who wordlessly thrust a copy of the paper under my nose.

'Take a look at this, Edward, and count yourself lucky you weren't there . . .'

'Mods arrested in riot at rugby club,' was the headline, and underneath it said: 'Police arrested nine teenagers following a disturbance at Bancroft's Rugby Club on Saturday' – and sure enough, there was the roll call of shame plastered all across the front page, with people's ages in brackets after their names. It turned out my sister, Vicky, who was by now 15, had been there and she filled me in. It was a birthday party and all of the Woodford mods had been invited. The DJ had been spinning jazz-funk all night, but regular nagging requests had prompted him to eventually play 'Geno'. As soon as the intro came on, all the mods in the room jumped up and started dancing in the middle of the floor. A group of men in their twenties – members of the rugby club and not invited to the party – took exception to this and immediately steamed into them with chairs and tables. There followed an almighty ruck, which was eventually broken up by bouncers. It was at this point that the rugger-buggers pulled out their warrant cards and introduced themselves as off-duty policemen. All the mods were arrested for affray – and when it later came to court, the main witnesses had perfectly coordinated statements that saw four of my friends sent to adult prisons for upwards of three months each.

Lucky I wasn't there indeed!

'Geno' was a powerful song – iconic and rousing. Once heard, it was never forgotten.

The more discos and gigs we went to, the more people we met. Eventually trips outside of London became something we wouldn't think twice about. And it was here that we realised that mod wasn't as southern-centric as we'd thought it was. Sure, I'd seen a number of bands playing the circuit who weren't from London, The Circles (Birmingham), The Killermeters (Yorkshire) and Seventeen (North Wales) among them, but on those early Bank Holiday trips we met northern mods for the first time. It turned out that things were different up there – a legacy of their scooter clubs, who'd carried on an unbroken tradition dating all the way back to the Sixties. It seemed that when mod in London floated away on a sea of paisley and patchouli oil in 1967 (or even shaved its head and pulled its skinhead boots on), in the north it just retreated underground and morphed into something else. Of course, the fashions changed from those of the Sixties, but the principles were still there: scooters and soul music.

The lads we met told us about dozens of bands from north of Watford, many of which had yet to make it down to London. Sema 4, the Salford Jets, The Cherry Boys, The Gents, The Name – turns out there were dozens of them and in many ways they were further along the path than we were because of their inherited cultural roots. They also had their own Bank Holiday destinations. While Brighton and Hastings might have attracted a few hundred scooters at most in 1980, Rhyl and Scarborough could boast over a thousand, because of the long-existing scooter clubs.

I began to see that the mod revival in many ways saw the south catching up with something that in the north had never really entirely gone away.

17

YOU NEED WHEELS

Maybe because she was sacked from the Small Faces fan club by Don Arden, my mum was dead set against me working in the music world – the only thing that excited me in life – and arranged an interview for an insurance job with a City broker.

Fuck that! I thought, but went along to keep her happy. It was easy to fail the interview – I just turned up late and acted surly! The interviewer wasn't impressed, but I'd bought myself a couple of brownie points at home.

Trouble was, I was told in no uncertain terms to get a job and pay my way. This was the typical East End world view and I was soon working in a sawmill on the Brooker Road industrial estate in Waltham Abbey, just three miles from my house in Loughton. Work started at eight in the morning and was tough. I toiled for a tenner more than I'd been picking up from Mister Byrite's, but I wasn't given a choice; I had to earn a wage. Aspiration had been drummed into me even as my parents delegated my upbringing to teachers and housemasters.

I paid rent and used the rest to further my mod life. But I hated it. It was hard work and hearing the bell ring at 4.30 on a Friday was the only thing I had to look forward to.

Time for change.

It was the end of the summer in 1980 and my sawmill job had earned me enough money to buy a classic mod motor. I found a 1966 Triumph

Herald in peacock blue to which I added the obligatory green sun visor with the legend 'Woodford Mods' in sticky white letters where 'Sharon and Dave' would normally be. It cost 150 quid.

I also realised that after four months I hated hard work so much that I left and signed on the dole. How much worse could it be? Well, the DSS paid a handsome £14.25 per week, which wasn't even enough to go to the Marquee regularly. The bloke at the job centre told me that if I enrolled at the local college to do the Enterprise Allowance Scheme I'd get money for that and could also pick up the dole. In other words, this particular initiative would let me trouser a heady £49 a week: a fortune! It sounded appealing. The only problem was, I had to set up a business.

I'd been running the *Extraordinary Sensations* fanzine in my spare time for almost a year and asked the man if this counted. Miraculously, he said that it did and I was immediately up and running.

I went to Loughton College to have a sniff about, but there were only a couple of weeks till term time, so I had to make a snap decision. Plenty of my scooter-riding mod mates were taking courses to avoid work and I eventually plumped for a BEC National in Business Management. A number of the other Woodford mods had signed up for college, Julian Abbott, Woody, Lanky (John Graham), Rob Jacobs, Louis Bacchus, Paul Regan and The Praill brothers among them, and that made it an easy decision for me. The Winston Churchill in Debden was our daily drinking hole and I have to say, it was a real crack. We spent most of our time socialising with the girls in the art school while avoiding work!

But fuck me, the college course was crap. I was gone within a term and a half.

The one thing the college did do was to teach me how to type. One of the course modules was touch-typing and it was the best thing I ever did because it meant that the fanzine just rolled off my newly acquired electric typewriter. To boot, I put most of the fanzine together at the back of the class while Julian Abbott created regular distractions. Genius.

Surprisingly, the Enterprise Allowance Scheme, Margaret Thatcher's gift to the indolent, wasn't withdrawn when I left college, so I used it to build up *Extraordinary Sensations*, which by now was on to its ninth issue with a healthy circulation of around 5,000 copies a time. It was still being printed by Dave Stokes, who'd managed to expand the print run without too much trouble at work. I began to recruit other people to write articles that were beyond my experience: Brian Betteridge on the poetry of John Lennon, Ian Clark from the 6Ts on soul music and various international stringers who would send in localised articles from around the world. As the sales increased and I got more into the habit of doing it, production values and the number of pages increased substantially.

My relationship with the eternal vision in white, Paula from Wembley, had gradually fizzled out. To be honest, it was impractical as she lived an hour and a half away on the Tube, which meant a whole night just to get there and back. I soon met a pretty local girl called Penny, who was, bizarrely, a skinhead. Of course, by now skinheads were normally our sworn enemies, to be avoided, but she lived round the corner and, in spite of the obvious difficulties, we were well suited. We spent a few months together (she was probably only my third girlfriend, after Julie Dear and Paula), but it didn't last and eventually I met Sandra.

Sandra was a regular at the Marquee and went to all same gigs as me. She was by far the best-dressed mod girl I ever met and approached Sixties style in her own unique way, with a silk scarf worn as a choker as her trademark. She was always exquisitely attired and wore her hair in a blonde pixie crop. She was another bloody Catholic. Were we constantly pulled into each other's orbits, like dysfunctional lonely magnets? Or just so fucked up by our upbringing that we naturally flocked together, forever searching for an escape from guilt?

We dated for several months, and it was wonderful to experience having a real and beautiful mod girl-face on my arm. We took in most of that year together, but she lived in Stockwell, which was again an enormous distance from Loughton, and sadly, like most long-distance relationships, ours gradually petered out. I always remember Sandra as the most mod girl I ever met.

At home I realised I needed to make some changes.

The dole was starting to piss me off – I simply wasn't getting enough money. I needed a regular source of income that wasn't benefits and I needed it quickly.

I had to pin down that job. But not just any job – it had to be a record company job. Music was the only thing that interested me; everything else seemed incredibly boring by comparison.

I realised that if I was going to get a job in music, I'd have to use my contacts. Seeing as my mum had been out of the game since 1967, that left just one person: Jackie Curbishley, the beautiful mother of my friends Jackie and Mickey. Along with being married to Bill, who was still managing The Who, she herself was the manager of Golden Earring.

I rolled up at her front door in Chigwell one afternoon and threw myself at her mercy.

Sitting in The Who's manager's kitchen talking job options with his amazing wife wasn't how I thought I'd start my career, but I was grateful. Jackie soon made me her personal project. She called several of her industry contacts and within a couple of days had arranged some interviews, including one at Polydor Records, The Who's label, which seemed the best option.

I realise now that Polydor took her calls and arranged the interview to keep a valuable client happy – but at the time, I thought I really had a chance. I was keen and turned up at their offices early with a rudimentary

CV that included just my O-level results and my fanzine experience. Now, on reflection, I can see that I was never going to get the job, but what it did do was fire me up to get one. The rejection when it came a week later didn't surprise me, but how the fuck was I going to take this further? The other interviews went the same way and a month later I was back where I started.

Once again, I found myself in Jackie's kitchen and she tried hard to give me hope – even though her kind introductions hadn't paid off. 'You know what, Eddie?' she said. 'When we had our office in Wardour Street I remember that most labels, not just the majors but also the indies, advertise for runners in the local labour exchange, just opposite the Marquee. Might be worth keeping an eye on it . . .?'

It was a throwaway line, the best she had at the time, but I knew the place she was talking about. It was closer to the Ship than the Marquee and right in the heart of Soho's media community. I filed it in the back of my mind in the section marked 'useful information' and thought I might check it out next time I found myself nearby.

At the end of 1980 I was still going to as many gigs as I could. Most of the early revival bands had thrown in the towel, which just spurred me on to make more of a determined effort to see as many as possible of the groups that were still gigging. Particularly because this gave me the opportunity to keep knocking out the fanzine . . .

One bitterly cold December night, a few of us trekked over to Feltham to see the Purple Hearts. Known mainly for its borstal, Feltham was a seriously long way from Loughton. The Purple Hearts were in the middle of their second wind and had come up with lots of new material. Dabbling with psychedelic influences, they'd played songs like 'Hazy Darkness (on a Sunny Day)' and 'Let's Get a Burger Man' and had recently signed a new, post-Fiction record deal with the indie label Safari. Psychedelia had been an acceptable influence on the mod world for at least a year already, encouraging an interest in garage rock and those elusive paisley shirts – prompting Epping mod Ed Silvester and his brother John to start their own psych-influenced fanzine called *Kaleidoscope*.

The Purple Hearts played through their new set and we certainly enjoyed the direction they were heading in. Gig over, we mounted up for the journey back east. There were probably 15 scooters and they pulled out of the car park in a pack and turned right. I'd dropped my glove and so had to jump off the bike to pick it up – which meant that I was about ten seconds behind the others, who were rapidly heading up the road towards central London. I checked the first set of traffic lights and they were still green, so I pulled off in pursuit. BANG! There was a screech of tyres and from nowhere my Lambretta was hit a glancing blow to the rear Florida bars as a driver who'd obviously jumped the lights swerved to avoid me. The scooter spun round on an invisible axis and I was thrown 5 or 6 yards across the road, landing on my front. My trousers ripped and I scraped the skin off my right knee, but was lucky not to come off worse. I wasn't sure about the scooter, though; it certainly looked a mess.

I was momentarily winded as I rolled over to take stock of the bike, still on my back. All of the lights and mirrors were mangled and smashed off, and one of the side panels was destroyed, but the damage looked mostly superficial and I realised that if the driver hadn't taken evasive action I would most likely have ended up in hospital with the scooter written off. There I was, lying on my back in the middle of the road looking at the wreck of my recently acquired Lambretta GP150 (PGS 332W, purchased from John Silvester from Epping, made in India!), and thanking my lucky stars it wasn't worse.

The rest of the scooter group hadn't realised I was no longer following them and were already half a mile away. I was on my own. *Shit*. I was thinking about the scooter: would I be able to get it back on the road or would I have to dump it and try to find somewhere to stay?

I finally looked up to see what had hit me.

Fucking hell! It was a burgundy Roller.

Wait, who on earth was that? Expensive leather slip-ons daintily tiptoeing through the broken glass towards me. Oh my God! I'd just been run over by Leslie fucking Crowther! In the early Eighties, Crowther was simply one of the biggest stars in the country.

'Oh God, I'm really sorry about that. I just didn't see you . . .' He sounded most apologetic.

'Well, you did jump a red light . . .'

'Oh, I'm sure I didn't – it was still green when I drove through. Look, I'm very sorry; it was just one of those things. Is there anything I can do?' His familiar voice sounded genuinely contrite.

That set me off and I burst out laughing at the ridiculousness of it. 'Well, I've always wanted a *Crackerjack!* pencil?' I guffawed.

He took a quick glance over his shoulder. 'Look, are you hurt? Do you think you need an ambulance?'

'No, I'm just a bit bruised. There's a call box a couple of hundred yards up the road; I saw it earlier. Shall I call the police?'

Leslie looked at his watch, appearing agitated at my mention of the police. 'Look, I don't mean to be rude, but I am in rather a hurry. I'm on my way home to the West Country and I'm very late. Can we just swap details? I'm expected somewhere . . .'

As he walked back to his car to get a pen and paper, I dusted myself down and picked the bike back up. It was indeed a mess. I pulled it onto the stand and surveyed the damage. It needed new panels, some work on the mudguard and probably even new leg shields. As is the case with all scooters that have been tipped over, the engine wouldn't start. But I reckoned with luck I could get it the 30-odd miles back home to Loughton. Crowther returned from his car, took my details and passed me a card with his phone number on it and his registration number written on the back.

'Look, I'm sorry again,' he said. 'Do you think it's going to be all right? Of course, I'll make good the damage – just get it to a garage and let me know how much it is and I'll sort it out. I'd rather do that than go through insurance. That OK with you? Excellent. Well, good luck on the way home . . .'

With that, he walked back across the road, carefully avoiding the detritus from the scooter, threw me a wave and flicked the ignition.

Unfortunately for him, a few minutes earlier my compadres had noticed I was no longer following and had turned back to look for me. They'd eventually arrived back where they started to see the Rolls-Royce and my scooter looking the worse for wear. Before Leslie had a chance to pull away, the dozen scooters had surrounded the car and immediately recognised its driver. They all jumped off their bikes and began rocking the Roller with him in it, shouting and laughing while the poor television presenter crapped himself. It was funny for a couple of moments, but I could see that he was genuinely scared, so I limped over and asked them to stop. Reluctantly the raucous chanting died down and the scooters were moved, allowing poor Leslie Crowther to roar away into the night.

I limped through our front door at two in the morning and went straight to bed, knowing that I'd have to phone the office in the morning and take a day off while I tried to find a temporary ride to borrow. Without a scooter I wouldn't be able to get around.

I did a ring round the next morning and eventually discovered that Steve Jarvis had just taken delivery of a Lambretta SX 200. Trouble was, it was a 'cut-down' and as such was frowned upon by us mods. However, needs must, so I jumped on the Central Line to Wanstead and 15 minutes later was ringing his bell round the back of the shops where he lived with his mum over a Wimpy.

'My God, Steve, I don't know how you cope with that smell – just a whiff and I'm Hank Marvin. What I'd give for a "Bender in a Bun" right now!'

Steve laughed. He was not as tall as me but more muscular, charming with girls, good at fighting and always impeccably dressed – on this occasion he was wearing a pair of shorts and a target T-shirt. He was regarded as one of the local 'faces'.

'You get used to the whiff. In fact, I'm sick of the Wimpy. I doubt I could force another bloody hamburger down my throat if you paid me. Now, what's the problem? Why d'you need to borrow a bike?'

I ran through the previous night's accident and, just like everyone else, he laughed when he found out it was Leslie Crowther driving a Roller. He asked how my leg was.

'Well, borderline stitches, but I couldn't be bothered to go to Whipps Cross on the way home; it was late enough as it was. It's scabbing over nicely. So what's this about a cut-down Lambretta? I never knew you had one.'

Steve walked over to the corner of the yard and lifted up a tarpaulin to reveal this odd-looking blue scoot. It turns out that the Lambretta wasn't actually a cut-down; it was what was called a 'skeleton-scooter', the kind ridden by original skinheads and suedeheads in the early Seventies. A cut-down would have the panels removed and the leg shields trimmed down, which reduced the weight somewhat, whereas a skeleton-scooter had absolutely everything removed. Not just panels but leg shields and mudguard. Rather than gaining a few extra mph, this totally changed the dynamic.

Steve's new bike, now little more than a frame with an engine bolted to it, had been sprayed a dull metallic Oxford blue and featured a tiny aluminium mudguard, the kind you'd see on a Raleigh Chopper. Most impressively, it sported a large chrome exhaust pipe and a Dell'Orto 32mm carburettor.

'Bloody hell, Steve, what the hell is that?'

I was exclaiming because I'd never seen one before, but he answered the question as if I was being serious.

'Well, it goes like shit off a shovel, so I assume it's a re-bore, a 225. It's pretty scary, to be honest. You've got to be really careful pulling away, keep the revs low or you'll wheelie and it'll fall back on top of you. I reckon I got about 85 out of it, but the speedo has been disconnected, so I couldn't tell. If you promise to be careful you can use it for a couple of weeks while you get yours repaired.'

'I wouldn't have thought it was your style, how come you got it?'

Steve laughed at this and said: 'You're not going to believe it but just before the Bank Holiday, the last one a month ago? About ten of us were sitting in the Green Man on Leytonstone roundabout with the scooters lined up outside. At about half ten a couple of northerners wearing parkas and carrying crash helmets came into the pub and asked if they could buy us a drink. They said they were from Bradford and were on their way to Hastings for the run. They begged us for somewhere to stay for the night and as Mum was away for the weekend I said they could doss down in the flat.

'In the middle of the night, I could hear them moving about, so I got up to see what they were doing and – fuck me! They were going through her jewellery box, fully dressed and ready to scarper. I went fucking doolally and attacked them, shouting my head off. They panicked and ran for the door. I was just in my pants and chased after them barefoot, getting a couple of decent cracks in . . .'

Steve was laughing as he continued.

'In their haste to escape, not only did one of them drop his crash helmet but he even left his scooter here as I chased them two's up down Wanstead High Street . . .'

Later as I rode the SX200 back to Loughton I resolved to be super careful because *fuck me*, it was terrifyingly fast!

The next morning was a Saturday, so with Steve 'Buster' Andrews in tow I rode my broken GP slowly up to Edmonton Scooters. After much scratching of heads, the guvnor, Phil, gave me an estimate for new panels, a mudguard and a general tidy-up, which was just shy of 200 quid – not quite enough for a write-off, but more than I could afford to front. I jumped on the back of Steve's P Range and he took me home, where I pulled Leslie Crowther's card out of my bedside drawer and rang the number.

A woman answered the phone. 'Bath 3762, can I help you?' That was usually how people answered the phone back then – stating the number.

I asked for Mr Crowther and the lady asked if he would know what it was about. Trying to be polite and not talk about what happened, I replied: 'Oh, nothing specific. I met Leslie a few days ago and he asked me to give him a call . . .'

A minute later the familiar voice came on the phone. 'Crowther. Who's this?'

I briefly explained who I was and that I'd had an estimate for damage to the scooter. He was very polite and didn't balk at the figure of £250, just took my address and asked who the cheque should be made out to. A week later, it arrived in the post.

A year later, Leslie Crowther rolled his car and was arrested for drink driving.

A few weeks after I'd handed the Lambretta back, Steve Jarvis was pulled up by the Old Bill, who informed him he was riding a stolen scooter. Surprisingly, in this instance, once he'd explained what'd happened, they chose not to arrest him for handling stolen goods but just took the bike off him and made sure that it was returned to the original owner in Bradford, where it had been lifted three months before.

The police weren't always that understanding, though.

18

LIFE ON AN L.I.

B y 1981 scooters were everywhere. In fact, prices started to increase dramatically with demand and it soon became impossible to pick up a scooter of Sixties vintage for less than 200 quid.

This meant the specialist scooter shops who'd been clinging on with an ever-decreasing turnover throughout the Seventies were given a new lease of life by servicing and rebuilding old bikes and, more importantly, selling brand-new machines. The legendary Eddy Grimstead's in Gants Hill, famous for their bespoke Sixties mod custom jobs, had by now gone, but there were still plenty of others dotted around London. Woodford Scooters, Royspeed in Hornchurch, Humphries in Upper Street, Mason's of Wanstead, Etty & Tyler in the East End, Edmonton Scooters and most importantly the family business, R. Agius in Maida Vale (who'd been selling Vespas since the first British-built Douglas models hit the streets in 1952). These were the ones we patronised, and the shops soon became Saturday-morning destinations in their own right.

The scooter you rode was extremely important, and as we went down this particular rabbit hole we found we learned more and more about them.

The bottom line was that there were only two manufacturers with any real credibility: Vespa and Lambretta. A few British companies cashed in on the Sixties boom and you'd occasionally see Triumphs, BSAs or the Velocette Viceroy with its 250cc engine knocking about. You might clock a handful of the incredibly ugly German-made Zündapps too, but it looked like a bath and spare parts were impossible to get. There was also the Garelli Capri, another Italian scooter from the Sixties, which looked like a cross between a Vespa and a Lambretta; that was picked up by a few mods at the time but never caught on because its 80cc engine was seen as slow (although my mate Mick Callaghan swore by his).

The more affluent could always plump for a bubble car and there were a few models available at the end of the Seventies, made by Isetta, Heinkel and Messerschmitt. Isetta had begun life as a fridge manufacturer, while the other two were better known for making planes for the Luftwaffe. That didn't diminish their cars' popularity, but there were so few left by the time of the revival that they were never a serious option and only Garry Moore from Ilford and Mick Taylor from Chingford had one.

The most exotic three-wheeler on the scene was the incredible-looking Bond Bug. There were not many around, but I did see a convoy of four on their way to the Great Yarmouth run in 1981. The Bond Bug looked amazing, like a space-age Reliant Robin; they were only ever produced in bright orange, with a 700cc engine and a top speed of around 80mph. Sadly, they were in production only briefly, from 1970 to 1974, so there was already a shortage by 1980 – and although they had a devoted following, there were never enough around to make a proper splash. You could even drive them on a motorbike licence!

If you wanted to buy a scooter, though, unless you were a niche collector it had to be a Vespa or Lambretta.

Based in Milan, Lambretta had by the early Seventies long given up the ghost as demand for new machines fell through the floor. The brand's owners, Innocenti, had already licensed production to Serveta in Spain in 1954, and a host of other international companies built their own versions, but it became apparent that Lambretta's days were numbered. The market was increasingly switching to small, cheap cars like the Mini, the Fiat Cinquecento or the Citroën 2CV and, with no apparent technological developments since the mid-Sixties, scooter production was wound down.

The company, which had been producing the Mini under licence for a number of years, was bought by British Leyland in the early Seventies and scooter production was finally halted. The factory's production lines were flogged off to the Indian government, who moved the whole kit and caboodle to the subcontinent and introduced the Jet, the first new model since the GP in 1969.

Unfortunately, the build quality was poor and all Indian Lambrettas had reliability issues. You could get a Serveta Lambretta from Spain, but again the quality (though better than those from India) wasn't as good as the Italians'.

Vespa on the other hand was owned by Piaggio, who'd continued to introduce new, innovative designs – so by the time of the mod revival their scooters were the only real 'new' option, with the 50 Special and P Range. These had improved brakes, lights and indicators; the P Range was available in three models, the 125, the 150 and the 200, and boasted the luxury of an oil reservoir that fed a steady stream of two-stroke into the engine. Launched in 1946, the brand had long dominated the market and their SS180, SS90, Rally and (most famously) GS models competed with Lambretta's TV and SX as the most desirable mod scooter. There was certainly fierce competition for the best accessories. In 1980 and 1981 it was lights and mirrors with whip aerials, foxtails and flyscreens, but within 18 months scooters were stripped back to basics.

Here's the thing: Lambrettas looked better, but Vespas were reliable, and for me it was reliability that won out. I'd owned four LIs, two SXs, a

Starstream and an Indian GP, but by 1982 I'd had enough of breakdowns, poor lights, crap brakes and terrible ignition, so bought myself a couple of Vespa P Ranges. From then on, I didn't look back and have, at one time or another, owned all but the very early Vespa models. If I had to choose a favourite, it would be a toss-up between the beautiful SS180 and my rare US Rally Special from 1976, which featured an on-board oil tank used as a test bed for the soon-to-be-introduced P Range.

While scooters had doubtlessly liberated the original Sixties mods, when it came to the early Eighties the scooter revival was unstoppable – and so popular that scooters arguably transcended the music, the clothes and the mod lifestyle, leading to another splinter group, the scooterboys. These were kids who rode a scooter but decried the mod scene; they could be rockabillies, psychobillies, casuals or even skinheads.

Scooter clubs proliferated rapidly in our area, with new ones popping up seemingly every week. They weren't usually real clubs with a treasurer, secretary and membership subs; although many of them started with those noble intentions, it was just a bit of a ball-ache to properly organise. Instead, scooter clubs were usually loosely affiliated groups of mates who chose an appropriate name. Ours was called the Essex Cougars Scooter Club and I proudly displayed the club's name on the side panels of my Lambretta in white plastic letters. F.A.B. Scooter Club – named after *Thunderbirds* – were from up the road in Ilford and Romford; England's Own and the E4SC came from Chingford; and the Debden Royals were based at the Royal Standard, the hardest pub in Loughton.

The sight of 20 scooters roaring down the road often inspired others to go out and buy one. Clubs soon became very fashionable and anyone who owned a scooter (and many who didn't) joined one. There were hundreds of scooter clubs in London alone, with names like the Fulham

Wasps, the Paddington Scooter Club, the Nomads, the Enfield Shitheads Scooter Club, the Britannia and the Viceroys. But this was a national phenomenon and we soon realised that many of the clubs based in the north could trace their roots back to the Fifties and had a number of national associations already in place as well as a structure that provided a modicum of organisation.

The most important thing scooters did was to turn Bank Holidays from a Monday-afternoon train ride to a whole weekend of mayhem. In this respect, the scooter really came into its own in 1981. Organised months in advance, often with entertainment provided by Tony Class, these five or six sporadically spaced weekends became the focus of our calendar. Many thousands of kids would descend on a down-at-heel, flyblown dump living on past glories to get drunk, dance and cause chaos.

The destination for these nationally organised scooter rallies was initially chosen by the National Scooter Riders Association, which had its roots in the original northern scooter clubs of the Fifties. The idea was that all the clubs who were affiliated to the national committee would send a delegate (their 'number one') to a national meeting where all potential destinations were debated and voted upon.

Unsurprisingly, this was of limited interest to impatient young London mods, and very few made the trips to Rhyl, Scarborough or Skegness! Who cared where northern scooter clubs wanted to go? Londoners generally plumped for Sussex (Hastings or Brighton), Essex (Southend or Clacton), Kent (Margate) or Norfolk (Great Yarmouth) and we wanted towns that were just two or three hours away. There were some exceptions, like Bournemouth, Weston-super-Mare and the Isle of Wight – the latter eventually becoming our main destination. For a while these excursions had been dubbed 'pirate runs' to differentiate them from the so-called 'official runs' organised by the National Scooter Riders Association, but even that practice died out soon enough. In the end our town of choice was dictated by wherever Tony Class was hosting his Bank Holiday events.

By 1981 the organisation of these Bank Holiday weekends had been perfected and they were eagerly anticipated. Many young teenage kids were going away on their own for the first time.

Easter was first out of the traps and the destination was Brighton. Because of *Quadrophenia* and its historical connotations, the town seemed to embody what our weekend should actually be like and the film gave us a template of how we were supposed to behave. I rang a cheap B&B and booked myself a room. B&Bs at the turn of the Eighties were worse than basic, with nylon sheets, mouldy bathrooms, rubbish foam pillows and inedible breakfasts, but they gave you somewhere to park the scooter, wash, change and occasionally sleep.

I pulled into the Castle car park in Woodford at eleven on Good Friday morning.

We weren't due to leave till one, but there were already more than 20 scooters parked up along with a handful of cars. More bikes were pulling in all the time, in ones and twos and the occasional group of five or six. The pub opened and we sat drinking pints on the terrace, waiting for others to arrive.

We were buzzing, chatting to mates and drinking in the atmosphere. By the time the convoy pulled out of the car park, we numbered at least 50 scooters, many of them two's up, with almost a dozen cars following in our wake.

The ride through London was amazing. People stopped and stared at the procession, wondering what the hell it was all about. Who were these kids on their weird machines? Some waved while others hooted as we chugged past in a pulsating two-stroke train, always cruising at the speed of the slowest scooter.

Riding in a big convoy is an extraordinary thing. We felt unstoppable, as if we could do absolutely anything. The convoy was 100 yards long at times, with us travelling three abreast; there were so many of us we could remove our helmets, safe in the knowledge that our numbers would protect us from solitary traffic cops.

Other groups and clubs joined us as we made our progress to the West End; from Manor Park, Ilford, Bow, Bethnal Green and Hackney they came, and as we cruised along the Thames Embankment towards the Westminster tea bar our number had swollen to more than a hundred.

This is how every Bank Holiday started in 1981. Scooters from all over London would congregate locally and meet up at a tea bar just outside the Houses of Parliament.

Tea bars are a long forgotten thing now but were once a London institution. Scattered around the city and open all night, they provided a haven for clubbers, taxi drivers and late drinkers in search of sustenance on their way home. They looked like green painted garden sheds with a serving hatch, and appeared to have been dumped randomly onto the pavement with little or no strategic thought. We tended to patronise the one in Shoreditch and would often meet there for a 'cowboy' – an overloaded French stick stuffed with two burgers, a sausage, bacon, cheese and onions – on the way home from a club in the West End.

The Shoreditch tea bar was perched next to the toilets outside Hawksmoor's incredible neo-Byzantine church, by the Ten Bells pub. This was real Jack the Ripper territory and still a magnet for the brasses who touted their wares on the pavement all the way down the Commercial Road, just as they had in Jack's day. Most nights at around half eleven you'd see a handful of scooters parked up while their riders sipped hot tea, and inevitably there'd be the odd rows with the smacked-up or drunken streetwalkers waiting for custom in one of London's oldest and most established red-light districts.

In Rotherhithe with Terry Rawlings.

Wearing tweed trousers with velvet-lined
frogmouth pockets!

(Left to right) Me with Steve Jarvis, Tony 'Mappy' Matthews and Ray
Patriotic Margetson outside Right Track Records, Carnaby Street.

(Left to right) Paul Green, Steve Jarvis, me, Mick Tomlinson and Tony 'Mappy' Matthews, posing for the *Daily Mirror*, 1982.

Suited and booted with Jamie Rave. Note the cane-handled umbrella.

(Left to right) Tony 'Mappy' Matthews, me, Steve Jarvis and Ray *Patriotic* Margetson, posing for the *Daily Mirror* outside the Carnaby Cavern, 1982.

ANDY ORR

My suedehead period – the only time
I ever wore a bowler hat.

JEFF SHADBOLT

On Carnaby Street with the enemy!

Fast Eddie playing at the Regency Suite in Chadwell Heath.

The vibrancy of the mod revival is captured here, in London in 1982.

In the Regency Suite car park with my flatmate Bunny.
Note Steve Jarvis's 'skeleton-scooter' behind me.

Modelling Terry Rawlings' question-mark T-shirt on my Sportique.

The tea bar on the north side of Westminster Bridge was normally patronised by most London scooter clubs and was the main meeting point for scooter runs. It was perfectly placed for the Embankment, which then took us down to Lambeth, Stockwell and Brixton.

By 2 o'clock on Good Friday we were ready to leave for Brighton, helmets on and engines kick-started. The roar of 800 two-strokes spluttering into life was an extraordinary assault on the senses and the cacophony continued as we made our way along the Embankment. The sun was shining and it felt incredible to be a part of it; I'd never seen so many scooters in one place. Other riders from all over the south were joining the convoy as they caught us up.

Fifteen minutes later and we found ourselves in a different world.

Brixton.

There was an increasing edge to things and in the country at large a general dissatisfaction with *how things were* thanks to the Thatcher government and the police. A tense atmosphere and a general sense of expectation, as if something was going to happen. And of course, in Brixton something *had* happened, just a few days before we rode through it, when the area exploded in flames as the black community, long the focus of police oppression, had finally fought back.

Over 250 police and 50 members of the public had been injured on the first day alone. Thirty Brixton properties had been razed to the ground and fierce street battles raged, first in South London and then throughout the country as more inner-city areas joined the riots. While the genesis of the riots had been almost a week earlier, with the shooting of Cherry Groce in front of her child by a police officer, the youth were still out and the uprising was very much alive. People were still on the streets throwing things and the police were still armed with riot shields and batons.

This was the scene that greeted the scooters as we passed through Stockwell into Brixton on the A23.

The main road was blocked with metal barricades, but these were ignored as we rode around them and made our way through the middle of the riot-battered Brixton streets. The place looked like a dystopian wasteland or a war zone. Many of the rioters stopped and just stood still, amazed at the sight of the convoy. At the time there was a definite sense of solidarity among people who represented 'otherness' – those outside the normal, establishment world. And we were most certainly that. It was an incredible experience.

The roar of two-stroke engines was truly deafening. We waved and hooted as we passed through but we didn't stop, and five minutes later we were out the other side, open-mouthed at the sheer drama of the situation.

Brighton is a long way from Woodford and many of the scooters weren't up to the task. But people were incredibly organised. On that particular trip, I saw a complete Vespa engine changed by the side of the road in under an hour. A van pulled up and several people gathered round as the offending engine was removed, a suitable replacement chosen from a van and whacked on minutes later!

Most of us pulled into Brighton mid-afternoon. The local Old Bill were caught napping and had no idea that a few thousand mods would be rolling into town that Good Friday. They eventually threw up barricades but it was too late – by the time reinforcements arrived, most of us were already there.

People parked up, unloaded their scooters and made their way into The Lanes for a drink.

The atmosphere was tense. Almost as if we'd been affected by what we'd seen in Brixton. The police were certainly heavy-handed as they tried to clear the pubs, but there simply wasn't enough of them to make a difference. Most scooters were lined up on Madeira Drive and there must have been a couple of thousand of us spread throughout the town. The evening passed in good-natured drinking and catching up with mates.

Tony Class was hosting an event at the racecourse, slightly out of town, so by 8pm the kids with tickets had made their way down there, some of them using the golf course as an impromptu campsite. There may have been thousands of mods in Brighton, but only a lucky few had tickets and I was one of them. Classy had certainly shifted more towards northern soul by now and the place was packed with kids practising that crab-like shuffle that they'd seen the experts perform down at the 100 Club 6Ts all-nighters. It was a brilliantly atmospheric night with no trouble, and when the music finally stopped at about half past one, everyone retreated to their digs, tents or down onto the beach for a slightly chilly parka-clad night with some beers and a sleeping bag.

Saturday, though, was different.

By lunchtime two things became apparent. The first was that the police had brought in reinforcements from around the country to bolster their numbers and the second was that skinheads were pouring into town on trains. This changed the dynamic from something relatively happy to something that wasn't happy at all.

By late afternoon there were five or six hundred marauding skinheads in town and things were turning ugly. As it got dark, they congregated on the seafront and charged the young mods who were hanging around by the scooters. The police tried to keep the two sides apart, but things developed until there were mass brawls between mods and the Old Bill. They'd put up more barricades and tried to keep the mods corralled into a small area by the aquarium, but it hadn't worked. The skinheads melted away and soon it was a running battle between an undermanned constabulary and a rampaging gang of more than a thousand mods.

Police snatch squads were arresting whoever they could but there were far too many for custody, so they were simply removing people's shoelaces to limit their movement before releasing them back into the mayhem.

I sneaked away back to the B&B before I got lifted.

The next day broke bright and clear, but the police had decided to kick the mods out of town. Many were herded to special trains while scooter riders were harassed until they left. I kept my head down and after a Sunday roast in a small pub up the coast in Rottingdean I set off back to London on my own in the late afternoon.

It's odd but I often rode home on my own after a Bank Holiday. I think it's because it was faster, not waiting for others, and the only thing you can think of on a Bank Holiday Monday is your own bed.

On Tuesday, several of us met at the Castle in Woodford and without exception we were buzzing about the weekend. It seemed like the experience was the ultimate expression of being a mod, the pinnacle of everything we had done up to that point. Sure, we'd all been to Bank Holiday weekends before and some of us on scooters, but this was the first occasion there had been thousands of us on scooters, all descending on the same place. It instilled an incredible sense of camaraderie and excitement, especially that incredible journey of a thousand of us riding through riot-torn Brixton. From that point on we became more determined to live what we saw as the 'mod life' – completely apart from what was going on in the rest of society. In turn, this attitude fuelled a desire to dress better, find rarer and more authentic music and travel absolutely everywhere by scooter.

19

THE BRITISH WAY OF LIFE

was 17 and the mod lifestyle was costing me money – something I still didn't have anywhere near enough of.

I'd hooked up with a few lads from Eltham. Normally we avoided south of the river like the plague, but these lads were great. They also had a few nicknames: Rick the Kip (because he seemed permanently asleep), Steve Roadrunner (named after his fanzine), Nick the Comb (he sported the biggest back-comb I'd ever seen and never missed an opportunity to comb it in front of a mirror) and the remarkably normal-sounding Martin Hollylee. These new mates joined forces with a couple of other young mods from Gants Hill called Martin Smith and Andy Gilbert and, together with my original schoolfriends, we formed an enthusiastic gang of gig-goers who transcended the local boundaries and were united in both style and substance.

The fanzine, while still successful, wasn't making much cash. I definitely needed proper employment.

I'd had a number of part-time or temporary jobs since walking out of college but was still searching for that elusive music-industry career when bizarrely, and in the most coincidental manner, my luck changed.

In the summer of 1981, I was standing on the platform at Leicester Square after a Chords gig. I was sweating profusely because I'd been jumping about down the front, and wasn't in a great mood as the venue was far too crowded and I'd somehow been separated from my mates. Suddenly, standing next to me on the platform was another young mod. As you did in those days, we looked each other up and down and he nodded, so I said hello. His name was Mario and he was a second-generation Italian immigrant whose dad was a Soho tailor. He'd been at the gig too and was on his way home to Marylebone. Unbelievably, he told me that he worked in the Wardour Street labour exchange as a clerk . . .

'You what?'

This was indeed the opportunity Jackie Curbishley had briefed me about and I took it.

I asked him about West End record labels. Was he aware of them advertising jobs in his labour exchange?

He laughed at my keenness but I managed to convince him I was totally serious. Mario realised the commercial possibilities of helping me get a job and a slightly avaricious glint came into his eye.

Straight out I asked him if he could put me to the front of the queue when it came to record-label jobs. We settled on a fiver. I handed it over and scribbled down my phone number. He promised to call me if anything came up. I flew home, ecstatic.

A month later, I assumed it was a fiver wasted. I'd heard nothing.

I'd been reduced to digging a large cesspit in the garden for a snotty couple in Chigwell, which wasn't the most inspiring of jobs but paid well. One night I got home from work literally covered in shit and my mum said, 'Edward, some Italian boy phoned for you – Marco . . . Maurizzio . . . Mario? He left you a message, it's here somewhere . . . Ah yes, can you go and see him tomorrow lunchtime – The Ship at 1 o'clock.'

I bumped into Mario just as he stepped onto Wardour Street for his lunch break. Unbeknown to me The Ship was a go-to music-industry pub frequented by bands, producers, road crew and record men. We walked through the swing doors and stood by the bar.

'Right, Eddie, here's the card. I've hung onto it for a few days; haven't even put it out yet, so you're the only one who's seen it. A motorcycle messenger's job for an indie label called . . . erm . . .' He glanced down. 'Yeah, Avatar . . . They're off Trafalgar Square. You've got a scooter, haven't you? Good.' He told me under no circumstances could I let anyone know he'd done me a favour – he could get sacked and he needed the job.

I promised to stand him a pint at the next Chords gig. The mod network had come good.

I inspected the card. Sure enough. 'Office Junior/Motorcycle Messenger for an independent record label. Avatar Records, Pall Mall, SW1 . . .' It was 70 quid a week with petrol and expenses; no experience necessary but must have own transport.

I got home and called the number. The receptionist seemed surprised – apparently I was the first person to call about the job. Mario had been true to his word. Could I come in a few days hence for an interview?

I pulled up outside their office on the Lammy. It was on Pall Mall of all places, just opposite St James's Palace, with red-jacketed guardsmen sporting bearskins standing outside in sentry boxes. Proper posh.

I was shown upstairs and introduced myself to the girl at the front desk, a stunning Scandinavian blonde in her twenties called Ellen. I was sopping wet and the GP175 had been playing up, so I looked like a grumpy drowned rat. I took off my parka and sat down until I was called up another floor for the interview. I took a deep breath.

Seemingly unimpressed by my CV, the boss grunted, frowned and looked me up and down in silence. I reckoned he was in his mid-thirties; he was dressed in a white linen shirt, unbuttoned just low enough to reveal the glint of a gold medallion poking out from his matted chest hair. Oatmeal jumbo cords with a kick-out flare. I noted his chunky gold watch and expensive zip-up cream leather Chelsea boots with a geometric pattern stitched on the front. Attention to detail.

This was real late-Seventies Kings Road disco chic.

To be fair, he was charming, eloquent and . . . surprised, like the receptionist had been. Surprised enough to tell me how surprised he was that I was the only applicant. The job'd been advertised for almost a week now and I remained the sole respondent.

I looked at the three-quarter-length fur coat hanging on the hook behind him and wondered whether it was his.

Focusing on the task in hand, I gave the interview my best shot.

He did what all bosses do in interviews and asked what I knew about the company. This was where the mod world helped me again. Just a year earlier, Avatar had released a single by a local band and I knew all about them: they were Sta-Prest and were fronted by Dick York from Billericay. 'School Days' was the single and I remembered they were arrested for playing an impromptu gig in Covent Garden. I'd even seen the band live at the Red Lion in Leytonstone.

I needn't have worried – the fact I'd even heard of them was all it took to secure the job.

Jon Brewer, the super-cool medallion-wearing playboy MD – whose dad had apparently been Lord Mayor of London – asked me to start immediately.

It was also obvious that the only qualification I needed was a bike and the *London A–Z*.

Now here's the thing. If you genuinely want a career as a motorcycle messenger, try not to use a Lambretta. They are absolutely shit.

On the third day in my new job, I got a real taste of what it was going to be like as a mod bike messenger in London.

Robert Patterson, another of my bosses, handed me an envelope and asked me to deliver it to an address in Fulham. It was bulky, so I shoved it down the front of my parka, zipped myself up and set off on the scooter.

I was tootling slowly down the Fulham Palace Road when I heard a siren behind me. I stole a glance over my shoulder, wondering whose attention they were trying to attract.

Oh, bloody hell. It was mine!

I knew I hadn't done anything wrong, but by now the Old Bill were constantly hassling mods on scooters. I assumed it'd just be a standard five-day wonder (they'd recently reduced the time you had to present your documents by two days) and I'd only have to turn up at Woodford Old Bill shop to prove my identity. I pulled onto the pavement, parked up and slid off.

I immediately realised that this wasn't a normal stop.

'Up against the wall!' He'd obviously had a bad day and was looking for someone to take it out on.

'Erm . . . I'm just on a delivery for work, what's the problem, officer?'

'Your chain looks very much like an offensive weapon. Put your hands on the wall and spread your legs . . .'

The other copper ran my registration through the central computer via a walkie-talkie. Although they seemed a bit over the top, I wasn't worried because I was completely legal – that was the one thing Brewer had insisted on. By now two further police cars had turned up, like I was going try and escape.

They searched me, properly.

It didn't take long for the lippy traffic copper to pull the envelope from the folds of my jacket.

'Well, well, sonny. What's in the envelope?'

'No idea. I'm just delivering it to an address in Fulham . . .'

'So, what's in it?'

'I really don't know, officer . . .'

Here things took a turn for the worse.

'Constable, pass me that envelope.' This was spoken by a sergeant who'd just climbed out of the second car. He pulled open the flap and peered inside.

'OK, son, so you expect me to believe that you have . . . What? Say five grand in cash and you didn't even know you had it? If it isn't yours, then whose is it?'

By now I'm in panic mode. 'Erm, actually, I'm not really sure . . . My boss gave it to me and I'm just delivering it . . .'

I was read my rights and arrested for possession of an offensive weapon. I'd been nicked before, so I was aware of the drill and this time I managed to avoid saying 'trousers' when they asked the bit about taking anything down. I'd made the unfunny quip once before when I got pulled for jumping a red light in Shoreditch and it'd made the arresting officer very cross indeed. There's nothing rozzers like less than having the piss taken out of them by teenagers.

Aggressive copper: 'OK, what's your boss's name . . .? Where d'you work . . .? What's the company called . . .? Give me the number . . .'

Fuck. All I could eventually stutter was that 'my boss's name is Robert, erm . . . Robert something or other. The other one's called Jon . . . The address, erm, I'm not actually sure. It's right at the top of Pall Mall, near the palace, and the company . . . Yeah, I think that's called Avatar . . .'

I genuinely couldn't answer him, but at least I got the company name right.

By now I was in the back of the police car, three days into a new job without a clue of my firm's phone number, address or my bosses' names with five grand in used fivers stuffed in my bin . . .

The other copper called the station on his radio. I could tell they didn't believe me – why should they? I was in deep shit. They obviously thought I was on a drugs run. I mean, five grand was more than a year's wages.

The desk sergeant at the station was asked to phone Avatar to verify my story. I didn't know the number, so he had to get it off directory enquiries. The message came over the radio: 'Can't get through to anyone at his workplace. Bring him down and we'll book him on suspicion and for the offensive weapon . . .'

Twice more the police phoned my office and twice more Ellen left them on hold for five minutes.

Eventually, three hours after my arrest, the police let me go. Apparently my story checked out and as I'd produced a key to the padlock and stuck to the excuse that the chain was used to lock my scooter (if I hadn't had a key for padlock I'd have been guilty of the offensive-weapon charge). I had to get the bus back to where they'd left my Lambretta and eventually pulled up outside the office in Pall Mall at half four, somewhat shamefaced and with the undelivered envelope.

Ellen buzzed upstairs. 'He's back . . . Yeah, I'll send him up . . .'

I knocked and entered Robert Patterson's office. I hadn't even spoken to him properly before now. He held his hand out and I could tell that he didn't want to shake mine, so I handed over the envelope. Next, he gestured to a chair. I sat down. He was red in the face. It looked like steam was about to come out of his ears.

'What the flying fuck were you up to? Arrested in the street with an offensive weapon and five grand of our money. Are you some kind of fucking idiot? That's the last thing I need, the bloody police sniffing about. What the fuck happened?'

I ran through my defence, stressing that the 4-foot chain with the enormous padlock draped over my shoulder was genuinely used to lock up my bike and certainly wasn't a weapon. (This was an obvious lie; both he and the Old Bill knew that it *was* a weapon, but to be fair it was one I used in self-defence as we were always being attacked by skinheads.)

It transpired that when the police called Avatar's reception, Patterson refused to believe it wasn't a wind-up and wouldn't take the call. Eventually, Ellen insisted, so he picked up. He gave them short shrift and insisted they release his employee immediately. Apparently, the desk sergeant had the temerity to express the unsought opinion that it 'wasn't necessarily a good idea to entrust a teenager who'd only been working for him for three days and didn't even know the name or address of the company with enormous cash sums'. This just drove Robert Patterson towards actual apoplexy, most of which he took out on me. I obviously thought I was going to be sacked and after Patterson's bollocking (which ended with the phrase 'Now just fuck off . . .') I made my way back to the cubbyhole that had been assigned to me and started to clear my desk – or rather, the very small table that they had described as a desk.

'What d'you think you're doing?' asked a voice from behind me.

It was my other boss, Jon Brewer, the one who'd interviewed me a few days earlier. He was smiling quizzically.

'I'm packing up my stuff, I'm really sorry I let you down. Robert is really pissed off that I got the police involved in company business.'

I was gutted and carried on packing up my few belongings, assuming I'd been dismissed.

'Oh, don't be a prat. It gave me a right laugh. Don't worry about Robert; he'll be all right in the morning. Welcome aboard and I reckon there'll be far madder things than that going on. Now get yourself home and I'll see you in the morning.'

I'd secured that elusive job in the music industry at last.

By the middle of 1981 the destinations for Bank Holiday weekends seemed to be chosen by osmosis with no single group making a decision. There was always some debate as to where we were going, but in the end we tended to arrive at a general consensus and descended en masse on an unsuspecting seaside town. As long as there were pubs to go to things would be OK – in the early days we didn't have discos or gigs organised; it was just about being with other mods in a seaside town. Just like in *Quadrophenia*!

One scooter run in 1981 almost ended in disaster for me. We'd set off for Margate from the Castle on Friday afternoon as usual. We didn't bother driving into London and headed for the Blackwall Tunnel direct from Woodford. We'd phoned a B&B in advance and reserved a few rooms, which was normal practice. They cost less than 20 quid, and while two or three people might make the reservation, there would almost always be ten people to a room (unless of course there was a girl involved and then it would be a little more private). Sneaking out in the mornings was never particularly tricky either; it was just a bolt down the stairs two at a time, flick the Yale lock and out the door. If you were caught, you just feigned deafness and sprinted for the corner.

This particular weekend started badly, though. On Friday night I found myself a bit pissed in a pub called the Albion in the old town. The place was full of northerners along with a large contingent of the new scooterboys – basically, ex-mods who'd rejected the scene but couldn't quite let go of the scooters. On the whole we didn't mix with them but it was inevitable that we would often end up at the same places, especially on Bank Holidays.

Many scooterboys were psychobillies – but some were skins, some were into northern soul and on the whole they were united by their casual dislike of mods. They caused a lot of bad feeling that occasionally spilled over into violence, but we tried to keep them on side as we had enough trouble with skinheads.

Looking around I suddenly realised that everyone I'd come with had moved off to the next pub. The Albion was heaving, with entry-level northern soul blasting out of the speakers, and as I pushed my way through the crowd to the door I got a few slaps from behind. I thought it was about to get a lot worse, but suddenly I was out into the street and heading to the next pub, looking for the East London lot and feeling relieved that nothing too bad had happened.

The real trouble started the following night. I was staying in Trinity Square, just behind the police station, and had gone for a drink in the Rose in June next to the B&B and then made my way into the town proper. All the East London lads were out drinking, and as I walked through the old town I'd stumbled into a girl from South London who I'd been chatting to for the last month or so and had designs on. We were having a great time and at about 10 o'clock I put my arm round her and headed for the door. I nodded goodbye to the rest of the lads and set off up the hill to go somewhere quieter. We bought a bottle of wine and a few cans of lager on the way, but as we drew level with the Winter Gardens at the top of the hill a group of six skinheads walked around the corner. They were South London and knew her from the Tony Class pubs. It seemed they didn't like her being with one of the East London mods.

As they advanced, I pushed her behind me and immediately took a punch to the head.

She ran screaming and I shouted at the top of my voice: 'Come on then!'

It didn't last long. One of them grabbed the bag, the wine bottle hit me round the head and I went down. Soon they were all kicking me. I blacked out and apparently they picked me up, swinging me by the arms and legs over the wall into the small police station garden. I was out cold.

What I didn't know is that five East London mods were walking 50 yards behind me and had seen the attack develop. They came running up the hill screaming and took the skinheads while they were throwing me over the wall.

That was all I remember. I came round on the concrete floor in Margate police station with a copper telling me they were about to book me and dragging me to my feet. I signed a form and the arresting officer pushed me into another room and told me to sit.

After ten minutes he brought me a polystyrene cup of water but wouldn't answer any of my questions. Soon a pissed-off and tired-looking police doctor arrived and checked out my head wounds. He put in a couple of stitches and left. After photographing my head, the desk sergeant ushered me back to my cell and shut the door behind me. Why is it that cells in police stations always stink of piss?

Ten hours later I was shown into an interview room and in marched a couple of CID officers with a cup of tea. Good cop, bad cop. Textbook.

'Well, Edward, I am afraid you are in a substantial amount of trouble. You've been arrested for a serious crime and we've applied to extend the amount of time we can hold you in custody. Is there anything you'd like to tell us? It'll go easier on you if you cooperate. Would you like some food?'

'Well . . .' Remembering my father's advice, I asked for a lawyer.

They laughed.

'Of course you can have a lawyer. We've put in a call, but I'm afraid that it's a Sunday and the duty solicitor's office is rather busy with all your mod and skinhead friends. In the meantime, can we just go through what you did last night?'

I told them I was hungry and would talk if they got me something to eat.

Half an hour later, a takeaway Wimpy arrived and I decided to at least tell the police what had happened. For fuck's sake, I had been brutally assaulted and dumped unconscious in a front garden – in *their* front garden.

When I finished eating the two coppers came back into the room.

'Well, Edward, we're going to charge you with attempted murder and I'm sure you realise that this is a very serious offence. Would you like to make a statement? I'm sure we can clear this up . . .'

Attempted fucking murder? What'd happened?

'I want a brief.'

A duty solicitor arrived and I had no memory of being charged but must have signed the charge sheet at some stage. I was left alone in a cell all night apart from a brief check from the doctor. I had no real memory of the assault, nor even the arrest. The girl (my only witness) had obviously made her way back to London with her mates that morning. That meant I had no one to tell them what really happened. I was in deep shit.

Gradually the story came out. The two detectives were skilful and did their best to interrogate me, but I was still in shock and was slowly coming to terms with my situation. The solicitor talked me through my statement. The police were trying to dictate it but I was expected to write it in my own hand. I declined and the lawyer helped me do it a while later.

It transpired that while I was being beaten with a blunt instrument and knocked unconscious by at least five skinheads, a group of mods ('youths unknown') ran up the hill and came to my rescue. In the ensuing melee one of the South London skins was stabbed in the neck. I, however, was unconscious and covered in blood and knew nothing about this. By the time the police made it to the crime scene (5 yards from the front door of the station), everyone had disappeared apart from the skinhead with the knife in his neck and me. He'd been raced to hospital in an ambulance and I'd been dragged into the station and arrested. They assumed I'd stabbed him and they were now going to prove it.

I'd been wearing a white Levi's jacket, which was now covered in blood; the CID assumed that the blood belonged to the victim, so they took it away. Things seemed to progress incredibly slowly and I spent a lot of time reading the dog-eared copy of the Bible that'd been left in the cell. It was, after all, a Bank Holiday and the police were short-handed while trying to cope with hundreds of kids beating the shit out of each other.

I was locked down for a second night and eventually the duty solicitor came to see me again.

'I've got some good news. Someone came forward to confirm your version of events. The witness – who is incidentally someone who claims not to know you – has made a statement. The fingerprints on the knife handle aren't yours. The police have dropped the charges and you're free to go. If I were you, I'd steer clear of Margate for a while . . .'

I thanked him and left.

At the B&B the landlady had put my stuff into a bag with my crash helmet and stored it behind the little hatch where she spent most of her day. I picked it up, waved goodbye and walked back to the seafront to get my Lambretta.

There's nothing more depressing than an English seaside town on a Bank Holiday Tuesday. Everyone has left for home and the place is exposed for the shithole that it really is. And it's invariably raining. Always fucking raining. Things have improved somewhat in the last 40 years, but in the early Eighties every single seaside town I went to was in need of some serious attention.

The Lambretta was still where I'd left it, so I made my way back to London and the real world. I felt like Jimmy Cooper when he turns up at the agency a day late and gets the sack.

20

NITE KLUB

There was an excited buzz doing the rounds of the Essex mods. There was going to be a mod alldayer at the Ilford Palais! This was a prewar ballroom with a capacity of around 2,000 and a wonderful sprung dance floor. I'd been visiting the place for a few years with my Woodford soulboy mates for jazz-funk at the weekends and loved the venue, which had even hosted a mod night with Martha & the Vandellas a couple of months earlier. It had been promoted by Andy Ruw and almost a thousand people had turned up on a Thursday night. This had given him the idea to put on a Sunday alldayer at the same venue.

When the event came round on 16 August 1981, we were surprised by the number of people who turned up. The place wasn't sold out by any means, but the crowd was bigger than expected with people travelling from all over the country.

The bands on the bill were great and typical of the time. Small World were by far the biggest and they were supported by Distant Echo and The Heads. Trouble was, our music taste was changing. Dick Coombes had begun his 60s Rhythm & Soul Society residency (distinct from Ady Croasdell's 6Ts setup) at the Electric Stadium in Seven Kings, which had been one of the last great live mod pubs of the first wave. Coombes was playing out-and-out northern soul and by now this had had a huge impact on our scene and our tastes.

The event was OK, but we felt it hadn't really been good enough.

A chance conversation at a Keb Darge night in the Albany a week or so later between myself, the editor of *Patriotic* fanzine, Ray Margetson, Tony 'Mappy' Matthews from Walthamstow and Dean Port from Hainault prompted us to try and rent the Palais and do an alldayer ourselves. Ruw was a promoter who'd championed the early mod revival at the Crystal Palace Hotel and on Hastings Pier, but we had two issues with him: first, that he was an outsider (at least to us he was); and second, that he was old enough to be my dad. Oh, and he went by the DJ name of Mr Bear! He just wasn't cool.

Trouble was, the Palais was owned by Top Rank and in order to rent it we had to sign a legal contract. None of us were over 18, so a contract wouldn't have been valid. I had to persuade my dad to sign it for me. He laughed and said he'd love to help and would even come down on the day to keep an eye out. Apparently he had been a Palais regular and had fond memories of it in the Sixties.

Well, actually, he later told me that the memories weren't that fond . . . As a bit of a man about town, East London bookmaker, friend of both Bobby Moore and the British Heavyweight Champion Billy Walker (who'd owned the East End mod club the Upper Cut) in the mid-Sixties, my dad had been invited to the Palais by its then manager to discuss a mutually beneficial proposal. When Dad arrived he was shown to a table and asked to wait. He smoked a cigar and eventually the blond-haired, flamboyantly dressed manager came over, introduced himself and invited my dad to his office, located in the bowels of the club.

My dad followed, was led down some stairs and walked through a boiler room. As the manager pushed open the door to the next room, Dad couldn't help but notice two men who were gagged, stripped to their underwear and hanging from a pipe on the wall. Their hands were taped together.

'What's going on here?' he asked the man.

'Oh, don't worry about them. They've been naughty boys; I'm just teaching them a lesson.'

The casual way in which this was dropped, as if it was the most normal thing in the whole world, made my old man decide to have nothing to do with the manager or his proposal, whatever it might be. It was one of the first pieces of club-related advice that my dad gave me back in 1981: 'Son, never have anything to do with Jimmy Savile; he's a bad man . . .'

We chose the promotions name of M.I.N.D. (for 'mod is not dead'!). It seems extraordinarily cheesy now, but was based on the fact that the whole existence of mod was under attack from all sides: philosophically, in the music press, but also physically, from most of the other youth tribes around at the time. I think we saw the name as an act of defiance.

The idea had started because, at the heady age of 17, we'd decided that we'd had enough of 40-year-old promoters telling us what to like. Darryl Hayden was the worst and his nights often advertised 'topless dancers' as well as the usual bands alongside regular DJs like Keith Hurdle. Now, it may be true that pubs in the late Seventies, especially pubs in the East End, often featured strippers (who would trawl the floor with a dimpled pint glass after their performance, hoping to raise tips), but it simply wasn't appropriate entertainment for teenage mods, and to be honest, it grated somewhat. Things had to change and we decided that we would be the ones to change them.

We simply nicked Ruw's format and did it ourselves. We booked the date in September 1981 to hold the event early the following year.

Andy Ruw was apoplectic. He was pissed off that we'd arranged one of our own events in what he considered to be 'his' venue – you can see that from his point of view – but to our 17-year-old selves, we never thought we were treading on his toes; we simply saw it as taking back something that belonged to us.

As if to warn us off, he managed to squeeze in a second alldayer before ours, this time featuring the Purple Hearts.

We had four months to tell people about our gig, so stuck adverts in fanzines and, more importantly, bombarded Carnaby Street with flyers (the design of which we pilfered from Andy Ruw's, which was another reason he was so cross with us).

The event was scheduled for the beginning of February 1982, and as the date drew closer I began to panic. The venue held close to 2,000 punters and none of the four of us had ever tried anything like it before. What with the venue and PA hire, the security, bands and DJs and advertising costs, we could lose a lot of money.

I was encouraged by the fact that we'd received a few requests for bulk tickets from the regions for coach trips as well as a number of postal applications to *Extraordinary Sensations* and *Patriotic*. With just a week to go, I realised that we might just pull it off.

We arrived at the cavernous Palais at 9am to prepare for the doors to open at 2 o'clock. We'd arranged for half a dozen stalls selling everything from fanzines and patches to records and even a home-made mod-girl clothes stall called Ramones (run by the aforementioned Simone Lynch) that sold shift dresses alongside hand-knitted jumpers featuring the logo of the all-girl three-piece band Dolly Mixture, who we all loved. We set the stalls up around the edges of the dance floor, listened to the bands performing their sound checks and waited nervously to see what would happen.

We needn't have worried. By midday the first of the scooters began to pull into the enormous car park and by the time the doors opened there were at least 500 young mods massing outside the glass-fronted dancehall. We'd sold less than half the tickets in advance, but by half three the rest had gone to walk-ups . . .

Our Ilford Palais alldayers were phenomenally successful. The first one we put on made me realise that I might be able to make a living from this lark – from promoting mod, I mean.

Because my dad had volunteered to sign the rental contract, he also volunteered to come down on the day and keep an eye on things. After all, the prospect of 2,000 kids all paying £4 a ticket meant that we just might have bitten off more than we could chew.

There was one unforeseen problem with the Palais and that was the door.

The security at the venue was run by a cartel that included the legendary bare-knuckle boxer Lenny McLean. I'd been warned we should expect some trouble from the bouncers who would probably try to squeeze us. These men were serious gangster-type players and had an interest in most of the local club doors.

I was worried that as a group of enthusiastic teenagers we were well out of our league, but it turned out that McLean knew my dad and his team ended up being very respectful when they saw the old man standing by the entrance in a tux and bow tie. It was a weight off my shoulders. We gave the bouncers a bonus and I was pleased to do it.

It's difficult explaining what the Ilford alldayers achieved for our scene. Somehow we managed to galvanise the second wave of the revival and nationally bring mod kids together in a shared experience. We booked most of the bands that were still around and even persuaded a couple of them to get back together. For almost three years M.I.N.D. ran the most important and successful mod event in the country and the gigs developed an almost legendary reputation.

Our success led to us considering what other events we could turn our hand to.

*

By now I was starting to take *Extraordinary Sensations* more seriously. Some of the early issues had been rubbish and instantly forgettable, but I thought I'd try to secure some proper interviews with real mod bands, proper reviews and stuff.

Beautiful Paula from Wembley and her sister Tina came up with a wonderful zine called *Own Up Time*, while Vaughn Toulouse had been pushing me towards making more of mine. Of course, *ES* wasn't alone – in fact, dozens of new fanzines had been popping up all over the shop to replace *Maximum Speed* and *Get Up & Go!*.

Martin Dixon's *Northern Mod Scene*, Steve Whiffen's *Roadrunner*, Ray Margetson's *Patriotic*, Chris Hunt's *Shadows and Reflections* and Derek Shepherd's *In the Crowd* were the new kids on the block, but Dom Kenny and Mike Jones's *Shake*, Tony Fletcher's *Jamming!*, Bernadine Wood and Jackie Topham's *Go Go*, plus *Direction Reaction Creation*, *XL5* and *The Right Track* meant the market was increasingly crowded.

If I wanted *Extraordinary Sensations* to stand out, I had to up my game. I decided to interview my favourite live band.

I'd been to a couple of Long Tall Shorty's midweek residencies at the Marquee and after each show I'd hung around by the stage waiting for a chance to speak to them. I loved LTS for the music; they'd changed from hammering hard and fast punk-influenced songs like '1970's Boy' into an up-tempo mod R&B band complete with vocalist Keith Mono's excellent harmonica playing. They dressed well too and guitarists Tony Perfect and Stewart England could often be seen sporting the extremely fashionable three-button leather jacket.

Trouble was, the band completely blanked me. After the band's third Tuesday show I again stood patiently by the backstage door waiting for a chance to interview their founder, Tony Perfect. And this is where the concept of perspective comes into play . . .

I remember it as follows: Perfect comes to the dressing-room door, enthusiastically answers my half-dozen questions and waits patiently while I take notes. The interview ends and he gives me a cassette copy of the band's recent demo, recorded for Jimmy Pursey's new mod label. I'm ecstatic and take some pics of Tony and the band to accompany the interview.

Perfect remembered it like this: Long Tall Shorty's manager Jerry Floyd walks into the Marquee dressing room and says, 'Fuck me, Tony, that annoying mod kid is here again asking for an interview. That's three weeks on the trot. If you don't at least talk to him and tell him to fuck off, he'll be back next week . . .' Tony Perfect reluctantly leaves the dressing room to talk to me, finds a tape in his pocket and hands it over, hoping it will hasten my exit so that he can get changed out of his sweaty clothes.

See. It's all about perspective. The interview with Tony Perfect led to a lifelong friendship that far transcended the mod scene, but from little acorns . . . I like to think that rather than slipping me the cassette as a way of getting rid of me, he gave it to me because he might just have seen something in my enthusiasm. A passion for both the band and our shared scene. Tony was an inspiration for so many years. He kick-started my creative journey.

A few weeks later I set my sights higher. I blagged a number for Bob Manton from the Purple Hearts – after all, I'd named my fanzine after one of his songs, so how could he possibly object? Unsurprisingly, he didn't and I spent a day in Romford talking him through his amazing band's career.

Manton was followed by my (virtual) godfather, Steve Marriott, and from there, well, the world was my oyster . . .

Marriott was fascinating. At this point in his life he seemed to be at absolute rock bottom. I'd kept in touch since Terry Rawlings had reintroduced me at the Bridge House. Marriott again joked that he assumed Ronnie Lane was my dad and gave me three hours of his time in a small Essex village pub garden. He was humble, erudite and witty, everything I thought he would be. I transcribed the cassette and split the interview into two, to be published across a couple of issues. The trouble with fanzines is that they often take quite a few months to prepare . . . Here, the inevitable happened and soon after publishing part one I lost both the tape and the transcript. I could tell I was going to need to become more disciplined and organised if I was going to continue. Oh, and to my eternal shame, I realised after publication I'd misspelled Marriott on the front cover, using just one *t*. Idiot.

Then I went for the big one.

I knew that Paul Weller was brilliant to his fans. Mod mates like Gary Crowley (who'd made his name as a young cockney mod television presenter with *White Light*). Shane MacGowan, The Nips' vocalist who worked in a Hanway Street record shop, and Vaughn and Tony from Guns for Hire were constantly singing his praises. I mean, he'd even written me a personal letter explaining the intricacies of 'English Rose'.

I wondered how I should I go about it. Maybe approach him at a sound check? Write to his sister at the fan club? Ask Crowley for an intro? Nervously hustle his dad?

Me and Simone Lynch from Chigwell had been renting her dad's coach to take the pair of us and 50 of our mates to Jam gigs all over the UK and Europe. A year or so earlier the Woodford mods had made it to Paris to see the band and just two weeks later our coach turned up at the Paradiso in Amsterdam, where Rick Buckler got on board to thank us for making the effort. Our average age was still 17, but because Simone's dad was chaperoning us all the way to Holland our parents seemed OK with it. Maybe Rick could introduce me? I'd managed to blag his number as he handed me a signed drumstick!

In the end, securing the interview was much simpler than that. My fellow fanzine editor Ray Margetson, who ran *Patriotic*, had somehow got Paul's number and just phoned him up. His mum Ann answered the phone.

Although Weller was halfway through recording the new Jam album, he invited us to the studio for the day where we could interview him at our leisure. The end result would be published in both our fanzines.

Oh my god, we were going to interview Paul Weller!

Me and Ray met at Hyde Park Corner and made our way to the newly christened Solid Bond studio. I was absolutely terrified. I remember trying to make a sartorial effort, although I've no idea what I was wearing. I do remember that we spent ten minutes in the studio reception until we were shown into the control room. Paul was incredibly welcoming and friendly, but his mate turned his nose up at us.

'Oh, for fuck's sake, not *more* bloody mods? I dunno why you put up with them . . .' he said, and stomped out of the studio.

That was the bloody point. It was the whole bloody point. We *were* mods. That's why Paul had given us the interview!

With his casual dismissal of Ray and me, Paul's journalist mate had completely misunderstood Weller's motivation for asking us to come to the studio, and with it, Paul's entire existential being.

Paul Weller had *specifically* given us time *because* we were mods and it didn't matter that we were just 16 or 17. During this particular period he'd so deeply embraced the 'philosophy' of the mod way of life that he was keen to understand what others had taken from the same set of ideals. It genuinely didn't matter how the pair of us had interpreted the shared philosophy; all that mattered was that we had. This is the main reason that (in my view) his journalist friend never really understood him, although I suspect that he *thought* he did. Paul Weller has lived a mod life since his teens and I genuinely believe that most people have struggled to understand him because of it. 'Normal' people fail to appreciate the totality of the philosophy's overwhelming influence on *us*. Every single decision Weller makes is taken from that specific perspective, from the books he reads or the colour of the socks he wears to the cut of a random collar on any one of his shirts or jackets. That's what gets Paul Weller up in the morning.

Our interview flashed past in a moment. Neither of us were experienced in the art of asking questions and I still regard our time together as a wasted opportunity: we didn't elicit much more than could have been gleaned by reading the *NME*! Weirdly, the key thing I remember about the day was that Paul sent me down to the McDonald's in Marble Arch with some odd instructions – he'd thrust a pound note into my hand, asking for 'a Big Mac without the meat'. What the fuck was that? I'd never been to McDonald's before and the staff laughed in my face, explaining that Paul was pretty much asking for a cheese sandwich!

In the end, I used Weller's responses in a number of articles I published in *Extraordinary Sensations*, while Ray plumped for the more traditional word-for-word, question-and-answer approach. Thing was, I'd already tried that a number of times with the likes of Dolly Mixture, LTS, and Bob Manton from the Purple Hearts and I'd never been satisfied with the result – especially with the one-liner nature of some of the replies.

The Weller articles and front covers certainly led to an expansion in sales and I found that not only were the wholesale numbers increasing but also, at pubs and clubs like the Mildmay Tavern and the Phoenix, people would approach me for a copy as soon as I walked through the door. This led to a somewhat blasé attitude on my part, and I found it helped to delegate pub and club sales to some of my female mates. Girls could approach strangers in a much more neutral way; and even Kathy Burke, a regular at the Mildmay in Dalston, occasionally lent a hand.

All told, the people, the printing, the slightly different way of crafting the writing and the addition of some proper articles made it come together. And somehow, I found myself with the bestselling fanzine on the scene.

*

Unfortunately, we were running out of pubs who would host us!

Although we still used the Castle and the Horse & Well in Woodford, once we began mixing with the East London mods the Seagull cafe in Ilford and the Foresters pub in Stratford became two of our main non-gig meeting places.

But as with most of our hangouts, they didn't last long because we were always getting kicked out. In the case of the Seagull, the owners had long displayed a much-loved poster of Elvis Presley, which was mocked by us mods. Eventually, Steve Collett burned The King's eyes out with a cigarette, poked a hole in his mouth and stuck a lit fag in it. The Cypriots who owned the cafe weren't impressed and mods were instantly banned. For life!

The Foresters Arms was a worn-out boozer on a residential backstreet off the Stratford one-way system where scooter riders met midweek.

Like many East End pubs in the early Eighties, the Foresters was always empty except for a handful of broken-down old men dressed in grubby threadbare tweeds, nursing pints of bitter and staring emptily at their copies of the *Racing Post*.

Initially, the landlord was thrilled that the local mods had moved in, but as word spread, more and more scooters turned up – which meant more noise and an increase in complaints from the neighbours. The guvnor seemed happy enough for a while – in just six months of our patronage, he'd gone from driving a battered old Escort to taking delivery of a new Daimler Sovereign coupé – but I suspect that as things got louder for the neighbours he'd had enough of the hassle.

The final straw was when all of the pub's beer towels disappeared overnight. The landlord couldn't work out what'd happened until the following week when everyone turned up with the missing towels stitched onto their parkas.

Having been kicked out of the Foresters, we soon switched to another Stratford pub, the Chatsworth. By now the East London and Essex mods could easily round up 30 or 40 scooters to a midweek pub night. It seemed like our patronage was worth something after all.

Just six weeks later, the grieving Foresters landlord sent a message asking us to come back, presumably because he was missing the income we brought to his otherwise empty pub.

He was rebuffed because we were comfortable in our new home at the Chatsworth Arms, but once Mick Hanrahan rode his Lambretta through the public bar we got banned from there too.

We were trying to persuade landlords to let us play our own tapes at our meets, but for some reason our nights never seemed to last very long. They were often orchestrated by 'Big' Bob Morris from Forest Gate, who had an early obsession with R&B. The Three Pigeons in Forest Gate went for a burton when Bunny turned up in full combat gear wearing an eyes-only balaclava, pretending to rob the woman on the door in an Irish accent while pointing a very convincing AK47 replica at her head . . . The Sebright Arms off the Bethnal Green Road lasted only two weeks thanks to some argy-bargy with local skins. It was a common theme . . .

There was a pattern forming; word spread on the landlord grapevine and we eventually ran out of East End pubs who'd let us in. Although it went against our natural East End prejudices, we had to take the plunge and head south of the river or nip 20 minutes up the Mile End Road to the West End for one of Tony Class's pubs . . . or a Saturday-afternoon trip to Carnaby Street.

It was around this time that my parents split up. It happened virtually overnight and me and my sister had no warning at all. I came back from college to find much of the furniture and pictures gone from our house, and mum and dad sat us down to tell us the news. With the exception of my dad, the Pillers didn't have much to do with us after that, although my dad's sisters Pam and Angie, and Pam's husband Peter Daltrey (no relation), certainly kept in touch from Jersey and Portugal respectively.

CLEAN LIVING UNDER DIFFICULT CIRCUMSTANCES

A year later my mum met a man from Chester called John Mortimer while she was on holiday in Ibiza. He became our de facto stepdad for the next 35 years and, back in those days, worked on the North Sea oil rigs. He was about as far away from being a cockney bookmaker as it was possible to be.

21

CARNABY STREET
(NOT WHAT IT USED TO BE)

By 1982, every Saturday would see hundreds of mods heading for Carnaby Street to pick up the latest records and fanzines. Jimmy at Robot had been very supportive of the fanzine. From Issue 4, published at the end of 1980, he'd been taking decent numbers of *Extraordinary Sensations* and soon became my major stockist.

The last piece of the Carnaby Street puzzle was the need for a proper secondhand mod record shop. While Robot concentrated on clothes and fanzines, Jimmy had never been able to source a reliable supplier for Sixties and northern soul (apart from a handful of bootlegs) and so eventually that was taken care of by a scooter-riding Woodford mod Terry Stokes and his wife Belinda. Called Right Track (the same name as Jim Watson and Garry Moore's Ilford fanzine), it was also on the mezzanine at the top of the spiral staircase, just 10 yards from Robot.

The mods flooding Carnaby Street would not just be Londoners but keen young out-of-towners too. These regional day-trippers were often in their early teens, thrilled to be allowed into London for their big day out with their schoolmates. We would often ride up there on scooters too, to shop or hang around in one of the many pubs we frequented.

This dramatic increase in perambulating mods brought its own problems. Well actually, just the one.

The trouble with Carnaby Street was skinheads.

Robot and Right Track were the worst affected. They were off the beaten track in an area never patrolled by the Old Bill, which meant that skins could operate with impunity. Congregating at the top of the spiral staircase, they waited for ones and twos to walk unsuspectingly into an ambush – the younger the better. They tended to ignore the bigger or older groups of mods and go for more easy pickings.

The skinhead approach was always the same: 'Got a spare 10 pence?'

It didn't matter what the answer was: the demand was usually followed by a punch to the head as the skins robbed the kids of their pocket money.

This was becoming a serious problem and we soon realised we'd probably have to deal with it ourselves. On a number of occasions some of the East London and Essex mods turned up mob-handed on scooters, parked up in Great Marlborough Street and combed the area looking for the muggers. Somehow, we never quite managed to get the whole lot of them at the same time.

There were always a few knocking about, but as soon as they saw the scooters they seemed to melt back into the maze of Soho back alleys round Broadwick, Poland or Berwick Streets and the John Snow pub. This made shopping in Carnaby Street a risky business, especially for the younger mods.

Like it or not, our world was becoming increasingly coloured by violence. This wasn't exclusive to mods; it seemed a societal thing and there was no doubt that the increase in Oi! and skinhead culture was what was fuelling it. But there were now casuals too, bringing their hooligan violence to the streets in seemingly random ways.

Things took a horrendous turn for the worse one particular Saturday in 1982, at Tony Class's highly successful night at the Phoenix on Cavendish Square in the West End.

That morning, I'd collected my silver tonic mohair suit from Steve Starr. I'd been planning the cut for a couple of months, regularly putting money aside until I could pay off the balance. When I collected it, my heart leaped with the joy that only comes from taking possession of something of great beauty. It was exactly as I'd wanted it: red silk lining, a 5-inch centre vent, 15-inch bottoms with a tailored V on both sides of the seam (allowing the trousers to sit an inch or so lower on the shoe); there was a slight butterflying to the cuffs, which had three working buttons, plus a carnation buttonhole on the left lapel and a set of three silver-covered buttons.

By this time Class had added the thrusting young R&B mod DJ Toski to his line-up and it worked: numbers were up and the Phoenix became the top club to meet girls. I was in the toilet, applying the eyeliner I was experimentally using for the first time. I'd picked up an appalling VHS copy of a copy of a copy of Kubrick's banned movie, *A Clockwork Orange*, and was deep into my Alex/Droog period. It was only the left eye, by the way, and no, it wasn't something I bothered with again. It became apparent that I was allergic to eyeliner and it looked, well . . . stupid!

I heard a commotion just outside the toilet door and I ran out to see what was going on.

The toilets at the Phoenix were at the bottom of the stairs, and the noise of the music and the overwhelming smell of cigarette smoke hit me as I took stock of the situation. But what had actually happened? I could see nothing out of the ordinary.

Tony Sims from Cheshunt was standing halfway up the stairs talking to a couple of girls, so I walked up to him. I remember he was wearing a lovely dark-blue suit with a similar cut to mine.

'What's going on, mate?'

'Dunno, a group of 15 blokes pushed past me and ran downstairs. I think they were casuals.'

A few seconds later, the same lads came running back upstairs. They were indeed casuals and were in a hurry. We were still confused as to what they wanted, but as one drew level he punched Simsy to the side of his face. He didn't stop, just kept on running. I turned to run after them, but as I did, I caught sight of Simsy's face and froze. *Fuck.* The lad hadn't punched him, he'd cut him. And it looked bad.

Simsy's face exploded. Cut from the side of his cheek to just below the eye. The girls were screaming but the music was still pounding.

Tony hadn't felt the knife and didn't realise he'd been slashed. He immediately made to chase after his attackers, but as he drew level with the door, a bouncer gently grabbed him and pushed him back inside.

What the fuck could we do? This was in the days before hand-dryers, and I remembered there was one of those towel-roll dispensers in the toilets. I went and wrenched it off the wall and ran back, thrusting the roll into one of the girl's hands, shouting at her to keep pressure on the wound. A few mods worked out what had happened and were piling up the stairs after them. I followed and sure enough there they were, 100 yards away running towards Oxford Street. I was soon sprinting as fast as I could. Unfortunately, I was wearing a new pair of loafers and their lack of grip meant that my pounding legs couldn't keep up with the rest of my body. I went down like a sack of potatoes, landing on my left knee, and skidded along the road, destroying my new trousers. I got up and limped in the direction of everyone else, but by then it was too late. The lads jumped into some waiting cars and disappeared.

I got back to find the club in chaos. The music was off, lights were on and the crowd were either streaming up the stairs or waiting to grab their coats from the cloakroom. Tony Class's sister Janet had been running the door (as was her custom) and had called an ambulance. The manager rang the Old Bill, who arrived in minutes and started casting around for witnesses.

Simsy was whisked off to A&E. He was in a state and once they'd finished he'd received 30-odd stitches. We still had no idea what happened, who the blokes were or what the attack was about. I was told later they'd been looking for someone particular, but whoever it was, he wasn't in the club. The guy who'd flicked out the blade as he ran up the stairs had done so at random, probably giving it no thought. He might even have laughed as he jumped into the car, adrenaline surging. But that simple, throwaway act of bravado had enormous consequences for Tony Sims. Serious consequences.

It was about now that I realised I was beginning to question the whole idea of mod. The scene had been my life for the last three years, but I felt that the whole concept of mod was slipping away in a sea of violence. Yes, life in the early Eighties was fraught with danger, but it seemed that every single time we ventured out now something awful would happen.

By 1982, our area had divided into territories: Woodford, Chigwell, Chingford and Loughton were exclusively mod; Buckhurst Hill, Priory Court, Debden and Harlow were skinhead; Epping, Hainault and Wanstead were mixed; and Gants Hill, Ilford and Romford were mainly soulboy. To add to this patchwork of confusion, there were isolated pockets of different youth cults in every suburb. Fuck, life was hard in those days. It seemed that the violence that had begun at football matches in the early Seventies had subsumed entire swathes of working-class society. Whereas youth culture had once been a fun and exciting way to transition into adulthood, it had now changed to the point where it seemed to be all about violence.

Being chased by skinheads or chasing them in revenge in cars and on scooters was a regular occurrence from early 1980 and carried on for three or four years. It meant that we had to stop going to certain places or seeing certain bands and always had to keep a wary eye out for ambushes. Stations were the most popular place for attacks, but really it could happen anywhere.

Things were pretty shit in gig land and getting worse.

It couldn't get any worse than having your friends murdered. Things came home to me pretty sharply after that. Who could have thought that our cultural journey – something that was supposed to be fun, an easy path from teenage years to adulthood – could actually end in death? What the fuck was that about?

Sadly, a number of mods were killed during that period, but I'm only going to talk about the two that affected me most.

Andrew Burgess, otherwise known as Budge, was a young mod from the 'safe' part of Chingford. When I say safe, I mean the mod part, not the bits where the skinheads lived, which tended to be Chingford Mount and Priory Court. Budge was the same age as me and, like most of the others from Chingford, soon integrated into the ever-growing, loosely affiliated group of us who'd meet at Woodford's Castle pub to socialise or ride into London.

By this time Tony Class was promoting at least four or five nights a week, and while we couldn't go to all of them, people would gather at the pub, waiting for others who were going to a particular club, and ride up in a group. There were a couple of lovely girls from Chingford who I'd made friends with and one of them, Lynn Evans, gradually introduced us to more of her mates.

On this particular evening, only a handful of scooters made the trip into town. The gig was a DJ-only night in a famous boxing pub called the Thomas A' Becket on the Old Kent Road. While I don't have a problem with Southeast London (although some of the East London did), the Becket was never one of my favourite places. It was a rough pub in a tough area, full of real faces, and had once been Henry Cooper's training base. The place achieved legendary mod status when it was used as the location for the boxing scene in *Quadrophenia*.

In the film, the lads go to buy some blues from the (real-life) gangster John Bindon (playing himself), who instead sells them an enormous bag of paraffin fakes. As revenge they decide on the spur of the moment to 'do the bastard's motor' and smash up his lovely Mark 2 Jaguar in the car park.

Back in the early Eighties I certainly felt out of place, in both the Thomas A' Becket and Bermondsey in general. The mantra had been drummed into me by my dad as soon as I could walk: 'Son, never go south of the water.'

This was a view commonly held by East Enders, often repeated while I was growing up. I assumed it was something to do with postwar criminal gang rivalry but could never be sure. This didn't mean that I never went south of the Thames; it just meant that I went there less often.

It was Tuesday 30 September 1980 and I didn't go to the Becket on this particular night, but in so many ways it was a night like any other, and I'd certainly made the trip there from the Castle on a number of occasions. Budge was actually a pillion passenger on his mate Tim Boyle's Lambretta, having blagged a ride in place of Spike Hull, another local and a DJ at the Mildmay in Dalston. Spike's own scooter was off the road and he'd been hoping to jump on the back of Tim's, but Budge beat him to it. It's important that I get this right, so Tim takes up the story in his own words:

> I was late to the pub, and even though Spike was keen to jump on the back, Budge had been my best mate since school and, as I'd passed my test the previous day, I was now legal taking a passenger, so I offered him the ride. I knew the way to the Becket as my dad was from the Old Kent Road and I was always visiting my grandparents. My mum was

from East London, so when they were courting they used to meet at the Rotherhithe Tunnel as she would never cross the river!

The Becket was rammed for a Tuesday, faces from all over London and almost 20 scooters outside. Tony was playing a typical late-1980 set with 'There's a Ghost in My House' and 'Wade in the Water', but I noticed the locals were paying a bit too much attention to the parked-up scooters, so I kept popping out to keep an eye on them. At one point a kid walked over and warned me that a mod had been chased away from the pub and that a few scooters had set off towards the Elephant so as to avoid any trouble. I told Tony Class and as the night was winding down he announced that there might be trouble on the usual routes home and asked people to be very careful.

As we were leaving, I darted back into the pub for a quick pee. When I got out, I saw a group of scooters heading down Albany Road, but there was no sign of Budge. For some reason he was across the road standing outside Burgess Park (strange, as his name was Andrew Burgess), so I grabbed him and we set off to catch the others. I wish I'd waited for the next lot.

We'd raced half a mile up Albany in pursuit, but too late I noticed a gang of kids standing in front of a block of flats. Nothing out of the ordinary until I spotted debris in the road and realised they must've been throwing things as the scooters rode past. It'd been a well-planned ambush and was too late for me to stop or turn round, so I brazened it out. They ran into the road to throw their missiles, I yelled at Budge to duck and swerved as I speeded up.

We got through unscathed and I couldn't believe my luck.

Another 100 yards and the scooter began to list to the left. I initially thought it must've been a puncture from the broken glass in the road. To my horror I realised that Budge was sliding off the pillion seat – he'd been hit in the face by a rock. I yelled at him to grab the backrest and slammed the breaks on, but it was too late: my best friend fell into the road where he was hit by an oncoming car. The driver didn't have a chance to stop. And although it was only a glancing blow, as I jumped off I could see Budge's body lying in the road. I rushed back to him and remember feeling strangely calm. I checked his heart and realised there was still a pulse.

I jumped up and shouted at the gathering crowd, 'He's still alive . . .'

No one had mobiles then, so I sprinted to the nearest house, vaulting over the gate and banging on the door. The startled man who answered immediately phoned an ambulance and then the police.

I ran back to Budge, got him in the recovery position and covered him with my parka. Unsure of what to do, I ran into the pub opposite. As I kicked the doors open I realised I was wearing my West Ham scarf – not a great idea in what was at the time a staunchly Millwall area. It was surreal. I was expecting something to happen but everything went quiet. I must have looked wild-eyed, holding a crash helmet, and they just looked at me in silence. I heard the ambulance arriving, so I rushed back to see what was happening and instantly regretted not staying with him. They drove off at speed, taking him to Guy's Hospital, just five minutes up the road.

The police arrived and inspected my licence. They told me I wasn't allowed to carry a passenger, but I explained that I'd passed my test the previous day. One of them pointed out that Budge was 'unlucky': if I'd failed the test, he wouldn't have been dead. They then started asking me about the 'accident'.

They hadn't realised it'd been a deliberate act.

They weren't listening to me, so I made to leave – to go back to where the kids had thrown the bricks. They grabbed me, so I explained again. They finally understood that we'd been attacked and things changed very quickly. Someone took me to the hospital, where they gave me a cup of tea and I sat down to wait. Initially the news was good: he was still alive and fighting. After a while a sister walked into the room and

I could tell by the look on her face that he was gone. Two odd things happened. Firstly, Budge had his brother's driving licence in his pocket, so the wrong Burgess was pronounced dead. The second was that the WPC who informed his family hadn't told them we'd been attacked, so they arrived at the hospital thinking that I'd simply crashed and killed their son. It must have been an awful experience for them, and it was almost 30 years before they forgave me, but I eventually found out that they never bore me any ill will.

I sat in the hospital dazed, waiting for something to happen. The murder squad picked me up and took me back to the scene, where they found part of Budge's helmet some distance from where I assumed the incident happened.

The gang were rounded up pretty quickly and charged with murder. They kept quiet, so the charges were lowered, first to manslaughter and then to affray. Finally, they appeared at the Old Bailey and on the day of the hearing were acting hard, staring me out while I was giving evidence. As the story unfolded, the bravado went out of them and one by one their heads fell. They eventually realised what they'd done.

We never found out who threw the rock that killed him, and although they were found guilty, they were sentenced to between just six months and a year.

Tim Boyle and Budge's experience was far from unique. It appeared to be open season on mods. The other murder I'm going to mention was even more personal. For an hour or so on the August Bank Holiday weekend of 1982 I was under the impression that my sister had been killed.

I'd enjoyed a brilliant weekend at the Isle of Wight scooter rally with the East London mods and was sitting on the deck of the ferry back to Portsmouth enjoying the sun and drinking a can of beer.

One of the lads from Fulham called across: 'Eddie, you're from Woodford. Have you seen this?'

He thrust a copy of that morning's *Sun* into my hands and pointed to a small article with the ominous headline, 'Mod killed in Bournemouth'. The small print told the story of a 16-year-old girl from Woodford who'd been deliberately killed by a drunk driver who 'didn't like mods'.

Fuck. My sister was a 16-year-old mod girl from Woodford who'd gone to Bournemouth for the weekend. *Jesus*. My stomach fell through the floor.

It was the days before mobiles and obviously there were no payphones on the ferry. I had to wait an agonising half-hour as the ancient boat chugged its way into Pompey dock. As soon as we got off, I ran to the nearest phone box and rang my nan. She eventually picked up and I gabbled out my question.

'Is Vicky OK? I read the papers about the murder . . . What happened?'

It didn't take her long to fill me in. My sister was fine, if a little shaken up. It turned out that a lunatic with a grudge had mown down some mods in a car park and tried to flee the scene. He'd been chased and forced off the road by an alert Derwent Jaconelli (the drummer with Long Tall Shorty), who'd heard the situation develop while trying to sleep and was quick to react as the man tried to escape.

Of course, I wasn't there, so I must let Derwent pick up the story – something he has never spoken about before:

We'd met in St Aubyn's car park on the Saturday morning. We never had a plan but spent a while debating where we should go. There were half a dozen cars and we realised that if we followed the rest to the Isle of Wight it'd cost a fortune on the ferry. In the end we plumped for Bournemouth; not sure why, but it seemed like a good idea at the time.

The group were mainly Essex mods with a handful of East Londoners along for the ride. Malcolm Knox was there, Paul Green . . . Your sister . . . The usual crowd. There were also a few younger kids, some of whom I didn't know, and at midday we set off for the coast in convoy. I was in my Capri with the Bastock brothers as passengers.

I remember seeing Rebecca Haworth in the school car park and she bundled into one of the cars for the drive down. Apparently, she'd told her parents she was sleeping at a friend's house and they weren't aware she was going away for the weekend!

We didn't have anywhere to stay when we got to Bournemouth, so we parked up in the massive car park near the seafront, hoping to make the best of it.

It was getting late. There were three of us in the car and after a while we decided to get some sleep. We'd only been settled for five minutes when I heard some raised voices from the other side of the car park. An argument between some of our lot and this older man in a Jag was getting heated. When I heard an engine overrevving I finally sat up and had a look around. Sure enough, there was an old Jag on the other side of the car park, but something wasn't right. The driver had his foot on the floor, making a right racket. I heard some tyres screeching but I'm still sitting there half-asleep thinking, *Fuck me, that's going a bit over the top for a car park.*

Before I had a chance to move, I heard an almighty bang and this terrible, heart-rending scream.

I immediately realised what'd happened. I didn't see the crash as I was still winding the reclining seat back to its normal position, but [I knew] the driver must have hit someone.

The two guys in my car, Pete and Al Bastock, both scrambled out and in the corner of my eye I could see the Jag racing for the exit. I realised the driver hadn't stopped and wasn't going to.

'Pete, shut the fucking door . . .'

I reversed as quickly as I could, just missing Paul Green's unseen head where he'd fallen, having taken the full force of the car.

Paul had been chatting to Rebecca at the edge of the group. They were nothing to do with the argument, but Rebecca was wearing a parka, which marked her out as a mod. The Jaguar hit them both very hard. Rebecca was killed instantly and Paul was thrown high in the air, landing in a heap just behind my car. I didn't know he was there, and it was incredibly lucky that I didn't run him over a second time.

My only thought was to chase the bastard. I got to the car park exit but couldn't see where the Jag had gone. Someone ran towards me pointing frantically to the right, so I headed off and took the first roundabout as fast as I could. Two hundred yards ahead I could make out those odd, pear-shaped back lights, distinctively Jaguar. I immediately knew it was him.

For a while the driver thought he'd got away scot-free. He obviously hadn't worked out I was chasing him, but once he cottoned on he put his foot down. Fortunately, there are a lot of roundabouts in Bournemouth; if there hadn't been he would certainly have got away, as a standard Capri can't hope to match a Jaguar's speed on the straight. The Jag had a 4.2 engine and was absolutely flying, topping 100mph on the dual carriageway and braking suddenly for the next roundabout – where I'd catch him up but he'd pull away once we were round it. I couldn't even look at my speedometer as the Capri's engine was screaming and it was all I could do to stay on the road.

At each roundabout I was gaining slightly, making ground, and he realised I was going to get him sooner or later. Should I ram him? I don't know.

At the next roundabout he tried a different tactic. He pulled away to get some distance, turned his lights off and pulled over at a parade of shops, thinking he'd lost me. He assumed I'd miss him if he ducked down, but he was wrong.

I saw him pull over, so I drove straight at the Jag to try and block him in. Things were happening so fast I hadn't realised that the Old Bill were now chasing me for speeding and they certainly didn't know I was chasing him. The adrenaline was pumping and I pulled up next to the driver's door, wound down my window and he did the same as if to chat.

'What's up, mate?'

'I've fucking got you . . .'

He tried to brazen it out. 'What are you talking about mate?'

'You're not my fucking mate. I know what you've done and I've got you. Stay there.'

With that he threw the Jag into reverse, spun past the Capri and roared away.

The chase was back on and I was flat out after him again. This time, though, a police car with sirens blaring pulled level with me and indicated that I should pull over. I didn't. Instead I pointed frantically at the Jaguar and the copper in the passenger seat put two and two together, gave me a thumbs-up and pulled ahead. Now both of us were chasing the Jag through this never-ending succession of roundabouts.

We were both on top of him now, trying to pressure the driver into making a mistake and force him off the road, but he just wouldn't stop. At the next roundabout his car clipped the curb at speed, flipped and ploughed into a wall. I was out before the policemen, raced to the wrecked Jag and dragged the driver out. He was obviously drunk and was screaming, accusing me of attacking him for no reason. The Old Bill quickly pulled me off, but he gave them a lot of stick, shouting about 'knowing his rights'.

The copper pointed at me and said to the guy, 'Shut your mouth or we're gonna let him have five minutes with you. You're nicked.'

As things calmed down the officer pulled me aside and told me that Rebecca was dead.

I asked them how they'd worked out the situation and they said that initially they thought I was a joyrider until they heard a message on the radio about a hit-and-run in the car park with a Jaguar fleeing the scene and realised I was chasing the perpetrator.

The whole thing was a tragedy and a really traumatic experience.

Derwent had been a hero and without his quick thinking the murderer would certainly have escaped. In court, the driver chose not to explain his actions, merely stating that he was having relationship problems, was drunk and had a particular dislike of mods.

That one event affected so many lives.

It certainly wasn't the first time one of our group had been killed and it sadly wasn't the last.

22

I SAW THE LIGHT

'd been greatly affected by the violence as it increased on the scene in the early Eighties. As had so many others. I was beginning to question the whole point of it all – my commitment to the scene and to mod in general. If this was the sort of thing that happened, was it even vaguely worth it?

I ducked the question and instead applied myself to my Avatar job over the next few months, and once I got the hang of things found myself enjoying it immensely. I found that I managed to block out the worst elements of violence and tragedy. Jon Brewer even insisted that I step up and hiked my salary, making me take on more responsibility.

Gigs, bands, lunches and the occasional party, all with free drink. What was not to like? It was everything the music industry was supposed to be.

When I wasn't actually delivering stuff, Jon Brewer believed in furthering my education. He gave me tasks with the sole objective of breaking down my natural terror of speaking to strangers so that I could learn how the whole thing worked.

After two weeks he threw me a copy of the *Music Week Directory* (the industry bible) with the comment: 'Under the section labelled "Radio Stations" you'll find a list of all the stations in the country. I want you to ring them up, make contact with someone you can foster a relationship with and start to send them promos . . . All of them!'

There were over two hundred BBC and independent stations active in 1981 and as instructed I phoned them all, duly writing down the names of contacts who more often than not never took a call from me. It was scary but thrilling and taught me the nuts and bolts.

One of my more interesting new jobs was looking after Todd Rundgren's label Bearsville. Well, when I say 'looking after' . . . That's perhaps something of an exaggeration. In reality, I was doing nothing of the kind. I was simply taking care of Bearsville's filing! I was already a massive fan of Rundgren's first American group, The Nazz, and as Avatar were Todd's official European licensee I was encouraged to spend days at a time listening to his entire output.

The more I heard, the more I liked. Brewer decided it'd be a good idea for Avatar to reissue Rundgren's classic 'I Saw the Light' on the newly invented picture disc. In my mind this was a big pop hit, but strangely I can find no mention of the reissue on the Official Charts website, so I guess it wasn't.

I'd always regarded Todd Rundgren as having modish sensibilities, more so than most Americans, so it came as no surprise when he included a version of Marriott and Lane's 'Tin Soldier' on his next LP, *The Ever Popular Tortured Artist Effect*, and I worked on its release. I'd been given even more responsibilities by this time; I was still the post boy, but was also involved in press and radio promotion as well as a bit of A&R.

A&R-wise, Jon Brewer threw me in at the deep end. He sent me to a meeting at a major label clutching a cassette with instructions to 'Get me a licence deal on this master. I won't take less than 25 grand!'

Avatar were looking for a production deal for one of their signed artists whose album was already in the can. It was common for indies to sell unreleased records to major-label A&R departments as a fully formed project. This saved majors the time involved in development and could often provide them with instant hits without them having to put in the hard yards. The indies got the cash without the risk. Win-win?

Unbeknown to me, the whole meeting was a setup.

Jon Brewer had sent me to one of his mates to make a pitch for something musically crap. The meeting was with a senior A&R manager at RCA, who conducted it in all seriousness. He then reported back to my boss as to my strengths, weaknesses and general tactical nous. I was unaware of what was going on, so took the meeting as if my career depended on it. After all, it was my first face-to-face experience and I was determined to make a decent pitch. Although I was crapping my pants, it must have gone well (even though, as we listened to the tape, I immediately realised that the band were rubbish) and a few days later Brewer called me into his office to congratulate me. He told me that the meeting had been a test and I'd see the RCA man in the pub after work to laugh about it.

Coincidentally, this was a tactic used by Dave Robinson when I started at Stiff a few years later and by John Williams when I was at Polydor. It's actually quite clever, making the young A&R kid construct a serious pitch for the first time to test their mettle even though the product was shite.

I was allowed to host my own A&R meetings from then on, but I soon realised that this was a curse as well as a blessing.

A few days later, a blind man with a white stick lugging a very large case was shown to my cubbyhole. I was slightly relieved that he was blind so he couldn't see the paucity of my workspace, but what followed was awful. Awful and fucking heartbreaking.

The man was earnest and keen, but the meeting was just about the worst thing that could have happened in my first week of A&R. I guided him to the chair and helped him sit down. After a minute or so he opened the large box, pulled out an enormous accordion and launched into a 20-minute set of excruciating zydeco awfulness. He sang along and stamped his foot in time to the music despite the fact that he couldn't sing and certainly couldn't play the accordion.

Because he was blind, I really felt I couldn't tell the man to stop before he'd finished and definitely couldn't tell him he was crap. I felt so guilty. The man genuinely believed he was the next big talent. I tried to let him down gently, but he took it very badly indeed. He cried. I mean, he was a grown blind man in his late fifties, and I was an inexperienced 17-year-old telling him he hadn't quite cut the mustard. He fucking cried.

After I'd helped him to the lift and closed the cage door behind him, the fact of seeing those blind eyes shedding tears of inadequacy and his genuine heartfelt pain made me realise that A&R couldn't get much worse than this.

I approached a smirking Ellen and asked her, 'What the fuck was that about? You should never have given him a meeting. He was fucking awful . . . I felt terrible shattering his dreams . . .'

'Yeah, Jon said you'd say that . . .'

'What? You know that man?'

'Oh yes, Eddie,' she said in her bewitching Scandinavian accent. 'He's been coming here for meetings for at least ten years. Jon thought it would be good practice for you . . .'

For fuck's sake!

Everyone who wants to work in the music business actually wants to work in A&R – the artist and repertoire department is where the good shit happens. It's where the artists are discovered (by scouts), the songs are chosen (by A&R representatives), the albums recorded (by producers), the lunches taken (by managers) and the rock & roll fun is had (by everyone) . . .

In the early Eighties it was tough to land a job at a record company and virtually impossible to get one in an A&R department. Firstly, you had to prove you had the ears for it.

I was still the most junior employee at the company, but I gradually grew in confidence and set out to understand the business. There were so many old-school characters to learn from, not just my immediate bosses Pete Chalcraft and Geoff Thorne (a couple of heavy-metallers in their mid-twenties whose idea of a joke was to ask me to deliver non-existent parcels in the rain so they could look out of the window and see me bump-starting my Lambretta up and down Pall Mall), but a whole succession of older men (and they were always men) who'd cut their teeth in the Sixties. The women, though, were the real backbone of the place. Along with the Scandi beauties (Inga and Ellen), I became friends with Gina Carter and the all-knowing Kate. Kate was elegant, refined and . . . Well, seeing I was just 17 with very limited experience, she was unlike anyone I'd met before. She reminded me of Helen Mirren as Harry Shand's girlfriend in *The Long Good Friday*. I was never quite sure of her actual job title, but always assumed she was Jon Brewer's assistant as she seemed to run the place.

Bizarre situations were always cropping up and there was seemingly no structure to my working life.

I was sitting in my cubbyhole one particular afternoon when I heard the lift ping as the antiquated elevator pulled onto my floor. As the doors opened, I caught a glimpse of . . . *Fuck me . . . Can that really be Georgie Fame?* Now, Georgie was a major mod hero and I'd been to see him play live a number of times already. I came over all shy and didn't introduce myself. Then I had an idea.

Terry and Belinda Stokes's record shop in Carnaby Street had just taken delivery of a large collection of Sixties sheet music. I thought it likely that they might have something by Georgie Fame.

I told Ellen I was popping out for a bit, jumped on the scooter and roared up to nearby Great Marlborough Street, where I left my Lambretta outside the magistrates' court. I rushed into Right Track and asked Terry if he had anything appropriate. I had a very small window of time, so we got stuck straight into the job of flicking through the piles of sheet music.

Georgie was at Avatar for a meeting with Jon Brewer to talk about a single he wanted to make in honour of the snooker legend Alex 'Hurricane' Higgins. How long would that meeting take? Certainly not more than an hour, probably less. I didn't want to miss the opportunity, so scrabbled about as quickly as I could.

'Bingo!' shouts Terry. 'Here's one . . .'

I grabbed it, thrust two quid into his hand and ran to the bike before I got a parking ticket.

Back at Avatar, I tore up the three flights of stairs and breathlessly asked Ellen if Georgie was still in the meeting. He was.

Phew!

I sat down at my desk, slid the sheet music into the top drawer and waited. Five minutes later I heard an office door open and goodbyes being said.

'Thanks, and a pleasure. I'll walk you to the lift . . .'

This was Brewer again; apparently their meeting had been successful and Georgie was going to sign to the label.

I steeled myself and as the pair got to the lift, I stood up, poked my head round the corner and said, 'Erm . . . Mr Fame?'

I wasn't even sure if it was OK to call him Mr Fame. His real name was Clive Powell, and to be fair, he had a reputation similar to that of Van Morrison. He didn't like being approached and could apparently be moody. I couldn't have been more wrong.

Jon Brewer frowned and I could tell he wasn't pleased; I shouldn't be badgering our artists like some starstruck fan. But I couldn't help it – this was my big chance to meet one of my heroes.

'Look, I realise it isn't the done thing at work, but I'm a massive fan – I saw you play a Blue Flames set a couple of weeks ago at the Cambridge Hotel . . . Could I ask you to sign something?'

He had very friendly eyes and immediately agreed, speaking softly in a strange half-Geordie accent with a mid-Atlantic inflection.

'Sure, man . . .'

I led him over to my desk with my scowling boss in tow, opened the top drawer and pulled out the black and white sheet music to his Sixties hit 'Get Away' with its photo of Georgie mid-gig on the front.

He took one look and exclaimed, 'Woah, man, don't tell me you actually keep that in your drawer on the off-chance I might walk into your office?'

Never one to miss an opportunity, I meekly nodded and said, 'Well, I told you I was a fan.'

'Hey, I'm really impressed. That's cool, man!' The third time he'd used the word 'man'. 'Next time we play, just let my people know and I'll put you on the guest list. Looks like we might be working together soon anyway! Now, what's your name?'

I blurted it out. He picked up a red pen from my desk, looked up at me and wrote, 'To Eddie, Stay Fast! Georgie Fame.'

At the time I had no idea what the great man meant by 'Stay Fast'. It took a while to work out that he was making a play on the name of Paul Newman's character in *The Hustler*, Fast Eddie. How fucking cool was that?

Avatar wasn't all wine and roses, though. One particularly crap afternoon at about half three Brewer buzzed me up to his office.

'Emergency, Eddie. I need you to take a master tape down to Jacobs Studios in Farnham. They need it immediately.'

Now, a 24-track master tape comes in a box that's 11 inches square and 3 inches deep, and is extraordinarily heavy. I looked out of the window and it was pissing cats and dogs. I tried to cry off, but the boss wasn't having it.

Those unfamiliar with the vagaries of London's motorway system in the early Eighties wouldn't be aware that the M25 didn't exist and that the M3 was little more than a dual carriageway and still unlit. This meant that my journey would be in the dark and the pouring rain. Lambretta front lights were notoriously pathetic. I reckon you got more illumination from a fucking candle.

I wrapped the tape in a plastic bag, sealed it watertight and stuffed it down the front of my parka, securing the unwieldy package with the drawstring. So began one of the most uncomfortable journeys of my life. Dangerous too, as overtaking lorries tended to drive far too close to you and a scooter would get sucked along in their slipstream. I couldn't see the unlit road surface and raindrops were smashing into my face with such force that I had to wear sunglasses to protect my eyes. This made it even harder to see more than 20 yards ahead . . . Terrifying . . . After what seemed like an age (Farnham was outside the scope of the *A–Z*), I finally found the place and rode up the drive of Jacobs Studios feeling thoroughly dejected, shaking with fear and very pissed off. Water had pooled between my legs, so I was literally soaked through to my pants.

I rang the bell and waited. Nothing happened. I rang it again, this time keeping my thumb on the button for half a minute.

Eventually I could hear the fumbling of a lock on the other side of the door and it swung slowly open, creaking like something out of a Sixties Hammer film. The sight that greeted me was so unexpected that I stood there open-mouthed, dripping onto the doormat.

I was confronted by a man with long blond hair wearing what could only be described as a paisley cape/polo-neck combo. He was also sporting white corduroy flares and green stack-heeled shoes. It was fucking Rick Wakeman and as soon as he saw me he burst out laughing.

'What have we here, I wonder? It looks remarkably like a drowned mod? You'd better come in, mod, and we'll get you out of those wet clothes.'

He was ever so sweet. I never found out what he was recording . . . Was it Yes? Was it a Wakeman *King Arthur*-type solo project? I was ushered into the kitchen, de-robed and handed a cup of sweet tea while my parka was hung in front of a fire. He waited until I was settled and asked, 'So, what brings you here, mod?'

'I've got some kind of master tape for you.' I shook my head, half-laughing. 'It's taken two fucking hours to get here in the dark with no lights on my scooter and now I'll have to go all the way back again . . .'

Alerted to the commotion, the other musicians trooped into the kitchen to see what the fuss was about. And this was where Wakeman dropped the big reveal . . .

'I wonder why Jon didn't bring it himself? He only lives two minutes up the road and we don't need it till tomorrow afternoon!'

Bastard! The ride back to Mum's in Loughton took an uncomfortable three hours.

Avatar soon became the focus of my world and I would regularly meet interesting characters at the office. Jon Brewer and Robert Patterson didn't just run a record label; they also had a music publishers, a management company and, before too long, a movie division.

The one-time Rolling Stones guitarist Mick Taylor worked with the company at the time and was a very unprepossessing character. Apparently he didn't like being in the Stones and preferred playing 'the blues' (just like his predecessor Brian Jones and the late Keith Relf from The Yardbirds), so he'd recently rejoined his original group, John Mayall's Bluesbreakers.

I only met the man a couple of times, but he'd been storing his Fender Rhodes in the office and when I asked him about electric pianos he patiently explained the difference in sound between the Fender and a Wurlitzer.

'A Wurlitzer has a warm sound, while the Rhodes is cold with more pronounced attack and you can't beat the vibrato on a Wurly, it's incredible . . .'

Max Splodge from Splodgenessabounds was occasionally in and out too, but my absolute favourite was the blues-rock guitarist Alvin Lee.

Lee was known for having the fastest guitar-picking fingers in rock & roll and had earned a decent reputation. His band Ten Years After played at Woodstock and I greedily hoovered up his back catalogue. The band's sound was a take on up-tempo blues-rock and I could never understand why they weren't much bigger. I've long suspected his *Stonehenge* album was the inspiration for *Spinal Tap* both sonically and visually.

These artists were typical of the vibrancy and sheer randomness of the place. You never knew what to expect at Avatar and I fucking loved it. One day a soul singer, the next a metal band . . .

One afternoon Patterson poked his head round the corner and said, 'Eddie, I've got a package to drop off to Raf Ravenscroft. He lives in the Barbican. Crack on . . . he's expecting you.'

I'd never heard of either the Barbican or Raf Ravenscroft, so I pulled out my battered *A–Z* and looked it up. Turned out it was an enormous brutalist construction round the back of Liverpool Street. Ellen explained that Raf was a sax-playing session musician we worked with regularly and it should only take me ten minutes to ride there. I set off on the Lammy, and while it didn't take me long to find the actual Barbican, the place was a massive concrete rabbit warren that looked like the location of *A Clockwork Orange* and to my uninitiated self the circular apartment-numbering system read like absolute gibberish.

After 20 minutes stomping around in frustration, walking past the same block for the third time, I came across a janitor and asked him where I should go.

'Ah!' he said. 'You're almost in the right place, but Mr Ravenscroft lives in the penthouse. He has a special lift that opens directly into his flat. Very fancy, it is . . .'

The man rolled his eyes in what I perceived to be disapproval.

Now, Ravenscroft was a legend among session musicians. He'd played for hundreds of artists but really made his mark with the extraordinary saxophone solo on Gerry Rafferty's enormous smash hit, 'Baker Street', (for which he received the princely sum of £27.50 with no royalty percentage!). Avatar's publishing company owned the rights to 'Baker Street', but I couldn't be sure why I was delivering the man a brown envelope. I could only assume he must have liked being paid in cash, but the envelope didn't exactly feel like cash. Still, I was only the delivery boy and it was none of my business.

I eventually found the bell, pressed it and heard Raf on the intercom: 'Get in the lift. It's the top button. I'll see you in a minute.'

The elevator whirred its silent way up to the penthouse, taking an inordinate amount of time to get there. Eventually the doors slid open and I walked directly into his flat.

'Wow!'

The place was the ultimate rock star's pad, decorated with brown velvet wallpaper, thick cream shag-pile carpet and at least three gold-edged glass tables arranged around the room with the requisite number of leather sofas and gauche oriental prints on the walls. To be honest, it brought to mind a pimp's apartment in a vintage episode of *Starsky & Hutch*, but this wasn't 1975, it was 1981, and the place screamed sex and drugs and rock & roll. Unrecognisable yacht rock was playing from invisible speakers, doubtlessly hidden in the wall. Again, wow!

It was open plan, unfeasibly large and very impressive. At the opposite end of the room was Raf himself.

A vision. He was clad in a black silk dressing gown with red watered-silk edging and a dragon embroidered on the back. Very Hai Karate.

It was loosely belted with a red silk cord, revealing a pair of tight budgie-smuggler briefs poking forward. Now this was proper rock & roll! I'd never seen anything like it.

Raf sported a long King Charles Restoration-style curled hairdo with an Aussie cattle farmer's moustache (à la Merv Hughes) and was clutching a large brandy or whisky on ice in a straight crystal tumbler. Jesus Christ. What the fuck was going on here? This only happens in Hollywood movies. My heart was racing.

'Ah, you must be Eddie. I've heard good things about you. I thought you weren't coming. Shall I pour you a drink? Have you got my package?' What the fuck could be in the package? Drugs? Cash? I quailed; this was well beyond my experience.

Get the fuck out of here, I thought, *and now!* Patterson hadn't warned me about this. Was this going to be a rock & roll party with me as the only guest?

I spluttered that I'd brought his envelope but was late for my next job and sadly couldn't hang about.

Raf seemed disappointed, but I handed it over and he tore it open with enthusiasm as I made my way to the lift, frantically pushing the button with the misplaced conception that the more times I pressed it, the quicker it would arrive. The next 30 seconds ticked by infinitely slowly, but eventually the elevator pinged, the doors swept open and, like the journalists in the *News of the World* said, I made my excuses and left. I'd still got a long way to go before I'd feel comfy in the presence of rock stars relaxing (while dressed in silk dressing gowns!).

23

POLICE OPPRESSION

The route I took to work at Avatar was through Stratford, over the Bow Flyover, via Mile End and the City, which saved me 15 minutes of journey time. For some reason two traffic policemen took great exception to me and my scooter. I'd picked up a Lambretta GP150 and bored it out to a 175, and fitted a big carb and exhaust, which made it both temperamental and noisy and was, I presumed, why they decided to make my life a misery.

It started with a random tug after I came down the east side of the Bow Flyover one evening. They waved me over and spent 20 minutes going over the scooter with a fine-tooth comb. Much to their disappointment they could find nothing wrong, so gave me a five-day wonder and that was the end of it. Or at least I thought it was. To them, it was the beginning.

Three weeks later the same coppers flagged me down again. This time they discovered that my MOT had run out a few days earlier and I'd stupidly forgotten to renew it. Gleefully they booked me for it. This was an offence worthy of an endorsement, which was a real pain in the arse. Before 'points' were introduced on your licence there was a 'three strikes' endorsement system. If you picked up three within a two-year period, you were banned. The only advantage of the old system was that all offences committed on the same occasion counted as only one endorsement.

From that point on, these two coppers pulled me up once a week. Other times they would stand by their car and watch me drive past. It was a real hassle to ride the longer way home, as most of the East London arterial roads hadn't been built by then. It was also something of a lottery. I'd stagger my journey times, but somehow these two would find me. In the space of two and a half months they charged me for nine different traffic offences. I had no idea why they were doing it, but it was apparent they were trying to get me banned and I only had two strikes left.

The next tug was a few days later for my large chain and padlock. I had the key and told them I'd been nicked for this before and as it was genuinely for locking my bike it wasn't a weapon. They tried to get me to admit I used the chain for self-defence, but I was wise to that. A few months back I'd been with Steve Jarvis when they pulled us outside Victoria Station. One of the policemen went through his pockets and found a battery. A normal battery. They made a joke that it might come in handy if he ever got attacked by skinheads.

'Er, what do you mean?' Steve asked, sounding confused.

'Well, you know,' said the copper, laughing. 'You could throw it at them . . .'

Steve replied, 'Well, yeah, I suppose so.'

They immediately slapped on handcuffs and charged him with possession of an offensive weapon. I protested on his behalf and they threatened to arrest me too. If you have a normal object on your person, then it apparently comes down to intent. The moment Steve agreed with the copper that he *might* throw the battery at someone he was nicked. It didn't matter that he thought they were joking.

Over the ten weeks, the traffic coppers pulled me up three times for speeding, bizarrely accusing me of hoofing it *up* the Bow Flyover. Fortunately, they over-egged the pudding and claimed I'd been travelling at 70mph. They'd already nicked me for the third time before I'd even been to court for the first. At the initial hearing I produced the manual to show that the manufacturers claimed a top speed of 58mph for a GP150 and I'd been spotted going *up* the flyover, which would have made their alleged speed impossible. The magistrate agreed and the case was dismissed. The second time, I had to get a mechanic to test the bike and write a report for the court. Again, the case was dismissed.

Then it was for a 'dangerous accessory' – they deemed my whip aerial was over the permitted length and nicked me for it. I wasn't even aware this was an offence! Things were now getting serious and I was worried I might lose my licence. I hoped they'd get bored and move on to someone else. Unfortunately, they didn't.

A week or so later, they pulled me again, this time in Whitechapel for 'defective mechanical parts'. There were four different charges at least: the speedo cable was too long and insufficiently secured to the front fork, the factory hooter wasn't loud enough, there was too much play on the brakes and the headset was dangerous. I lost that hearing because all of those offences were 'subjective', with no specific benchmark to judge against. It was based purely on the witness statements of the traffic officer, in whose experienced opinion these offences warranted a charge. Fortunately, they counted as one endorsement, but this took me dangerously close to a ban, which would cost me my job . . . This carried on until they'd ground me down. The policemen seemed to be loving it, but I was increasingly pissed off and had no idea how to deal with the situation.

So eventually I called my dad and asked him what I should do.

The old man went doolally. 'Why didn't you tell me before? I'm not having this. Leave it with me.'

A couple of days later he called me at work, said the matter had been dealt with and I wouldn't be harassed by them again. The charges that had yet to come to court were all dropped.

The following week, I was surprised to see the same two Old Bill parked up in their usual layby and flagging me down.

I stopped the engine, took off my helmet and asked them what the problem was.

'Who do you think you are, you little shit? Special, are you? We'll soon see.' He then walked round the Lambretta making his usual inspection while the other one gave me a body search. I asked if they didn't have anything better to do with their time and this seemed to push the one checking the bike over the edge. He was always the nastier of the two and the one who wanted to book me.

He launched into a rant about my dad: 'I dunno who your old man thinks he is but he can fuck right off . . .'

There was more in a similar vein and by piecing it together I realised my dad had gone in to confront the superintendent at Leman Street station and made it clear that he wasn't going to let their officers bully his son. If it happened again, several people would regret it. Apparently . . .

When I got home that night, I asked Dad what happened at the police station and he just said, 'Never you mind, son. You won't be stopped again; let's just leave it at that.'

I laughed and told him they'd actually pulled me up on the way home from work that night.

He just said, 'Yeah, but did they nick you? It was just their way of saying goodbye, letting you know that they've won.'

'Well, actually, they didn't nick me but seemed pretty furious. What did you say to their boss?'

'Look, son, our family have been dealing with these idiots for over a hundred years. I'm telling you, you won't be hearing from them again.'

And he was right, I didn't.

We were still attending Bank Holiday weekends en masse, and this time word filtered down that we were going to Bournemouth.

I had a quick gander at the map and realised that the trip on a scooter would take at least half a day, so elected to jump in a car. I drove down as a passenger in Jacquie Wratten's Beetle with a couple of others, Scrape and Spencer. Jacquie was the sister of Small World's guitarist; she ran the band's fan club and had been helping me with the previous couple of issues of *Extraordinary Sensations*. She was also my girlfriend.

Bournemouth was incredible.

There were more than ten thousand mods there and we took over the whole town. Photos of the hordes even made it onto the front pages of the national papers the next morning. By this time the journalist Garry Bushell was slipping me a few hundred quid for a tip-off. It seemed like a fortune, but for a red-top tabloid it was peanuts.

'Where are the mods going this weekend?'

Telling him didn't seem too much of an issue at the time. All he did was dispatch a photographer and the local stringer to see if there was any trouble to fill the *Sun*'s quiet news days. Even if there wasn't, they could pretend there had been, but by this time, trouble with skinheads was so common anyway we didn't have to travel to the coast to find it.

That weekend in Bournemouth was probably the most mods I'd ever seen in one place. And the crowd were mainly mods – there were virtually no scooterboys and any casuals were ex-mods who'd made the trip down with their old mates. There was hardly any trouble, but for some reason the police still managed to arrest some people for what looked like imaginary offences.

The lads who were nicked were kept locked up until Tuesday, when they were released to appear in court a week later. A couple of days after I got back to my normal routine, I had a call from Steve Butler. He was one of those detained and had a favour to ask: could I take a day off work and drive him down to Bournemouth magistrates' the following Tuesday? I had a quick word with Jon Brewer, telling him I had to go to the dentist, and found myself flogging down to the south coast in the Triumph Herald.

Thank God I never attempted that Bank Holiday trip on my scooter because even in the car the journey took forever. I sat on the public benches in court and spent a fascinating couple of hours watching the hearings, which did indeed seem to mirror those of the Sixties. The beak might as well have read out the 'petty little Sawdust Caesars' speech from 1964. The situation was clichéd and depressing as a conveyer belt of 20 angelic-faced teenagers traipsed along, waiting their turn in front of an old chap in a wig who looked like he'd be more at home on the bench with Judge Jeffreys.

Most of the defendants were mods, with a smattering of skins who were generally ignored. Trouble in court was not a good idea, and besides, the kids were no longer buzzing and fizzing with adrenaline and pills – if anything, they were more concerned about their imminent sentence. Most were fined, but a few copped a short-sharp-shock sentence at a borstal, mainly for the more serious charges of affray or GBH. These youth prisons were well past their sell-by date and rumoured to be hard work for the inmates. The recent film *Scum*, starring Ray Winston and Phil Daniels, had caused a stir with its shocking portrayal of the life of a young man inside, and I certainly didn't fancy it. Fortunately, the borstal system was scrapped in 1982.

What a couple of hours' close observation made me realise was that most if not all of these court convictions relied entirely on the accused's *admission* that they'd committed an offence. There was no corroborating evidence to back up the arresting officer's statements and most of the accused stood supine and resigned to their fate.

It reminded me of the advice my old man gave me in case I came into contact with the police: 'Say nothing . . .'

In my mid- to late teens I'd seen people arrested enough times to work out what was going on. On the whole, the Old Bill weren't bothered who they arrested or why. They were in a results-based business and what mattered to them and their senior officers was a steady stream of uncomplicated convictions that looked good on paper. On the occasions I'd been nicked from 1980 to 1984, I can say with genuine honesty that only one of them was justified and I was found not guilty, and on one occasion I was even awarded compensation for wrongful arrest.

Police often saw an easily identifiable individual who may or may not have been from a group with a reputation for law-breaking but made an easy target for arrest. If these kids were out of their depth, intimidated or plain scared they could often incriminate themselves for a crime they'd not committed. Evidence is often easy to find – I'm not saying it's easy to fabricate, but that it can be made to connect the accused with a crime or even a non-crime that can be escalated to qualify as one. This is why a disproportionate number of visible minorities are arrested. At that time, the bias wasn't just limited to obvious youth cults like mods, skinheads, punks, football casuals or hooligans; it was also directed at the black community.

In the late Seventies and early Eighties I saw it happen time and again. One by one I'd seen friends give up and let themselves be carried along to the conclusion of the process. No proper access to lawyers, boys under 18 interviewed under caution without adults present, tricked into admitting 'intent' for an offence they didn't commit . . . It happened all the time and nobody cared because the system could simply say, 'Well, what would you expect from a skinhead/Rasta/punk/mod/football hooligan/black boy/gypsy . . .?' (delete as applicable). I understand that nothing is simple, and that the police have a tough job to do in difficult circumstances; I also realise that the majority of officers are fair and try to obtain the right result. But this kind of thing has always happened and will continue to happen for the foreseeable future. Taking the easy option is a fact of life.

I was relieved that the four of my mates who were in court that day were convicted of only minor offences: breach of the peace; threatening behaviour; or drunk and disorderly. They all entered a guilty plea and were handed small fines. Their offences weren't serious and the punishment was nothing. In truth, they were just unlucky, in the wrong place at the wrong time when the police were looking for someone to arrest. It could have been any of us. The whole thing was pointless.

If I was having doubts before, this day in court simply confirmed them and my trust in the police disappeared.

24

25 MILES

One Monday morning everything changed.

Jon Brewer walked into the office. 'Eddie, do you have a full driving licence?' he asked.

'Erm . . . Yeah, why?'

'We've just signed Edwin Starr and you're going to drive him on tour . . . Scooting round northern clubs and radio stations with him and his manager. Simple. You mods like all that stuff anyway . . .'

What the fuck?

'I've only got a Triumph Herald; I can't take him around in that!'

Brewer gave me a sharp look and said, 'Sometimes I worry about you. I've hired a Ford Granada. You get it the day before you set off.'

I was in shock. Of course I knew who Edwin Starr was – he'd had big mod hits with 'Back Street' and 'S.O.S.' (Stop Her on Sight) on Ric-Tic and '25 Miles' on Motown, both labels out of Detroit – but to be on tour with him? That was something else.

I quickly tapped up Ian Clark, *Extraordinary Sensations*' recently appointed soul correspondent, 6Ts DJ and Kent Records designer, for what he knew about Ric-Tic and the other side of Detroit – I certainly didn't want to appear out of my depth with Edwin.

The day came round faster than expected, and on a wet Wednesday morning in the beginning of January, Brewer stomped into my cubbyhole, threw me a set of keys and handed me an envelope: 300 quid and the itinerary.

At nine the following morning, I loaded my bag into the Granada and set off to meet a genuine legend.

His first gig wasn't until the weekend, but I had to drive up to Manchester, introduce myself to Edwin and his manager Lilian Kyle and run through the itinerary for the weeks ahead.

Lilian was his German-born manager. A sweet woman who spoke with a very pronounced accent, she fiercely protected Edwin. I had no idea how respected Edwin was on the northern soul scene before that trip; in fact, I wasn't even aware of the size and makeup of the northern soul scene. We'd heard of it of course, but that tour opened my eyes. The three of us had a lovely and relaxed dinner, and I produced the schedule with a flourish. We made a plan and agreed to meet the following day, when I'd drive the pair to the local BBC station for an interview and then back to the hotel.

I should stress here that I wasn't driving the tour van. That was left to the professionals. I was Edwin's personal driver and the tour wasn't just Edwin Starr playing a few gigs – it was a whole soul review pitching up at a host of venues that held up to 3,000 people. The thing was much, much bigger than I was expecting.

I'd just celebrated my 19th birthday and had been at Avatar for 18 months, and was by now more involved with press and promotion than anything else. I was no longer the office junior and had had a number of pay hikes, which had got me thinking about buying a new car. I was still young for the job and was often met with disbelief when I turned up with Edwin and Lilian in tow.

The tour was called the Ric-Tic Review and Edwin was the headliner. He was joined by J. J. Barnes, Lou Ragland, Al Kent and Pat Lewis, with a backing band led by sax player Snake Davis. While Edwin and J. J. Barnes knew what to expect as they'd already forged careers here, the other artists couldn't believe the reaction they received or the size of the crowds they were playing to. You heard this time and again in the Eighties: most of the smaller black American artists who came to Britain for soul weekenders had absolutely no idea what was going to happen. Their careers in the States had ended many years earlier and the best they could hope for was a few cabaret nights on the Chitlin' Circuit. In America they were forgotten, but here they were legends. It was beautiful to see their reaction, which would often be very emotional.

When I worked with Dean Parrish years later, he told me an incredible story. He'd been a tenor in a Brooklyn doo-wop street quartet. He had such a distinctive voice that it came as no surprise when he was picked up by Laurie Records in 1964 to cut some sides. Thing was, the label told him there was no interest in Italian singers, so pressured him to change his name from Phil Anastasi to Dean Parrish. The name change didn't help. Phil signed to four labels in quick succession without success and in 1967 gave up trying to make it as Dean Parrish, reverted to using the name Phil Anastasi and became a session guitarist and later an actor.

Fast forward to the year 2000 and Anastasi searched his former identity on the internet. What he discovered both amazed and appalled him. It turned out that his Dean Parrish single 'I'm on My Way', a flop on its minor, original US release, had been picked up by the Wigan Casino DJs as one of the famous 'Three Before Eight' all-nighter tracks and became *the* northern soul anthem, several years after its original release. So much so that the 45 had been reissued in the UK in the mid-Seventies and reached Number 38 in the charts, selling upwards of 250,000 copies. The trouble was, when British DJs tried to track him down, they searched instead for his alter ego, Dean Parrish, rather than Phil Anastasi and all roads led nowhere.

The single is now estimated to have sold 500,000 copies, but Anastasi earned nothing. The money went somewhere, but it certainly didn't end up with the man who made the record. In 2001, Phil made contact and was invited over to the UK by the DJ Russ Winstanley to perform live at a Soul Weekender, but there was one last surprise in store. When Anastasi arrived in North Wales for the gig, he was blown away by the 3,000 people who'd turned up to hear him sing. Trouble was, no one knew he was white and many of the crowd refused to believe he was the real Dean Parrish! Any doubts were dispelled as soon as he opened his mouth, and for the first time in his musical career, Phil Anastasi received the response and welcome he truly deserved. But not the money . . .

This story highlights a problem that has plagued the northern scene from the very beginning. The lionisation of music that failed on its initial release and may have sold less than a hundred copies in a regional US market created incredible demand in a rapidly growing scene. The available copies soon disappeared and fans followed DJs around specifically to hear the rare records they owned. Competition was intense and soon bootleggers stepped in to fill the vacuum.

A bootleg is an illegal record pressed without permission. This means the copyright owner and artists receive nothing. It's estimated there has been over a thousand bootlegs released on the northern scene and this remains a problem that refuses to go away. In November 2018, two men were jailed and two others received suspended sentences for running a northern soul bootlegging ring in Wales.

Admittedly, the scale of bootlegging has decreased since British indie labels like Kent have found it easier to license and reissue hard-to-find records, but the problem is more one of forgery. As the price of rare soul 45s has increased to the point where someone will pay £100,000 for an original copy of Frank Wilson's uber-rare and overplayed classic 'Do I Love You (Indeed I Do)', and where lesser records that may have been sold by John Anderson's Soul Bowl for just a couple of pounds in the mid-Eighties can fetch over £5,000, then the incentive for the bootleggers is to make exact copies and pass them off as originals, making hundreds of thousands of pounds in the process.

This was certainly a problem on the Ric-Tic Review and one of my new acquaintances took great pleasure in pointing out the fake Ric-Tic pressings in the record bars on the tour.

The first night was upon us and things got very busy.

I drove Edwin and Lilian to their hotel with a promise to pick them up in an hour and take them to the local radio station. It was the same format every time: Edwin would be interviewed by the local 'soul show' presenter who'd use the opportunity to promote both his show and Edwin's new album. On one occasion I had to take J. J. Barnes as well, and the pair were like a couple of kids in the back of the car, laughing about the old times in Detroit before the rapacious Berry Gordy snapped up all his city's competitors and incorporated them into the ever-growing Motown conglomerate.

The first gig blew my head off. It was at an enormous sports centre-type venue in Leicestershire, but the shocker was that there were at least a couple of thousand people crammed inside with many, many more waiting to get in. Once the doors opened, I had a chance to look around properly and took in the record bars and the dancers. The dancers were like nothing I'd ever seen before, totally different from the jazz-funk dancing we had in London. The oddest thing was the extraordinary mix of people: mods, soulboys, northern soulboys, scooterboys and, most extraordinarily, skinheads. And there was no fighting.

For all us mods in London and the south, violence was an everyday occurrence, but here in Hinkley, everyone was mixing together, dancing together and, yes . . . laughing together. I was shocked.

An expectant hush fell over the hall as the lights were dimmed and Snake Davis and his backing band walked on stage. There followed a magical couple of hours. One by one the succession of vocalists walked into the spotlight and held the crowd in the palm of their collective hands. The show was most definitely stolen by Lou Ragland, who ambled out with an oversized acoustic guitar and stormed through his up-tempo hit 'I Travel Alone'. Stolen, that was, until Edwin was announced and the crowd screamed their approval. The atmosphere was electric and I was hooked. Edwin Starr was a brilliant performer who held the crowd spellbound.

The rest of the tour passed in a blur. I remember Ray Margetson joined me at one of the gigs. We took in Manchester, Nottingham and a host of other northern halls. My 300 quid expenses quickly ran out until I got back to London and grabbed some more. Jon Brewer was sceptical that I'd gone through so much cash in just over a week, but I pointed out that Edwin and his mates had healthy appetites.

And then, before I had time to fully digest it, it was over and I returned to London, elated, clutching a phone book bursting with soul scene contacts and a copy of Edwin Starr's legendary rare 45 'Scott's on Swingers (S.O.S.)', which he'd gifted me for looking after him.

I'd been thrown in at the deep end but had an incredible time. Truth be told, the whole holiday – and yes, it was a holiday – was immense. And it had been amazing to see a world where there was so much joy in the room.

PART 4

25

I GOT BY IN TIME

Musically, there was a gap opening on our scene. The Q-Tips and The Step had recently split, and that left only Nine Below Zero playing soul or R&B on the mod circuit, but there was an increasing demand for that sound.

The Electric Stadium in Seven Kings had become a very supportive venue, hosting mod bands twice a week with a market on Saturday afternoons. We were often there watching groups like Small World, The Kick and Scarlet Party with 35 scooters in the car park every time.

It was there that I saw a band that blew me away.

They were called Fast Eddie and were from Benfleet, in the heart of the Essex blues delta. While they weren't necessarily mods, they immediately appealed to our crowd; an R&B four-piece in the mould of Dr. Feelgood fronted by a charismatic vocalist called Gordon Tindale. He was super sharp, dressed like an ace-face with a brilliant stage persona, and quite simply, he insulted his audience. And they loved him for it.

The first time I saw Fast Eddie I knew I wanted to manage them. Although I assumed management couldn't be difficult, I'd never done it before and had no idea what a manager was supposed to do. I approached the idea with some trepidation, but the band were certainly one of the best live groups I'd ever seen and I knew that to make them a success on our scene all I had to do was to get people to see them play live.

The band members were all a few years older than me and I suspect they were sceptical about whether a teenager could actually help their career move forward, but because they'd been playing the ever-decreasing pub-rock circuit I also suspect they thought they had nothing to lose.

At this point Fast Eddie had no live agent, so when I offered my services I took on the job of booking gigs too. The band quickly became incredibly popular and built up a large following, initially among the East London mods but soon around the country as word of their appeal spread.

Within months they were playing regularly at our nights at the Regency and further afield at the Bush Hotel in Shepherd's Bush and the 100 Club, always to packed houses. It was a very successful, mutually beneficial relationship, but after six months I was disappointed that I hadn't broken them to the next level. By the spring of 1982 I knew I had to do something to kick them up the ladder; the question was what?

I walked into Mike Everett's office at Avatar and asked him what I should do. There was a rumour at work that Mike had been involved in signing David Bowie to RCA and he was genuinely revered as an old-school A&R man. Up to this point my main contact with him had been to collect a small bag of change from his secretary every morning and walk to wherever he'd parked his car to fill the meter. Mike was an industry veteran and contemporary of the legendary Tony Hall who'd seen the original mod scene at close quarters. I was slightly in awe of them both. In his Sixties, Mike seemed to be an all-knowing oracle on the disparate vagaries of the music industry. He was seeing his days out at Avatar and for some unfathomable reason seemed to love the idea of helping this young upstart. I think I reminded him of his glory days 15 years earlier – after all, I was always harking back to the Sixties in the office. I suspect Mike was quietly pleased I'd asked him for advice.

'Erm, hello, Mike. I need to tap your brain somewhat . . .'

'Well, what about?' came the gruff reply.

I told him that I'd come up against something of a brick wall with my management clients and poured out the exact situation. 'We're getting great gigs but don't seem to be getting much further than that.'

He considered me in silence for what felt like five minutes but couldn't have been longer than 30 seconds. His advice was quite simple: 'Make a record.'

But how on earth did I make a record? I worked at a record company and didn't even know how to make a fucking record!

I spent the next few weeks researching what to do, and eventually came across an advert in the *NME* classifieds. It stated, quite simply: 'Make your own single, best prices'. The firm was based on an industrial estate near Stratford. I called them up and they told me it would cost 120 quid for 1,000 copies in a one-colour picture sleeve. The only problem was, I needed to send them a master and the artwork.

I knew what artwork was because I'd been producing the fanzine for a few years by now, but what was a master? I went back to Mike Everett and asked him to talk me through the nuts and bolts. He explained I'd have to put the band in a studio and record them. It sounded expensive, so I asked if he had anyone he could introduce me to. He gave me the number for PRT, Pye Records' in-house studio in Marble Arch. I called them and was told they could fit me in. It was £20 an hour to hire, which was pretty steep, but at least it included an engineer – whatever that was!

'We're free next Wednesday . . . Shall I book you in?'

I was still a bit worried about the cost, so mentioned I was a friend of Mike's and they put the price down to £17.50. An *hour*! That was more than I was earning a day!

I realised that the best way forward would be to take a partner in the record label; that way, if the thing didn't work, we could share the losses as well as the profits. I approached my DJing partner at the Regency and the editor of *Patriotic*, Ray Margetson. He loved Fast Eddie and seemed initially excited by the project, so while I still did most of the planning, I knew that he would be there to help me out.

I called the band and we decided to record the Little Walter classic 'My Babe' with a couple of B-sides. Fast Eddie all had to take a day off work, but it was agreed and in the diary. We'd pop up to Marble Arch the following Tuesday and record the band's first (and only) single.

While the modish Gordon Tindale played harmonica and handled the lead vocals, the other three band members were more in the tradition of Dr. Feelgood – although bassist Andy Waite had a penchant for three-button tailored jackets. The other two, Chris Page on guitar and Bob Fulbrook on drums, got around their lack of modness by wearing Hawaiian shirts. Fortunately, they were all able to bunk off work the following Tuesday.

I was certainly enthusiastic but didn't have a clue what I was doing. I was supposed to be the producer, but what did a producer do? The day was upon us and we turned up at the studio at ten. The band unloaded and set up in the live room. The engineer, a long-haired denim-wearer asked, 'So, Debbie on reception didn't fill in the time schedule. How long you gonna need, man?'

Well, £17.50 an hour was steep – I wasn't even on 80 quid a week. In my ignorance I replied,

'Three hours should be enough . . .?'

He laughed at me and I cringed with embarrassment.

'Mate, it'll take more than three hours to set the mics up. It'll probably take all day to lay three tracks down.'

It was my first studio session and I felt incredibly out of my depth.

The live room was larger than I expected. The walls were either covered in foam sound-deadening tiles or acacia-wood slats and there were microphones and cables everywhere.

'Listen, guys, we're on a tight deadline; can you crack on with setting up?'

I sat in what was called the 'control room' and observed the band through a soundproofed-glass window. Realising I was a complete recording virgin, the engineer encouraged me to relay my ideas by pressing a button on the mixing desk. The band would all hear me in their headphones and hopefully follow my instructions.

Well, it appeared to work!

We were ready to go in 45 minutes. I think we had a couple of run-throughs and that was it. I thanked the engineer and we were out within the three hours. He told me no one had recorded that quickly since 1969.

Jon Brewer had once made clear never to take a master tape on the Tube because the electromagnetic interference can cause what's known as 'drop-out', where the sound recording on the tape disappears for a split second. (I have no idea how or why this can happen!) With that in mind, I drove home on the Lambretta with the precious reel inside my parka, feeling very pleased with myself. I was now officially a record producer.

The next day, I dropped off the tape to the pressing plant along with the amateur artwork I'd knocked up with Letraset and a cheque. A couple of weeks later, the records arrived at Avatar in ten boxes. My extracurricular activities raised a few eyebrows at work, but Jon Brewer had always been all right about it; as long as I did my job properly, nothing was said.

I immediately delivered the discs to Merc, where Jimmy put one in the window. Rather pleasingly, 'My Babe' was well received and sold out in a couple of months despite us not having a proper distributor.

I'd called the label Well Suspect, after the original mod revival shop round the back of Carnaby Street. Well Suspect's super-cool status had been enhanced by their Lambretta, strategically positioned and cemented into place so that it appeared to burst through the shop's front wall. Sadly, the shop lasted less than 12 months, but it made such an impression on me that three years later, knowing nothing about copyright or intellectual property, I appropriated their name and logo for my first record label! I took a photo of the label sewn inside one of their jackets, which Terry Rawlings eventually redrew for our second release – because when we'd done the first single, I hadn't even known what a logo was!

Ray had been initially keen, but I soon realised that his heart wasn't in it. He had a proper job away from music, whereas I worked at a record label, and although we continued to run our nights at the Regency together, I soon found myself as the sole director of the fledgling Well Suspect Records.

The single was a success and did indeed lift the band's profile. Gigs were coming in from around the country and Fast Eddie were soon the biggest band on the scene after The Style Council and The Truth. It was an amazing time and seemed like things were going to get better. The fanzine was growing and now I had a record out.

Meanwhile at Avatar, I'd been promoted and was now 'head of press and promotion'! The label had diversified into the latest trend, the VHS video. Jon Brewer had connections in the States and landed the licence for a teen movie called *Screwballs*. It was pretty funny, in the tradition of *Lemon Popsicle*, *Animal House* and *Porky's*. I can still remember the line when one of the kids complains about the headmaster: 'Principal Stuckov can fuck off!' Almost perfect poetry.

The movie was an instant hit. It was one of the first-ever VHS releases and became an enormous seller. This taught me another important lesson. It doesn't matter how good or bad your product is; what matters is that people believe it's good and that they really need to have it.

This business was also about timing. Avatar had the right product at a time when a new market was crying out for it. It didn't seem to make any difference whether the films were crap or brilliant; the video rental shops appearing on every high street were crying out for tapes. Six months later would have been too late but, as it was, Avatar found themselves as market leaders, which meant that the next three or four releases were easy sells. This also kept the retail price for new VHS releases extraordinarily high: we could shift the product at almost 30 quid a pop. Jon Brewer was ecstatic and my stock climbed at the company once again.

However, a few weird things happened after that success, which got me thinking about my future.

Some were just mad. Jon unveiled the next couple of VHS releases and I was tasked with getting an axe made that could be worn as part of a cap that fastened under the chin. This would apparently make it look to the casual observer like an axe was embedded in the wearer's skull. What the fuck was he on about this time? When Brewer got something into his head (not an axe, obviously), it was hard to shake him off. Apparently, the next release was called *The Unhinged* and was a slasher movie in which the protagonist dispatched her victims with an axe to the head. Seemingly, my boss thought it would be a great idea to get some special-effects cap/axe combo made for the staff to wear at the press launch.

'They won't forget that in a hurry!' he said.

It was easier said than done. I had extreme difficulty even explaining what I was looking for but eventually found a special-effects/logistics company based at Pinewood. The prototype cost 100 quid and looked more like a child's comedy toy. Brewer was furious. Needless to say, the experiment wasn't a success, and the only thing that happened at the press launch was that I got drunk and made a fool of myself. I wasn't used to so much free drink.

*

One day I turned up for work to find the company had moved to a new premises over the weekend but hadn't told the staff. I never knew why but assumed there was some financial reason for this. Literally everything had been transported to our new headquarters, which were ready to roll by Monday lunchtime. Avatar had decamped to a decent building halfway down the Kings Road. Chelsea was a cool place to work in the Eighties and was where I came across my first example of that culinary delight, the pizza. People don't realise how utterly crap dining out was in London in the early Eighties. You had the Wimpy or the Aberdeen Angus Steakhouse. The Kings Road was a cut above.

However, my real problems at Avatar started a few months down the line when the *Daily Mirror* newspaper published an interview that I'd done as part of their 'Youth of Today' feature. It wasn't a great piece but it ran to a double-page spread with a large photo of me and my mates on scooters outside the *Mirror*'s building in Chancery Lane. I was glad I was on holiday when it hit the streets as I was embarrassed with what the journalist had come up with: hardly any of the quotes were accurate and they made me look stupid. It kicked off with the line, ' "Watch the threads, mate," barked Eddie Piller as the pint splashed dangerously close to his tailor-made suit . . .' and continued in the same vein. That particular quote had been lifted verbatim from *Quadrophenia* and was followed with other crap we hadn't said, like, 'We love the Sixties, even though we aren't old enough to remember them . . .' and 'We dance to The Doors and The Beatles . . .' You get the drift: all totally fabricated.

When I got back from my Ibiza holiday a couple of days later, I was called up to Jon Brewer's forbidding office where an open copy of the *Mirror* was laid on his desk. The first thing I thought on seeing it was that I needed a bloody haircut.

'Eddie, we've got to have a chat. Sit down.'

Then followed a 20-minute bollocking during which Jon complained about me running my own business from the Avatar office.

'You've garnered more coverage for yourself than you have for any of my acts over the last six months. I don't mind you doing it, but pull your bloody finger out. Don't forget, you work for me first and yourself a very distant second.'

Suddenly, we moved office *again*. The team was getting smaller and many of the original staff had moved to pastures new. It became apparent by my increasingly frequent trips to Avatar's lawyers (I was still forced to deliver the occasional letter) that in spite of the video successes there was growing cashflow pressure. Bill Newton, the company accountant, taught me about VAT, cashflow and, best of all, how to juggle non-existent cash with a bank.

The one advantage of the second move – this time to a new purpose-built media office building called Imperial Studios in Stamford Brook – was that I could spend more time with my mates from the Fulham Wasps Scooter Club. Such was the situation in London at the time that most of the different areas didn't get on, regardless of whether or not they were mods. I had a couple of mates who were active in the Wasps and we'd regularly drink in the same Kings Road pubs frequented by Georgie Best. There was Brian Miller, who lived right next door to my office with his two lovely sisters in Imperial Square; Graham Parsons, who was a bit of a face and who represented Britain in athletics but sadly died far too young; and the main man at the club, Andy Hilson, whose occasional dabble with casual led him to sport a tweed deerstalker with a red Fila BJ (this was sartorial suicide from my perspective!). We often met for a pint at lunchtime and the relationship between the East London and the Wasps was surprisingly good; this was one of the main reasons we never fought with them, which we unfortunately did with so many others . . .

26

MY EVER CHANGING MOODS

The mod scene continued to grow all through the autumn of 1982. So many young kids were doing their best to join us that it was impossible to ride a scooter past a school at kicking-out time without a dozen nippers pointing and shouting their approval. It seemed like mod just couldn't stop getting bigger. The media and the music establishment might have hated us, but youngsters were still flocking to the banner.

But then, out of the blue, something shocking happened that completely shook our world.

The Jam split!

When Paul Weller called time on The Jam in December 1982, there was a kind of collective disbelief. We had become so used to the band being the focus of our world that we were stunned. Most of the original revival bands had split already and, although there was a healthy London and localised national DJ scene, everybody expected that if The Jam split, mod would disappear with them.

I could understand why Paul Weller did it. He was becoming more fascinated with the theoretical *concept* of mod. Weller's musical taste had broadened too, and he was increasingly drawn to both soul and jazz – as evidenced in The Jam's later recordings like 'Move On Up' and 'Shopping'. Perhaps he just wanted a fresh start with musicians who were more in tune with his new personal direction?

Even so, when he announced the end of The Jam, none of us could really believe him. I can only compare the general feeling on the mod scene to some kind of mass mourning. I mean that people actually became depressed and it felt like our world was over. They were at the peak of their game and had delivered hit after hit in succession; they were probably the biggest band in the country at the time. So why would he throw in the towel?

Quite simply, Paul Weller had had enough. He'd been reading a novel, either *City of Spades* or *Absolute Beginners*, both by Colin MacInnes (the ultimate Sixties mod writer), while on holiday – the first holiday he'd been able to take for many years – when a light came on in his head: 'I can't do this any more. I need things to move forward . . .' Once Weller decides to do something he very rarely changes his mind, and in this instance that was never an option. After sitting on it for a few months, Paul eventually told Bruce Foxton and Rick Buckler of his decision and they were stunned.

Fortunately for us, the band had already scheduled a winter tour and confirmed they would honour the dates and split after the last gig, in Brighton. This prompted a massive rush for tickets. Everyone wanted to see The Jam on their final tour and it was hard enough to pick up tickets for their shows at the best of times. I managed to secure them for about half the dates. In the past, I'd occasionally been able to blag a guest list, but there was no chance on this tour as tickets were so scarce. However, even without tickets I managed to take in most of the tour, including the five nights at Wembley Arena. Like many others, we climbed through windows or sneaked in during sound checks and hid until the doors opened.

As the tour neared its conclusion the atmosphere became more hysterical. At the penultimate gig, in Guildford, the front doors were forced and hundreds of ticketless mods crashed their way in. It was absolute chaos.

Brighton was special too and I managed to climb up onto the stage for a brief moment until I was grabbed by the band's roadie, Kenny Wheeler, given a quick clump and chucked back out into the crowd from the side of the stage. It was to be The Jam's last-ever gig. What on earth was going to happen now? Was this the end of the mod revival?

The answer was a decisive no.

No one was expecting what came next.

Six months after The Jam split, Weller somehow reinvented mod for the next generation. Single-handedly he introduced new influences: jazz, poetry, literature and style. Kids still clung to the original revival look, though, and defiantly carried on sporting their parkas as a badge of belonging, much as we had in 1979.

For his next move he teamed up with former Merton Parkas and Jam session player Mick Talbot to form The Style Council and the pair were quickly joined by a teenage jazz drummer called Steve White and Paul's wife, the former Wham! and Animal Nightlife vocalist Dee C. Lee. The new band took the mod philosophy to new heights. As soon as I saw them, I realised that Weller had been right to end The Jam.

While The Style Council led the way with their explosively political soul-pop and a manifesto that was reinforced on all of their record sleeves, their new jazz-tinged sound split The Jam's fanbase, many of whom never quite forgave Weller for ending 'their' band.

Possibly the saddest photo of the mod revival is of a newly Jam-less Paul Weller leaving a recording studio in 1983 wearing a herringbone overcoat. Patiently waiting outside to greet him is a group of 13-year-olds proudly dressed in their parkas. Paul looks slightly bewildered and embarrassed while they gaze hopefully at their hero without quite realising that their newfound world had already gone and wasn't coming back any time soon. I'm not criticising them in any way – they were young and finding their feet by embracing the iconography of mod. We've all done it. But the look on Weller's face speaks volumes.

Somehow mod, the culture and the movement, kept evolving and it felt like Weller had given it another burst of energy by forcing The Jam's ending. As a result, by the middle of 1983 mod was back in the charts, and not just with The Style Council. There was another new band making waves. They were called The Truth and had an organ-heavy sound closer to what mods had become used to during the revival.

We had followed Nine Below Zero since 1979 and there was no doubt that their classic take on harmonica-heavy R&B had influenced our own Fast Eddie. The band were incredible live, but a lack of commercial success led harp player Mark Feltham and frontman Dennis Greaves to throw in the towel. Instead, Greaves met Mick Lister and, along with bassist Brian Bethell, drummer Gary Wallis and Hammond player Chris Skornia, they formed an out-and-out mod band.

To an extent, The Truth filled the gap for those among The Jam's fanbase who didn't like The Style Council (perhaps The Truth sounded more like 'Beat Surrender'-era Jam than it did the more jazzy Style Council) and had a string of chart hits. I'd known Dennis for a few years already, but he was one of Terry Rawlings' best mates. Not only did he ask us to design the first few single sleeves, but I also found myself on stage introducing the band at the 100 Club for their live EP *Five Live* – the first time I ever appeared on record! We helped out when the band were on the road too, by selling merchandise or roadie-ing.

While very different, these two bands, The Truth and The Style Council, ensured that mod retained a musical profile and – along with newer groups like The Times, The Moment, The Kick, The Direct Hits, The Scene and The Jetset – gave birth to something that could only really be called the second mod revival.

This one was different to 1979. The clothes were much better, for one; there was more tailoring and sartorial style rather than just parkas and desert boots. The music was different too. Bands would still play, but the DJs would pretty much exclusively spin northern soul and R&B. Scooters played a much bigger part in mod life in the second revival, as many of the youngsters from 1979 were old enough to ride them by this point.

The bands of the second revival somehow filled the vacuum left by The Jam, while Fast Eddie managed to link the DJs' club sound with their live performances, something only they could only do because of their retro R&B style.

Meanwhile, with the exception of Long Tall Shorty and Small World, pretty much all the original 1979 bands disappeared without a trace. This new soulful, sharper environment just wasn't right for them. Almost without exception, the first wave of mod bands had formed long before *Quadrophenia*'s release. And following the film's success and subsequent impact on the scene's demographic, many of the revival's originators fell away – feeling very little in common with the much younger crowd that suddenly appeared. Those bands had also experienced a pretty horrible post-revival backlash. To mod bands in 1980 and 1981, it must have seemed that slogging away on the live circuit offered little real chance of success, because every band that made it into the music press would be treated with disdain and contempt.

So, by 1983, everything felt purged, and the new younger, hipper, more soulful scene felt ready to reinvent itself. Undeniably, the real understanding of what mod was actually about had changed, helped by the burgeoning scooter scene and the discovery that Sixties mods, the faces at least, had been more into soul music and R&B. The first mod revival bands were simply becoming less relevant. They stood aside and made way for the next wave.

In mid-1983, the mod scene was in very rude health indeed.

*

One of the key differences between this second revival and the first was that – despite some very good and inventive bands – proper mod nightclubs with sussed, knowledgeable DJs and a clued-up, equally knowledgeable dance-floor crowd increased in dominance.

By now, the shape of our mod weekends was familiar, but the flavour had definitely changed into something less punky and (for many) a lot more authentically Sixties.

Friday nights were often for drinking with my local mates, out in Ilford at one of the jazz-funk clubs or if not, then up West on scooters to a night at the Ben Truman or the Phoenix. There were always a few Sixties or northern soul nights to visit. We'd take our pick and descend en masse.

Saturday morning and a few of us would meet in the Castle car park in Woodford to begin our 'trawl'. We were on the hunt for records or clothes. Mintz & Davis in Romford was great for schmutter but was risky because boneheads roamed the shopping centre looking for mods to attack. It became like a game of cat and mouse as me, Dave Palmer, Spencer, Les Howard, Bunny or Bullshit Bal were chased around by tooled-up skins in Anglias or Mk2 Cortinas trying to ride us off the road. Romford gradually became out of bounds.

Instead, we'd cruise around on scooters, maybe taking in a different scooter shop every week; there were still plenty in London or Essex where you could rely on meeting like-minded travellers on the path.

From there we'd head down to Forest Gate, Manor Park or East Ham to check out the dozens of what would now be called junk shops that provided a treasure trove of Sixties 'stuff'. Secondhand records, clothes, tie pins, badges, patches and, if you were lucky, new-old stock. This was old gear that had been stored in the backrooms or warehouses of East End fashion shops and had seen better days.

The stock was 'new', so was perfect for us but needed a dry-clean to get rid of the smell of being left unloved in storage for over 15 years. You could dress like you'd been to the tailors for the fraction of the price. Denson shoes were also a revelation, super-cool Sixties styling that could be snapped up for a fiver. When the shopping was done, we'd pile into a pie and mash shop by midday for a 'double-double'.

Pie and mash was our own cultural delicacy and in the early Eighties there were still dozens of these exotic eateries scattered around the East End offering cheap and instant food for the working classes long before McDonald's raised its ugly head. They sold minced-beef pies and mash with a unique green-tinged liquid called liquor in place of gravy. This was apparently a mixture of eel water, potato starch and parsley with the consistency of, well . . . I'll leave that to the imagination. They also sold that legendary East End delicacy jellied eels. The shops were so incredibly popular in my youth that when Terry Rawlings joined me at *Extraordinary Sensations* we published a Top 10 Pie and Mash chart. Changing demographics and the East End diaspora has seen many of these shops close in the last ten years, although some have relocated to Essex and Kent.

By 1 o'clock we'd be parking our scooters outside Great Marlborough Street Magistrates' Court for a few beers in the Shakespeare's Head, the Coffee House, the Clachan or the Blue Posts. There would always be lads from all over London milling around on Carnaby Street and it gave us a chance to catch up with friends and find out what was happening in the clubs.

Then it was football.

Saturday nights were usually spent at mod events in the West End. Your smartest clobber was essential and by now I was driving most places in my full-up Herald. We'd either check a band or go to a club like the Royal Oak in Tooley Street or the Bush Hotel and then maybe on to the 100 Club for a 6Ts soul all-nighter. I'd drive to Walthamstow to pick up Mappy, Wanstead for Jarvis, Hainault for Dean Port . . . I'd have clocked up 70 miles before we even got into town!

Most of the London clubs were organised by Tony Class, who had single-handedly kept the mod scene alive as the live scene collapsed. But he wasn't entirely alone. At this time the majority of mod events were held in the upper rooms of London pubs, with budget sound systems, no security and carpet on the floor. We loved it! We could be mods with no interference or hassle. The nights thrived but were always getting closed down because eventually skins would track us down and there'd be trouble.

Next-generation mod DJs like Paul Hallam, Toski, 'Big' Bob Morris, Andy Orr and Richard Early were popping up with a more early soul- and R&B-based sound. It immediately took off. They'd dropped the Sixties pop that Classy dipped in and out of and stuck close to the Randy Cozens formula.

The soundtrack was changing fast. Paul Hallam, seen by many as the heir apparent to Classy, was certainly digging deeper. His first club was at Feltham FC (the very place where I'd been knocked off my Lambretta by Leslie Crowther!) and he then played at the Dolphin in Kingston. By the time he opened Sneakers with Richard Early he'd been guesting at the Outrigger in Birmingham and was bringing their more Sue Records R&B flavour back to London with him. Tracks like John Lee Hooker's 'I Love You Honey', 'Juke' by Little Walter, 'Don't Start Me to Talkin'' by Sonny Boy Williamson, 'I've Got a Woman (Part 1)' by the organist Jimmy McGriff, 'Hurt by Love' by Inez & Charlie Foxx and 'Who's Afraid of Virginia Woolf (Parts 1 and 2)' by Jimmy Smith. This sound was definitely more rootsy than the stuff we were spinning in Essex, where we'd been more influenced by the northern soul sound introduced to us by the likes of Keb Darge, Dick Coombes and Simon Cento.

In fact, Hallam and his Sneakers night certainly fuelled the drive to a more 'authentic' look and feel to both clothes and scooters. Very few of the original bands fitted into the new direction. There were a whole host of younger kids into the scene by now and they seemed to prefer this new stylistic direction. It was especially popular with the girls. They'd been looking at the pictures in Richard Barnes's book *Mods!* (published by Pete Townshend's Eel Pie imprint to provide some authentic flavour alongside *Quadrophenia*). I think that by this time, in late 1983, the mod scene had reappraised Barnes's work, especially the photos, and began using it as a reference manual for how the next generation should dress. While I was becoming more comfortable in jeans and polo shirts, those coming onto the scene at this point were obsessed with dressing like it was 1964.

This is the way of the mod world.

Ray Margetson and I had been approached to move our Tuesday rhythm & soul night at Barons up the road to the Regency Suite in Chadwell Heath. To be fair, Barons was too small (it was simply a terraced house converted into a nightclub) and in a tiny backstreet, so we jumped at the chance. Ilford was a really heaving party town with clubs on every corner, and of course, it was where we had been hosting our alldayers. We were on the ladder and success was beckoning.

I knew the Regency Suite as it was where my jazz-funk DJ hero Froggy played a Saturday residency and I'd been many times. Moving our night there was very appealing.

Originally the owner, Brian, boasted that he'd been a mod in the Sixties and offered us Mondays, but within three weeks we were selling the club out. Brian was amazed that our crowd were turning out in such numbers on the hardest night of the week, so he offered us a Friday too. For a while we did both and they were almost always full. We'd already recruited Mappy, our partner in M.I.N.D., to join us on the decks; the music was a mixture of northern soul interspersed with tunes lifted from Cozens' Mod Top 100 and the new sound they were calling 'modern soul' dropped by Mappy. Typical northern tunes you might hear were 'What's Wrong With Me Baby?' by The Invitations, 'Breakout' by Mitch Ryder & the Detroit Wheels and 'I'll Be Loving You' by the Soul Brothers Six. Some of the more mod tracks were things like 'All About My Girl' by Jimmy McGriff, 'The Wah-Watusi' by The Orlons, 'Soul Sauce' by Cal Tjader and 'You Can't Sit Down' by the Phil Upchurch Combo. Examples of the latest 'modern soul' sound we were playing included 'How Can I Tell Her' by Curtis and 'It Takes Heart' by Greg Perry. We even got to play British mod tracks like 'Almost Grown' by Small Faces or 'Bert's Apple Crumble' by The Quik. As you can tell by these tracks, the playlist was incredibly varied and, to our surprise, remarkably popular.

We called the night Sound & Rhythm and within a couple of months it was pulling people from all over the south of England, with 50 scooters lined up in the car park every time. We soon caught the attention of the BBC, who sent down a film crew to document the rebirth of yet another mod scene for a BBC Two culture show. The programme was presented by Perry Haines, the manager of King (and the man who pioneered the rebirth of Dr. Martens in a non-skinhead way), and although he was from the Wag Club's New Romantic scene, he understood soul and mods and the piece was sympathetic, giving the club serious kudos.

The worm was turning.

27

PHOENIX CITY

I n 1983 we saw the foundation of an extremely successful and galvanising mod newsletter called 'The Phoenix List', which had been set up by an American called Mark Johnson.

Johnson washed up on these shores and within six months literally took control of the mod scene. I often wonder how he managed it. After all, we were an enormous but disparate, amorphous collection of young men, women and kids who were into a specific way of life called mod. We were united by a love of the Sixties, scooters, bands – all of it.

'The General' (as he was universally known) was an odd fish. He had been a PR man on Ronald Reagan's campaign team and was apparently married with a family, but suddenly walked away, relocated to London, bought himself a scooter and – completely out of the blue – started to organise the mod scene. Of medium height with a sparse frame and an East Coast twang to his voice, he was also ten years older than the rest of us.

We never really gave much thought to the *why*. It was more about the *what*; what Mark Johnson was actually doing for *us*. He took over Tony Class's newsletter 'What's Happening Fer Mods' and improved it. What had been a handwritten flyer publicising Class's clubs suddenly morphed into a comprehensive newssheet covering every mod club in the country and was published weekly. 'The Phoenix List' was organised, nationally distributed and was incredibly useful.

Even Tony Class was on board with it, and then Paul Hallam joined up too. For our part, we were running the Regency and Hallam had Sneakers, and it soon became apparent that Johnson's newssheet was an indispensable promotional tool for everything to do with the mod scene. We'd long had no coverage from the real press and fanzines were sporadic and surfaced only every couple of months. 'The Phoenix List' soon became how kids around the country found out what was happening – it was reliable, accurate and regular. It became our diary, and our mouthpiece.

The list soon spawned a society. For some reason the mod scene was big on societies back then. It started innocently enough: we (the 'steering committee') would meet every other week in a room above a pub, usually in Shoreditch or the East End. It seemed slightly odd. We had things like minutes, a treasurer, a secretary and quorums, and various business was discussed by the committee members. Johnson was the chairman. The Phoenix Society reminded me of a type of 'mod masons' (a joke idea long discussed by Paul Hallam and me but never instigated). It was initially concerned with fairly basic stuff, like deciding Bank Holiday destinations and venues.

A couple of interesting things developed from this. The first was the Buckingham Palace Scooter Run, held on the anniversary of the first one in the Sixties, when a bunch of random mods had descended on the palace for an event that ended up with a pilled-up rider ramming the wrought-iron gates on a clapped-out Vespa. The other was something called the National Mod Meeting. It was a good idea in principle and Johnson suggested holding an alldayer at a North London Irish ballroom where a panel of mods would discuss the scene's direction in front of the audience and then party the night away with bands and DJs, with prepared statements from the likes of Ronnie Lane and Steve Marriott read out to the crowd. Before long, 'The Phoenix List' established itself as an important cog in the London mod machine.

While the Phoenix Society was initially just a collective of mates and DJs, it eventually became apparent that Mark Johnson had always intended it to be a commercial vehicle for his business ideas; this became increasingly obvious once the society was established. But still, the rest of us weren't bothered as we too were all involved in selling fanzines, records or hosting club nights. Johnson was obviously making money out of the society, but I went along with it because he was convenient. He advertised my gigs, sold my records and promoted my fanzine. What's not to like?

The Buckingham Palace Scooter Run was an extraordinary event. Hundreds of scooter riders from around the capital and Home Counties headed for Carnaby Street for it. On the day, I made a sartorial effort and wore a Steve Starr pink suit (à la Camp Freddie in *The Italian Job*), a tab-collared shirt with white collar and cuffs from Harrods and a burgundy tie, all topped off with a brown full-length leather trench coat and burgundy loafers. My Vespa was providing a pillion ride to a young photographer from the *Sunday Mirror* called Caron Malcolm who was shooting the event for the paper. Caron was already a mod and was so impressed with our crowd that she soon embedded herself with us, visually documenting the scene for a few years.

The event itself was incredibly exciting and the scooters soon headed down The Mall until a few hundred were riding around the Queen Victoria Memorial on the roundabout outside the palace front gates. The police were taken completely by surprise and had no idea what was going on, but eventually managed to summon enough officers to direct us into Hyde Park, where we parked up next to the Serpentine.

Life was very, very good.

This is a story about how some of the violence started to dissipate a little bit. This wasn't exactly down to me, but it serves to illustrate that by this time things felt different and were changing for the better in many ways.

The Paddington Scooter Club was one of the crews we didn't get on with. There was bad blood and I never really found out why. Tension had been building over a number of months until it exploded in spectacular fashion on Sunday night at another Tony Class club called the Sols Arms in Euston.

An argument between some of the younger Chingford (East London juniors) mods and the Paddington lot had got out hand at the Mildmay. No one really knew how it started, but a few weeks later around 25 East London mods turned up to sort out the situation once and for all.

The East London cars and scooters parked up round the corner from the pub. The Sols Arms was surrounded. At a prearranged signal the windows got put through with dustbins and bricks to the surprise of those inside. People were attacked as they tried to leave the pub, and found themselves quite simply unable get out of the doors. It was absolute mayhem and the pub got bashed about a bit. Not all of the people inside were our enemies, but in that kind of situation, when a pub is under siege, there's always going to be collateral damage. I heard later that people were hiding under tables as others were charging in with chairs and more were trying to get out to fight.

It's not something I'm proud of but, like many of these things, it happened regularly back then. Sometimes to us and sometimes by us (I once hosted an under-18s Saturday-afternoon disco at the Notre Dame Hall with Georgie Fame's agent and original mod Chris O'Donnell that got smashed to pieces by a scooter club who took exception to the event). There was a lot of fallout because of the Sols Arms 'incident' and for quite a while Tony Class made it clear that we weren't welcome at any of his clubs.

This was a big price to pay, as we visited his gigs at least once a week, but after a month he relented as we'd been following him around London since his very first night at the Hercules Tavern. He made one condition, though: we had to patch things up with Paddington SC. We did reach out but things were certainly strained until the August Bank Holiday a few months later.

The Isle of Wight was by now our regular August destination, and everyone met at a Tony Class do at the White Lion on Tottenham Court Road to get the weekend started in London.

Just as 30 scooters pulled away from the White Lion to head down to the coast, my throttle cable snapped. It was 11 o'clock on Friday and Classy's night was finishing, so I told the others I'd change the cable and catch up en route.

With the cable sorted, I eventually headed off on my own, driving through the night down the badly lit A3. And that's when I hit a curb head-on at about 30mph. Both tyres burst and the wheel rims were so severely buckled that they had to be dumped. For some added comedy value, the two side panels blew out sideways as the frame contracted on impact and ended up 10 feet away from the broken Lambretta.

As I was on my own when the accident happened, I thought I'd probably have to leave the bike by the side of the road and doss down in the porch of the Happy Eater services I'd passed a few hundred yards back. My best hope was that someone I knew would pull in for petrol in a van, let me chuck the scooter in the back and give me a lift.

But first I had to get back to the services. It's virtually impossible to push a Lambretta with two flat tyres and a whole host of gear strapped to it, but I knew I had to manage somehow.

I eventually made it back to the services thoroughly dispirited. It took me 40 minutes of serious effort to get there and by the time I arrived it was almost 1am. Would anyone be making their way down to the island in the middle of the night?

Fifteen minutes later I heard the distinctive *pop-pop* of a couple of approaching scooters. Thank fuck.

But my excitement was short-lived. When the two scooters pulled into the garage and parked up, I recognised them by their club patches as members of Paddington SC and instantly felt like Gary Shail in the scene from *Quadrophenia* when rockers gather around his broken-down Lambretta and give him and his girl a kicking. *Shit.* Of the 6, 000-odd scooters expected on the island, these two blokes just happened to be from our enemy. The Sols Arms bust-up was only a few months in the past and I was expecting the worst.

I realised they'd clocked me as soon as they pulled onto the forecourt but instead of reacting as I'd expected they made their way over and asked what the problem was. Surprised, I explained and within minutes they'd got their spare wheels out and were replacing my broken ones, which was generous and slightly unbelievable. I expressed my eternal gratitude and before long we set off in company, riding the rest of the way together until we finally arrived at the ferry crossing 40 minutes later. It was odd, sitting together in near silence for a quarter of an hour, waiting for the boat to pull in. I didn't really know how to start a conversation with them – after all, we were supposed to be enemies. But it soon became apparent that we weren't. They might have been from the wrong part of London, but they were both kind and friendly.

By the time the ferry docked at the pier we were knackered and set off for the official campsite. It was a bit of a schlep across the island and we'd been riding for four hours at this point, so decided to pull up and pitch the tents wherever we could find a space. Our *entente cordial* was going well, so we decided to share one tent rather than set up two at three in the morning, and eventually spotted a field surrounded by a thick hedge. The night was pitch-black and moonless, and once we'd parked up on a verge, we squeezed through a gap in the hedge and whacked up the tent as soon as we could. Fortunately, the field was very flat with surprisingly few lumps. Thank heaven for small mercies! The three of us jumped into our sleeping bags fully dressed and immediately fell asleep just as the sun was coming up.

'Get up! Come out of there – what on earth do you think you're up to?'

The shout woke me but I ignored it and burrowed deeper into the sleeping bag. Then I heard someone trying to unzip the tent flap. 'Are you deaf? I said come out or I'll phone the police.'

Oh, for Christ's sake. We'd only managed three hours' shut-eye!

We were all awake by now, so I unzipped the flap and stuck my head out. I was immediately confronted by an old lady in a Barbour jacket wearing wellington boots and a headscarf accompanied by a Jack Russell. She was indignant and shaking her walking stick.

Did we know we'd pitched our tent on the square of the Ryde Cricket Club ground? They were due to start play in a few hours, so we'd best clear off before the team turned up. 'The square is sacred, don't you know,' she said. 'You're not even supposed to walk on it, let alone pitch a tent!'

A rude awakening indeed, but the sun was out and it was a glorious day, so we laughed at the sheer joy of it all and scarpered as soon as we could pack the tent up. We drove to the scooter-run campsite, said our goodbyes and sought out our own people. And that was the end of the violence between the Paddington and East London scooter clubs.

Writing this 40 years later, it seems obvious, but we had so much more in common than we realised. It tells you a lot about the times, that it took a situation like this to realise it. The sad thing is that after all this time I can't remember the lads' names.

Unfortunately, while there was something of a softening of attitudes within the mod scene, we still had a problem with our newer 'friends', the scooterists.

The very idea of scooterists (or scooterboys) had been growing for a year or so already. While most had begun as mods, they had soon split away from the scene and by this time had already established their own rallies and events. Openly hostile to mods, they opted for a much more regressive and aggressive stance on just about everything. They appeared to be made up of every youth cult except for mods but, like us, they all rode scooters. This led to much antipathy between the two groups and from 1983 you would often see handwritten signs on venue doors that spelled out: 'No Jeans, No Greens, No Casuals'.

With the demise of Oi! and skinheads in general, the scooterboys' ranks were boosted by many from those former groups. Why they would want to ride scooters now, having spent the previous few years attacking people who rode them, we could never find out. But skins had certainly disappeared, to our great relief – although this didn't spell the end of violence against mods. Far from it.

In the summer of 1983, I'd been booked by Tony Class to DJ at an event at Cowey Sale in Walton-on-Thames. It was an under-18s gig on an island in the middle of the river and I'd borrowed my dad's car so I could take a few of the young Woodford mods with me. At this point the old man owned a Granada estate and I could fit seven of the nippers in without effort. Perry Quai aged only 15 was already a face at West Ham and, along with my next-door neighbour Roger 'BJ', was a member of the Under 5s – the junior branch of the Inter City Firm. I was only 19 myself but felt like some kind of elder statesman with all these hard kids in my car.

It was a glorious day and perfect to be down by the river. Tony Class was in his element as usual, bouncing around with his cheeky grin and filming everything (this was an annoying habit of his) with a large Sony video camera.

The open-air event was just around the corner from the Sixties mod club on Eel Pie Island and Classy had set everything up perfectly. The island had been home to one of the first R&B clubs in the Sixties and had a very mod reputation. I arrived to see a few hundred youngsters enjoying the sunshine and the disco with a smattering of older mods on scooters and in cars. The atmosphere was fabulous and kids were even jumping into the river to cool off.

At 3 o'clock things changed.

Fifty or so scooterboys came charging over the hill, looking to smash up the gig. They were all in their twenties or thirties and many were members of the Bad Boys Scooter Club, an offshoot of the A23 Crusaders. The kids at Classy's event were in their early teens, so it wasn't really an equal fight at all. The scooterboys were soon in among the kids and hitting out. Tony kept the camera running and the fight quickly became serious. A few older boys tried to defend the event and I was particularly concerned about my records, which were on the table by the decks. Soon we were surrounded by scooterboys turning over tables and steaming into us. The young West Ham lads were straight in with fists flying, but we were always going to lose. There were about 20 of us, most under 16, up against 50 of them. I traded a few punches and took a couple of hits over the back with an iron bar but nothing too serious.

Sadly, others were not so lucky. A teenage mod kid called Keiron Sergent had an eye poked out when he was hit with a Vespa front rack that had been ripped from a scooter during the fight (he was hospitalised for a month with over a hundred stitches to his face). A holidaying German mod had his leg smashed with an iron bar and a girl called Tabitha had her arm broken.

And then suddenly it was over. Just five minutes later we were left standing among the debris and helping the wounded.

I got my charges into the car and set off back to Woodford, pleased that none of them had been seriously hurt. Even though it was a horrible end to a really good day, this kind of thing happened every weekend, so I didn't give it too much thought.

Two days later I pulled up outside my house on the Lambretta, having just ridden home from work.

My mum walked into the kitchen as I was hanging up my parka and said, 'Edward, a policeman came round this afternoon looking for you. Apparently they issued you with a five-day ticket and want you to take your insurance straight down to the station.'

Not a problem, I told her, and walked the 300 yards to the Loughton Old Bill shop.

'Erm . . . Hello, my name's Edward Piller and I've been asked to drop off my details . . .'

Well, fuck me. Judging by the desk sergeant's expression, the Yorkshire Ripper had just rolled up. He pressed a button and a bell went off in a back room.

'He's here . . .'

Immediately, two uniformed officers ran out and wrestled me to the ground.

'What the fuck is going on? I've only brought my insurance down . . . Owww . . . Get off me!'

They bundled me into a cell and left me there for a few hours. I asked to call home and they reluctantly agreed but would tell me nothing. Eventually, a police car arrived to collect me and I was led out, handcuffed and thrown onto the back seat. Not a word was spoken and I still had no idea what was going on.

At Barkingside police station, which was apparently the main local custody centre, I was handed over to some different coppers and put into another car. We set off and they told me they had a warrant for my arrest issued in Walton-on-Thames and were taking me there to be interrogated. They'd tell me nothing else. After about half an hour we pulled into a garage for petrol. Bizarrely, after they'd filled up the Rover wouldn't start. Pure, absolute farce. Somehow the battery had gone flat and I was reluctantly pressed into bump-starting a police Rover while in fucking handcuffs. This broke the ice somewhat and the copper in the passenger seat lightened up enough to talk to me.

'Look, can you just tell me what's going on?' I asked. 'Where are we going and what have I done? I came home from work and was asked to take my documents to the station. Next thing I know I'm nicked?'

He told me I'd been arrested for affray and GBH – apparently, a complaint had been received about me hitting someone with a weapon the previous Sunday.

It was pointless trying to find out more and so in the early hours, after the clapped-out Rover pulled into Walton police station, I was thrown into yet another cell.

Next morning, I was interviewed under caution about the fight at Tony Class's Walton event. The police had arrested three scooterboys from the Bad Boys SC who'd given my name as a ringleader for the opposition. The police didn't seem to be aware of exactly what happened on the day, so I put them right. I was the only non-scooterboy to be arrested and I was pissed off that they'd grassed me up. From my perspective, I'd done nothing but defend myself and my records from marauding psychobillies and scooterboys.

According to the Old Bill, they had cast-iron evidence of me attacking someone with an offensive weapon. The police had seized Tony Class's video tape and it showed the punch-up in all its awful glory.

I wasn't allowed to see the film and neither was my duty solicitor, but he pushed hard and a week later I was shown a 40-second video clip of me hitting someone with a crash helmet, stripping off my shirt and then boxing – I kid you not – with someone for about 20 seconds. It was straight down the line jabs and hooks. I thought I came out of it quite well.

That was all there was. Or so the police told me.

I was arraigned for trial a month hence and was shocked to find out I'd be sharing the dock with the scooterboys, who were all on the same charges: affray, ABH and GBH. Some serious shit here that could result in me going down for a couple of years.

My lawyer had been constantly on to the Old Bill for access to Class's film, but they were dragging their feet. In the end he received the copy of the relevant section just a day before I was in court, which was an obvious attempt to rig the case by denying me access to evidence. It was revealing and fortunately looked like it would put me in the clear.

The court was intimidating, and standing in the dock on the day alongside the people who'd been smashing the fuck out of children just a month earlier and who'd then grassed me up to the Old Bill was not a good experience. They kept whispering that they were going to give me a hiding. The man on my immediate right was a tall, blond and tattooed psychobilly who constantly threatened me out of the side of his mouth. I ignored him for the rest of the trial until the verdict was announced. Then I laughed in his face.

The prosecution showed the film in its entirety. The police had somehow got wind of its existence and raided Tony Class's house. Obviously, they'd seized it against his will, but the whole thing brilliantly revealed how the scooterboys had swarmed over the hill and attacked the event.

There were also some hairy moments on the tape. While I was in the dock they ran a clip that showed a mod pulling a hammer out of his parka pocket and hitting a scooterboy around the head. It was a shocking incident and demonstrated that there was violence on both sides. The judge asked me if I recognised the man with the hammer; I thought I maybe did but I couldn't be sure and told him I wasn't prepared to guess.

The clip featuring my own actions also clearly showed a man with a metal bar chasing me and hitting me over the back and shoulders with it a number of times. That part of the clip lasted just 20 seconds, and then you saw me pick up the helmet and hit the very same man with it.

He'd chased me first. He was still trying to hit me with the iron bar and I'd been using the helmet to fend him off. The police hadn't wanted my brief to see this because it vindicated me completely. It was a real shocker. The only evidence the CPS had against me was a doctored video and some hearsay from the very people who'd attacked me in the first place.

My lawyer made them play the relevant part of the tape three times and I was again given an absolute discharge. I'd acted in self-defence and the film proved it.

I looked at my co-defendants in the dock next to me. The sad and crazy thing about all of this is that these scooterboys were effectively from an offshoot of the mod revival. Whether they were ex-mods or punks or skins or what, I don't know, but these men loved scooters and had decided, on a whim, that they hated mods enough to launch an almost military-style attack on a teenage disco. The judge delivered his verdict. The scooterboys who'd attacked the under-18s event in the first place got between 9 and 21 months each and were led from the dock in handcuffs.

28

KNOW YOUR PRODUCT

A few weeks after the Fast Eddie record sold out, I cast my eyes around for Well Suspect's next single. I loved the kudos of having a record label and was keen to keep it going. I had the fanzine, to which I'd added a mail-order record list – selling many of the singles that I'd reviewed – the Regency Suite DJ nights, the Ilford alldayers, band management and now a label. I was becoming quite the little mod entrepreneur! On top of that I'd got myself a new girlfriend. A scooter-riding suedehead from Sunbury called Nicky. She had a very long feather-cut and a penchant for Fair Isle jumpers and three-quarter-length tonic jackets. Before long we became inseparable. Oh, and I was still enjoying my time at Avatar.

At an industry function back in late 1982 I'd met a bloke from Beggars Banquet called Steve Webbon and we got on well. Although they'd started as a record shop, by this time Beggars were a pretty substantial independent label based just over the river from the Avatar office in Chelsea. Surprisingly, Steve was enthusiastic about Well Suspect, so we swapped business cards and agreed to meet for a pint in the near future.

The number of times I've said that and immediately forgotten the conversation are legion, but in those days I was still green and keen. Steve knew I was a mod and said he'd have a think about a project we could work on together.

Two weeks later he called and said he'd got an idea; he wondered if I had a Revox tape player in my office at Avatar. Revox made quarter-inch tape players, one step down from a proper mastering machine like a Studer A80. Steve told me he was bringing some tapes over for us to listen to. How exciting!

I went upstairs and asked Mike Everett if I could use his office for the meeting and he agreed, telling me he might as well go out for a long pub lunch and that the tape machine was all mine.

Steve turned up with a bag of quarter-inch tapes and was shown up to Mike's office to find me sitting behind an enormous desk. It was an impressive room and I couldn't help thinking he actually thought it was my office! I didn't disabuse him. Ellen popped her head round the door to offer us coffees and I felt like a real A&R man rather than a jumped-up office boy. I was soon brought down to earth when he handed me the first tape to thread into the machine.

'So, Steve, what have we got here?' I asked, cheerfully enough.

'I've been thinking how I can get involved and help Well Suspect progress to the next level. You told me you liked The Merton Parkas, yeah? Well, have a listen to this lot . . .'

Fuck! Fuck! I thought. I had absolutely no idea how these tape machines worked. It wasn't like playing a cassette; quarter-inch tapes were complicated. I wasn't about to let Steve know that I didn't know what I was doing, though. I was supposed to be proper A&R. It was a fucking disaster.

'Brilliant, Steve, give me the first reel . . .' I held my hand out, waiting.

Steve had brought me some unreleased Merton Parkas masters. The band had recently split, and to be honest, they'd had something of a hard time of it. The first single, 'You Need Wheels', had been absolutely slaughtered by the press and the mod scene in general. Although it was the first hit of the revival, it was pretty dire and coloured the band's whole career. People didn't give The Parkas a chance after that, which in my opinion was unfair. I thought their LP, *Face in the Crowd*, wasn't a bad record and they were always brilliant live. I'd seen the Parkas at least half a dozen times at places like the Marquee or the Wellington and had got to know the frontmen Danny and Mick Talbot and their younger brother Steve slightly.

I was very keen to hear the tapes but stood there over the machine like a lemon, not knowing what to do.

Master tapes are unique. There's usually only one of them and they're the end result of everything that goes into a recording session once the multichannel recordings have been 'bounced down' onto the two-track master. They are what you make actual records from.

'Great, Steve. I've always been a fan of the Parkas . . .' I said, staring at the tape machine.

I eventually managed to figure out how to thread the tape so it played OK, but soon realised that it was at the wrong end and needed to be rewound to the beginning before we could hear it. I switched the knob so the arrow pointed to 'REV' but the Revox burst into life at five times the speed I was expecting and the tape seemed to be travelling far too fast on the spool. I panicked and did the worst thing I could possibly have done. I quickly reversed the knob to 'FWD' without pressing 'STOP' first and there was an agonising slow-motion screeching noise as the spindles turned in opposite directions, the tape stretched and then snapped. Jesus. What had I done?

'Oh fuck . . .'

Steve's face was a picture. He looked horrified. I'd broken the master tape, *his* master tape. Of an unreleased Merton Parkas track. That it was indeed the only copy of the tape soon became apparent. Then he saw the look on my face – one of panic and terror – and burst out laughing. That broke the tension just as Ellen came in with the coffee. I had no option other than to confess I'd never used a quarter-inch machine before and was very sorry I'd broken his master. He then explained that the problem wasn't the break itself but the stretch. Tapes run at 15 (or 7.5) inches per second and a stretched tape would be unusable because that particular section would be out of time. A simple snap could be easily repaired, but to make right a stretch would entail an engineer identifying the section, finding a similar part elsewhere in the song, copying it and splicing it in to replace the stretched section. If the part that I'd ruined was in the middle of a verse, I was fucked; if it was an instrumental section or a chorus, it could probably be repaired. I was chastened and embarrassed, but it taught me another valuable lesson. Don't try to blag or bullshit technical stuff as you can do much more damage than you'd expect. Learn how to do things before you make a tit of yourself.

Steve then outlined his idea.

Since The Merton Parkas had called it a day, Beggars Banquet intended to release a career-defining compilation LP, but Steve was very aware that the band had an image problem. Quite simply, they weren't loved like The Chords, the Purple Hearts or Secret Affair and he was worried that no one would buy the record. He wanted to go some way to restoring their credibility before Beggars released the LP (which eventually turned out to be a mini-album of just the singles). *Extraordinary Sensations* was respected on the mod scene and by association Well Suspect would be too. How did I feel about choosing one of the band's unreleased masters for a single on the label? Beggars Banquet would generate the artwork and even manufacture the singles, putting the cost down as a marketing expense for the forthcoming album.

I was thrilled. We went back to the tapes and listened to them all, with Steve operating the complicated machine this time. Sod's law, it was the tape I'd snapped that I chose as the A-side, a track called 'Flat 19'. Unfortunately, we could only listen to the first bit, the section before I broke it. Steve said he'd take it to an engineer to see if it could be repaired and I kept my fingers crossed. The B-side would be the band's version of the Freda Payne classic 'Band of Gold'.

A week later, Steve called to inform me that the tape had been fixed and asked me to send him a Well Suspect logo for the sleeve. Suddenly we were in business! I didn't even see the artwork before it went to the factory, but when the finished records came back I was thrilled. The single looked fantastic and Steve had even arranged a distribution deal for me with Rough Trade, who were then part of the Cartel operation. The single was really a badged promotion opportunity for Beggars Banquet, but this had the added advantage of not costing me much. Along with the Rough Trade sales, I supplied all my usual wholesalers myself – everyone was a winner.

Steve's idea had given me a huge leg-up. The record label was up and running!

It was around this time that it started to feel like the mod network was really spreading internationally. I'd just returned from my extraordinary trip to Dublin, Crossmaglen, Belfast and Bangor. As if to prove that mod was internationalist, in May 1983 I received another airmail letter from an *ES* subscriber – this time a fellow fanzine editor who lived in the northern suburbs of Sydney.

Fanzine editors in the UK and indeed around the world seemed to have banded together into some weird community, sharing – via the old-fashioned postal system – ideas and articles as well as our own magazines. This particular missive arrived on that super-thin blue paper with the striped edges on the envelope that denoted international airmail. Glyn Williams was the writer's name.

He asked if I fancied a trip to Australia to check out the mod scene. *Fuck yeah.*

I'd always dreamed of travelling to Australia to see The Saints play live before it was too late. Bassist Kym Bradshaw had already decamped to the UK to join Small Hours and had been replaced in Australia by

Algy Ward from The Damned. I was worried that the band's creative genius, Ed Kuepper, would quit too as the rumour was he wasn't getting on with vocalist Chris Bailey. If I left it much longer, all I'd end up seeing would be a Saints tribute band.

It turned out that Australia had developed a thriving mod scene with its own bands, nightspots, scooter clubs and, most importantly, its own way of doing things – a way that was completely different from what I'd been used to in the UK.

Glyn Williams was extremely helpful with the details, suggesting I stay with him at his parents' place in the idyllic northern suburb of Roseville. He sourced the dates for The Saints' next tour, so we set about planning my month Down Under.

This involved finding some space away from my working life, as I was feeling increasingly jaded. I was working full weeks at Avatar as well as DJing at our Sound & Rhythm nights at the Regency twice a week, and increasingly felt like I was on a self-perpetuating treadmill. I was managing Fast Eddie, organising the Ilford alldayers and running *Extraordinary Sensations* (which had published four new issues the previous year and was now the biggest-selling mod publication in the country, shifting 4,000 copies an issue – my secret printer Dave Stokes was now having to sneak into the print shop after work to run off the pages) and its companion mail-order business . . . And on top of that, Well Suspect Records had just released its second single. All this in what little spare time I could find away from the office.

I could also tell that my time at Avatar was coming to an end. The company had been moving increasingly away from music towards the emerging VHS market. I'd been promoted a couple of times and was now head of video marketing with a responsibility for organising screenings and obtaining reviews for our new releases (one of which was the Smokey Robinson Motown film *Big Time*, a run-of-the-mill blaxploitation piece released in US cinemas a few years previously), but my heart wasn't really

In my bedroom with Ed Silvester, late 1980.

(Left to right) Richard Habberley, John Silvester, me and Ed Silvester
in paisley overload.

Millions like us – Bournemouth, 1982.

Carnaby Street on a Saturday afternoon.

Marion McKee and friends outside Merc and the Carnaby Cavern.

Dancing at Scamps club, Southend-on-Sea, 1981.

Mick Taylor shaking his tail feather at the Regency Suite.

With Terry Rawlings in Berwick Street, London.

DIANE PORT

'Who me, officer?' Getting arrested for a traffic offence
for the first time by the police in Brighton, 1981.

DARREN MORRELL

In the Australian outback with Malpractice and M16 semi-automatics, 1983.

(Left to right) Ricey, Garry Moore, Andy Orr, me, Kim, and Jim Watson
at the Ben Truman pub near Southwark Bridge in 1985.

Me and Terry Rawlings at a James Taylor Quartet gig.

'Just Jeff' (Jeff Shadbolt), Terry Rawlings and me with my Lancia Spyder.

in it. I wanted to be making records. I was on a decent salary but was just a month past my 19th birthday and often felt like an imposter, out of my depth dealing with experts who were often twice or even three times my age. Don't get me wrong, it was an incredible job for a young mod. I got to work with all those brilliant artists and learned the machinations of the industry at the coalface. I also realise that working for Jon Brewer taught me everything I needed to know about music as an industry. Nevertheless, I was beginning to feel that it was time to move on.

The final straw for me at Avatar was when I was alone in the office with Jon's latest PA and fixer, an extraordinarily pretty girl (as were they all, actually) by the name of Gina Carter. We were in the new building in Stamford Brook at about half six one evening and most of the staff had already left when a wild-eyed lunatic who bore a striking resemblance to Bob Hoskins in *The Long Good Friday* marched in carrying a shotgun and screaming at the top of his voice.

'Where the fuck is he? Come out, you bastard . . . I know you're in here . . .'

Gina attempted to pacify the lunatic but he was having none of it. Who he was searching for we never found out.

I realise now from my own experiences that men brandishing guns can be a regular occurrence in the world of the indie record label, having been threatened with shooters on at least three occasions (and one baseball bat, which made me burst out laughing; when you've had a fully automatic ArmaLite pulled on you by a mafioso in Los Angeles, a fat lump with a baseball bat storming into your office can provoke that reaction, no matter how hard he thinks he is!)

We eventually persuaded the irate, foaming-at-the-mouth interloper that we were alone and got the man to leave – I say 'we' but I was hiding behind a desk while Gina had grown a pair of man-sized testicles and confronted him. I realised then that this was the end of the line for me and I told Jon the next day that I would serve a month's notice.

That was it. It had been a brilliant place to work, but I had so many mod things going on in my life that there was hardly room for anything else. Maybe I'd have to get another job, but I'd deal with that problem when I got back from Australia.

29

LET'S GET A BURGER MAN

I didn't have to wait too long.

There had already been tentative overtures in my direction from the management of MCA Music Publishing, a division of MCA Records, and pretty much as soon as I left Avatar I was summoned to an interview at their swanky offices on Hyde Park Corner. Now, MCA were rumoured to be heavily connected to the music-industry mafia, but that was Stateside and in the UK they were seen as just another major label. I was taken to lunch at the Hard Rock Cafe, which at that particular time had achieved something close to legendary status. Burger joints were not common in London in the early Eighties (unless you counted the Wimpy, which in spite of childhood memories of coke floats and the 'Bender in a Bun' I did not) and the Hard Rock arguably had the best burgers in the capital.

I breezed the interview but was in no hurry to take up a new position. What swung it for me was that I'd get a tab at the Hard Rock to 'entertain clients'! I'd also be given my own office. The salary was four grand more than I'd been getting at Avatar and, to cap it all, my immediate superior was to be Mark Warrick, who'd been the co-manager of one of my favourite (but recently disbanded) mod groups The Directions, whose 'Three Bands Tonite' single would go on to be one of the great rarities of the revival. We agreed on a start date some seven weeks hence and I was immediately down the travel agent to book my flight to Oz.

While I'd been on a goodish salary for a couple of years, I was going to have to support myself on holiday for a month, so plumped for the cheapest flight I could get. It helped that my good mate Julian Abbott worked in his dad's travel agency (Julian rode a Lambretta and lived round the corner from me – that's how our network functioned) and could always get a decent discount on flights and hotels.

'Garuda are certainly the cheapest with the one advantage that you get a number of stopovers,' he said, making this sound like a bonus! 'I can sort you out a hotel for a couple of nights and you can hang out in Jakarta or Bangkok. They're the Indonesian carrier – food's crap, though . . . Well, actually the whole airline's crap, but they're certainly the cheapest . . .'

Julian charged me £220 and two weeks later I found myself at Bangkok airport thrusting the scribbled address of a budget hotel into a tuk-tuk driver's grasping hand.

Had I known what an awful journey I was going to experience I'd have tried hard to raise the extra money to fly Qantas.

The plane stopped eight times to refuel and it took us 24 hours just to reach Thailand. I was mentally and physically exhausted, so remember very little of my 48 hours in Bangkok other than the tuk-tuk; the prevalent mode of transport for Western tourists was based on the chassis of the Vespa Ape (or 'Bee', to give its English translation, and surprisingly nowt to do with monkeys – plenty of which I was amazed to see running wild on the streets outside Bangkok) and I made a mental note to try to buy one of these scooter-based three-wheelers back in the UK if I ever had the chance. Fortunately, that chance never arose. I also had a three-piece tailored suit made to measure in 24 hours flat for 30 quid.

Four days later I was walking down the plane's steps at Kingsford Smith airport in Sydney, a dishevelled and broken man.

*

Wow. A sweltering Sydney blew my mind. It was hot but it was a dry heat, punctuated occasionally by heavy, short bursts of rainfall.

I was collected from the airport by my hosts, who did their best to put me back together again. Along with Glyn Williams there were several other Sydney mods in the welcoming committee, with Mike Vaughn, Johnny Ball and Steve Dettre among them. They collected me in a Mercedes stretch limo with three bottles of champagne on ice in the back.

Now stretch limousines weren't a common sight in London back then and I'd never seen one before, let alone sat in one. I was immediately freaked out: all this for little old *me*?

'It's the least we can do for you, brother. We've lined up a host of surprises while you're here,' Glyn told me, beaming. He was gregarious, with an open, friendly face so typical of his countrymen at the time. He was also a super-cool mod.

The first surprise was how *absolutely* different Australia was to England in the early Eighties – I mean, it looked the same but so much was strange to English eyes. I realise I might be making no sense with that statement, but to me Sydney was like a cross between Seventies London and the America I'd seen on *Starsky & Hutch*. Big US-style cars called Holdens rubbed along with the odd Mk3 Cortina (known as a Taurus), with a few little Japanese cars thrown in. They also had shopping malls. Oh, and no nightclubs; instead they had big old Victorian pubs where bands played and you could buy warm roast-beef rolls until one in the morning . . . And there were plenty of scooters on the streets too.

The next surprise was lovely and showed me how much effort the lads had put into making me feel at home. I'd let slip to Glyn that I was a massive cricket fan; the Ashes weren't being contested during my visit, but I was hoping I could visit a cricket ground at some point in my stay. Well, 40 minutes after they'd picked me up from Kingsford Smith we were sitting down with a picnic and some VB tinnies at the Manly Oval watching Bob Hawke, the recently elected prime minister, playing for his own all-star XI in a charity game. Hawke was actually batting when we arrived. It was extraordinary; there were 1,000-odd people sitting round the boundary watching the game in what was basically a public park. I couldn't imagine a high-profile English politician taking part in a public sporting event – although, to be fair, Labour leader Hawke was untouchable. He'd just won an enormous landslide in the election and was much loved. He was a unique politician who wore his emotions on his sleeve, even breaking down in tears on television over his daughter's drug problems. The Australians love a straight talker, and this admission of family fragility just made them love him more. Oh, and he'd once held the world record for downing a yard of ale. The perfect Australian politician! This was shaping up to be a brilliant trip.

Eventually, we arrived at Glyn's place in Roseville. I was hitting the wall by then.

'Mate, you should grab an early night and see if you can shake off the jet lag. We've got a big one lined up for tomorrow, so you're gonna have to be on form. Did you bring your suit? Good, because Mike Vaughn's gonna pick us up in the RX4 at seven and you'll be expected to dress for dinner; then it's cocktails and champagne at the Regent Hotel and then off to the Quarrymans for some dancing.'

I spluttered out, 'What do you mean, dress for dinner?' I had no idea what he was on about and was completely bemused by this turn of events. I was also trying to process the news that Mike Vaughn collected Seventies Mazda RX4s, the ones with a rotary engine (previously only found in the German NSU). They looked like a mini-American muscle car and had the most extraordinary acceleration I'd ever experienced. Incredibly cool and very rare in the UK.

Glyn laughed and answered: 'All the lads from Malpractice are coming out to welcome you and we make a point of dressing for cocktails. Most will be in black tie and tuxedos, but you can just wear your suit. Now get yourself to bed and I'll see you in the morning . . .'

Malpractice? Cocktails? Tuxedos?

And so began one of the most extraordinary months of my life.

To understand the Australian take on the mod scene, I should give you some background.

Mod was introduced to Sydney in early 1979 almost single-handedly by the Hosie brothers, Donald and Gary. They were fiercely proud of their British heritage and had been born to Geordie parents who'd emigrated from the British northeast as part of the 'Ten Pound Pom' campaign of subsidised relocation in the Sixties. In 1979, the boys had returned to the 'mother country' (as England was affectionately called back then) for a family holiday, during which they'd discovered and fallen in love with The Jam and the emerging British mod revival.

The brothers hoovered up as much info and music as they could and set about creating their own Antipodean version of the revival, like some kind of new religion. There were already a few mods in Sydney, but somehow the brothers galvanised them and helped pioneer an actual scene. They bought scooters and formed an out-and-out mod band called The Sets, whose debut single's B-side was called 'Life on an L.I.'.

While mod had been huge in Sixties Australia, with a host of bands such as The Atlantics, Phil Jones & the Unknown Blues, the Purple Hearts (the original ones, not our lot from Romford) and even The Easybeats playing alongside a thriving home-grown soul and R&B scene, mods had faded from view in the late Sixties to be eclipsed by their own uniquely Australian successor, the sharpie.

The nearest we had to sharpies in the UK were the working-class bootboys who appeared in that glorious but brief period between suedeheads and smoothies; where skinhead fashion with longer hair was giving way to the high-waisted flares, spoon shoes, grandad shirts, Fair Isle yoke jumpers and football hooliganism.

Sharpies had their origins in the mid-Sixties and were immediately in conflict with mods. Their rough-and-ready appearance and willingness to ruck garnered an enormous amount of bad press, which seemed only to add to their appeal for working-class teenagers. As a youth cult, they were popular and enduring, and were a regular sight right up to the mid-Seventies. They wore Levi's and dressed in many of the outfits worn by British skinheads, but they had the most incredible and unique haircut – a type of proto-mullet with enormous sideburns. As a subculture they threw their weight behind the Aussie pub-rock scene and adopted their own groups, like Lobby Lloyd and Billy Thorpe & the Aztecs (who originally started as a mod band), and as time went on adopted AC/DC and Rose Tattoo.

Once mods faded away at the end of the Sixties, sharpies were the main working-class movement in Seventies Australia, proportionately a much bigger scene than bootboys were in the UK. Indeed the 'sharpie menace' was seized by the Australian media who used it to create moral panic akin to that surrounding our own 'mods and rockers' shenanigans as invented by the press on a quiet news day in 1964.

In fact, memories of sharpies totally overshadow the legacy of their mod predecessors Down Under. So much so that when the Hosie brothers and their friends first started riding scooters and forming bands in 1979, no one had a clue what they were up to.

Quadrophenia came out in the autumn of 1979 and this had a galvanising effect on the burgeoning movement, with other local mod scenes, bands and fanzines appearing in Melbourne, Perth, Brisbane and to a lesser extent Adelaide and the ACT. The thing that was most different from their British counterparts was that the Aussie scene appeared extremely well organised, even codified (at least that was how it appeared to me at the time). There were faces and tickets, and just about everyone else in between. The faces were the organisers; they were respected and copied, and tried their best to dress as smart as fuck. They also rode at the front on scooter runs, with the tickets spluttering through the cloud of two-stroke in their wake. It was an impressive take on what we were doing in the UK. Even better and fresher in many ways.

By the time I arrived, the Sydney scene was firmly established, with its own fanzines such as Glyn Williams' and Steve Dettre's *Shake & Shout* and Anita Janelsins' *Get Smart!*, as well as regular club nights at pubs like the Quarrymans or the Trade Union and an interested age range going from 14 to 30.

Speed, as in amphetamine sulphate, was everywhere – to such an extent that it was seen by many, especially Don Hosie, as a serious problem. There were a few kids who'd been mainlining it (something I'd never heard of before), which led to a handful of tragic deaths on the scene.

The Sydney mods also had a gang. And I mean a proper gang. It was called the Malpractice Organisation and boasted around 50 to 70 active members and their girlfriends. And it was Malpractice who hosted this wonderful night of cocktails at the Regent Hotel and dancing (with bottles of champagne on ice!) at the Quarrymans.

The Quarrymans was one of their enormous Victorian pubs where bands played and people congregated. I suppose the Aussie scene seemed so fresh to me because I knew very few people there and they all treated me incredibly well. Super friendly with a very open take or interpretation on the mod ethos. Smart too. But what impressed me so much was that there were hundreds of them and the music was as good as anything we were playing in London at the time. Soul but with a lot of jazz mixed in and the occasional Australian beat record. The enormous mod scene the country had hosted in the Sixties was a heritage they were proud of.

The next day, a Saturday, we had a barbecue at The Don's house. (All the Sydney mods seemed to have nicknames: The Vogue, The Don, Bedders, Bovver, Lofty, Dusty, The Dentist, Ball-o – you know the kind of thing . . .) Several of the mod girls made wonderful cakes and everyone else brought crates of beer. This was looking like fun. I was falling in love with Australia.

The real reason I'd embraced the trip so enthusiastically was so I could get to see the band that had changed my life all those years ago. While Kym Bradshaw had left them in 1977 and turned mod in London, The Saints were in the middle of a ten-date tour of New South Wales with Algy Ward on bass. I first saw them the following Wednesday at the Coogee Bay Hotel, a vast Victorian barn of a pub, and they simply took my breath away. The place was packed and the atmosphere electric. The friction between Chris Bailey and Ed Keupper on stage made the set edgy and exceptional, hard and fast. I was in heaven. What surprised me, though, was that The Saints didn't appear to be as revered in their home country as they should have been, despite being on a par with the Ramones as one of the few bands to invent punk rock in 1974. They played all my favourite songs – '(I'm) Stranded', 'Know Your Product', 'Messin' With the Kid', 'This Perfect Day' and even 'Kissin' Cousins' – and I knew every word. I caught them twice more on the tour that month, but many of the people I met had never heard of them! Had they received so little support in Australia? Among music lovers in the UK they were almost household names.

A week into the holiday and the following Sunday gave me a better understanding of what the Malpractice Organisation was really about. Five-a-side football (soccer was still frowned on and almost non-existent in Australia at the time, but this was The Don's contrary Englishness kicking in) followed by military training . . .

Eh? Military training? What the fuck were they on about?

Well, that afternoon it was just a little abseiling. You know the kind of thing: running down a sheer cliff face, a rope attached to your waist with a full pack on your back while crapping your pants. But that was just the first part of my Malpractice exercise; there was an awful lot more to get to grips with.

Let me explain. Here was a gang of 50 or so Australian mods who were engaged in proper military training. It turned out that there were a few Malpractice members who'd been in the Australian Army and even one who was a serving member of their Special Forces. It was starting to get a bit weird.

But – and this is a big but – they were deadly serious about it. All of it. The military training, the dressing like James Bond for cocktails at Sydney's most expensive hotel, the all-encompassing mod world that they'd created. And you know what? I fucking loved it.

The skinhead wars had only just started in Australia and the Malpractice approached the problem with some serious and practical strategies, far ahead of anything we'd even thought of in the UK. They planned things tactically and somewhat incredibly had developed the use of a weapon that was if not lethal then certainly dangerous and could be guaranteed to stop any marauding skinhead in his tracks.

The Hosie brothers had a family farm up beyond the Blue Mountains, some 200 miles west of Sydney in a small outback town called Mudgee. Their dad specialised in the cultivation of pure-bred Angora goats – known for producing mohair, for God's sake, the mod fabric! During the course of their goat husbandry, the lads had come into contact with a new import from New Zealand that was used mainly in sheep farming.

In the early Eighties, paintball guns were practically unknown in the UK, and definitely not for the leisure use that came a few years later. I'd certainly never seen one. In my first week in Sydney, I was given a demonstration of their effectiveness by one of the scooter-riding mods.

'Eddie, mate . . .!' he started.

Australians use the word mate as punctuation.

'Eddie, mate, we've been having a bit of trouble from some fuck'n skins lately. It's tricky because there's plenny we get on with and some we don't – kinda depends on where they're from. Westies are the worst . . . Anyway, mate. The Vogue is gonna give you a little demo of how we've been dealing with it . . .'

The Vogue was thin and rangy, sporting an army crewcut with the hint of a quiff, and he pulled open his jacket to reveal an oversized pistol with a three-quarter-inch bore sitting in a holster.

'Ah, mate, it's simple . . . We just give 'em some of this . . .'

With that, he whipped it out and fired three quick shots in succession. I followed his aim to a wall 25 yards away to see three red splurges in a 4-inch grouping.

What magic is this . . .? I wonder.

'That's fucking incredible – can I have a go?'

If only we had these back in London.

Into the weapon's handle was screwed a metal compressed-air cylinder (like we used in soda syphons), which propelled round pellets of water-based paint in cellulose at high velocity. The pellets exploded on impact, marking the target with the paint.

It wasn't rocket science, but you could imagine how useful they were for sheep farmers trying to mark their flock.

'Ah, mate, the only thing is that they're not strictly legal . . . You need a licence to import them from the Kiwis and you can only get one if you are a proper farmer . . . Luckily for us, a few Malpractice are!' He smirked. 'Well, at least we *claim* we are . . .'

As the trip progressed, I was taken to a number of gigs in Sydney. Garage rock was still pretty big in New South Wales, but there were plenty of mod bands playing the circuit too; during my stay we watched The Sets, Little Murders, Cockroaches, The Allniters, Mustard Club, the Dynamic Hepnotics, Stupidity and Lime Spiders all play live.

*

Two days after the paintballing I was on a scuba-diving exercise.

A Malpractice member serving in the Royal Australian Navy was holding a scuba-diving class down in Sydney Harbour. Forget about the sharks, this was bloody insanity.

I was several years away from taking my PADI diving qualification and yet here I undertook an intensive but informal scuba course. Needless to say, it takes at least a week to qualify for the right to use oxygen underwater, but after a brief ten minutes' instruction I found myself exploring the harbour – the instructor made me very aware of potential problems, but I seemed to navigate the experience OK.

A week later and a party of seven of us travelled the 200-odd miles through the Blue Mountains to the Hosie farmstead in Mudgee for a few days 'walkabout'. Rather than hanging out with the beautiful Jenny Agutter (my teen crush), this entailed some serious bush walking. Equipped with a map, compass and a selection of semi-automatic weapons, we trekked 20-odd miles through the bush – sleeping in the open and communing with nature. I never saw another person the whole time and breakfasted on yabbies pulled from crystal-clear streams and then chucked, still alive, onto glowing campfires. I saw plenty of wallabies, kangaroos and snakes – the tiger snake, red-bellied black snake and the inland taipan were three I remember – but I didn't see any of the legendary drop bears, in spite of the lads telling me to keep my hat on at all times in case one jumped out of a tree and went for my throat.

Most interesting were the abandoned mines that dated back to the gold rush of the 1850s. We passed at least three of them on the Hosie property as well as the remains of a genuine ghost town of deserted wooden buildings.

The mines were marked by piles of rock and spoil and had apparently been worked by Chinese labourers in Victorian times, while the ghost town was abandoned when the gold rush moved to fresh pastures in the mid-19th century. The Don told me that a gold nugget weighing

285 kilograms (one of the largest ever found) was dug up just a few miles south of his property in 1872. Sadly, none of the lads seemed particularly interested in looking for gold! I did briefly pan the streams but saw nothing glitter. Regardless, it was an exciting few days.

The rest of my first trip to Sydney rushed past in a daze, but I was inspired and the Aussies had completely reinvigorated my passion for mod. I'd had the most extraordinary month and realised that these guys really knew how to make the *concept* of mod work for them. The girls were amazing too and I fell into company with half a dozen real winners. Karen Parker and Natty Cheek became lifelong friends; Carolyn Smee came to work for Acid Jazz ten years later; and I asked a beautiful South African-born rockabilly called Renee Acker out on a date. Sadly, we eventually realised that a trans-Pacific romantic relationship could never last more than the year it did. I was in love with everything about Australia and couldn't wait to come back.

I returned to the UK refreshed and ready to start at MCA.

30

YOU'RE LYING

Based on Piccadilly, MCA Music Publishing was an interesting place to work. I knew little about the publishing business, which is very different from making records – although both are concerned with the exploitation of copyright. While Avatar had a successful publishing portfolio, the nearest I got to it was an occasional pint after work with one of their clients, Max Splodge from Splodgenessabounds, who took us (well, and him actually) by surprise with his chart hit 'Two Pints of Lager and a Packet of Crisps Please'.

No, publishing was a mystery to me. It was mid-1983 when I rocked up for my first day at the MCA offices, a nervous but enthused 19-year-old industry veteran of two years' standing. The first surprise was that it was true: I did indeed have an office and, even more impressive, a secretary, although I had to share her with my immediate boss, Mark Warrick. It was a step up nevertheless. My role, once it had been explained, was what used to be known as an MCA 'song-plugger'. Song-pluggers were once the lifeblood of the publishing world, and their sole purpose was to persuade artists, or more regularly their managers, to cover MCA's copyrights – that is, the songs that had been written by MCA writers. There was an enormous amount of money involved in this. The goal that was drummed into me was to place one of our songs on an Elton John or even a Cliff Richard album, although I could think of little that was less inspiring.

Competition was incredibly stiff and even persuading people to listen to our songs was tough. Song-pluggers (not to be confused with *radio-pluggers*, a completely different industry role) tried all sorts of backdoor methods to gain an upper hand, including (but not limited to) bribery, with either 'presents' (expensive tour jackets, VIP tickets, lavish meals and even weekends abroad) or drugs. Famously, cocaine often appeared on certain major company expense accounts as 'flowers'. Not, I hasten to add, at MCA (as far as I knew).

I'm no salesman and selling average songs to muppets was something I struggled to get excited about, but MCA was a great place to learn about publishing. Mark Warrick was a brilliant boss and very encouraging. We regularly drank in the pubs of Shepherd Market and even had our own table in the Hard Rock next door. Shepherd Market is a funny old place; in those days you were as likely to see high-end brasses looking for punters as you were Princess Margaret buying a shirt or Jeffrey Archer passing envelopes around. Allegedly.

It was a vibrant 'secret village' tacked onto Mayfair and an exciting place to be.

I'd traded up my Triumph Herald for a Lancia Beta Spyder and felt like I was cock of the walk. I should have known that it wouldn't last, and it didn't.

Like all major publishers, MCA had a coterie of in-house songwriters, and they were mainly crap. The days of a bank of faceless men (and they were almost always men, with some notable exceptions) writing songs to order were gone; the trouble was, MCA hadn't yet quite worked this out. The songs simply weren't very good.

I was briefly enthused by a couple of Mark's projects. The first was David Grant, vocalist with the Brit-funk band Linx, who'd had a big hit with 'You're Lying' a couple of years earlier. Grant delivered hit after hit for the company and was a cool guy but wasn't writing songs for other people. He was an 'A&R signing' who wrote songs for himself and so there wasn't much for me to work on.

The other project Mark was developing was a brilliant post-mod soul group called Big Sound Authority. As soon as I saw a picture of them I recognised the Burke brothers, who'd fronted The Directions. 'Three Bands Tonite' had been a self-released masterpiece that sold just a handful of copies at the time. The song itself was an odd and highly critical tale about a cancelled gig that featured both The Teenbeats and Sta-Prest, and was melodic with some great production.

The lyrics moaned that The Directions insisted on playing the gig while the other two bands refused because the sound system wasn't good enough. I have since asked both The Teenbeats and Sta-Prest about 'Three Bands Tonite' and neither of them have the slightest idea about the song or what it meant!

As I said, it was odd.

In the early revival days, The Directions were always playing at the Greyhound on the Fulham Palace Road and I thought they were great. Super-cool dressers but, like many of the first wave of bands on our scene, a lack of commercial success and fierce, unwarranted press criticism did for them, and they split up soon after the single was released.

I was thrilled to get the chance to work with what was left of them. The brothers had been busy building the new project over the previous year. I thought Big Sound Authority deserved to break through as they had some fabulous songs, like '(Call Me) Soulman' and the minor hit 'This House (Is Where Your Love Stands)', but they never quite crossed over. At the time I thought they had the potential to sit alongside The Style Council, The Bureau (Mick Talbot's post-Merton Parkas group) and Dexys Midnight Runners.

However, it was a throwaway remark that Mark made in the pub after work that got me most excited. He mentioned that he still had

300 copies of 'Three Bands Tonite' sitting in his shed. Would I be interested in buying them cheap to sell through the fanzine?

Fuck yeah!

Now, *Extraordinary Sensations* was flourishing and one of the ways I raised the money to pay for it was to run a record-mailing list that I sent to my subscribers on a monthly basis. I regularly trawled the 'cut-out' warehouses for cheap and long-deleted singles, and called up labels like Safari, Whaam! and Rocket to buy up dead stock of bands like The Teenbeats, the Purple Hearts, The Times or The Lambrettas. Thing was, I sold the singles at £1.25, which was cheaper than you could buy them in the shops. I treated it as a kind of complementary service that ran alongside the fanzine and would engender brand loyalty. Something of a mistake, I realise now.

I bought all 300 copies of 'Three Bands Tonite' off Mark for 20p each and ruthlessly set about repositioning the record as the great lost anthem of the revival. I flogged them all in just six months, but when the copies dried up, the price went through the roof. I wish I'd kept a box but I didn't. When I finally got rid of my personal copy a couple of years ago, it fetched the outrageous price of £375.

Working at MCA's offices had some upsides. I was particularly intrigued by their tape library. It was a largish walk-in cupboard close to my office and was stuffed with reel after reel of quarter-inch tapes of the songs MCA owned. The archive stretched back to the Fifties and I spent days and days playing tapes of (often unreleased) demos by incredibly cool American soul and R&B artists. They owned the ABC Dunhill catalogue and had hundreds of songs by groups like The Four Tops and Dusty Springfield. Thinking back, I wish I'd nicked them as they probably got chucked into a skip when CDs came into fashion. Seeing as I'd finally been taught to use a Revox by Steve Webbon from Beggars, this soon became my favourite part of the job. However, although it was legitimate, it wasn't what I was actually employed to do. I was supposed to be placing songs with Elton John or Cliff Richard.

Well, as you can imagine, that was a completely thankless task and I never really got anywhere as a song-plugger. I remember my time at MCA as the least interesting job I'd had in the music industry and the experience certainly went some way to inculcate my lifelong dislike of the major corporations.

One interesting thing – in fact, the *most* interesting thing – that happened to me during my short stay at MCA was when I was sent to an Ivor Novello Awards dinner. I'd never been to an industry function before and had no idea what to expect. I was told to wear a suit and present myself at the Park Lane Hilton at 12.30 the following Tuesday lunchtime. There were a couple of others from MCA present, but they were sitting at important tables; I'd been consigned to the outer reaches, as far away from the award presentations as it was possible to be.

After a couple of solitary pints at the free bar, I threaded my way through the great and the good to my designated place. It was at a large table on the fringes of the room; only one of the ten seats was occupied so far and after checking the place cards I discovered I was sitting right next to its inhabitant, an old fella in a grey suit. *Oh fuck*, I thought. *This is going to be boring. Just my luck.*

I sat down, slightly embarrassed, and poured myself a glass of red. My neighbour, wearing the most outrageous, enormous old-fashioned square glasses, leaned over and introduced himself. I didn't quite get his name and just sat there, trying to think of something to say. He reminded me of Denis Norden off the TV.

I didn't have to wait long. My new friend wanted to open a conversation and launched in.

'So, son, what is it that you do?'

'Erm, I work at MCA Music . . .'

'Yeah, that's as maybe, but what is it that you *want* to do?' He endowed the word 'want' with exaggerated gravitas.

Well, that was an easy question. 'I've got my own label and run a little fanzine, but I think I want to be a manager. I've already got one band and I'm looking for more . . .'

At this revelation the man rolled his eyes, took off his glasses and began polishing them on his polka-dot breast-pocket handkerchief. He looked at me for a few seconds and said, 'Management? Management . . . Forget it, son. Let me tell you a story about management . . .'

Oh, that's all I need, I thought. *A boring old git wants to tell me how to be a manager.* But he didn't. He had a proper story for me.

'See, son, management always goes something like this . . . You're approached by four disparate and probably untalented boys who spend their days working on building sites, in pubs or in sundry dead-end jobs. They're incredibly persistent in their pursuit of you. They tell you that they're in a group and want you to be their manager. You think about it and tell them that, yes, you could indeed become their manager, subject to just one condition. Your new clients must pay you 20 per cent of their earnings in commission. You explain that in the music business this is standard, completely normal. They agree to the terms with what sounds like desperation. You plug them into your system and work incredibly hard to build their brand. Press, radio, live, styling, clothes the whole bloody thing . . .'

Where was he going with this? I looked at my watch, poured another glass of wine and let him continue. The place was gradually filling up.

'The four of them are so grateful. "Oh, yes, sir; thank you so much, sir; anything you say, sir . . ." You help them get a set of songs together and book their first live gig. Two pounds, second on the bill at the Marquee. "Oh, thank you so much; here's your eight shillings commission . . ." Before too long they're headlining for a tenner. "Oh, thank you so much. Here's your two quid . . ." You land them a singles deal with Decca. There's a 100 quid advance. "Oh, Mr Page, you're the best. Here's your 20 quid commission . . ."'

Hold on a minute – what did he say? Mr Page? I leaned in, strained my ears and listened attentively.

'The LP deal comes in from Decca. It's a grand. "Oh, Mr Page, you're wonderful. Here's your 200 quid . . ."'

Page, Page . . . I knew that name but just couldn't place it. Who was he?

'Big tour, the band earn ten grand and gratefully pay you your two-grand cut. Everyone's happy. They're building well and you all have your eyes on the prize. *Ready Steady Go!* absolutely love the band and they're now chart regulars. You work harder keeping their dalliances out of the public eye and their faces in the papers . . .

'A Number 1 album follows and the band's first proper royalty cheque tops 100 grand. Hmm . . . For some reason they become harder to reach on the phone and grudgingly pay across the 20 grand with what appears to be some reluctance. "Oh, yes, can you invoice our accountants. They'll sort out your invoice . . ."

'Then – bingo! You hit the jackpot and your charges receive their first-ever million pounds . . . They aren't taking your calls. Three days later you get hold of them. "Hey, lads, about my commission . . .?" They reply with: "Commission? What the fuck have you ever done for us, you thieving bastard!"'

The old fella sat back in his chair laughing, still polishing his glasses.

Then the penny dropped and I defensively replied, 'But that would never happen to me. My band are my friends.'

'Son, it might not happen with *that* band, but it *will* happen. It always does; it's human nature and there's always a gang of bottom-feeding lawyers ready to take them on once you've done the work. The ungrateful bastards.'

I thought about it. Nah, it wouldn't happen to me. I'd make sure it doesn't. I asked him the obvious question. 'So, I suppose you've been a manager, then? Anyone I might've heard of?'

'Probably not, son, but here's my card. If you ever need any advice on management, give me a call.'

Fuck me. I knew I'd recognised the name. I'd just been delivered the most accurate truism on band management by Larry Page. He really is a mod legend. Page One Records was his baby, but he'd managed The Kinks and The Troggs. I was dumbfounded to be in the presence of industry royalty. And the worst thing? Larry Page was absolutely right.

It *always* happens.

The end at MCA when it came was spectacular.

I was sitting in Mark's office quietly reading the latest copy of *Music Week* and consequently my own room was empty. That's when I heard my shared secretary make a call.

'Hello, Serena. Just to let you know, he's made three phone calls about Fast Eddie this morning and a couple to Rough Trade about his label . . . Yes, I'm certain . . . Maybe one to his friend at Beggars Banquet too . . . I'll fill you in on what else he does before I leave . . .'

Now, I heard all of this very clearly. Serena was the overall boss and my secretary was apparently spying on me! The thing was, I'd been working reasonably hard on getting to know the catalogue and making pitches to labels and producers, and I was fucked if I was going to put up with this. I walked out of Mark's office and over to the girl's desk. She visibly blanched when she realised I'd heard every word. She couldn't hold my eye.

'I hope you're proud of yourself?'

I grabbed my bag and coat from my small office and ran up the stairs three at a time, fuming. I didn't care how much they were paying me;

I was doing my job well enough but these fuckers were actually spying on me. For fuck's sake.

I marched up to Serena's office and knocked on the door.

'Come . . .'

She was on her own and I can't remember what I said because I was so angry. In my mind it was something like Jimmy Cooper's resignation speech towards the end of *Quadrophenia* . . . 'And you can take that franking machine, those letters and that other shit I have to deal with and you can shove them right up your arse . . .' In reality, though, it was probably much more polite. Something along the lines of, 'Look, if you think having my secretary spy on me is appropriate, then I certainly don't want to work here. I think I'm doing a pretty good job for MCA and have already secured a decent cover with The Pretenders, but I just can't work in an atmosphere like this. I quit . . .'

I got two months' salary and made the decision never to work for anyone else. I never wanted to be on a payroll again. I was going to work for myself. I'd show these wankers.

Rather unsurprisingly, my departure made not the smallest splash. It's all well and good walking out of somewhere in principle, but what the fuck was I going to do now?

I was officially unemployed!

31

LEAVIN' HERE

ncredibly, *Extraordinary Sensations* was still the country's biggest-selling modzine (I was shipping at least 4,500 or 5,000 copies an issue) and the Regency Suite was the most successful club in our orbit. The trouble with turning out so many copies of the fanzine was that it took an inordinate amount of time to collate and staple each issue together. The printed pages arrived from Dave Stokes separately and I had to rope my nan in to help me put the whole thing together. Even with her working full time, it took a few weeks and thousands of staples to come up with the finished article. We arranged the paper in piles and walked round and round her dining-room table taking the pages off one at a time and then stapling the finished article.

I realised that I needed to be more organised and finally admitted to myself that I had to recruit some help. But from where? What I needed was a creative, intelligent mod who was good at design and writing – but to be honest, they were few and far between.

I reached out to my old mate Gary Crowley, who I'd met while following The Jam and The Chords in 1979. He'd had a lot of fanzine experience with *The Modern World*, a quasi-mod/punk hybrid and I thought he might have a couple of ideas. He immediately came up with a name.

'You remember my old mate Terry Rawlings? You know, The Chords obsessive who doesn't travel north of the Thames?'

Of course I remembered Terry. He'd written the Small Faces book for Paul Weller's Riot Stories publishing company and was the man that reintroduced me to Steve Marriott at the Bridge House a couple of years back. I saw him on a casual basis but never realised he could be my partner in *Extraordinary Sensations*.

Gary enthused: 'I used to work with him at Decca; we did the *London Boys* mod EP together. He's a great designer and artist, and I happen to know he's not up to much at the moment . . .' Gary read me his number and I resolved to give Terry a call the next afternoon.

From our previous acquaintance I remembered him as stubborn, grumpy, facetious and rude. Nevertheless, we arranged to meet in one of the Carnaby Street pubs, where I soon discovered he was also generous, funny, talented and . . . unique.

We talked through my plans for expanding the fanzine and Terry came up with some great ideas. The meeting turned into an all-day drink, and by the time we left the pub, I'd invited him to join me as the co-editor of *Extraordinary Sensations*.

The fanzine was now up to Issue 8 and had grown in circulation to 5,000 copies, but I'd not had enough time to devote to building it up as a commercial enterprise – and after all, a copy sold for only 30p (15p wholesale with an average of 5p a copy printing). With a partner I could share the workload and get back to releasing a new issue every couple of months. Terry agreed and I set about getting us an office of our own where we could base our operation.

It turned out that my new partner had been a mod from the very beginning of the revival and featured in Janet Street Porter's legendary London Weekend Television broadcast. Porter had been an enthusiastic original Sixties mod but like many of her kind was suspicious and sceptical of the revival.

The trouble with Terry was that he was fiercely territorial. All through 1979 he'd been an absolute, every-week regular at the

Wellington in Waterloo, where his main love was The Chords, but he couldn't be arsed to go anywhere else apart from Jam gigs, let alone to the Bridge House in Canning Town. Therefore, he always treated my prolific revival gig attendance list with thinly veiled scepticism. Still, we got on like a house on fire.

A mate of my dad's called Ernie Brain owned a haulage company based in Dagenham. He had lots of space and offered us a free room with a telephone line. While Dagenham had a Wild West reputation and was hardly local to either of us, it was the perfect base for the new reconstituted *Extraordinary Sensations*. The number of letters in the *ES* postbag had risen to over a hundred a week, from all over the world, and we settled down to something akin to a full-time job.

Unfortunately, Terry didn't have any transport. My Dagenham day began with me riding the P Range (or very occasionally driving the Lancia Spyder, but the traffic was shocking and it took twice as long) from Woodford to Rotherhithe (where he lived in his flat on the Thames) to cart him all the way up the A13 to Chequers Lane and the biggest industrial estate in London. We'd arrive at the office, answer the post, pack up the mail order and go to the pub. Two hours later we were back on the A13 and making our way to the Mayflower, next door to his flat. Life became a succession of pubs and we soon worked out where we could buy corned beef and chips for ten bob. We were obviously still on a budget.

Within months the move was paying dividends. The mail order was making good cash and the fanzine soon reached the heady circulation figure of 8,000 copies an issue. I was becoming a regular in the pubs of Bermondsey and we were making some money. Not a lot, admittedly, but we were making some.

One morning I turned up at Terry's flat and he said, 'We're not going to the office today – I've got a surprise for you. I'm gonna take you to meet some people. Head for King's Cross . . .' He pulled on his crash helmet, climbed on the back of the P Range and we set off to cross the Thames at Tower Bridge. Ten minutes later we pulled up outside a massive Victorian pub in Holloway. Terry tapped me on the shoulder and indicated I should park.

It was early but the pub was already open. We weren't meeting his friends until 12.45, but Tel wanted to get a few glasses of wine down him before they arrived. He was being mysterious and wouldn't tell me who we were waiting for. By 12.30, the place had filled up with a dozen or so broken men in their Sixties. All sitting on their own, nursing a pint over a copy of *Racing Post* and watching the horses on the television.

At quarter to one on the dot the leaded glass doors swung open and one of Rawlings' mates walked in. I didn't recognise him and wondered why Terry had been so mysterious. I was standing at the bar, so the pair of them came over and pulled up some stools.

'Eddie, I'd like to introduce you to my old mate, Art Wood.'

Fuck me, Art Wood of The Artwoods. A mod legend from a legendary mod band. I was impressed. He was engagingly friendly and we were having a general chat when the doors swung open again.

Fuck me, Ronnie Wood of The Birds. Art's brother. A mod legend from a legendary mod band. I was even more impressed. But the most impressive thing about Ronnie Wood was that he beckoned the barman over, handed him a £50 note and said in hushed tones, 'Don't mention it, but any time anyone wants a drink, it's on me. Let me know when that runs out and I'll give you another one.'

I hadn't even seen a £50 note before; they'd only been out a year and a bullseye was a lot of money. Top man.

It turned out that Terry was indeed good friends with the pair. We spent a fascinating and relaxed couple of hours talking about mod while the Wood brothers enthused over their memories of the original scene.

In two and a half hours, Ronnie never mentioned The Rolling Stones once, and neither did anybody else.

The rejuvenated fanzine was now selling almost 10,000 copies an issue, so I had a little money in the bank. I knew I could leave Terry in charge for a month, so what did I do?

I took the opportunity to go back to Australia.

I'd spent nine months evangelising about Sydney and this time three of my mates came with me. Colin, Spencer and Darren Morrell were Woodford mods who'd also joined the London Scottish at the same time as me and as such had the basics of military training.

After a few days in Indonesia, where I accidentally killed a village dog and was chased for several miles by a car crammed full of apoplectic Balians, Garuda's decrepit 747 finally limped into New South Wales, where we were welcomed with open arms.

We had a few days acclimatising while the other English lads got acquainted with the locals and settled in. We were all stopping at Don Hosie's this time; there was plenty of room and I could tell that the other three were as blown away as I was when I first came.

The Malpractice Organisation soon set up an extensive training schedule to cover the whole of our trip; 60 or so mods would make their way to Mudgee in combat gear for a full-on exercise the following weekend. The lads had a Land Rover Defender and were scheduled to work on coordinated section attacks on enemy trenches. One half would be dug into defensive positions and the others would be attacking in half-sections, very similar to British Army tactical deployment. The three London lads couldn't quite believe what was going on.

'I told you it was going to be mad,' I said.

'Yeah, but we didn't actually believe you . . .' came the incredulous reply.

Don Hosie was in charge of the whole thing and planned the coming trip meticulously. He also carried himself like a British officer (small arms only and a Sam Browne belt!). As before, there were a number of Australian Army regulars and TA present, including a couple of NCOs. They all wore Malpractice shoulder flashes on their DPM uniforms and badged berets, just like a real military unit.

But why? What was the point? We never found out.

What was most bizarre was that we were issued with real weapons. Not modified blank-firing weapons but actual *guns*. There were dozens: British Army FN 7.62 SLRs, M1 carbines of Korean War vintage, M16s, ancient Mauser rifles, Lee Enfield 303s, Colt CAR-15 (the lightweight Commando version of the ArmaLite), AK47s and even a Bren light machine gun. Not everyone had a proper rifle, so some carried high-powered .22 air rifles. The 'officers' were issued with pistols and everybody had live ammunition.

Whaaat?

This was extraordinary. In the British Army, live ammunition was very, very strictly controlled and only ever given out on a range or a supervised live-firing exercise. It was also very dangerous. The Malpractice were out on section patrols with a round up the spout. *Jesus fucking Christ*. We were crapping ourselves. The Aussies, though, were completely relaxed about it. They'd been doing it for years and had their own protocols.

It soon transpired that there was a legitimate reason for the weapons being loaded. Feral goats in the outback were a major problem; they got in among the Angoras and shagged them. The resulting half-breeds were useless for wool and so, once a month, various members of the Malpractice headed to Mudgee for a cull. Don's dad needed the lads to get the goats off the farm and it was a very big farm with many inaccessible valleys, streams and lakes. It was apparently a never-ending chore . . .

But that didn't make the fact that there were men with real loaded weapons walking along behind you any easier.

They practised army tactics for their own enjoyment, in order to make fun weekends of the culling outings. To make the section attacks more exciting and realistic they had an interesting method of making their own grenades. Basically, they would collect the small canisters used for 35mm film, just bog-standard plastic canisters about 2.5 inches high with a rubberised lid. They'd pack them with a mixture of gunpowder and tightly scrunched newspaper, binding the loaded canister tightly with tape. Then they'd make a hole in the lid, insert a length of paper straw filled with gunpowder through it and push it down into the body of the canister so it acted as a fuse, close off the end of the straw with masking tape and – hey presto! – you had a home-made hand grenade.

Bear in mind, all this was completely legal at the time – even owning a fully automatic weapon wasn't against the law in NSW and gunpowder could be bought anywhere. However, it also transpired that just before our arrival, the mods had used some home-made grenades against a group of skinheads, which *was* illegal. In fact, in preparation for our trip to the farm, the making of grenades lasted a whole day and in true Sydney style was done at a barbecue at The Don's house in Duntroon Avenue, just north of the Harbour Bridge. It was here that we realised that Malpractice was a lot bigger than we'd initially assumed and got to meet some of the next generation of troops. People like Mick Franz (who was actually a skinhead) and Karl Veisas, who both came to live with us in London a couple of years later. Mick's dad was German born and a real character; he'd been drafted into the SS from the Hitler Youth as a 15-year-old in the last months of the war. Turning his back thoroughly on all that, he subsequently spent a number of years as His Imperial Majesty Haile Selassie's bodyguard in Ethiopia in the Fifties and had a presentation sword engraved from the emperor displayed on his wall – this fascinated me as I was very interested in Rastafari and by this time owned several antique swords. I tried to buy it off him but, needless to say, it wasn't for sale. I spent a couple of months with Mick and his family a year or so later up on the North Shore.

The grenade production line functioned well enough until a couple of lads started lobbing them over the hedge into the street. This being a Sunday afternoon in a quiet Sydney suburb, eventually a neighbour called the police. While what we were doing wasn't technically illegal, someone at the police station might have made a connection with the attack on skinheads a few weeks earlier and soon a patrol car pulled up to investigate.

Wow: immediately a clean-up operation akin to the removal of alcohol from a Twenties American Prohibition-era shebeen clicked into place. A trunk came out and all the grenades and their unbuilt parts were swept into it. The automatic weapons followed and the trunk was thrown into the garage before the policeman had even asked to come into the garden. When they did, of course all they found was a group of 30-odd kids having a barbie complaining about a neighbour's car backfiring.

Phew, that was a close shave.

The next morning was bright without a cloud in the sky: perfect Mudgee weather. We made the journey up through the Blue Mountains in Mike Vaughn's Mazda RX4 among a convoy of cars and scooters. It was an amazing sight. I can remember seeing an orange GP200 belonging to a lad called Lofty, two petrol cans on the rear rack (there weren't enough garages in the outback for a scooter to make the journey on one tank) and a Mauser of World War II vintage strapped to the side panel. One of the mods proudly showed me a lovingly kept Schmiesser submachine gun that was oiled and wrapped in a towel. This was absolutely insane.

A year or so later, a very drunken Lofty aimed the loaded Mauser at me with the safety catch off and then slid back the bolt. *Jesus fucking*

Christ. I almost crapped my pants. No, that's not true – I *did* crap my pants. I'd been hanging out in a shared Victorian terraced mod house on Eton Street, Paddington for a drinking session and he took exception to my presence because he claimed that I was 'getting too close to Anita . . .'

Anita Janelsins was a letter-writing friend of some years' standing and the editor of Sydney's influential *Get Smart!* fanzine. She was also Lofty's housemate and obviously his unrequited love. I hadn't read the signs at all and it came as something of a surprise when he pulled out the rifle and pointed it at my head. He was massively pissed and I genuinely thought he might just pull the trigger.

That was the first time I felt the cold fingers of absolute terror squeeze me, but fortunately Anita stood between us to spoil his aim and firmly prised the weapon from his hands. Thank fuck for that! I stepped forward and slapped him round the face, hard. He was stunned, but that was the end of it.

At Mudgee, bivouacs were established, lunch was eaten with some tinnies of Victoria Bitter (our preferred Aussie tipple) and we were presented with our Malpractice berets and shoulder flashes. The exercises weren't due to start until the following day when the rest of the crew were expected to make an appearance, so that first afternoon we went on a goat hunt . . . With a round up the spout, for fuck's sake – criminally irresponsible. We never saw one of the feral goats as they were very canny and took some real sniffing out, but again I saw a number of kangaroos. Colin even managed to cut the head off a red-bellied black snake that was chasing him. He used a shovel. A very brave man, as a bite could have killed him.

I'd never fired a semi-automatic pistol before and wasn't going to turn down the opportunity to put a Heckler & Koch P7 9mm into my hand.

That day I also fired a Browning pistol and a Webley Mk VI short-barrelled revolver of World War I vintage that had been adapted to fire .45 rounds and had a kick like a donkey. Seriously exciting stuff.

That night's grub was a mix of barbecue and something Aussies seemed to love, called Maggi Meals – they came in foil containers and you just had to add boiling water. I never quite worked out what I was eating, but it certainly tasted better than the standard British Army ration packs of shit biscuits and some kind of reconstituted bacon in a can.

At dawn the next morning, the remainder of our private army of weekend warriors rolled into camp. We were divided into six squads, and each one was given a different task and objective that culminated, after copious patrolling and target shooting, in the section attacks we'd been originally briefed on. Us four London Jocks had been looking forward to putting our superior training into practice against what we assumed would be a load of Aussie chancers who knew nothing about infantry tactics.

Needless to say, we were wrong and things didn't turn out how we thought they would. Spencer, always a naughty chap, had a surprise up his sleeve. He'd obtained a 12-inch bottle of Sunny Delight (at that point unseen in the UK), then emptied the contents onto the floor and surreptitiously replaced the radioactive brew with gunpowder and compressed newspaper, wrapping the whole 'super-grenade' in masking tape and thereby creating a monster that was at least ten times larger than the small film canisters everyone else was carrying. Unfortunately for him, later that night as he crept up to the defender's trench and lit the fuse, he held onto the bottle for a second too long and it blew up in mid-air, 3 or 4 inches from his hand, just as he'd launched it.

The explosion was so loud and blinding that no one noticed Spencer had been blown off his feet and was lying in the ditch quietly moaning to himself. The duty medic (yes, the Malpractice actually had one) was an Australian Army dentist known as Big Richard, the proud owner of the Heckler & Koch. Hostilities were temporarily suspended while he got his medical kit from his tent – but not before the defending troops fired rockets (of the firework kind) through shoulder-mounted drainpipes at us attackers in a similar manner to how we fired the Carl Gustaf 84mm anti-tank weapon in the British Army. This kept us pinned down until someone heard Spencer's beleaguered wailing.

Poor Spencer was now in some pain. His hand had swollen to three times its normal size and everybody crowded round to see what'd happened. It turned out that the explosion had shattered a couple of the bones in his hand and broken his thumb in two places!

The Don was furious.

'See, this is what happens if you deliberately disobey standing orders! The size of the grenades is *specifically* regulated and enforced to stop this kind of thing happening!'

He called off the operation and we all retired to a farm outbuilding to enjoy a beer.

The rest of the trip continued in a similar vein and lifelong friendships were made between the Sydney mods and their London counterparts.

I left after five weeks as I couldn't justify any more time away from Terry Rawlings and the forthcoming edition of *Extraordinary Sensations*. Our mod-based enterprise had become a relatively successful business that required my presence to ensure that Terry wasn't spending all our reader's subscriptions on pie and mash.

These two initial trips to Sydney led to an awful lot of two-way traffic. Many London mods like Garry Moore, Steve Butler, Jim Watson and the photographer Darren Russell crossed the world to stay with various Malpractice members while I had an open-door policy in London, initially while I was still living with my mum and then later once I'd moved into my own place.

The first man who rocked up on my mum's doorstep was a full-on skinhead wearing a Crombie, boots, braces and windowpane check shirt. He had a missing front tooth and carried a suitcase in his hand, and once my mum opened the door he said, 'Ah, you must be Mrs Piller. G'day to you . . .' And then, without waiting for an answer, walked straight into the front room and took his coat off, braces standing proud on his shoulders. Whatever my mother had been expecting, it wasn't that. Up to this point she was very aware that I'd been in trouble with the police for fighting skinheads on a regular basis and it was unthinkable that one could knock on the door *and be polite*.

She ran straight upstairs. 'Edward, you'd better come down. I think you've got trouble. There's a skinhead asking for you at the door.'

'Aw, don't worry, Mum, it's Bedders; I forgot to tell you he was coming to stay . . .'

'What? How long for?'

'Erm, sorry, Mum . . . About two months . . .'

She spluttered with rage but before she could say anything I chipped in with, 'Don't worry, Mum. He's one of us, not one of them – lovely bloke and quiet as a mouse . . .' And I shot off to show him to the spare room and then to the pub.

And that's how it was with our Australian mates for the next five or six years. Open doors on both sides.

After he'd settled in, Steve Bedwell came up with a proposal: 'Look, Eddie, a couple of my mates from school are playing for Australia at Lord's next week and I've got us a pair of tickets in the MCC members area. D'you fancy it?'

Does the pope shit in the woods? Of course I fancied it. Ashes tickets at Lord's were like gold dust. The best I could ever hope for was the fifth day at the Oval. Lord's in the fucking MCC stand? Happy days . . .

It turned out that his classmates were the Waugh brothers, who were making one of their first appearances at Lord's in the baggy green. Bedders sent a note down to the dressing room and – *fuck me!* – a reply came back asking us to pop down at lunch on the first day. They were grumpy and quiet, and obviously in some kind of zone, so completely ignored me, but they did seem to love Steve. Tickets were forthcoming for the whole week. Many years later, my Aussie skinhead mucker ended up presenting *Saturday Night Live* and becoming Australia's leading stand-up comedian!

The world of mod never stops throwing surprises at you.

And that was the extraordinary thing about the world that I now found myself in. Mod – something that had taken my fancy a few years earlier as a fun alternative to punk – seemed to keep delivering. The fanzine, in particular, was the starting point for one surprise after another. It was being read globally and taking me on a journey all around the world, meeting new people and visiting new places.

Towards the end of 1983 I was invited to DJ in Rome along with the East London band Small World. One of the second wave of mod bands, they had recently changed their line-up when drummer Andy Orr left to join the newly formed band The Scene. I was good friends with the band as their guitarist, John Wratten, was my girlfriend Jacquie's brother. Bizarrely, our hosts for the event were the Italian Communist Party.

I'd never been to Rome and was looking forward to the experience.

Italy already had a healthy mod scene that had thrown up a number of bands, like The Underground Arrows, Statuto and Four by Art, but its politics seemed to be a bit fucked up. After my Irish trip I determined to steer clear of any kind of politics, but couldn't really avoid the fact that I'd been brought over to DJ for the Communist Party! It transpired that the far left ran an enormous network of what we would call 'social clubs', except that these were almost mini-sovereign states that apparently weren't answerable to either local government or the police. It was an extraordinary situation; people openly took drugs and the alternative community organised their own social events, art exhibitions, gigs and general 'happenings'. I was minded of the world that Crass had been striving for back in the UK, but here in Italy it was a reality. I was fascinated.

That weekend I was staying with an *Extraordinary Sensations* contact called Stefano Bellezza. He was the guitarist in The Underground Arrows and offered to put me up. He lived with his grandmother in an incredible apartment in the posh part of Rome. She even had a butler who served our food. The grand old lady spoke not a word of English and looked like she certainly wouldn't have approved of her grandson's dalliance with the communists! The conversation was extremely stilted. I was certainly out of my depth and things were about to get a whole lot more uncomfortable.

'Ah, hEddie . . .' Stefano pronounced my name like so many other Italians have done over the years, with an H at the front, phonetically 'Heady'! 'My grandmother has arranged a special meal for you. She cooked it with her own hands and this is an honour as she rarely ventures into the kitchen these days.'

'Oh, how kind, please tell her I am very grateful and looking forward to tasting it. By the way, what has she prepared for us?'

At that moment the butler walked into the room carrying a cloche, a large silver dish with a domed lid to keep the heat in.

'hEddie, she has made pasta vongole for you. Her speciality.'

My mind raced. What the fuck was pasta? I'd certainly never heard of vongole. With great reverence, the butler put the silver platter on the table and lifted the lid. Steam gushed out as he took a step backwards. Shit, what the fuck was that funny-looking round stuff? Oh god, there was some kind of seafood on it.

I absolutely hated all types of seafood and I'd certainly never seen pasta before. I had no idea what it was. They were both staring at me encouragingly. Fuck, I was going to have to eat it. There followed one of the most uncomfortable 20 minutes of my life. The old lady didn't take her eyes off me and made sure I was eating it all up while expressing the appropriate pleasure in doing so.

I took a small, tentative spoonful and shovelled it into my mouth. What did pasta actually taste like? I couldn't really imagine as I'd never seen anything like it. That first mouthful put me right. Ah, I knew now: it tastes like cold rubber smothered in a particularly strong fish paste. I began to chew but felt nauseous.

She was still smiling at me right up to the point where I gagged on the second mouthful. Then she looked confused and eventually concerned, glancing across at her grandson. Was something the matter with this strange English boy? He doesn't seem to like my pasta . . .

Stefano had worked out I was having a hard time and said something to distract his grandma, while I spat the pasta into my hand and stuffed it into my pocket. The next time she looked away I grabbed another handful and shoved it straight in. I managed to get another couple in without her noticing, but to my horror the butler was standing over the other side of the room, waiting. And smirking.

He'd seen it all.

As soon as I got back from Italy, I was pleasantly surprised to get a call from a young mod in Germany called Leif Nueske. He was one of my international contacts who helped sell the fanzine and he also had his own record label, called FAB. Just like in the UK, German mods were beginning to move away from the Sixties-influenced garage rock sound in favour of the burgeoning northern soul scene. Unlike in England, however, these two styles of mod were happily coexisting.

Local German bands like The Chocolate Factory and Dateline Diamonds (named after the film starring Small Faces) rubbed shoulders with Scandinavian mod-psyche groups like The Backdoor Men or The Stomachmouths and the scene in Hamburg, a Hanseatic port city in northern Germany, hosted a vibrant mod community.

Leif asked if I wanted to come over and DJ at the first-ever German northern soul weekender. It didn't take much to persuade me and a month or so later I got on a plane for the short journey. It was much harder to DJ abroad at the time as we were still in the era of the highly regulated and price-controlled national airlines and so air travel was out of reach of most DJ promoters.

Leif collected me from the airport and took me round to his house, where I was to stay with his family. His sister Svenia was also a mod and her boyfriend Jan Kohlmorgen was one of the Hamburg faces. A super-smart dresser with a penchant for polka-dot scarves, he played guitar in one of the local mod bands.

The mod scene there was massive and the all-nighter was held in a large theatre building down in the docks. Groups of young mods clutching all-nighter holdalls were arriving all day, dressed either in parkas or more smartly. Hamburg was a vibrant city that possessed a very active red-light district stretching from the Reeperbahn (once home to the Star Club, made famous by The Beatles in the early Sixties) all the way down to the Elbe and Alster rivers.

I'd already seen a European red-light district, when I'd travelled to Amsterdam to see The Jam, so this one didn't hold any surprises. I just found it odd. We didn't have legalised prostitution in Britain; instead sex workers plied their trade on street corners. In Europe, or at least in Holland and Germany, the city fathers handed over a small and strictly controlled area where women sat in shop windows displaying their wares looking bored.

As the number of mods gathering outside the venue grew, the atmosphere became something akin to a party. By 7 o'clock there were a few hundred of them milling around drinking. Most looked to be around 17 and a few even younger. Suddenly the open square was charged by a highly organised gang of skinheads, many giving the stiff-armed salute. They were older and bigger than the young mods and cut through them like a knife through butter.

Bloody hell, I thought. They even had the skinhead wars in Germany, where it was actually a criminal offence to make a fascist salute or wear swastika imagery. The police were slow to arrive and when they did the skins had already run off, so no arrests were made. Unfortunately, the damage had been done and many of the kids were nursing black eyes and cut faces. The skins were dressed like their British counterparts and, because of their age and size, didn't experience much resistance. They were also wearing Third Reich insignia.

I watched the whole thing from the front window of a cafe and it certainly put a downer on the evening. When Leif and his DJ partner Olaf Ott opened the doors an hour or so later, quite a few of the kids had already gone home. It didn't stop me DJing, though, and after an hour or so, the dance floor was full and the incident forgotten. The German mods instantly took to northern soul and copied the crab-like sideways shuffle with enthusiasm. It became apparent that northern soul would soon be the dominant force in the mod world.

32

COOL JERK

While I'd been away in Australia, Rome and Hamburg, trouble had been brewing at the Regency Suite.

The Regency was just one of more than 20 Ilford nightclubs in an arc from Gants Hill to Seven Kings. It was a typical large, old-fashioned pub that at some point in the distant past had been turned into a bone fide nightclub with a 2 o'clock licence. By now we'd been hosting the Sound & Rhythm nights for over a year and the venue had become one of the main mod clubs in the south of England. The Regency Suite was packed every Friday (we'd long since dropped Mondays as being too much like hard work) and people came from as far afield as Peterborough in the north or Guildford in the south every single week.

The manager never really realised how lucky he was. The club was spread over two rooms and already looked tired when we first moved over from Barons; now, 12 months later, the place definitely needed refurbishment. The thing was, though, it was always packed. The majority of the crowd were 16- to 18-year-old Essex mods, but they were always joined by contingents from Ealing, Paddington and other random pockets of stylists or even scooterboys. The car park would always boast at least 50 scooters joined by a dozen or so mod cars like Mk2 Cortinas, Anglias, Heralds, Mini Coopers or Dolomite Sprints. There was also a hefty contingent of big old Rovers from Garry Moore and the rest of the Ilford crew.

The Regency Suite had two rooms, which meant people could cool off and drink in the outer bar before coming back into the main room to dance. We often had guest DJs with us too, like Peter Young from Capital Radio's Soul Cellar, Dick Coombes or Gary Crowley, and were soon joined by other locals like Andy Orr (the drummer in The Scene and host at the R&B night at the Westmoreland Arms) or the fanzine editor Jim Watson to provide some soulful variety.

The most amazing thing was that the Regency was where young mods practiced and then honed their 'special dances'. In the Sixties there were numerous dance crazes that swept the country via *Ready Steady Go!*, but it seemed to me that the mod boys and girls at the Regency took this concept to new heights. They mainly (but not always) invented their own based on what they assumed Sixties mods would have liked.

Some of the most popular were the Watusi, which always accompanied 'Wah-Watusi' by The Orlons. Our version of the dance bore no relation to the original Sixties Watusi craze but instead allowed a packed dance floor to raise a regular 'jazz hand' left and right in time to the music. The same dance was employed every time 'Last Night' by The Mar-Keys was played. Seeing a few hundred 17-year-olds performing a syncopated dance move to a record that had been recorded before they were born was a wonderful thing and we made the most of it.

Another quite extraordinary and complicated routine accompanied James & Bobby Purify's classic 'Shake a Tail Feather', which we copied wholesale from the Ray Charles version that featured in *The Blues Brothers* film. It allowed the dancers to work their way through almost a dozen different moves until the song culminated in dancers bending over with their hands behind their backs, replicating how they assumed a tail feather would look when it was shaken. Not only did we not know what a tail feather was, we certainly didn't know how to shake one!

The love of *The Blues Brothers* led to a couple of mods taking it a step too far. Trevor Blackett and Mick Taylor from Woodford often turned up dressed as Jake and Elwood Blues and led the dancing with their own routine copied move for move from the film.

'Cool Jerk' by The Capitols was always a popular dance track but usually led to the bellowing of 'Hornchurch!' in place of the chorus, whether the dancers were from Hornchurch or not! The novelty northern tune 'Skiing in the Snow' by The Invitations always resulted in a mock slalom on the dance floor, while 'Hawaii Five-0' (or Sammy Davis Jnr's infinitely cooler vocal version 'You Can Count on Me') would often see someone lying on the floor while a friend used his prostrate body as a surfboard!

These songs weren't the only ones, though. 'Land of a Thousand Dances' had its own moves, as did 'Night Train' and 'The Madison', but the ultimate dancer at the time was 'Hitch-Hike' by Russell Byrd on Symbol. The floor was always packed for any of them. You have to understand that we were playing fundamentally unsuccessful records released 20 years earlier to white kids from East London and Essex who suddenly gave a shit. It was certainly weirder than the northern scene whose records would often have been released just a few years before. The mod love of obscure R&B and soul had become all encompassing. Most importantly, at the Regency it was fun!

By this time, girl DJs like Sue Brick, Val Palmer and Amanda Sullivan were beginning to make an impact at the 100 Club and it seemed as though they were starting to stamp their authority on our scene more.

There was an all-girl mod gang known as the Ugly Buglies on our scene, who took the love of obscure to new levels. They produced their own fanzine and pioneered a look and a number of original dances. They were really a bunch of self-deprecating female faces, including Anita, Annabel, Hannah, Anne-Marie, Diane and Lucy, who regularly set the agenda at the expense of some of the male mods on the scene. They were rather anarchic and championed the 'knee-length socks and A-line skirt' look while pushing their own particular dance floor move that we christened the Birmingham Bendy Dance. I can only describe it as an alternative take on the 'shake a tail feather', but you had to be there.

To be fair, we had absolutely no idea about original Sixties dances like the Block, the Camel Walk, the Alligator, the Mashed Potato, the Watusi or the Boogaloo; the important thing was that we *imagined* we did and made them up as we went along. It was a fabulous time.

Trouble was, our days at the Regency were numbered.

Although Mappy had already left (he'd argued the toss with Ray about 'modern soul', an issue that also led to Keb Darge leaving the 100 Club 6Ts all-nighters around the same time), me and Ray Margetson had been running the Sound & Rhythm night there for well over a year and it was still the most successful mod club in London, having been recently joined by Paul Hallam's Sneakers in Shepherd's Bush and Classy's Royal Oak in Tooley Street. Our night was working and the guest DJs were keeping it fresh. And then greed reared its ugly head.

When we'd moved into the club, Brian the manager had taken great pride in telling us he'd been a mod in the Sixties and was still a bit of an 'expert'.

Not content with his half of the door take on (initially) two sold-out nights and then a Friday with 400 punters every week, Brian had been quietly fuming that we'd made such a success at *his* club. Why were we taking half? I mean, it wasn't difficult to do what we were doing. Any idiot could do it – and after all, Brian had even been a bit of a DJ himself back in the day. Nah, those bloody chancers Eddie and Ray were ripping Brian off. Anyone could see that, and it just wasn't fair. He'd show them . . . So he did.

All that hard work building the club over time counted for nothing. Brian could pay a couple of warm-up DJs a pittance and keep all the door money himself. We were unceremoniously kicked out – and sure enough, Brian booked a couple of young'uns to open the evening and did the main sets himself.

In hindsight, we reacted in completely the wrong way, but we were angry. I was angry. Me and Ray booked another Ilford nightclub, Dukes in Cranbrook, for a Friday a couple of weeks later and hoped that our crowd would follow. Many of them did, but we hadn't planned for the casuals who came down to smash the place up. We called it a day then – after all, we'd had a great run – and sat back to see what happened up the road at the Regency Suite.

For a few weeks, Brian held things together and even went as far as to book a couple of the special guests we'd brought in a few months earlier, but the damage had been done. He wasn't a DJ, and while his junior support jocks could set things up, he couldn't hold the floor and within two months it was over. The Regency soul nights were gone for good.

I've seen this happen so many times over the years. Nights in unestablished clubs become successful, then owners become jealous and forget why the nights were popular in the first place; they want all the money for themselves and think they can do a better job. They can't. The simple fact that they only want to do it for money is usually enough to kill things stone dead – but even if they do manage to replace the originators and string the punters along, it never lasts. People aren't stupid. They want something real. Something genuine. And Brian for one couldn't give that to them.

With the Regency gone, my main source of income disappeared overnight. Thank God I still had *Extraordinary Sensations* and the occasional alldayers at the Palais, but I needed another way to make a bit of cash.

Help was at hand.

I'd joined my first band at school. An out-and-out mod group of 15-year-olds called The Speed. I played guitar, badly, and we were rubbish. I realised I had slightly more talent at the drums but didn't last too long in my next group, who didn't even have a name. Then came an R&B outfit called The Rhinos with Andy Donoghue on harmonica and Steve 'Buster' Andrews on bass. We played Yardbirds and John Lee Hooker covers with a couple of originals and furiously rehearsed at my mum's house in Loughton with me on the organ. Rather unsurprisingly, we weren't much cop either and split within three months. I realised that if I really wanted to be in a band, then I'd have to concentrate on the one instrument that I could actually play: the alto saxophone.

In 1983 I joined a mod soul band called The Mighty Marvels, who'd first met at the 100 Club 6Ts all-nighters and at the Regency. We nicked our name from the rare soul group The Mighty Marvelows, whose up-tempo R&B smash 'I Do' had been a hit at the Regency the previous year. Except for me, they all lived in Ealing – a bit of a schlep from Woodford but I'd been practising the bloody sax for years and really wanted to try to use what I'd learned. The important thing was that the band were outright, smart-dressing mods and featured Mark Leech from The Onlookers on bass, the future soul DJ Ivor Jones on vocals, Rick Blackman (who later became an author and university lecturer) on guitar, Joff McKellow on tenor and my old mate Arron Jones on drums. We dipped into the Lou Rawls, Clarence Carter and Otis Redding songbooks and also had a few numbers of our own, completely different from any of the other bands on our scene. Sadly, The Marvels lasted just a year; we rehearsed furiously but things never got much further than that. It was a tragedy as we were pretty good! The demo tapes recently surfaced and I have to admit that I'm disappointed we never put a record out.

The drummer, my close friend Arron, was a ducker and diver in the classic sense. He was the son of a West London car dealer who'd worked out a number of impressive scams and fast-move hustles. He wanted to put his ill-gotten gains into something more substantial and get out of the game, so, with us both at a loose end, we decided to open a record stall in Kensington Market.

Kensington Market had been a go-to destination since the mid-Sixties but was in a state of genteel decline when we moved in. A collection of independent stalls selling clothes, records and a cornucopia of weird shit all gathered together in the one emporium. You could buy punk bondage trousers or studded leather jackets, hippy Afghan coats, Teddy-boy drapes, mod parkas and psychedelic paisley corduroy. In short, the place was unique. There was already a record stall there but they weren't going to be competition as they concentrated on punk and we were going to sell Sixties soul. The rent was cheap, we secured a great position on the first floor near the front and both decided it was a brilliant thing to do.

I was already selling a substantial number of records by mail order through the *Extraordinary Sensations* monthly list, but our trump card was Moondog Records. This was the Teddy-boy shop three doors down from my dad's bookie's in High Street North, where I'd bought my soul and R&B DJ set for peanuts a few years previously. Sure enough, they were still in business and had a damp basement packed with shelf after shelf of US import 7-inch 45s that had apparently been used as shipping ballast in the Sixties. Had I known in 1983 what I know now, I'd have bought the whole lot (maybe 150,000 singles) and long retired to the West Indies, but I didn't and instead settled for just 1,000 or so to start.

The Teds who ran the place might as well have sold them by weight. From memory, the basement singles were just a couple of pence each, maybe 10p and certainly under 30p. All the best independent Sixties black music labels were there from Sue to Specialty and from

Okeh to Golden World. It was a veritable Aladdin's cave with a smell to match. We bought as many singles as we could store and prepared Marvel's Records (named after our band, of course) for its grand opening.

Arron and I photocopied some flyers, bought a couple of cases of beer and waited for the appointed day.

We got off to an incredible start.

As the shutters came up on the first morning, we were confronted by half a dozen teenage mods who were bunking off the school just over the road. Both boys and girls, they came every day just to keep us company. All day. None of them ever bought any records and we soon realised that they were playing truant.

Our first real customer was the Radio 1 DJ Mike Read. We were gobsmacked. I mean, how on earth did he know about our little stall? Read eventually revealed he'd seen the flyers around the market and was determined to come along before anyone else to hoover up any rarities we might've had in the racks. He spent over 75 quid that first morning and became our best regular customer.

I'd always thought Mike Read had more than a bit of mod about him, with his boating blazers, general clobber and love of the Sixties. Arron and I often engaged him in conversation about the glory days of pirate radio as he'd started on local radio with Steve Wright before moving to Radio Luxembourg and was always full of stories. Read told us that he had indeed dabbled with mod as a teenager. Like The Jam, he came from Woking. I told him that I'd seen him compere one of The Jam's last-ever gigs, at Guildford Town Hall just nine months earlier. He confessed that he'd hated the evening and thought his presence had taken some of the gravitas from the situation as it was the band's last 'hometown' show.

When Mike Read had walked out on stage to pick numbers for The Jam's raffle (the band had donated many items of memorabilia to raise money for local charities), the crowd, swollen by hundreds of ticketless liggers, started chanting his radio jingle. Incessantly.

'Mike Read, Mike Read, 275 and 285 . . . Mike Read, Mike Read, National Radio 1 . . .'

I remembered it well. The crowd wouldn't stop, Mike couldn't get anyone to listen to the ticket numbers that he pulled out of the bag – but then that wouldn't have mattered anyway as the table with the raffle prizes on got stormed and everything was stolen.

'Mike Read, Mike Read, 275 and 285 . . . Mike Read, Mike Read, National Radio 1 . . .'

The crowd were relentless, and continued chanting until he appeared again ten minutes later to try to introduce the band.

'Mike Read, Mike Read, 275 and 285 . . . Mike Read, Mike Read, National Radio 1 . . .'

When it became apparent that they weren't going to stop, John Weller walked out, grabbed the mic and shouted his catchphrase: 'And now . . . The best fucking band in the world . . . The Jaaammmm . . .'

Read came to our stall at least once a week. I was pleased to think that a Radio 1 DJ who famously owned many, many thousands of records would still be obsessed enough for us to help him scratch the singles itch. He lived for records.

I'd work a couple of days on and a couple of days off. The rest were done by Arron or occasionally by a mate of his when neither of us could make it. There was a great community at Kensington Market and most of the stallholders drank together and patronised each other's stalls. Paul Daley (later to form Leftfield, and who I signed when he was in A Man Called Adam) was a hairdresser there. I was particularly taken by Sweet Charity, the psychedelic girls' fashion shop. The incredible Regal, its male equivalent, had long moved to Newburgh Street.

I was also making plans to release another record on Well Suspect.

It had been Mark Warrick's idea when I was still at MCA.

Had I ever thought of putting out a compilation album of unreleased masters and demos by the original mod revival bands? He was sure there would be a market for it, and after mulling over the idea, I agreed with him.

He kicked the album off by chucking in a few Directions tracks, so I called up many of the friends I'd made through the fanzine to see if they had anything lying about that might be appropriate.

Kym Bradshaw and Neil Thompson from Small Hours found some demos, as did Derwent Jaconelli from Les Elite, and the Purple Hearts discovered an unreleased tape of their psychedelic masters. Steve at Beggars Banquet gave me some Merton Parkas material and the compilation was completed by Long Tall Shorty's Tony Perfect, who donated the masters for the free flexi that came with *Direction Reaction Creation.*

The album was called *The Beat Generation and the Angry Young Men* after a Fifties beat-poetry anthology that had always caught my mod eye.

I set about getting the record released. A compilation was a much tougher proposition than the Fast Eddie or Merton Parkas 45s of a year earlier. An old colleague from Avatar called Frank Neilson stepped up.

Bizarrely, Frank had been the manager of Bryn Gregory from Beggar, the Leyton-based mod band from South Wales. Beggar had been local heroes and we followed them from gig to gig in the East End back in 1979. At one stage I had a Union Flag with their logo on it sewn onto the back of one of my parkas. Neilson immediately set about manufacturing *The Beat Generation* LP through an independent broker in Portobello called MayKing Records.

I still needed some artwork, so me and Terry put our heads together. We made a collage of an existing couple of beat poetry books and hand-drew the label. I sent it off to MayKing and we sat back and waited for the LPs to turn up.

*

The period of 1983 moving into 1984 was great, with so much going on. Unfortunately, not all the enterprises could last. The new owners of Kensington Market had doubled the rent overnight. While our stall had been washing its face, it couldn't meet the new cost, so me and Arron reluctantly called it a day. The Mighty Marvels didn't last either. I had to drive 50 miles every time we rehearsed and we weren't getting much better. The rehearsal tapes show a band of great promise, but that promise never seemed to convert into gigs. I admit that I wasn't the best sax player but could hold my own in a section (they'd only let me have one solo, on our version of Etta James's 'Security', 16 bars I can still play today). Nah, the game was up. Arron told me he wanted to doss around India for a few years with his new girlfriend and our partnership was dissolved. (He married her, so obviously made the right decision!)

I was skint.

Terry had a plan.

Being from one of London's more colourful areas, he was always coming up with scams that he'd picked up in the pub – usually from his brother Mickey, who was something of a Millwall face. I was often roped in as some kind of dupe. One scam in particular lasted a few weeks and helped fill the coffers between *ES* issues.

Terry had had it on good authority from one of his Bermondsey mates (who went by the name of Ferret) that there was a scam going and it was *totally legal*!

Yep, that's right: the criminals of Southeast London, well known for their charitable disposition, had given Tel the nod to get involved in something slightly dodgy . . . All we had to do was weigh Ferret in for a third.

'But, Eddie, it's not bent. We aren't stealing anything – we're recycling!'

Now, this was 30 years before recycling became anything like normal practice . . . If you'd even mentioned it down the pub in Rotherhithe on a Friday you'd have been laughed at or, worse, asked to take your business elsewhere.

While we were using Ernie Brain's office rent free, cash was always an issue. I was now in the position of having to pay the bill to MayKing Records for *The Beat Generation* LPs. And with the record stall gone, and the Regency having folded too, I was struggling – especially as the next edition of the fanzine was months away at best.

The Friday following the closure of Marvel's, Ferret outlined his plan in the Ship Tavern in Rotherhithe. All perfectly legal, mind! Over the third pint of Carling, Terry cajoled me into a reluctant yes. What the fuck had I got myself into?

Ferret drove his own van but was contracted to a minor hauliers, so whatever driving job he had he still received a weekly wage. Apparently this particular scam wouldn't even affect his wages. He leaned over conspiratorially, drawing us closer so he couldn't be overheard.

Had we ever come across computer paper? Wide, green-striped stuff of amazing quality with holes on either side?

Of course we hadn't. We hadn't even heard of fucking computers; it was 1984, and although Avatar had run to a telex, even the concept of computers was way out of our pub-based orbit. It turned out that this stuff was extremely valuable and was the only type of paper that could be 'recycled' – which apparently meant 'pulped and turned into more computer paper'. Nothing else was of the requisite quality, so ended up burned or in landfill. There was a fortune in this recycling lark, or so he said. All we had to do was pick it up and deliver it to the paper mill at the other end of Rotherhithe Street.

Ferret looked round the bar, playing a spiv-crook in an Ealing comedy. He reached into his inside pocket and pulled out a handwritten list of addresses and times.

In a stage whisper, he said: 'Here's my route for next Wednesday. All you have to do is get to the addresses half an hour before me and load the paper into your van.'

Terry: 'But we don't have a bloody van . . .'

Ferret: 'Well, borrow the one from the garden centre; they'll let you have it for a day for a tenner . . .'

Terry: 'Well, I suppose I could . . . What do we have to do?'

Ferret: 'Just act like you're official. Turn up and chuck the stuff into the back the van. No one'll even ask what you're up to. The paper is usually left on the pavement, so you're not even nicking it . . . You're just concerned citizens clearing up rubbish.'

These days, to hide in plain sight you'd wear a hi-vis jacket. In 1984 we chose donkey jackets.

While it might not have been actual stealing, I still felt mildly uncomfortable. The pair of us did Ferret's round and sure enough the paper was on the pavement. Tel was driving the garden centre van, so we covered their logo with tape and sheets of paper. We'd pull up next to the back doors of whatever property it was, open the Transit and chuck the boxes of paper in the back and then bugger off as quickly as we could.

It was actually very easy, but I did draw the line at the next part of their plan. The paper would be stored in the van overnight to be taken to the mill the following morning. When you arrived, you'd drive the full van onto a weighbridge, the operative would note the weight, you'd chuck the computer paper onto a pile outside the van and they'd weigh the van again. The difference between the two totals would be paid out at whatever the going rate was. Trouble was, Tel and Ferret worked out that wet paper was heavier than dry, so they regularly pulled up, opened the doors and pissed on it!

33

DAGENHAM DAVE

*T*he *Beat Generation and the Angry Young Men* album came out in early 1984 and was an instant success. The network of independent record shops that we'd built to distribute the fanzine took copious copies direct from us but the game changer was that, thanks to Steve Webbon and the Merton Parkas 45, Well Suspect had secured a national distribution deal with Rough Trade, which meant our records were available in almost every shop in the country. The LP sold out in two weeks and I ordered a second pressing.

The album itself was well received and garnered some sympathetic reviews in the music papers. I've since been told that *The Beat Generation* helped breathe new life into the concept of 'mod bands', and it's true that soon a new generation of kids were forming groups to fill the void of all those we'd lost over the previous couple of years.

Things were genuinely looking up. But of course, it couldn't last and in the summer of 1984, me and Terry suffered a major blow.

Things had been changing in Dagenham. Unbelievably, the place was moving up in the world and rumours of imminent gentrification abounded. Our patron, Ernie Brain, decided to cash in and sell his yard for redevelopment. We couldn't really complain as he'd given us a free workspace for a year and even told us we could stay until the sale had been finalised. We figured this would give us six months at most. What were we going to do after that?

First things first: we decided to knock up a new *Extraordinary Sensations*. We'd been working on an issue for a month or so, but now its completion assumed a greater importance.

Surely our luck would change soon . . .

I was also trying hard to push Fast Eddie further up the ladder. The band had grown into a seven-piece, having recruited a couple of young girl singers and a tenor sax player. The move had worked and the fresh sound saw a whole host of new fans and bigger gigs coming in. Jo Sullivan, known as 'Little Jo', was a crowd favourite – she was indeed little and became a great foil for Gordon Tindale's on-stage wit. A beautiful, tiny waif of a torch singer who rode a small-frame Vespa, she regularly stole the show with her version of Peggy Lee's 'Fever'. Jo was joined initially by Gina Guarnieri, another scooter-riding mod girl and long-time scenester. The new line-up was completed by Al Tracey, Gordon's rockabilly mate from Southend, on tenor sax, which allowed the band to introduce some Louis Jordan-style jump-jive into the set. Pressures of work meant that Gina soon left and her place was taken by Tracy Kilrow, a soulgirl from North London.

With the Regency Suite now closed off to us, the band had fewer opportunities to play live and I didn't want them thinking I'd lost interest. I certainly hadn't. Alongside The Truth, they had quickly built up the biggest live following on the scene.

After the success of *The Beat Generation* and the cash that its sales generated, I decided to put Fast Eddie back in the studio. But rather than produce an album myself, I asked my old Avatar contact Frank Neilson to run the session. In the end he co-produced alongside the legendary Vic Maile, who had during the course of a glittering career worked with the likes of Dr. Feelgood, Small Faces, The Kinks and Motörhead. I booked four days in a country-house studio and roped in

The Truth organist, Chris Skornia, to put down some Hammond. The album was shaping up perfectly.

Fast Eddie's new line-up had gone down well and had given the band a new lease of life. The recording session was very successful, although we'd run out of time and managed to put only seven tracks down on tape – a mixture of covers and originals, but all of them popular live numbers.

The failure to finish a whole album's worth of material caused me a major problem and I had just two options: I could wait another month and get back in the studio to cut five more tracks, or we could change the release to a 12-inch mini-album and choose a release date just a couple of months away. I chose the latter option. The artwork, knocked up by Terry in an hour, was a blatant rip-off of the Donald Byrd Blue Note LP *A New Perspective*, with the band standing around an E-Type Jag.

We sent the master and artwork to the factory and sat back to wait for the records.

Then disaster struck again. Serious this time.

The first problem was with the Ilford alldayers. The local soulboys, led by a firm called the Gants Hill Riot Squad, decided they'd had enough of their town being taken over by gangs of mods twice a year and unfortunately for us they resolved to do something about it.

The local paper had written a big piece about the coming event and it had given the Riot Squad enough time to arrange a reception committee. The alldayer started as normal but at around 5 o'clock 150-odd soulboys and casuals began gathering outside. Unfortunately, the Palais had left around 30 empty beer barrels stacked up against the wall in the car park. Arming themselves with these, at a prearranged signal the interlopers began to batter the doors in from the outside. Taken by surprise, the bouncers, helped by many of the mods, began a battle to keep them out. The violence was indeed shocking and many were injured on both sides.

After only 15 minutes, the police arrived. Some of the attackers were arrested, but the rest melted away as quickly as they'd arrived.

The damage was done. The police closed the event and the venue manager was furious. I tried to explain that it wasn't our fault, but he was having none of it. I suspected that this would be the end and I was right. A week later I received an invoice for £4,000 and a legal letter insisting that I pay for the damage to the venue. Unsurprisingly, all our future dates were cancelled too. After much toing and froing the Rank Organisation eventually dropped their demands as I made it clear that I wouldn't be able to pay, but our incredibly successful event was no more. We were gutted.

If that wasn't enough, the next bit of bad luck looked like an absolute death blow.

A company that owed Well Suspect a few thousand pounds for export sales went bankrupt before we'd been paid – and while I didn't know how these things worked, I realised that it probably wouldn't be a happy ending for Well Suspect Records.

Lots of bills were falling due. I tried hard to raise some cash but had absolutely no experience of finance and the label didn't even have an overdraft at the bank. Had the Regency, the record stall and the Ilford alldayers still been running I might have been able to swing it, but they'd all been closed and we'd been running on empty. I had been depending on this money to pay our outstanding liabilities.

Two months later, Well Suspect was gone and all our hard work with it.

I now had no label for the Fast Eddie album I'd just made. Although London Records showed some initial interest in the band, nothing came of it and for a short time I desperately tried to start a new imprint called Soul Stylist. I put in a new order with a different manufacturer, hoping I'd be able to raise the rest of the money before the finished records were due to be delivered. Fingers crossed . . .

After we got the test pressing back from the factory, Terry mused in his usual deadpan 'glass half-empty' way: 'Why on earth did you choose the name Soul Stylist? It's bloody crap. Possibly the catalogue number SS1 wasn't the best idea either . . .'

Sadly, I couldn't raise any more cash and we quickly realised that the game was up. All we had from everyone's hard work was a couple of white-label test pressings sporting the catalogue number SS1.

A few days later I broke the news to the band. Their label was bankrupt and the long-awaited Fast Eddie album wasn't going to come out. They were devastated, and while we kept going on the live circuit for another six months (which included a sold-out headline at the 100 Club for my 21st birthday, 8 November 1984), within a year they'd thrown in the towel. It was a tragedy but one that I could do nothing about.

Terry and I were broke and with very few options. Was this to be the end of our partnership?

My old mate Tony Perfect from Long Tall Shorty offered me the opportunity to be a guitar roadie for Angelic Upstarts and I jumped at the chance. Shorty, one of my favourite bands, had recently split and Tony had been recruited by vocalist and band leader Mensi to join the punk stalwarts on bass. Roadie-ing was something I loved because life on the road can be the most exciting thing imaginable, full of unexpected pleasures. All your hotels, food and drink are free, you cruise around Europe having fun and get a nice cash lump sum at the end of the dates. The Upstarts needed me for just one European tour and a handful of UK gigs, but the offer certainly got me out of a hole.

I'd always loved Angelic Upstarts. I'd bought 'The Murder of Liddle Towers' on Small Wonder in 1978 and 'I'm an Upstart' a year later. I thought they were still coming up with great songs and, best of all, my old mate Kev the Hammer was also in the road crew. Even Si Spanner joined us for a few of the gigs.

The tour started and finished in Holland, and if I thought the skinhead wars were big in the UK, Europe was absolutely mind-boggling. It was the same at every gig. The Oi! phenomenon was at its peak there, and although the Upstarts weren't intentionally part of that scene, they did attract a similar crowd. The gigs were always banged out with skins and punks, but the trouble was nearly always political. You'd get right-wing skinheads and punks who assumed the Upstarts were fascist sympathisers because of the song 'England', and left-wing punks and skins who loved the band for 'Police Oppression' or 'The Murder of Liddle Towers'.

Halfway through the set, the Upstarts would launch into 'England' and the right-wingers would push to the front and give the Hitler salute. Mensi would tell them to fuck off and sometimes jump into the crowd and kick off. The stage crew had to be on their toes because once he'd decided on something there was no stopping him and we had to make sure he was safe. Then the left-wing skins would attack the Nazis and the whole place would explode. Golf clubs, baseball bats, chairs and tables . . . They used absolutely everything. These battles were a regular occurrence and very often the crowd would try to storm the stage in a frenzy. The Upstarts road manager was a punk called Chuck and it was his job to protect both the band and the equipment. He tried enthusiastically to do so, but it was occasionally touch and go.

Two things come to mind when I remember my time with the Upstarts. The first was that I was reunited with Max Splodge, who'd joined them at the same time as Tony Perfect. Tony stood on the right side of the stage with Max, and if anything went wrong with their guitars, one of us would have to run on and swap them or change a lead. Mensi thought it would be funny to make me wear a target T-shirt.

Every fucking night. This drove the skins absolutely mental and I became a target for the relentless missiles.

The second memory was at a gig in Swindon, after we'd got back from Europe. Fascist skins had taken great exception to the end of the set and stormed the stage. We had to take refuge in the dressing room as there were 25 or so trying to force their way in. The dressing-room door was just to the right of the stage in a kind of small corridor that created a funnel effect. Only three skins were able to push the door at the same time, but this didn't stop them trying and all 25 were squeezed into an area about 9 feet long by 3 feet wide, the ones at the back pushing forward so that almost none of the skinheads could move.

Although we were physically trapped backstage, Kev the Hammer had an idea. He pointed up at the dressing-room window and asked, 'D'you think we can get out of that?' I thought it might be a tight squeeze but he said, 'Follow me.'

Sure enough, Kev pushed a table against the wall, climbed up and squeezed himself out of the window and we dutifully followed. The four of us ran quickly round to the front of the venue and walked straight in through the front doors. Most of the crowd had left, but those 25-odd skins were crushed into the small area to the right of the stage still trying to force the dressing-room door.

Kev put his finger to his mouth to indicate silence and then carefully walked across the stage on exaggerated tiptoes.

At once we realised what he had in mind.

The stack of PA speakers was perched on the edge of the 4-foot stage, just in front of the dressing-room door. This conveniently shielded our approach, but even if it hadn't I doubt the skinheads would have noticed us. They were far too intent on trying to attack the band. Kev used hand signals to indicate on the count of three that we should go into action.

'One . . . Two . . . *Three*!', this last shouted at the top of his voice. Too late the skinheads looked round, just in time to see the massive stack of speakers teetering off the edge of the stage. A second later, before any of them had a chance to react, the stack toppled and three extraordinarily heavy PA speakers landed on them.

It was mayhem. They were squashed and screaming. Kev just climbed over the bodies and opened the door. 'Come on, lads, let's load the van.'

I got back to London refreshed by the break in routine and determined to find some work. Terry had persuaded Dennis Greaves to let us design some artwork for The Truth's record sleeves, and we did some crew work for them on their first British tour too. There wasn't really any money in it, but it did give us an opportunity to see just how the second mod revival was shaping up at first hand.

Then you had the scooter scene, which had also exploded. If you defined it broadly, by late 1983, there were more mods in Britain than at any time since 1966. These kids were young, in their mid-teens and at 11 or 12 had been too young to take an active role in the mod revival based around The Jam and two-tone. Now they were 15 or 16 and finding their feet in ever-increasing numbers.

This was best illustrated on a wet Tuesday night when The Truth played a gig at the New Ocean Club in Cardiff. As the tour van pulled into the car park at five in the afternoon, we were greeted by at least 400 young mods waiting for the band to arrive. It was extraordinary. A local group called The Colours opened for them and we sold at least 300 copies of *Extraordinary Sensations* that night alone. On a Tuesday!

This was the next generation of mod kids who bore such wonderful fruit with the next wave of bands, fanzines and DJs who were shaping up just around the corner.

We rushed back to London enthused to concentrate on selling more copies of the current issue of *ES* and were amazed at how warmly the fanzine was received. With that issue we'd topped 8,000 sales for the first time, proving that the second mod revival was an underground reality. This time the media hadn't even noticed!

There was enough cash to keep us going, but we were both conscious that Ernie Brain's free office was soon to go. We vowed to complete the next issue sharpish, setting ourselves a two-week deadline.

I'd taken a weekend job moving furniture round West End offices for 40 quid a day, cash in hand. But then, when we thought things couldn't get much worse . . .

Fortune came a-knocking.

I read the letter. It was from *Twist* fanzine from California. It turned out they'd recorded a local mod band and were so pleased with the result that they thought it deserved a British release. They'd recently reviewed *The Beat Generation* and realised that, for this sort of music, Well Suspect was the only game left in town. No one was signing mod bands, no matter how good they were.

We knew the label had closed, but the Americans obviously didn't.

Aw, fuck it. For a couple of days we didn't even bother to play the cassette – we couldn't afford to release it, so what was the point?

Then a week or so later, Terry pointed out that we needed a few reviews to fill the 'new music' space in the next *Extraordinary Sensations*. We might as well review that American band.

Good idea, Tel.

I took the tape out of the box. It was very amateur and similar to the dozens of crap cassettes we got through the post every month. I wasn't sure why this one should be any different.

I slid it into the machine, popped a can of Fosters, unwrapped my sandwiches and sat back to listen.

Fuck me! I wasn't expecting this. I looked across at Terry and could see he was also impressed. It was up-tempo, bouncy and most of all positive. It was also very different to any of the British bands on the circuit. The music was an enticing mixture of soul and ska with a big hook for the chorus.

'What are they called again?'

I picked up the box and looked at the cover. 'The Untouchables . . .'

I reached for the copy of *Twist* that accompanied the tape and gave it another look, this time in much more detail. It was impressive. Well produced with some great photos. One that caught my eye was the shot of a local face called Billy Zoom standing by his beautiful GS. I looked a little deeper and it turned out he was the frontman in a punk band called X who were making noises on the West Coast. It seemed that the American mod scene was deserving of further investigation.

The band looked absolutely amazing. Multiracial, smartly dressed mods certainly, but there was also a funky dread who wore mod gear too. Some of them even had scooters. They looked like the real deal and such authenticity would go down really well over here in the UK.

In those pre-internet days, the only way you could find out about anything to do with the scene was by reading fanzines. I moved over to the filing cabinet and pulled out every American fanzine I could find. There were at least a dozen titles, mainly but not exclusively from California. I flicked through the first, a six-month old copy of *Whaam!*, and sure enough, there was a terrific live review of The Untouchables. 'Terry, have a look at this . . . What do you reckon?'

'Looks like they're a good live band too . . .'

We listened to the tape a couple more times and the music seemed to get better with each play. It really did seem like the band – who I was now thinking of as 'our' band – had something great going for them. And I wanted a piece of it.

We left for home and when we pulled into Rotherhithe Street made the unconscious and mutual decision to enter the Mayflower and talk about the band.

'So what the fuck are we going to do? We haven't got a label any more and this lot deserve the proper treatment.'

I got a round in, put Terry's glass of wine in front of him and waited. I could tell that he was mulling over the basics of an idea.

'Go on then, tell me?'

'Well, I've got a friend who runs the UK Sire Records office at WEA. Until recently her old man was number two at Stiff and she still has contacts there. I don't think Seymour Stein will go for this as he's got Madonna blowing up and this lot aren't his type of band. He's more of an Anglophile. No, I reckon Stiff might bite. I'll get a meeting with her for tomorrow; we can take her to the Royal George, have a few drinks and pitch it. If she likes it, she can get us in with Dave Robinson, the boss.'

The more I thought about it, the more I thought Stiff might go for it. Dave Robinson had had an enormous amount of success with Madness, so knew the potential in a band with some ska flavour. He was also aware of the size of the new underground mod scene, or at least if he wasn't, we'd certainly tell him. Most importantly, he was a maverick marketing genius who could sell pretty much anything. Yeah, it was a great idea. I congratulated Terry on his far-sightedness.

Terry was true to his word and at half past five the following day we were sitting in an empty Royal George, just next to the EMI office on Charing Cross Road, waiting for Maxine Conroy. I'd never met her but I knew she'd been friends with Terry for years and he was always singing her praises. Ten minutes later she breezed into the bar and sat down. I bought her a glass of wine and waited for Terry to introduce me.

I was surprised to discover that Maxine was from New York and had been working for Seymour Stein over there until she'd married Paul Conroy and moved to London, where she was looking after Sire's UK office. You'd think she'd love her current job; Ramones, The Undertones,

Talking Heads and Madonna – what's not to like? It turned out that Maxine was looking for a new challenge.

Terry gave her the pitch and I handed her the Walkman headphones and pressed play.

She was obviously impressed, and before the first track, called 'Free Yourself', had even finished, she put the headphones down on the bar and said simply, 'I'm in. What do you want me to do?'

I told her that they'd sent us a master to release, so we were looking to place them and get some kind of cut in the back end. They hadn't asked for an advance from Well Suspect, so we figured that if we could get even a small one out of Stiff, the band would sign. We mentioned our Dave Robinson rationale and at that she waved her hand to stop us talking and asked, 'But what do you two want out of it?'

We explained to her that our label had been forced out of business by someone else's bankruptcy and that we were about to lose our office too. We also realised we didn't have a clue what we wanted to achieve strategically.

'Well, losing your office is an easy one to rectify. You can come and work out of Sire. It's right next to the Blue Posts, the coolest pub in Soho. I'll let Seymour know – Sire's in the WEA building and he won't mind. He's always been a champion of indie labels. As to the record label, that's a slightly different challenge. I'll think about it for a couple of days. Leave me the cassette and I'll get you a meeting with Robbo for next week. If he agrees, you've got to be at the top of your game. Think through all your marketing and promo ideas too. And you'd better call the band and tell them you're about to get them a deal with Britain's coolest indie!'

Stiff certainly were Britain's coolest indie. From their early marketing slogan, 'If it ain't Stiff, it ain't worth a fuck' through to launching the careers of dozens of household names: Ian Dury & the Blockheads, Madness, Elvis Costello, Lena Lovich, The Damned and most recently The Pogues. This list was seemingly endless and, more than that, Dave Robinson had that special and extremely rare knack of turning average and sometimes even bad records into hits.

Stiff had just moved from West London into the Island Records building in Chiswick, where Dave Robinson had taken on the role of Island's MD alongside Stiff. He'd put the Bob Marley *Legend* album out and overseen U2, both of which were incredibly successful.

A week and a half later we were sitting in Robinson's office making our pitch. Surprisingly, Maxine had insisted on coming in with us and she was unusually quiet while I was explaining the musical side of things. I'd outlined how the band joined so many creative dots that would lead them directly to an enormous, ready-made fanbase with the mod scene. All we had to do was release the record, sit back and count the chart hits.

Dave Robinson had the habit of raising a quizzical eyebrow while he waited for you to answer a question. It could make him appear somewhat demonic. I saw that eyebrow for the first time as I finished the pitch.

'I can see it. It's a good idea and that track you played could even be a hit. I'll do it; we'll sign them to Stiff. But here's the thing – what do you lot want out of it?'

Before I had a chance to answer, Maxine sprang to life and cut across me. So was this why she'd insisted on coming to the meeting?

'I wondered when we were going to get to that, Dave,' she said. 'The band already have a manager, so we can't get involved there. Commission for placing the deal is great, but I have a better idea. This underground mod scene is enormous. I've been researching it for the last week and I really think we can come up with something special. There are plenty of bands out there with a decent following and no record deals. We can pick up the best of them. What we want is our own label as part of Stiff.

Not a subsidiary, but licensed to you with us as owners. The three of us get a salary, you fund us an office and we sign you some mod bands.'

I looked at Terry open-mouthed. We had no idea she was going to come up with this, but fuck it – it was a great idea. It got Terry and me a new job with a real salary and, most interestingly, it got Maxine out of Sire with her own, totally funded record label. She would be my partner. Well, blow me down. What a great idea. All we had to do was get Dave Robinson to say yes. It was a big commitment and I could see him turning it over in his mind, weighing the pros and cons.

After half a minute of silence he said in his lilting Dublin accent: 'Here's what we'll do. I'll take a serious look at the band. The Untouchables, is it? I like the name, they look good and they can write a song too. If I work out a deal – and it's a big if – I'll set you up a label. You can sign a total of say . . . four bands, but we have approval on costs. You can have A&R independence, all the press, promo and marketing comes from in-house at Stiff. Oh, and Maxine – it's in your interest to persuade this American band to sign, so I suggest you get on the phone to the manager and sell it to him. Leave the finer points to me, but if it works, you've got a deal.'

With that, Dave Robinson stood up, the meeting suddenly over. We stumbled out of the Stiff office and into the nearest pub, shell-shocked.

'Fuck me, Max, you could have warned us!' exclaimed Terry. I was just staring at her, amazed at what'd just happened.

We sat down to a round of drinks and she said simply, 'Gentlemen, if I'd have warned you, then you'd have fucked things up. I knew what Robbo wanted to hear and I knew the best way to tell him. It was important that I pitched him or I might not have been able to cut myself in as a partner. All you've got to do, Eddie, is find us some bands.'

And this is where it started . . . Terry and I used to trek over to Chiswick a couple of times a week to see the Stiff team. The Island office was a great place to be and we certainly made the most of it – especially the vegetarian cafe that was run by a beautiful American whose name was Lovely Previn, daughter of the conductor André.

Stiff soon moved again, this time to a desolate and derelict Hoxton in the old East End, so Maxine sourced us an office at Greenhouse Studios round the corner from them in Provost Street, right next to the Duke of Wellington. She also chose a name for us.

'We're going to call the label Countdown Records. Terry, you get on with designing a logo and this time next month we'll be in business . . .'

Crikey, I'd only met the woman four times and she was now my business partner. I loved the way Maxine went about things; she was organised in a way that Terry and I most definitely weren't. I knew immediately it was going to be a great relationship – and best of all, she shared our sense of humour.

Ernie Brain's sale came through just a few days later. With Maxine serving her notice at Sire, it wasn't appropriate for us to share her office. We needed somewhere to finish the next issue of the fanzine, somewhere that we could use as an office. Help came from an unexpected quarter.

Paul Weller had recently moved to Nomis in Shepherd's Bush. This was an enormous warren of studios and offices in Sinclair Road. It even had its own canteen. I'd bumped into him in the West End a few weeks earlier and mentioned we needed a stopgap to nail down Issue 15 and he immediately offered us a room rent free. We could have our own office within his office with access to the phones and the receptionist. This was a really generous gesture and one we grasped with both hands. We soon moved in.

Paul had always supported fanzines, and of course I'd first interviewed him way back in 1980. I'd got to know him better since he set up The

Style Council, and to be honest, I knew I didn't even have to ask. He just offered. I reckoned it'd be for three weeks, enough time to finish the new issue, but he told me to take as long as we needed.

Sure enough, when the fanzine went off to Dave Stokes for printing we moved ourselves out of Weller's HQ and into the upstairs room at Greenhouse Studios.

Countdown was a real label and we had real jobs. All in the space of two months.

5-4-3-2-1 Go!

34

FREE YOURSELF

A week later we interviewed a couple of people for the role of office junior. I chose Jon Cooke. He was a progressive-minded mod from Hornchurch and a skilled designer. He fitted in perfectly. The office was taking shape too. We'd constructed an enormous collage of black and white photos from the Sixties that was stuck to the wall; it stretched over 20 feet across and 10 feet up, and completely dominated the office. We also got hold of an Asteroids machine and had use of the recording studio's pool table. It was an amazing space for an office. The only slight drawback was that all through the summer of 1984 Katrina & the Waves were recording their album downstairs and we had to endure listening to 'Walking on Sunshine' a few hundred times in quick succession. Consequently, I've found the record very difficult to put up with since!

Now we needed to find some music.

Just before Well Suspect went tits up, and when Fast Eddie were still going, I'd also been working on another project. Six months earlier, on holiday in Ibiza, I met Karen, a 16-year-old mod girl from Willenhall in the West Midlands. She was sweet and we got on well. I told her about the fanzine and promised to send her a copy.

She responded with, 'Oh, I know a band you might like from my town, right proper mods. Makin' Time and they've just made a demo. You send me a fanzine and I'll send you the tape, deal?'

Well, to be fair, I didn't hold out too much hope. I received a dozen cassettes a month from aspiring bands, most of which ended up in the bin after the first chorus. I sent her the fanzine and a week or so later Karen's promise came back to me when the demo arrived. I reluctantly whacked it on.

The music was surprisingly good, but very raw and underdeveloped. Plenty of song ideas, but nothing that blew me away. I had a look at their photo and realised they were a five-piece who looked so young they were probably still at school. Notably, they had two singers. One was a girl who played the organ; the other a male guitarist.

The band's music nagged away at me until I eventually called the number scrawled on the tape.

I spoke to a lad with a broad West Midlands accent called Martin Blunt. He told me he was the bass player in Makin' Time and said if I wanted to see them live they were playing their local pub the next week.

I'd drove up to Willenhall and introduced myself to the kids (and they were kids) just before they went on stage. They played a competent set, but it wasn't good enough for me to take them on. They needed to rehearse and most of all needed to play live. I told them I'd get Makin' Time a gig supporting Fast Eddie in London and we'd see how the audience took to them. I also mentioned I might be interested in managing them if they garnered a favourable response from Fast Eddie's notoriously difficult crowd.

They definitely weren't the finished article but had improved massively in just a month. Vocalist Mark McGounden (a former punk nicknamed Sid Gounden after his one-time icon Sid Vicious) told me that there had been a comprehensive programme of rehearsals and routines, with the band determined to make the most of the opportunity. Makin' Time were a typical example of the second mod revival. They were ridiculously young but impressively smart, all vintage knits and white Levi's.

Fay Hallam wore her hair in a short, dark pixie crop and played a Farfisa organ, giving the band a very Sixties feel that drew numerous comparisons with Brian Auger, Julie Driscoll and The Trinity. There was also no ambiguity about their dedication to the mod cause. All five were out-and-out travellers on the path.

The crowd at the London gig took to them straight away, so I signed them for management. I decided to record a couple of tracks in the studio. Really, they were just demos, but if they came out well enough, I'd put them out as a single on Well Suspect. As a favour, I persuaded The Truth's Dennis Greaves and Mick Lister to produce the session and the day went well. The lead song, 'Honey', was a duet where both vocalists shared the lead with some great harmonies. Both songs turned out brilliantly, but before I had a chance to do anything with them, Well Suspect collapsed and I was forced to put Makin' Time on the back burner.

Six months later, Dave Robinson wanted some bands, so were Makin' Time good enough?

Before we had a chance to make that decision, Robbo called us over to his office for a production meeting. He'd had an idea and I thought it was a good one. He suggested a compilation album featuring new tracks from some of the bigger bands on the mod scene. We'd use it to launch the Countdown label and then sign the band (or even bands) whose contribution got the best reaction.

I got busy sourcing the acts while Maxine came up with a title. Our first release was going to be called *5-4-3-2-1 Go! The Countdown Compilation*. Within three weeks we had a track list and two weeks after that we had the masters.

The sleeve was more complicated. Terry set his heart on using a particular David Bailey image; I couldn't understand why but he was crazy about it. It was a photo of a girl's legs encased in mismatched Sixties-style meshed stockings, with flat white pumps on her feet that had studs on the sole and . . . Oh. She was wearing gloves. Bailey's people wanted well over a grand for permission to use it so, after much gnashing of Rawlings' teeth, I convinced him we could recreate the pic for less than 100 quid. He didn't want to but eventually sense prevailed and we set about making the shoes, sourcing the tights and altering the gloves so it looked just like Bailey's shot.

The finished image was substantially different from the original, but Terry had such fun working on the sleeve that I'm not sure he noticed. We persuaded a tall and leggy label manager at Ace Records called Vicky to model the outfit and she did a sterling job. Garry Bushell was recruited to write some suitably aspirational sleeve notes and an upbeat press release. He was probably the only major journalist still giving mod the time of day and his recent feature in *Sounds*, 'The Face of Mod in '84', featured me modelling a question-mark T-shirt designed by Terry.

We plugged into the Stiff setup and were genuinely part of the team. The staff seemed to like what we were up to – and if they hadn't got it on the pitch, by the time The Untouchables had hit the charts they were convinced.

Philip Hall was Stiff's press officer and we hit it off immediately. He was laconic, laid back and very funny, and taught me everything I hadn't picked up as Avatar's press officer. But the place was full of characters and working with such a team was an education that couldn't have been bought. Stiff Records had more hits than any other indie in the modern era, with over 20 gold singles in the nine years they were in business. Maggie taught me production; John Whyton the basics of contract law; Alan Cowdrey encouraged me to think outside the A&R box; Alison Donald demonstrated the importance of personal contacts in an ever-changing industry; and Dave Robinson himself showed me how to market a record. It was thrilling and every day was a schoolday!

Less than three months later, *5-4-3-2-1 Go!* was released. It sold over 30,000 copies worldwide, and was consequently pronounced a success by the Stiff team. Each copy included a pre-addressed postcard with instructions to return it to the label in order to receive a free subscription for our regular newssheet, 'Countdown News'. Mark Johnson had convinced me of the importance of direct marketing with the success of his 'The Phoenix List' and all we did was to copy the format but populate the newsletter with stories about what our bands were up to.

The mod scene flocked to support the new LP in spite of the fact that there were no real big-hitters involved. All of the early bands had given up and the coming generation simply weren't yet sufficiently established. As for picking a band to prioritise from the ones included on the album, I didn't fancy any of them as being the finished article. I thought The Kick and The Moment were OK as development projects, but I made the decision to go elsewhere for Countdown's first real signing. I knew that whatever the label did, it would have to be superb in order to get over the antipathy the press had towards mod bands.

I quickly realised that I'd already begun the development process with Makin' Time. If I was going to try to develop a band commercially, I might as well go back to them. They did seem to be the most promising group I'd come across in recent years – and I was thrilled with the Dennis Greaves and Mick Lister recordings already in the can, so I resolved to use the tracks as demos to present to Robbo as a means to demonstrate the band's potential. But there was a slight problem. My career with them as manager hadn't worked out particularly well.

When I'd first begun managing them a year or so earlier, I'd told the band that only by playing constantly would they learn how to manipulate a hostile crowd and properly learn their craft. That way they could reach the level needed to have a serious crack at crossing over. I'd arranged some German shows through my mate Leif Nueske from FAB Records in Hamburg. The band hadn't been able to afford a driver, and as I'd done it before (to Belfast, among other places), I'd offered my services again.

It was a mistake. Being locked up with them for days on end was tough. I wasn't particularly getting on with one of the band at the time and the inevitable eventually happened: we had a row (at the sound check at the Grosse Freiheit in Hamburg) and I was sacked. I wasn't best pleased and flew home the next day while they recruited another driver. I'd put a lot of effort into building Makin' Time and had virtually nothing to show for it. But at least I still had a record contract with them – and it was this that I fell back on when I suggested putting them on Countdown.

I told Maxine I thought they should be our first signing and she eventually agreed.

The band appointed a new manager, Will Birch, who was the perfect fit. Will was a drummer with more than a foot in the mod camp, having been in pub rockers the Kursaal Flyers and The Records. He was also highly organised. A month later, Robbo chose Will to produce the band alongside the former Vibrators bass player Pat Collier.

Makin' Time were duly signed to Countdown and spent a month recording what was to be their debut album, *Rhythm and Soul*, underneath our office. I'd withdrawn somewhat from the process, more than happy to let the producers do their job. The atmosphere was still a bit prickly with me around and I didn't want the band to have any distractions . . .

Then *bang*! It was in the can and off to the factory.

We had hooked The Untouchables up with Stiff in early 1984, but it took almost nine months before the first single was released. 'Free Yourself' hit the UK Top 30 chart and was soon followed by their *Wild Child* LP, which hovered around the edges of the Top 50 for a month. The team at Stiff were suitably impressed with our A&R ability and Countdown's stock rose overnight. The Untouchables delivered the last two chart hits of the mod revival and things were once again on the up.

But for how long?

*

However, just as Countdown was on track for our first big release, strange things were happening at our parent company. A year earlier, Stiff had moved in with Island Records and Dave Robinson had taken on the role of Island's managing director. No one really understood why. Sure, it was an exciting place to be, and I assumed that there'd been some kind of business hook-up between the labels at the executive level, but really we were in the dark.

Stiff slotted into the Island setup pretty well. The label was storming along with The Pogues, whose new album, *Rum Sodomy & the Lash*, had finally established the band as contenders after a long period of gestation. I'd known Shane MacGowan since the beginning of the revival and we'd regularly check out his band, The Nips. They were originally an out-and-out punk band called The Nipple Erectors, but by 1979 they'd calmed down somewhat, changed their name to the marginally less offensive The Nips and released some of the best singles of the mod revival. I'd always reckoned Shane had more than a bit of mod about him and even in 1977 he would be seen at gigs in Jam-style suits or Union Jack jackets. His fanzine, *Bondage*, was the first punkzine to get behind The Jam, putting them at odds with Mark Perry's *Sniffin' Glue*, which dismissed their mod sensibilities. After the demise of The Nips, Shane kept his hand in by working at one of the rare-record shops in Hanway Street.

Always moving forward, he'd formed an Anglo-Irish band called Pogue Mahone (which means 'kiss my arse' in Gaelic). It was a truly original idea as no one had thought of mixing Irish folk with punk, and as soon as they released 'The Dark Streets of London' and 'Boys From County Hell', it was obvious they were destined for greater things. The band soon changed their name to the (less offensive) The Pogues and under the direction of their enigmatic manager Frank Murray became Stiff's great hope. When Countdown joined Stiff, the band had just released their debut LP, *Red Roses for Me*, to general indifference. They had a lot of credibility yet weren't particularly selling records, but they had yet to go to America, which is where everything fell into place.

Even their hits didn't really chart. 'Sally MacLennane' and 'Dirty Old Town' were both incredible singles from the *Rum Sodomy & the Lash* LP, but neither broke into the Top 50. It was after the Americans woke up to the band that they reached the dizzy heights. MacGowan's incisive lyrics and the band's blend of punk sensibility and traditional Dubliners Irish folk found a market with generations of lachrymose ex-pats yearning for a link with their beloved homeland (even if most of them had never been there). It was an incredibly successful formula! I'd long loved Irish folk and had played the penny whistle on a regular basis, so The Pogues soon became my favourite band. (Later, Spider Stacy, the penny-whistle player who stepped up to lead vocals with Joe Strummer when Shane left, became a drinking partner and I still occasionally play the whistle he gave me.)

While Island were on a roll, there was still an odd atmosphere and I felt the Stiff staff were never really accepted by the Island employees. It wasn't anything overt, but I occasionally felt we weren't welcome.

It didn't make any difference to Countdown, though, as we had our own office in Hoxton.

As the Makin' Time LP hit the streets, the pressure was on from Stiff Records, who were pushing us to sign another band. We were committed to releasing four albums a year and needed two more bands in order to hit our target.

But who?

There was one band I'd been following for years but knew they'd be difficult to work with. They were called The Prisoners.

An old-school promoter called Jim Driver booked me to DJ some mod/garage nights at the Cricketers at the Oval and the band were regular headliners. Before long I was hooked. The Prisoners appeared just as the mod revival was running out of steam, and although they were ambivalent about their mod roots, their 1982 debut LP, *A Taste of Pink*, was about as mod as you could get. Of all the groups I've ever seen play live, I can safely say The Prisoners were far and away the best.

The 'Medway Scene' had coalesced around the enigmatic, guru-like Svengali Billy Childish and other core musicians like Bruce Brand and Russ Wilkins in the early Eighties. Childish's early punk band, The Pop Rivets, seemed to have paved the way for almost 50 others who followed in their wake. Even at the height of punk the Pop Rivets were flirting with the mod revival, and it was natural that they should dictate what would later become known as the 'Medway Sound'. It was brash, fast and Sixties-influenced, with an emphasis on authenticity in both style and sound. The Dentists, The Milkshakes, Thee Headcoatees, Thee Mighty Ceasars and The Daggermen were just a few, but for me The Prisoners stood head and shoulders above the lot.

The most important thing was that they were a real band who oozed personality and style. Graham Day was the singer and guitarist, a perfect frontman with chiselled good looks, an aggressive playing style and a fabulous voice. James Taylor used a harsh-sounding Casio keyboard with a substantial nod to the Sixties US garage rock sound. Bassist Allan Crockford was solid, a whole heap of unsmiling cynicism who steadied the ship. And then there was Johnny Symons. Often dressed in a striped Breton shirt, Symons played a ferocious and idiosyncratic drum kit in a style that was closer to Keith Moon than it was to Charlie Watts; he literally attacked his kit with real venom. They were the perfect band.

Trouble was, they were prickly and positively anti-success – they didn't like doing interviews, disliked photo sessions and in short seemed determined to sabotage their own careers. Nonetheless, their records sold well with no promotion and they'd built up a substantial and fanatically loyal fanbase (that included me). Weirdly, they were often lumped together with the emerging psychobilly bands and regularly appeared at John Curd's Klub Foot nights at the Clarendon.

Whatever the band might have thought about it, the bulk of their following were mods and Europe was also going through a second, garage-flavoured mod revival. The Prisoners were constantly gigging and inspired a dozen young Continental bands like The Creeps, The Backdoor Men, The Stomachmouths and The Chocolate Factory in their wake.

The Prisoners had released three previous albums, two that they'd made themselves and *The Wisermiserdemelza* for Ace, which was produced by Phil Chevron from The Pogues and hated by the band. They were grumpy, contrary, sometimes just plain rude. They refused to be told what to do and wouldn't even promote their own records. I dreaded signing them as I had a good relationship with the band and just knew it would most likely end in tears. Against that, they were worth the risk because they were one of the most exciting bands I'd ever seen.

What to do?

I chewed it over. If I could be the one to harness their talent, imagine what we could achieve? If we could record an album in a month rather than three days. Make them take the whole thing seriously for once. Do things like photo sessions and interviews and tours. If I could direct that incredible passion and point it in the right direction, well, they would be unstoppable.

The four of them were in their own little Medway Sixties bubble. I decided I was going to be the one who burst it and drag the band kicking and screaming towards the thing that they feared most. Success.

They'd recently finished a small tour of Holland. I'd flown over for a couple of gigs, but it was the last one, in Eindhoven, that stuck in my memory. The band came back onto the stage for the encore stark-bollock naked. Worse, they just stood there and refused to play a note until I'd bought them a bottle of brandy from the bar, heckling me on the mic until I reluctantly put my hand in my pocket and placed the open bottle on James Taylor's organ.

A few weeks later, at the band's gig at the Medway Indian Club, I broached the subject with frontman Graham Day, who I had a great relationship with. To my wonderment, after some toing and froing and Graham's delicate convincing of the other three, the band agreed to a record deal. A contract was duly signed and before I knew it we were looking around for suitable studios.

But before they began recording Dave Robinson had another idea – and again, it was a cracker.

The Countdown Compilation had been such a success that Robbo decided he wanted to try to do it again. He'd heard me eulogising the Australian music scene and decided that I should fly over there for a month, see a whole host of bands and put an Aussie Countdown compilation together.

Sent on an extended holiday to the far side of the world with the company credit card? The stuff of dreams!

I stayed with Malpractice member Mick Franz and his family near Manly and trawled the clubs of Sydney for a month before returning home with at least 30 tapes, headed by an incredible garage track from The Saints.

A week later, the album was submitted and off to the factory.

It was here that I breached my own first rule of the music business: avoid puns. We called the compilation *Party at Hanging Rock*, a play on the 1976 outback movie *Picnic at Hanging Rock*. I still cringe at the title!

Again, sales were good – but not as good as for the first compilation. Nevertheless, as a label Countdown was performing much better than expected and Stiff were convinced that The Prisoners album *In From the Cold* was going to be a very big record indeed.

*

Too late, I realised the mistake I made with The Prisoners.

Stiff put them into Wave Studios (coincidentally above the Bass Clef in Hoxton, which I purchased and turned into the Blue Note club just eight years later) with the producer Troy Tate, who'd been in the power-pop band Advertising. Had I been in the country I might possibly have been able to diffuse the situation. Unfortunately, and stupidly, I was in Australia. The band wanted to work only with long-term mentor Russ Wilkins, who was more of a mate than an official 'producer', but Stiff insisted, so the session started off on the wrong foot.

Graham Day told me later that the problem wasn't having a producer per se; it was that Tate forced them to run through the tracks time and time again until the band were thoroughly sick of the songs, which made the final recordings sound flat. Familiarity obviously bred contempt. Worse, he added a brass section against the band's wishes. The final ignominy was that once the band had finished mixing with Troy Tate and made what they assumed would be the master, Dave Robinson unfortunately disagreed and went in over a weekend to remix the album. This was the last straw and The Prisoners were furious.

They didn't like the sleeve photo, they didn't like the clothes they were wearing, they didn't like the sleeve itself. In fact, they didn't like any of it.

My one fear when I'd signed the band had become a reality: they didn't like the record. Still, we had to make the best of a bad job, and internally, Stiff still had high hopes. Phil Hall secured a decent press campaign and, possibly against their better judgement, the band cooperated.

At this point, Stiff officially split with Island Records and while this was happening the label found themselves moving their office to the space above their warehouse in Hoxton, just around the corner from Countdown. This should really have alerted us to what was just around the metaphorical corner. Even so, we weren't aware of any greater problems and continued preparing for The Prisoners' album release.

Soon, release day was upon us and *In From the Cold* came out to great fanfare. The album was far more popular than even Stiff had predicted, and both the vinyl LP and cassette sold out within a month. The first time we at Countdown became aware of any problems at our parent label was when we were told we couldn't order a re-press from the factory. How could this be? We had an LP on the verge of the charts and couldn't make a second pressing?

No answers were forthcoming from Stiff, but we had an ominous feeling. Word filtered down that Stiff and Island were at loggerheads and in a serious dispute. I never found out the actual reasons behind it, but Stiff eventually filed for bankruptcy and our Countdown dream was over. We soon realised that without our parent company the game was up!

In From the Cold, released in May 1986, was to be Countdown's last release.

The three of us wound things down a couple of months later, relinquished the office and made the staff (well, our tiny team of Jon Cooke and receptionist Lisa Seeley) redundant. *In From the Cold* never made it to a second vinyl pressing and Countdown Records was finished. We'd released a total of five singles and four albums, hosted dozens of parties, printed eighteen months' worth of 'Countdown News' but there was no getting away from it: the collapse of Stiff was intensely personal and heartbreaking to the team, and once they'd gone, we were left with no choice but to call it a day.

PART 5

35

THE HIPSTER

After a year building up the mailing list and contacts for 'The Phoenix List', and perhaps encouraged by the success of The Untouchables and the Well Suspect releases, in 1984 Mark Johnson had set up a label, Unicorn Records, and became even more present on the scene. It was odd having a man ten years older than us hanging around, but I wasn't particularly bothered as long he was helping my events. 'The Phoenix List' was selling hundreds of my fanzines through his well-organised and efficient mail-order setup.

He also came up with the idea of Mod Aid, a fundraiser established to support Ronnie Lane's multiple sclerosis charity, Action into Research for Multiple Sclerosis (ARMS). To this end, the Phoenix Society recorded a single, released on Unicorn, with all profits donated to ARMS. The single was a version of the Small Faces hit 'All or Nothing' by Spectrum and featured the combined talents of the likes of Steve Marriott, Eddie Phillips (from The Creation), Kenny Lynch, P. P. Arnold, Chris Farlowe and Bryn Gregory from the revival band Beggar. Dozens of other established musicians were involved. It was a great thing to do and reasonably successful, managing to break into the Top 100 of the pop charts.

Inspired by this success and the money raised, Mark Johnson arranged a Christmas alldayer in mid-December 1985 at Walthamstow Town Hall featuring dozens of bands, including The Change, 5.30, The

Direct Hits, The Co-Stars, The Threads and the Purple Hearts. The event attracted a couple of thousand young mods and was packed, but there was something about it that felt a little bloated and spoon-fed. To me, it didn't feel quite right, and the gig marked the beginning of the end of this particular part of the scene.

I couldn't put my finger on it, but it felt slightly like the scene was going round in circles. I certainly didn't feel such a strong part of it any more. Maybe that's because this guy was running everything. Or maybe it was because the way he did it felt overorganised and somehow a little hollow.

Musically, Weller's post-Jam outfit The Style Council had introduced me and most of my mates to the concept of modern jazz. It had always been there in the scene, especially the organ jazz of Jimmy Smith, Jimmy McGriff and Jack McDuff, but I felt out of touch with the bands and what the DJs were playing. Not only was it the last alldayer I attended but it was also the last major alldayer on the scene. Mod had changed and at the same time I'd had a huge amount of fun with my record labels and various ventures. I instinctively began looking for other things to do.

Mark Johnson released the concert as a live album in the spring of 1986 under the title *Dedicated*. It was his final moment of glory.

With Countdown gone, and because we'd stopped *Extraordinary Sensations* when the three of us launched the record label and the newsletter, I was left for the first time in five years with absolutely nothing to do. But somehow, against the odds, the Countdown team found a second life.

Maxine had settled into a job at ABC/ID Records, which was owned by music-industry legend John Curd – Sixties mod, former manager of The Action and the biggest independent gig promoter in the country. Would there be space for me and Terry too?

Maxine was always looking out for Terry and a couple of weeks after she started there he got a call. Did the pair of us fancy coming in to work for John Curd? She suggested Terry could do artwork and I could be a label manager.

Curd ran his empire from a ramshackle terrace on Cheyne Walk in Chelsea, right next door to Jade Jagger's house. I'm not so sure that the neighbours were thrilled to be sharing one of the most expensive residential streets in the country with the unorthodox and eccentric Curd, but I absolutely loved him. A font of mod knowledge, he often regaled me with stories of his early life and some of the scrapes he'd got himself into. Curdy lived on a houseboat just round the corner, which he shared with his dogs and an enormous collection of Converse trainers.

While John made his living from promoting live shows, he had fingers in an awful lot of pies. If you wanted a theatre ticket or a flyposting campaign, John or his wily hustling sidekick Ray could sort it for you.

I know I said I was never going to work on a payroll again, but needs must. Everything had gone tits up since Stiff's demise and I needed some cash to fund my next label, which I'd already decided would be called Re-Elect the President. It was an odd name for a record label and one that bizarrely came from a pin badge. I'd been riding the scooter through Hackney one day when (as I often did) I stopped at a junk shop, right by the Dolphin pub. A 2-inch button badge in the window leaped out. It featured the peanut-shaped face of the disgraced President Richard Nixon with the words 'Re-Elect the President' round the edge. I found the idea extraordinarily amusing. I mean, who on earth would vote for Richard Nixon? I scanned the badge and set up a new hobby label while I was running around for John Curd.

And so began my last-ever job. Curdy was amazing to work for and had a great team. As well as Maxine there was Jeremy Thomas, Lillian, Craig and Lucy. I used to work in the Kings Road for Avatar, so knew exactly where the office was and was looking forward to revisiting some of the Chelsea pubs I'd frequented with the Fulham Wasps and George Best three years earlier. When I say 'frequented with', I mean that George was often propped up at the bar surrounded by admirers while we were drinking a few yards away!

Bizarrely, I was to be the new product manager for Curd's indie record label. In fact, it turned out that ABC/ID was actually a rockabilly label – or rather a psychobilly label. These were an offshoot of the rockin' scene and blended punk sensibility with basic rockabilly rock & roll. I'd seen plenty of them around the scooterboy scene and the main thing I knew about them was that they had an extraordinarily violent way of dancing, which just seemed to involve punching people in a melee. WTF? I'd seen The Meteors a few times and genuinely liked them, but I drew the line at the chicken blood, flour and vomit-inducing antics of King Kurt. I had to work with a number of psychobilly bands, including Restless, Guana Batz, Demented Are Go, The Stingrays and Frenzy, but despite the general antipathy between psychobillies and mods, on the whole they were a great bunch (albeit mainly country bumpkins). I regarded The Highliners especially as brilliant blokes. They had a skeleton riding a surfboard stuck to the top of their van and hit the outer reaches of the chart with their chaotic theme song 'Henry the Wasp'.

We were also hosting the regular and heavily psychobilly Klub Foot nights at the Clarendon Ballroom in Hammersmith, which occasionally featured The Prisoners or The Milkshakes on the bill.

I suspect that the collapse of Stiff and Countdown had really pissed The Prisoners off. I mean, I'd finally persuaded the four of them to compromise for me. Against their better judgement, the band had eventually recorded and released a pop record and I'd made them do it. Countdown had taken a band at the top of their game and, as The Prisoners saw it, damaged their credibility to make an album that was on the verge of the charts but that they weren't keen on. I was gutted. Not only did I know it was going to happen but so did they.

After they walked away from the car crash that had become Stiff and Countdown, The Prisoners' final recorded offering was a song with the chorus 'We don't wanna go to your pop star party', which I'd always assumed was aimed at me. I found out later that it actually wasn't – it was a V-sign to their unhappy experiences with Stiff. It might as well have been about the collapse of Countdown, though, and that particular disaster was on me.

Although I'd known it might go wrong if they signed to us, I was still disappointed because they were one of the most exciting bands I'd ever seen. 'Pop Star Party' was a terrible epitaph. Looking back, I wish I'd never signed them. Maybe they would have carried on. I'm not saying that their split was my fault, but they left too small a legacy for a truly great band. I wish there was more than those four albums.

While I could handle the psychobilly stuff at ABC/ID, when I was handed the Nordic black metal band Celtic Frost to look after, I realised the time had come to leave Chelsea and concentrate on my own label again.

Meanwhile, on the mod scene something particularly dark had happened.

On a Bank Holiday weekend in 1986, Mark Johnson was caught red-handed. There had been rumours, of course: he was maybe a bit too friendly with younger boys and was often seen with a kid riding pillion. But nothing concrete emerged. People didn't like him much but, as I said, he helped things work, so was tolerated. He'd been confronted on a couple of occasions about the rumours but swore blind there was nothing to them – after all, many kids liked getting a ride on a scooter and none of them had revealed anything untoward when questioned. The end for me had come over something as pedantic as the official mod 'scene' regulations. The Phoenix Society started to make rules and attempted to make us follow them. *Whaat?* This wasn't cool and a few of us started weighing the balance of usefulness against embarrassment and soon realised that embarrassment won out. He was a liability.

Mark Johnson had signed a dozen young mod bands to Unicorn Records, and 'The Phoenix List' had upwards of 5,000 weekly subscribers, then suddenly, in Lowestoft on a Bank Holiday weekend, his world came crashing down.

I was staying in a hotel on the seafront with my American girlfriend Marion when, at two in the morning, we heard a commotion outside the room. It had been a brilliant weekend and I was looking forward to the next day when I was DJing. I reluctantly dragged myself out of bed and walked over to the door to listen. Shouting and banging. What the fuck was that about?

I ran out to see what was going on in time to see one of the East London lot kicking the door of a room on the landing above. There were a couple of men shouting and trying to break it down. I quickly asked one of them what was happening but he just pointed at the door and said, 'We gotta get in there . . .'

He ignored any other questions and put his shoulder back to the door. It suddenly gave.

I took in the room in a split second. Johnson was wearing underpants and trying to force the door shut, but behind him on the bed was a boy. He looked a young 16-year-old and was obviously upset. Johnson was barking out some excuse and saying that it wasn't what it looked like but that he was helping him find something.

We were horrified. This American 'organiser' who'd inserted himself into our scene, provided a service and became mildly useful had abused his position to seduce teenagers. The kid was bundled out of the room and Johnson was dealt with. His scooter, a Vespa P Range in white with the legend 'Behold the Pale Horse' painted on the panels, was taken to the end of Lowestoft Pier and thrown into the sea.

It was the last time I saw Mark Johnson.

There was a dark side to Johnson and in retrospect it should have been obvious he had a thing for young boys. Hindsight is a wonderful thing, but had he really set the whole Phoenix/Unicorn Records thing as a cover for nefarious ends? From then on, every time he turned up at an event it was made clear to him that he wasn't welcome, and when this didn't sink in, both him and his scooter were regularly dumped in the sea. The penny finally dropped when his Vespa was cut in half with an angle grinder.

While he didn't disappear completely from the scene, he certainly kept a much lower profile.

Were we complicit in enabling him? I never really thought about it until sitting down to write this book. After a while of being cold-shouldered he eventually turned his attention to the skinhead scene and the Phoenix Society faded from view. Mark Johnson was still around but was increasingly mocked and ignored, a pale shadow of the man who set up and ran 'The Phoenix List' all those years ago.

In 1986 I had my first experience as a professional journalist. Print was a closed shop back then, so I joined the National Union of Journalists and applied for a feature-writer vacancy at *Sounds*, the paper I'd been reading since I was 13. The staffer's application was unsuccessful, but they did give me a few live reviews to write. I enjoyed it. Writing creatively about music you didn't like was a challenge. This led to a more regular position at *Underground*, a glossy music monthly set up by Dave Henderson when he left *Sounds*. I considered trying to make a career out of writing. After all, *Extraordinary Sensations* had been much more successful than I'd ever imagined it could be and Chris Hunt from *Shadows and Reflections* and Tony Fletcher from *Jamming!* had both made a seamless transition from fanzine to professional print journalism.

In the end, I realised that the NUJ rate of £77 pounds per 1,000 words was never going to be enough to keep me in the style to which I wasn't yet accustomed, so I gave up and concentrated on records again.

I continued with the mod-type stuff, releasing a couple of (post-label) Countdown compilations and an album by the amazing Swedish garage rock/mod group The Creeps, but it was with my next signing that I started to see a new direction for myself.

Quite simply, the mod scene (rather than the *concept* of mod) had for me and many of my long-term mates begun to turn sour. While fun could still be had, there was an increasing feeling that a specific type of mod 'tunnel vision' had begun to dominate. Mark Johnson's huge influence on the scene – even ignoring the dark stuff – had seemed to water down the fun quotient and make things *too* organised. On the club side, it often felt like there were no new ideas and, worse, no new people, and the music seemed to have disappeared into a very specific rare R&B rabbit hole. Also, while the skinhead wars might have petered out, the general violence on the scene was still an issue, bubbling away in the background.

There had often been problems between mods and scooterboys – which had led to regular 'No Jeans, No Greens, No Casuals' signs outside clubs – but by 1984 things had got serious and black artists like Eddie Holman and Edwin Starr were occasionally booed at rallies. After Desmond Dekker was attacked on stage by boneheads and scooterboys at the Great Yarmouth rally in 1985, I got really worn down by it. Ashamed actually. I was done. Laura Maloney from the Woodford mods had been hit in the face with a bag of ammonia at the Isle of Wight and spent two weeks in hospital and another month in Queen's while her sight gradually returned. What the fuck was that about?

I still wanted to be a mod, but only on my own terms. Marion came over for the summer and we began to explore other, more disparate elements of mod. The Palo Alto scene seemed to be open to many more influences than London. She helped me search for a new direction, if you like. We settled on jazz.

I'd met Steve White when he was in The Style Council and he'd recently got a new band together called The Jazz Renegades with some of the best players in the country. Alan Barnes was on sax, Dave Newton on piano, bass was Alec Dankworth (son of Johnny and Cleo Laine) with White himself on drums. They'd carved a niche for themselves in the burgeoning London jazz scene where I'd been spending more and more time listening to the likes of Paul Murphy on the decks at the Electric Ballroom. I'd actually brought incredible modern jazz drummer Tommy Chase to Stiff, where he recorded a great version of 'Killer Joe', but again the campaign was cut short by the label's demise. The Tommy Chase Quartet LP was one of the last-ever releases on Stiff.

Tommy Chase was utterly insane. He was an original mod who'd built up an untouchable persona around himself and his band. Usually a quartet, they played 100mph hard-bop jazz at venues like the Wag Club and Ronnie Scott's. Thing was, Chase was flying a solo flag for modernist be-bop dressed in a tightly cut, dark-blue tonic suit, while the rest of us were starting to find our own feet (have you ever noticed that jazz drummers from Art Blakey to Charlie Watts *always* wore tailored suits?). We followed him from gig to gig and through Chase began to discover the music of Blakey, Buddy Rich, Gene Krupa and Cozy Cole.

Following the collapse of Countdown, Marion went back to the States and I had to admit to myself that, while I was undoubtedly still in love with the *concept* of mod, the scene had ceased to inspire me creatively. By 1986 jazz was my main influence and I revisited my dad's old record collection, which included the likes of Jimmy Smith, Jimmy McGriff and Ramsey Lewis. I found some gems there, among them his almost impossible to find green RCA demo of 'The Hipster' by Harold

McNair! I never knew where my dad got this insane, hard-pushing mod-jazz flute instrumental from but, fuck me, it's rare. Another of my mod heroes, The Rolling Stones manager Andrew Loog Oldham, told me that McNair – known in 1965 as the 'Little G' – was the hippest mod he'd ever met. His Jamaican heritage made him look so much cooler than the pale suburban hipsters. These were the details we aspired to, whether they were true or not, but in Oldham's case, we knew they were true.

By mid-1986 our scene had split down the middle. There was the growing influence of the 1967 psych and freakbeat mods, who dressed rather like we had at the Groovy Cellar five years earlier – all Marriott hair, Austin Powers and paisley. We called them 'swirlies', but that take on it wasn't really my thing.

For me, the scene had been regressing (although some would say it had been progressing) into an ever-purer take on what we imagined the Sixties to have been like: overtailored clothes for the boys and puritanical A-line skirts with knee-length socks for the girls, as epitomised by Lucy Muccini, Diane Daly, Daisy Clark, Anita Stinton and the evergreen Ugly Buglies. They looked cool, but to me it didn't feel like my world was moving forward.

One thing was new, though: there had been a surge in popularity of the style of Latin American music called *bugalú* – or 'boogaloo', as we called it. This was brilliant dance music, a Puerto Rican/New York hybrid that was briefly a real driving force in the Sixties and Seventies Latin ghettos of Spanish Harlem and the Bronx, recorded by artists like Ray Barretto, El Gran Combo, Joe Cuba and Joe Bataan. Yet even when new music like this entered the mod scene, it always seemed to result in more tunnel vision – for a brief six-month period, all the DJs wanted to play was boogaloo. I needed a break.

36

SUBWAY JOE

I was now 23. I'd had three record labels, managed three or four bands, owned around 20 scooters and had been seeing the same tailor since I was 16. Was I just getting too old for all this?

I was definitely becoming uncomfortable with what I saw as the ever-tightening Sixties straightjacket of the 'mod scene'. I certainly wasn't finished with mod itself, far from it, but at times I wondered where I fitted into it all. Surely mod was a young man's game?

Jazz and soul provided our salvation, though. Especially jazz.

I remember going to Andy Orr's Soulful Shack at the Westmoreland Arms and thinking that those who were left from the old East London mods were all moving forward together.

A succession of Australians turned up to stay with me and my flatmates John Halls and Bunny at the house in Woodford. First was the Sydney face Don Hosie. Don, always ahead of the game, had also arrived at the conclusion that jazz was the modernist way forward. We spent six weeks touring the capital's jazz haunts, places like Ronnie Scott's, the 101 Club and the Wag Club, and falling in love with the new 'hard-bop' sound of Tommy Chase and The Jazz Renegades – which we all agreed was far more interesting than the ever-decreasing musical boundaries of Sixties R&B. Next up for a visit were a couple of the younger Malpractice, Karl Viesas and Mick Franz, who spent the whole summer embedded as honorary East London and Essex.

We had a real riot, taking in every scooter run, club and pub for the whole summer – pushing the envelope as far as possible. But once they left for home, I found the scene increasingly flat.

One night in late summer I was driving my Vauxhall Astra GTE to the Warren Wood, our local pub in Woodford, scanning the radio looking for pirate stations. There were only a few on FM at the time, stations like Horizon, Kiss FM, Studio FM and JFM, who played black music across the spectrum. In 1986 it was virtually impossible to hear jazz, funk or soul on mainstream radio unless you caught the specialist shows on BBC Radio London, Kent or Essex – and even then it was just a couple of hours a week. Pirate stations were completely illegal and subject to increasing government sanctions.

They all played better music than the crap on Capital or Radio 1 but were pretty unreliable. Mainly broadcast from an inner-city tower block by a dedicated but unlikely alliance of techies and DJs, they usually concentrated on reggae or dancehall and were peppered with adverts for 'Dougie's Nightspot' in Clapton or revival reggae nights in East London social clubs. But there were a few DJs who played old American black music and these were the shows I was looking for.

Suddenly the car radio ceased crackling and picked up a signal. More interestingly, it had chanced upon a record that was coincidentally in my DJ box – someone, somewhere, was playing 'Ain't There Something That Money Can't Buy' by Young-Holt Unlimited. A mod jazz classic.

Whaaat?

This faded into 'Subway Joe' by Joe Bataan, another rarity that featured in my set and a boogaloo monster that had enjoyed a good run on the mod scene just months before. (Admittedly, the mod scene was still digging up some of the best tunes in terms of northern soul and R&B, but I was becoming bored with the scene itself.)

Who on earth could be playing mod records on the FM dial? The DJ still hadn't said a word and I had no idea who it could be. After all, it was the wrong frequency for Peter Young and the wrong time for Charlie Gillett, who, despite being one of my favourites, probably wouldn't be playing mod stuff anyway. I'd long arrived at the pub but stayed in my car with the radio on, listening to hear what the bloke would play next. I wasn't disappointed, it was 'Come With Me' by Tania Maria, a beautiful Brazilian-tinged mid-tempo two-step. This show was a revelation, but who on earth was the DJ?

Eventually he spoke. Soft and quite posh-sounding for a pirate. The DJ's name was Gilles Peterson.

All thoughts of the pub evaporated as I drove to the off-licence, picked up a few cans and headed home to listen to the rest of the show on my hi-fi. This was the kind of DJ I wanted to hear on the radio.

Two weeks later I was playing a rare guest spot for Tony Class at his regular Saturday-night club in London Bridge. It was late summer in 1986, I was feeling like I was on a treadmill and my time on the mod scene had come to an end. The venue was an old-style, two-storey pub called the Royal Oak in Tooley Street, which nestled up against the banks of the Thames.

Before I played my set, I'd been standing outside moaning about my growing complacency to Big Jason, Tony Class's bouncer, when he suggested something that was to change my life.

'You know what, Eddie? If you've had enough of this, you wanna check the place out on Fridays. Jazz and soul upstairs with go-go and more commercial shit in the basement. It's rammed and the music's great.'

'Oh yeah? You reckon? Who's playing?'

He had my interest.

'It's called Special Branch. D'y'know Nicky Holloway? It's him and a load of his mates. Erm . . . people like Pete Tong, Bob Jones, Paul

Oakenfold, Chris Bangs, Kev Beadle and Gilles Peterson – changes every week.'

That name again. Gilles Peterson. The Special Branch . . . I checked out the Royal Oak the following week with Bunny and Jon Cooke and was totally sold on the club and the crowd.

From then on, I was a Special Branch devotee – after all, it wasn't like I was leaving mod behind; I was leaving the *scene* behind. I was wearing the same clothes, but by now we'd discovered the Duffer of St George over in Portobello. A mod ex-girlfriend from Woodford called Jacquie had been dating one of the founders and she tipped me off. It was amazing clobber. As well as selling the usual new-old stock, they were churning out their own take on Sixties mod gear, but instead of nylon, they were using terrific materials with a nice cut. It was as if they were dressing this new rare groove scene with clobber I'd been wearing since I was a kid and it fitted in down at the Special Branch perfectly. By this time, mod had become such a broad church that we were mixing Seventies Italian knitwear by Gabicci, maybe taken-in Farah's, the odd polo-neck and basket-weave shoes, Adidas Gazelles, Stan Smiths or Puma Romas. Even Big E Levi's made an appearance. Mod but not mod, if you know what I mean?

It was funny. In that world, the Special Branch world, I was nobody. I'd been DJing for five or six years on the mod scene and was used to guest lists and parties. At the Special Branch, I didn't DJ and had to pay to get in. It was like I was starting out again as a punter. It was inspiring.

By 1986 the Hammond organ was becoming the biggest sound in the 'late mod' clubs that me and my friends were hosting and going to. I'd recently opened a night in a basement between Covent Garden and Leicester Square at an old Sixties club called the Formula One. It had a black and white chequered floor with its original Sixties layout preserved in aspic and was the perfect place to host our new 'stylist' venture. The records I was playing were almost exclusively the jazz of Jimmy Smith, Jack McDuff and Jimmy McGriff from the States and Brian Auger, Graham Bond and Georgie Fame from the UK. Once you added some Chicano boogaloo from Joe Bataan and Ray Barretto, or some Young-Holt and Ramsey Lewis, you had what I felt was the mod sound of 1986. For me, it felt good. The music was cool, creative and maybe more in the spirit of the original 1964 mods than anything I'd really done so far.

This shift away from northern soul and R&B was incredibly popular with a very small number of my peers and proved to be a breath of fresh air. It also gave me an idea.

Mods of all sorts were in love with the Hammond, and The Prisoners' organist James Taylor had switched to a Hammond and Leslie combo a few years before. Why didn't I put him in the studio to record some mod instrumentals for release on Re-Elect the President? I called James, and while he thought it a good idea, he said it was pointless as he'd already made a decision about his post-Prisoners life.

He told me he was moving to Stockholm with his Swedish girlfriend, Ellen, the following month. 'I'll be studying classical piano at university!' he said. 'I fancy something different.'

'C'mon, James, I know it's a great idea. You won't even have to write any songs; I just want you to cut a version of "Bring Down the Birds" by Herbie Hancock.'

At this he instantly brightened. The track was one of the great mod classics, better known as 'The Theme From Blow Up'. I suggested a Jimmy Smith-type cover for the B-side. James told me that he'd give it a go and, a week later, was in a tiny Medway studio with Prisoners bassist Allan Crockford and two members of the Medway garage band The Daggermen with his brother David on guitar and Wolf Howard on drums.

Three days after the session, a cassette arrived and the end result wasn't what I was expecting. While all the musicians were great players, the finished article didn't actually sound like the stuff I was playing in Covent Garden (which had been my plan). Instead, it sounded exactly like it was – young garage rock musicians playing jazz. And 'Blow Up' was brilliant. The recording was magical and unique. Totally fresh. They'd put down a jazz standard called 'One Mint Julep' for the B-side and it ripped the speakers off the wall with pure excitement and energy.

I immediately called James. 'You've got to do some more before you go!' I pleaded and wheedled, and eventually he agreed. We decided to record as many movie themes as the band could learn and record in one day. The James Taylor Quartet was born.

A week later James was gone to Sweden for his new life. I sent the 'Blow Up' tape up to Derek at Backs in Norwich, who were my record distributors, and they agreed: this was something special. So I resolved to release it as soon as I could. It became Re-Elect the President's first 45.

I sent a copy to Gary Crowley, who by this time had popped up on BBC Radio London with an influential show. He gave it a resounding thumbs-up and hammered the record in the month before release. I was pleasantly surprised at the reaction and so had moderate hopes for the single. James, firmly ensconced in Stockholm and immersed in the world of classical piano, was blissfully unaware. He had genuinely forgotten all about it.

Suddenly everything changed.

I was in the bath in the house I'd just bought with a hefty mortgage in Woodford, just a few hundred yards from where I grew up.

The phone rang and kept ringing. I was annoyed. I eventually got out of the bath, slopping water everywhere, but the caller hung up just as I reached the phone. Frustrated, I got back in the bath and as soon as I lay down the bloody phone rang again. This time I gave up, grabbed a towel and stomped back over to the phone.

'Whaaat?' I asked gruffly.

'Well, I certainly wasn't expecting that!' exclaimed a warm and friendly voice with faint northern tones.

Hold on a minute – I recognised that voice. *Fuck me.* It can't be, can it . . .?

'Is this Eddie Piller? Good, I've called a few times but not got hold of you yet. My name is John Peel and I'm phoning about your new record . . .'

'Erm, crikey, how can I help?'

' "Blow Up", James Taylor Quartet. I love it. I'm going to play it to death. Fabulous mix of punk sensibilities and jazz. I'd like to get the band in for a live session – when can you sort that out?'

A Peel session? These were legendary with serious kudos attached. They could be the making of any band lucky enough to get one. Trouble was, I didn't have a band. There wasn't a James Taylor Quartet and James was a thousand miles away and unlikely to come home any time soon. What should I say?

'Well, thank you very much, er . . . Mr Peel. It'll be an honour. Let me talk to the band and get back to you . . .'

He told me that his producer John Walters would be in touch and rang off. I ran around like a headless chicken. I didn't even have James Taylor's Swedish number.

I eventually got hold of James's brother Dave, who gave me his details, and I then left a message with Ellen, James's girlfriend. A sceptical Taylor phoned me back a day later. At first, he refused to believe me, but once I'd convinced him that John Peel was genuinely interested, he listed his objections.

'I don't have a band, it was just for fun, I'm in Stockholm, it's the middle of term, I'm skint . . .!' Those were top of his list.

This went on for a couple of weeks until James saw proof of the record's success. We'd made it into the indie Top 20 chart. This was indeed serious kudos, so James relented and arranged to come home for half a day's rehearsal and then to record the Peel session. I got back to John Walters and we arranged a date. I immediately agreed with James that we should bundle the film demos together to release as a mini-album, which we eventually called *Mission Impossible.*

Sure enough, the Peel session was an enormous success – and this was where the fun started.

I immediately looked for opportunities for my new management clients, the newly constituted James Taylor Quartet.

We booked a gig at the Limelight Club in Shaftesbury Avenue. It had been put together by a mate of mine from the Wag called Jason Jules from Manor Park, who lived round the corner from my dad's shop. A smart jazz modernist, he was working at the new venue as a booker and, for a short time at least, it was one of the coolest places in Soho. Cookie knocked up a flyer announcing the band's debut gig and in the end none of us could quite believe how oversubscribed the night was. Could we really be on to something? When I turned up, the queue stretched a good 100 yards down to Wardour Street and was crammed with 'celebrities' (well, mainly Gary Crowley's mates, like Patsy Kensit and the occasional member of Bananarama). Even James Taylor was blown away at the response. The James Taylor Quartet's first-ever gig was a sell-out!

A live agent soon followed. Nigel Hassler stepped in to take control and within a couple of weeks I was beginning to understand the music industry in a way that you never do until you actually have success. It was an odd experience, but one I was determined to make the most of.

I was back in the game.

37

TIGHTEN UP

I f I needed any further confirmation that my time on the mod scene was over, it came at the next Lowestoft Weekender in 1987. This was a mods-only event held at a small holiday camp and I'd been booked to play an hour-long set on the Saturday, early evening.

The weekend started well. I'd been to Paul Hallam's competing weekender on Hayling Island on the Friday. I was driving a full car with my housemates John Halls and Bunny along with Karl and Mick, my two Australian guests. We left for Lowestoft first thing Saturday morning and rocked up mid-afternoon. There was a different vibe from Hallam's gig, and although I had been doing my best to get into the spirit of the event, it was hard. I'd been listening to the different DJ sets as the weekend progressed with increasing impatience. I was just about sick of hearing the same old shit played by every single DJ and wanted to get my set over and fuck off. They'd all been spinning Sixties R&B or entry-level northern, and to be honest, I had a short attention span and had been bored of that for years. Unfortunately, these young mods were totalitarian about it: music had to be recorded before *this* date, have *that* particular tempo and (very often) be on *that* yellow and red label that Guy Stevens used on his Sue Records. It was Groundhog Day (again!).

This seems incredible now, but it was 1987. As the sound of rare groove had long taken over London's cooler clubs, no one in that Lowestoft holiday camp had ever heard 'Tighten Up' by Archie Bell &

the Drells. The record had never been played by anyone in the mod world and I'd come across it when Jay Strongman span it at a warehouse party I'd been to with Jon Cooke a year earlier. But hey, what's not to like? 'Tighten Up' was released on Atlantic and recorded in 1967. It had a brilliant dance beat and I was looking forward to playing it to this crowd.

My set started off OK with a mixture of boogaloo, soul and Jimmy Smith's mod jazz. About three-quarters of the way in, the floor was heaving. I was spinning that old Peter Meaden-produced chestnut 'Ain't Love Good, Ain't Love Proud' (the Tony Clarke cover), recorded by Britain's first black mod band, Jimmy James and the Vagabonds.

The song was up-tempo, worked well for the dancers and I judged that the time to play 'Tighten Up' was upon us. After all, the floor was packed – what was the worst that could happen?

I was about to find out.

The tune kicked in with that superb walking bass line, soon to be joined by the fatback drums and eight bars later by that awesome guitar riff, which complements the intro so perfectly.

'Hi, everybody, I'm Archie Bell of the Drells from Huston, Texas. We don't only sing but we dance just as good as we want . . .'

I closed my eyes and let the music wash over me. Absolute perfection. When I opened them again, the dance floor was completely empty. Not a single person. *What the fuck?*

If these people can't understand this incredible record, then I'm in the wrong place. That was the only conclusion I could come to. That was it. I was done.

I told the next DJ that I was cutting my set short. I packed up my records and walked out, never to return. As I got to the door, the DJ who took over played some crappy entry-level northern soul bootleg like 'The Snake', 'Tainted Love' or 'The Night'. Sure enough, the floor was packed once more and I drove back to London vowing never to DJ again.

38

VOICE YOUR CHOICE

I embraced Nicky Holloway and the Special Branch. While the Royal Oak was their regular base, his little firm (helped by Chris Fanning and Lisa Blofeld) also promoted gigs at London Zoo, Streatham Ice Rink, the Natural History Museum, the Bournemouth weekender, Rockley Sands near Poole and plenty of other unusual venues. The Special Branch was like a family. Yes, it was a scene, but it was a scene that was different from the one that I'd just left. The DJs played every single type of music: jazz-funk, breakbeat, disco, electro, go-go, jazz, easy listening, northern and modern soul, boogaloo, bossa nova, funk, soul and proto-hip hop. It was all good.

For me, the revelation was that I could be a mod in a completely different world. Looking back on it now, the Special Branch DJ list read like the future of club culture, all shepherded by Nicky Holloway: Pete Tong, Trevor Fung, Chris Brown, Paul Oakenfold, Chris Bangs, Gilles Peterson, Johnnie Walker, Bob Jones and half a dozen more. All playing records that I loved. It was an interesting turn of events.

Suddenly, plenty of the more progressive mods in my world – people like John Halls, Andy Orr, Bunny, Mark Lovett, Paul Newman, Dom Bassett, Big Bob, Cookie and a handful of others – realised that we could still be mods without the strictures of a 'mod scene'. It was liberating. Mod wasn't what I'd thought it was; it was actually a state of mind, something we'd all been fleetingly touched by.

That made this new world all the more exciting. Mod was whatever we wanted it to be . . .

Within six months of me meeting Gilles Peterson, he persuaded me to start DJing again, warming up for him at the Wag Club on the Monday jazz night. I'd already had a residency at the legendary Soho venue, having been recruited by Chris Sullivan to host a Friday soul night when I was just 18. Peterson, his partner Chris Bangs and, to be honest, the great Paul Murphy too all allowed me to rediscover my modernist roots.

I'd met Peterson properly when I pitched him the JTQ's *Mission Impossible* mini-LP for his *Mad on Jazz* show on BBC Radio London. I could tell he wasn't keen. Why should he have been? He was sponsored by the City Sounds Jazz Chart (compiled by the City Sounds record shop in Holborn and made up of 100mph hard bop or jazz fusion), whereas all the JTQ offered was punky jazz played by mods. Still, I persisted and he melted somewhat. The turning point was the *Mad on Jazz* 'Record of the Week' slot, where Gilles would play four new releases and open the telephone lines for a public vote.

I remember the evening quite clearly.

I approached the BBC security guard with slight trepidation: 'Erm, I've come to see . . .'

He cut me off mid-flow as if expecting me to finish the sentence with 'Gilles Peterson'. 'It's through there; just head for the noise . . .' The obviously put-upon receptionist buzzed the security door while simultaneously pointing with his head and rolling his eyes.

We'd only met a couple of times at the Special Branch, so I wasn't sure what to expect – especially knowing that he wasn't taken by the record. I pushed open the soundproofed doors to discover that Gilles had an enormous number of friends ensconced in the studio with him, all answering phones, making the tea or just hanging out. It reminded me of a *Steve Wright in the Afternoon* show, but without Steve Wright.

He welcomed me warmly enough and I handed him an extra copy of the JTQ mini-album in case he'd (purposely) left his one at home. Gilles beckoned me to a seat and I sat back to watch him at work. He had an incredibly loyal listenership and an extraordinarily eclectic musical taste.

Sure enough, when the 'Record of the Week' slot came up he span 'Mission Impossible' without too much enthusiasm. Against the odds, though, the track won the public vote and became the *Mad on Jazz* Record of the Week.

I enjoyed my evening sitting in on *Mad on Jazz* and as I left Gilles invited me back the following week. I took him up on this offer and again the public voted for the record. And again the week after that . . . It seemed like the JTQ already had the makings of a following!

Eventually, a casual friendship developed and I attended many of his gigs. By now a few more of my open-minded mates were joining me. Malcolm Knox from Epping, my flatmates John Halls and Bunny and the distinctly non-mod Matt Richardson from Limes Farm made up the numbers and we would take a couple of carloads 'up town' on a regular basis.

I also found myself drawn towards his partner Chris Bangs' sets. If anything, Bangsy seemed to spin an even more wide-ranging selection of records that had a sense of humour and a greater reach. He invented the famous 'dodgy bossa' (or 'shitty samba') sound (which included fabulous tracks like 'The Crickets Sing for Anamaria' by Marcos Valle, Quincy Jones's 'Soul Bossa Nova' and 'Cacara' by Nancy Ames). They were both playing an enormously wide variety of styles. Two girls in particular – both ex-mods – became my friends. The first, who came to be known as Janine Jazz, ended up as Gilles' right-hand woman; the second, Martha from Acton, became my girlfriend. It was such an exciting time.

At last, here was the eclecticism I'd been looking for.

After a couple of months of hanging around, I found myself a regular guest at Gilles' flat in Brownswood Road in Finsbury Park, which was in the basement of Simon Booth's house. Booth – or to give him his real name, Simon Emmerson – was not only Gilles' landlord but was also the founder member and the musical brains behind Working Week, the 'agit-pop' jazz group who released the single 'Venceremos (We Will Win)' in support of Chilean opponents of Pinochet.

Gilles had been growing out of the flat and was casting his eye around for a place of his own. I knew that Terry Rawlings was looking for a tenant for his Thames-side apartment, so introduced the pair and within the month Peterson had moved in. I was surprised he took it, because once he'd had the place racked out, his LP collection took up three quarters of the space. But the view over the Thames up to Tower Bridge was priceless.

After the success of the James Taylor Quartet on Re-Elect the President, Polydor Records approached me with the idea of signing James direct to their 'rare groove' label, Urban.

Polydor's head of A&R, John Williams, realised there might be something to the new live bands being thrown up by the jazz-funk scene that was bubbling along under the radar. Cooltempo had signed The Brand New Heavies, and JTQ, although instrumental, were coming from the same place. Taylor's view on mod had broadened substantially following exposure to the Hammond funk of Brother Jack McDuff and Clarence Wheeler & the Enforcers.

John Williams wanted me to stay on as the band's manager and I agreed. I thought I'd taken the JTQ as far as I could on my bedroom label. I had no staff, no office and no money. Polydor were offering a substantial advance and, as manager, I'd get a hefty share in commission. What's not to like? The icing, as it were, was that John Williams offered me a consultancy with Polydor and actively encouraged me to bring him ideas for release. So it wasn't only management commission: I was getting a salary too!

Once James signed to Polydor I knocked Re-Elect The President on the head.

Taylor was given a brief to head into the studio and make a Hammond instrumental album in a rare groove style.

Jazz and the move towards it had completely taken over my life. Along with an old drinking buddy from the Queen's Head in Ealing called Jan Kincaid (who was also the drummer in The Heavies), I became a member of Ronnie Scott's. It cost peanuts but gave you either free or subsidised entry to many of their midweek shows. Horace Silver, Art Blakey, Georgie Fame, Joe Henderson, Airto Moreira and any number of classic jazz greats played there. I even took my new girlfriend Melanie (who later became my wife) to Ronnie's on a first date to see the amazing be-bop vocalist Mark Murphy, which was memorable mainly because it was a hot and sweaty night when Murphy's wig-tape came unstuck and his toupee fell off.

This was a new world and, in my opinion, far more mod than the one I'd left behind.

By 1987, most London clubs, including the Special Branch, featured two rooms. The main one would be hosting a more mainstream and commercial vibe, often playing electro and the b-boy sound, while the smaller rooms were usually jazz, funk and rare groove. There was an amazingly warm and vibrant sound going on in London and a new generation of groups were appearing, often embracing a Seventies look and funky feel. The Brand New Heavies, Diana Brown & the Brothers and The Pasadenas led the way, but they weren't alone. Groups like PUSH and The Explosions were playing out-and-out funk to ever-growing audiences and the sound of James Brown and The J.B.'s was dominating left-field clubland.

But then, almost overnight, our wonderful jazz and rare groove existence was completely blown out of the water and everything changed.

A few Special Branchers like Johnnie Walker and Chris Butler (both of whom I worked with at Polydor) had gone over to Ibiza with Holloway to check out some venues for the forthcoming Special Branch holiday, and it was then that our world got its first taste of a new sound coming out of the underground clubs of New York and Chicago. It was a revolutionary type of dance music, electronic but with a tempo that mirrored the disco of Ripple and Sylvester, and it was enhanced by a new drug called MDMA or, to give it its street name, ecstasy.

The sound was called acid house.

39

MY FAVOURITE THINGS

A couple of months later, in May, the Special Branch holiday to Ibiza saw around 400 of us head off to San Antonio for a couple of weeks' hardcore partying. Most of the main DJs from our scene were there whether they were playing sets or not. Pete Tong, Gilles Peterson, Bangsy, Simon Dunmore, Bob Jones, Chris Brown, Johnnie Walker, Bob Masters and Nicky Holloway himself were the headliners and we took over clubs like Es Paradise, the Star Club and Café del Mar (Café Mambo was still a private house and I remember a little old lady sitting on the terrace watching us). It wasn't just club nights but also football matches, on Ibiza Town's pitch, where Maggot knocked six shades of shit out of Gilles with an awful, bone-crunching tackle. (Peterson was quick on his feet and had represented the south of England as a schoolboy Rugby Union player; Maggot, on the other hand, was a great jazz-funk DJ but a bit of a lump who wouldn't let Gilles past him on principle – West Ham vs Arsenal, of course!) Chris Fanning and Lisa Blofeld helped Nicky with the away-day boat trips, barbecues and beach parties. I can safely say that it was by far the best thing I'd done in my life to that point. I went with a couple of mod mates from Chingford, Mark Lovett and my flatmate Bunny, and we all felt that things would never be the same again.

Sure enough, the people on the Ibiza trip became polarised. And not just the DJs but the punters too. It was impossible not to be affected by the atmosphere that came with acid house, but I can understand that the music wasn't for everyone and people broadly split into two different groups. There were the ones who totally embraced the sound and the people who still loved their classic black-influenced music of jazz and soul.

When we got back to London, everything had indeed changed. Nicky Holloway immediately opened The Trip at the Astoria and shortly after that Danny Rampling followed with Shoom. 'Aciiiid!' became the capital's buzzword and house – or rather, specifically acid house – became the most important cultural revolution Britain had seen since The Beatles. Hundreds of books have been written that try to explain the impact the movement had on culture, so I won't try here. All I can say is that it was enormous and everything, literally *everything* was cast aside to make way for the new zeitgeist.

I can remember standing next to Simon Dunmore (who at the time was head of A&R at Cooltempo/EMI but went on to set up Defected) at Dingwalls in Camden Lock a few weeks later while the incredibly rare jazz-funk masterpiece 'Sweet Power, Your Embrace' by James Mason was on the decks. Simon turned to me and said simply: 'I've seen the future and it's not this . . .'

He was right, of course.

Acid house was our 'year zero'. Most of the traditional youth cultures disappeared overnight – as did football hooliganism – in a sea of peace and love and MDMA. Sartorial dressing wasn't far behind. It was impossible not to be caught up in the acid revolution because pills were everywhere that year. But what had happened to rare groove and jazz? The bands were still there: James Taylor Quartet and The Brand New Heavies hadn't gone away, and Gilles Peterson and Bangsy were still among the best and most popular DJs in London. Our music just seemed a bit . . . well . . . old-fashioned. From being super cool, it now had something of an image problem.

What the fuck were we going to do? Suddenly, for a couple of months at least, our gigs were half-empty. The answer was just around the corner, and when it happened, it was just a joke.

One of our regular haunts was the Watermans Arts Centre in Brentford. Quite a schlep for us, but well worth the trip to see DJs like Steve Hobbs, Mick Farrer and Bob Jones playing soul and jazz. It was also a venue that hosted one of the new acid house nights.

Bangsy and Peterson found themselves coming on to double-deck after a banging acid house set from Pete Tong with a psychedelic light show and day-glo banners draped around the venue.

'How the fuck do we top that?' asked Gilles as he cued up 'The Better Half' by Funk, Inc. as their first record. The track has a long guitar intro, and as Gilles pressed 'play', Chris Bangs frantically pushed the varispeed slider on the Technics turntable up and down so the record sounded wonky and a bit more psychedelic. Bangsy famously then grabbed the microphone and shouted: 'If that was acid house, then this is acid jazz!' The pair dissolved into hysterical laughter.

It was only a joke, but what a prescient joke it was. The name stuck.

Chris Bangs used the term 'acid jazz' alongside 'wah-wah funk' on the flyer for his forthcoming Cock Happy night in Smithfield Market, and suddenly the phrase was everywhere. Jazz, funk and soul seemed current again; it became cool. The updated jazz sound along with the Duffer of St George late Sixties- and early Seventies-style fashion attracted large numbers of mods and ex-mods to this new scene.

But just what was acid jazz?

It wasn't really anything, to be honest. The music could be as random as Stetsasonic, John Coltrane, Naná Vasconcelos or Jimmy Smith. It was nebulous and indefinable, which only added to its appeal. Hip hop, bossa nova, boogaloo, be-bop, funk, salsa, fusion, jazz dance, breaks, gospel . . . The list was pretty broad. The important point was that it was all mixed up together.

Suddenly the Wag Club and Dingwalls were revitalised by the new 'acid jazz' tag, and more and more of the progressive element among the mod scene were turning up at our gigs and club nights wearing mod gear with a twist.

Gilles Peterson taught me a number of important lessons about DJing as a vocation. Two things in particular stand out. The first was that you should always play to the crowd: who cares how rare your record is if no one dances? The key is to find a tune that is both obscure *and* danceable.

The second, far more pertinent, was that you don't play the artist or the vibe; you play the individual record. This was a revelation. I'd always thought that if people liked a particular record, then I'd be on solid ground if I played other tracks by the same group, as long as they fitted the night. Peterson disabused me of that almost immediately. I'd heard him play a Jeff Lorber Fusion track at the Special Branch, so I picked up one of the band's LPs at Ray's Jazz and chose a track I thought was a pretty good fit to spin at the Wag. Gilles walked over and explained that it being by Jeff Lorber didn't automatically make it credible. I needed to think about where the vibe was travelling and project four records ahead. This was an important lesson and I tried not to make that particular mistake again.

This sort of interaction is a great example of two scenes mixing and benefiting from one another. And in this new environment, mods suddenly realised that they had somewhere to go, where they could still be mods but without the tunnel vision that had taken over the scene.

Rob Gallagher, the budding jazz rapper who became Galliano and was Gilles' DJ roadie, described acid jazz thus: 'Acid jazz was simply a mixture of mods and casuals who came together to make something new. The mods came from Eddie and the casuals from Gilles. It was that simple.'

*

A host of things happened that summer.

The first was that me and Gilles decided to start a little label so we could release some of the music our wider circle of friends were making. The Brand New Heavies had been dropped by Cooltempo after just one single and, with the exception of the James Taylor Quartet, it didn't look like anyone we knew would be picked up by a record label any time soon. No one was catering for our kind of music. But I understood how to make a record and we both knew enough thrusting artists who wanted to make one. It seemed like a good idea.

The second thing was that James Taylor, having been encouraged by Polydor to experiment musically, parted company with half of his band midway through the recording of the *Wait a Minute* LP. This actually shocked me, but Taylor began to work with a number of session musicians and Simon Booth was brought in as a producer. It was hard trying to come up with an instrumental with chart potential, so I suggested covering Tom Scott's 'Theme From Starsky & Hutch'. James Taylor and John Williams agreed, so we put a band of session musicians together that featured Fred Wesley and Pee Wee Ellis from The J.B.'s. These two had been the trombone and lead sax player who provided the horn lines for most of James Brown's best-known material. Who else's backing band had become legendary for the performances they made without their frontman? I can't think of any. Only The J.B.'s.

The afternoon they arrived at the studio to lay down their respective parts, I was to discover why they were rated as two of the best session musicians in the world.

A taxi pulled up outside the studio and to my surprise, as I was helping the pair with their instrument cases, Fred Wesley leaned through the black cab's front window and said, 'Man, keep the meter running; we'll only be ten minutes.'

Eh? I'd never, *ever* heard anyone come in and out of the studio in such a ridiculously short time. They must be joking, surely?

'Hey, are you Eddie? It's cash, right? Have you got it?'

I pulled out the envelope. They'd asked for a grand each, but to be honest, we thought it was a small price to pay for two of The J.B.'s. I handed it over. Wesley quickly counted the money and handed half to Ellis. They both made it obvious that they didn't want to sign a receipt.

As soon as the fee was sorted, the pair walked into the control room and immediately asked where they would be recording. The engineer showed them into a small booth with just one mic and they both took out their instruments and tuned up.

'Who's first?' the engineer asked.

Wesley shuffled the microphone and replied: 'Hey, man, just play us eight bars of the track and we'll go together. How long do you want the solos?'

The engineer replied that we wanted about 64 bars and that we could cut and shuffle the take after they'd finished.

Pee Wee Ellis laughed. 'Just roll the tape, man . . .'

They had an eight-bar lead in and then just played. I'd never heard anything like it. One take, one mic.

The pair of them walked out of the booth, out of the studio and straight back into the waiting cab. They'd been in the studio less than 15 minutes. They didn't even ask if we were happy with the take; they knew we would be. It was genius.

'Theme From Starsky & Hutch' was probably the first contemporary record to be described as acid jazz and it was recorded by an out-and-out mod called James Taylor. Things were changing in our favour.

The third significant thing that happened that summer was that I persuaded my boss at Polydor/Urban to make a compilation of some of the bands who were starting to make a name for themselves on our scene. Gilles gathered together the artists and the package was produced by the aforementioned Simon Booth. We called the album *Acid Jazz and Other Illicit Grooves*. It came out in a bright-blue sleeve with Chris

Bangs' famous Acid Jazz smiley logo embossed in day-glo pink. Bangsy had basically graffitied the standard acid house smiley by drawing nerdy glasses and buck teeth on it and it became the iconic image of the emerging scene.

The album had got the Acid Jazz name out there and became a critical success.

A couple of months later I put James Taylor into the studio with one of the last remaining live mod bands. They were called The Clique and featured my mate, a progressive mod called Paul Newman. He'd been with the Acid Jazz programme for a couple of months and suggested that I produced his band with James sitting in on the Hammond. The recordings went well, but I found myself arguing with the rest of the band, who seemed to be stuck in the late Sixties. In the end I walked out of the session and vowed that unless the mod scene could step outside that particular box, I was done with it.

But things had moved quickly with our prospective new label! At the same time as the Polydor/Urban *Acid Jazz and Other Illicit Grooves* LP was being recorded, we realised that Polydor didn't actually want to sign anything else we might come up with, so Gilles and I pressed on with our own musical vehicle.

The aforementioned Rob Gallagher was a cool scenester and a jazz dancer as well as Gilles Peterson's DJ roadie, but he was also something of a jazz poet who regularly grabbed the mic when Peterson was DJing at the Wag Club. He'd occasionally belt out his poems over the top of appropriate jazz and soul instrumentals live and off the top of his head. We suggested to Rob that he might like to cut a version of the Curtis Mayfield classic 'Freddie's Dead' for a 7-inch 45 on our (subjective) new label. We took him down to Rooster Studios in Kensington (the same one that I'd walked out of during the Clique session) for an afternoon's recording and he delivered a stone-cold classic that he called 'Frederic Lies Still'. A star was born that day, but before we could release the single, we needed a name for our new venture. The pair of us decided that the label was only going to be for fun, maybe just a handful of releases, but it still needed a name. We considered dozens but whittled them down to just the two Chris Bangs came up with on his original Cock Happy flyer: Acid Jazz or Wah-Wah Funk. The former won in the end. Neither of us had the slightest idea that the label would explode in quite such a spectacular fashion. The fact that our forthcoming Urban LP shared its title with the new label didn't even occur to us!

We cut just 500 copies of the Galliano 45, all of which had a large American-style dinked hole in the centre. Someone who was visiting New York on holiday posted a few review promo copies to British journalists from a fake American address with a made-up press release claiming that Galliano was a US jazz rapper from the Bronx. It was only ever supposed to be a laugh and we sat back to see what happened. (This was a trick copied from the perennially uncool Stock, Aitken & Waterman, who had fooled the world with their incredible rare groove smash 'Roadblock' just a year before.)

Sure enough, poor James Hamilton, one of the most experienced and well-liked black music journalists with a long tradition of championing artists in the mainstream media, took the bait and reviewed 'Frederic Lies Still' as an incredibly brilliant jazz poetry release out of New York. I felt awful that it had been him and he was furious when he realised what we'd done. He never forgave me and I'm sure he never reviewed one of our records again. No one likes to get caught out!

His review did the trick, though, and we soon secured the services of Marc Lessner, who ran a small, specialist dance-music distribution service called Soul Trader. Marc sold all of the Galliano first pressings in just a couple of days.

Almost by accident, the Acid Jazz label was up and running, the *Acid Jazz and Other Illicit Grooves* compilation was released to critical acclaim on Urban and 'Theme From Starsky & Hutch' was a minor chart hit on the same label.

All of a sudden, I was experiencing real entrepreneurial success. I couldn't quite believe it.

But who or rather *what* was I now? This sort of thing doesn't worry most people – but if you've ever been a mod, you'll probably understand. Acid house was king and we were trying to carve a new, mod-influenced path. Did that idea even make sense?

In reality, I was a dissatisfied modernist who'd walked away from our scene and for the first time had reached something of an earth-shattering, paradoxical conclusion.

I finally understood that mod was just a state of mind.

It wasn't the cut of a pair of trousers, the collar of a shirt, a rare scooter or even a fight against people who hated us. Well, actually, it was all of those things – but it wasn't *just* those things.

The truth was, away from the scene I'd grown up in, no one gave the slightest fuck how I dressed or what I was. Yes, it was important to me and 30 of my mates, but not to anyone else. And that just reinforced how important the *concept* of mod was to me personally. But I'd come to understand that it was about personal choices; it was about a certain outlook; it was about how you approached music, and life. I would always be a mod – I couldn't help it. But that was because of the way I approached and appreciated life. Not because I rode a scooter.

What was it Paul Weller said? 'You can bury me a mod.'

I always felt he was talking about me. Or rather, about us.

And this is the completely unsolvable dichotomy of mod.

Mod was a concept I'd embraced as a teenager and that had been invented in 1958 by forward-looking kids who were searching for *the new*. The reality was that our take on mod was nothing of the kind. It was a set of icons and sound bites that we'd adopted to *avoid* the new. 'The new' was properly shit and we had totally rejected it for an imaginary culture that never really existed. We were looking back on some kind of perfect period that only ever existed in our imagination. Let's be honest, the Sixties were shit. All inequality and outside toilets. But somehow we created a world out of our *perception* of the Sixties! What on earth did we think we were doing? All I know is that we and a few older kids were the first generation that refused to turn into our parents. But once you've tasted it, you never quite let it go.

In 1987, I started the first acid jazz mod club at Corks Wine Bar in Mayfair. It was called Voice Your Choice and was where fellow DJs Jon Cooke, Dom Bassett and Paul Newman and I introduced the hip hop of Stetsasonic and the jazz rock of Brian Auger to the next generation of mods. They were mainly younger than us, usually clad in Gabicci, vintage Levi's and Weejuns, but with beads around their necks. The most important thing was that they all appeared to get with the new modernist programme.

Within a month, *Touch* magazine came down to photograph some of our punters and a week or so later *The Face* got in touch to write an Acid Jazz article. The bandwagon was certainly picking up speed.

Acid Jazz had also been given the mod seal of approval by Paul Weller. He certainly understood what we were trying to do and was a supporter from the very beginning, usually turning up at Dingwalls, the Wag or the T&C2 *as a punter.*

Acid Jazz had breathed new life into a moribund mod world and when DJs like Paul 'Smiler' Anderson, Andy Orr and Dave Edwards stepped across from the mod 'scene' and began to take things into a new, mod-jazz-influenced direction, I finally saw that as proof that, as a mod, you could be into just whatever you like. Regardless of when or how you originally got into it, the mod spirit always wanted more and would always keep you changing as a person.

'I don't wanna be like anyone else; that's why I'm a mod, see?'

Jimmy had nailed it in *Quadrophenia*, and now I finally understood what he meant!

It had been an incredible ten-year journey, learning all the time. Looking out for new things, meeting new people, making connections. We'd always been hungry for the next thing, but with our own agenda, driven by something special to us personally, and yet that was so hard to define.

But then, even my dad had it right all those years ago when he dropped me off at school in 1979.

'What's this rubbish, son?'

'It's mod music, Dad!'

'This isn't mod music. Mod music is modern jazz. Tubby Hayes, Art Blakey, Gene Krupa and Cozy Cole . . .'

Yes, people a lot wiser than me had come to the same conclusion: that mod is an attitude, an outlook, a way you live your life. Whatever you want it to be – this was what it was all about. It was who I was, it was where I was from, and I was where I was going.

This was mod. Clean living, under difficult circumstances.

CHAPTER TITLES PLAYLIST

PART 1

1. 'Alternative Ulster' – Stiff Little Fingers
2. 'Eddie's Dreaming' – Small Faces
3. '(I'm) Stranded' – The Saints
4. 'Marquee Moon' – Television
5. 'Do They Owe Us a Living?' – Crass
6. 'British Hustle' – Hi-Tension

PART 2

7. 'The Modern World' – The Jam
8. 'The Real Me' – The Who
9. 'Millions Like Us' – Purple Hearts
10. 'The Kids Are Alright' – The Who
11. 'If the Kids Are United' – Sham 69
12. 'Whatcha Gonna Do About It' – Small Faces
13. 'In the City' – The Jam
14. 'I Can See for Miles' – The Who

PART 3

15. 'Time for Action' – Secret Affair
16. 'Geno' – Dexys Midnight Runners
17. 'You Need Wheels' – The Merton Parkas

This **monoray** book was crafted and published by Jake Lingwood, Leanne Bryan, Monica Hope, Mel Four, Rachael Shone, David Eldridge at Two Associates, Jouve, Elise Solberg and Lisa Pinnell.